Freedom North

Freedom North: Black Freedom Struggles Outside the South, 1940–1980

Edited by
**Jeanne Theoharis and
Komozi Woodard**

First published in 2003 by Palgrave Macmillan™
175 Fifth Avenue, New York, N.Y. 10010 and
Houndmills, Basingstoke, Hampshire, England RG21 6XS.
Companies and representatives throughout the world.

Palgrave Macmillan is the global academic imprint of the Palgrave
Macmillan division of St. Martin's Press, LLC and of Palgrave Macmillan Ltd.
Macmillan® is a registered trademark in the United States, United Kingdom
and other countries. Palgrave is a registered trademark in the European
Union and other countries.

ISBN 0–312–29467–0 hardback 0–312–29468–9 paperback

Library of Congress Cataloging-in-Publication Data

Freedom north: Black freedom struggles outside the
South: 1940–1980/edited by Jeanne Theoharis, Komozi Woodard.
     p. cm.
     Includes bibliographical references.
     ISBN 0–312–29468–9 (alk. paper)—ISBN 0–312–29467–0
     1. African Americans—Civil rights—History—20th century. 2. Civil
rights movements—United States—History—20th century. 3. United
States—Race relations. 4. Northeastern States—Race relations. 5. Middle
West—Race relations. 6. West (U.S.)—Race relations. I. Theoharis, Jeanne F.
II. Woodard, Komozi.

E185.61 .F8397 2003
323.1'196073'009045—dc21   2002029892

A catalogue record for this book is available from the British Library.

Design by Newgen Imaging Systems (P) Ltd., Chennai, India.

First edition: February, 2003
10 9 8 7 6 5 4 3 2 1

Printed in the United States of America.

Contents

Acknowledgments

We are immensely indebted to all of the authors of the articles collected in this volume: Beth Bates, Jon Rice, Adina Back, Robert O. Self, Angela D. Dillard, Ula Taylor, Felicia Kornbluh, Scot Brown, Johanna Fernandez, Evelyn Brooks Higginbotham, and Robin D. G. Kelly. Moreover, Kevin Gaines, Matthew Countryman, and Timothy Tyson participated on the American Studies Association panel, where the idea for this collection was born.

Matthew Countryman played an invaluable role in the creation of this book, helping to lay the groundwork logistically and intellectually for its genesis and development. *Freedom North* would not exist without him.

At Palgrave Macmillan, the editors have been enormously patient, helpful, and committed to furthering a new civil-rights historiography, including Deborah Gershenowitz, Sonia Wilson, Jen Simington, Nadine Dumser, and Jennifer Yoon. Deborah Gershenowitz recognized the need for this book perhaps even before we did and provided us the encouragement, vision, and support to make it possible.

We also need to thank a number of people whose contributions are less visible: Manning Marable, Kathleen Cleaver, Fanon Che Wilkins, Peniel Joseph, Tara James, Amina Baraka, and Amiri Baraka. Indeed, a book such as this cannot happen without generous institutional and emotional support. We are thankful to Sarah Lawrence College for a grant supporting the publication of this volume. And we are immeasurably grateful to a wide circle of family and friends who enable us in countless ways to imagine the power of the word to transform society.

Foreword

Evelyn Brooks Higginbotham

There is no greater symbol of the civil rights movement than the March on Washington in 1963. The power of the March as metaphor, as emblematic of the dream of freedom continues to resonate with Americans of all races—in books, television documentaries, Martin Luther King, Jr., birthday celebrations, and even in television commercials having nothing to do with issues of racial equality. As a heuristic device, the March serves also as a window onto the historiography of the black freedom struggle in the 1950s and 1960s, allowing access to the shifting focus of historical interpretation. From this perspective, it is interesting that historians initially studied the freedom movement by looking not at the 250,000 marchers, but at the leaders on the platform high above the crowd gathered at the Lincoln Memorial. Despite the complex and diverse character of this massive demonstration on August 28, 1963, historians assessed the civil rights movement according to the speakers on the raised platform and heard a voice that was singularly nonviolent and integrationist. So great was the platform participants' desire for both racial harmony and homogeneity of message that Malcolm X would strongly condemn the revision of John Lewis's speech during the actual march—the excising of what was perceived to be harsh and militant language by the Student Nonviolent Coordinating Committee (SNCC) leader.[1]

Historians' focus on the platform, thus, presented a top-down, even "heroic" vision of the movement. Research drew overwhelmingly from presidential archives, judicial opinions, legislative records, and the papers of national organizations and their leaders. This important, foundational scholarship emphasized the personality and ideological differences between national leaders, assessed the impact of Supreme Court decisions on the dismantling of Jim Crow practices, analyzed the transformation of political institutions in light of the passage of civil rights legislation, and examined national civil rights, labor, and religious organizations in confrontation and coalition. Yet the focus on the leadership proved to be limited, since it overlooked the immense phalanx marching for jobs and freedom. Like John Lewis's original speech, the range of voices present was silenced.[2]

As a teenager and a Washingtonian, I stood among the many demonstrators on that historic day. The sight of hundreds of buses, the thousands of banners, and the sea of people en route to the Lincoln Memorial remains in my memory no less vividly than the figure of Martin King perched above and afar, eloquently and intimately proclaiming my own and other African Americans' unfulfilled dream of freedom. Today, I see these images through the eyes of a historian who interprets their meaning based on primary sources, especially the newspaper accounts of the event. Such sources capture the motivations that led relatively obscure individuals to the March, and they capture as well the uniquely local efforts of hundreds if not thousands of organized groups from all over the United States.

It was not until the mid-1980s that scholars began to look more closely at community-level protest. Led by sociologists such as Aldon Morris, Doug McAdam, and Charles Payne and by historians such as Clayborne Carson, John Dittmer, and Adam Fairclough, this scholarship forced a rethinking of social movements and their theoretical and methodological frameworks.[3] Attentive to grassroots activism in southern cities and in rural areas deep in the Delta, the new scholarship explored human agency, moving beyond the charisma of a single personality to discover unheralded, previously unknown men and women in a spectrum of leadership roles and perspectives. The local movement scholars uncovered the influential, at times problematic, role of existing community organizations and institutions, such as labor unions, barbershops, colleges, fraternal organizations, and churches. Their attention to grassroots activism has facilitated important new work on black women's roles in the movement.[4] Although there is certainly more to be done, the study of Southern communities in the struggle for racial equality has persuasively challenged the earlier scholarship's overemphasis on external political forces, leaders, and funding. Yet from the standpoint of the 1963 March on Washington, even this path-breaking work proved limited, since its regional focus unwittingly reinforced the idea that similar goals and tactics were not pursued outside the South during the 1950s and early 1960s. Rendered invisible were the many delegations from the West Coast, the East Coast, and the Midwest— men and women who converged on Washington with banners and placards that identified the civil rights issues of their locales: "We March for Integrated Schools Now;" "We Demand an End to Police Brutality Now;" "We March for Higher Minimum Wages, Coverage for all Workers Now;" and "We Demand an End to Bias Now."[5]

For example, the large number of Philadelphians at the March participated with the knowledge of their own successful fight for jobs and freedom. Between 1959 and 1963, black Philadelphians waged 29 consumer boycotts. According to Leon Sullivan, the black Baptist minister who spearheaded the "Selective Patronage Campaign," thousands of skilled and unskilled jobs opened to blacks as a result.[6] Several thousand New Yorkers traveled to the March in buses, cars, and trains.[7] Twenty-four buses left from Harlem alone. Some of the buses were filled with black and white members of the Congress of Racial Equality (CORE). One-third of the Harlem buses contained unemployed blacks whose fares were paid by donations and button sales. The bus riders were instructed: "Remember our obligation of dignity and responsibility. Eliminate emotionalism … no drinking and no alcoholic beverages on the bus. Most important keep a level head."[8]

More than 1,000 persons from Boston participated in the March on Washington. Under the leadership of local National Association for the Advancement of Colored People (NAACP) activists, such as Kenneth Guscott and Ruth Batson, the Boston group rode in 30 buses and in private cars.[9] They were in the middle of their own decade-long fight against de facto segregation in the public schools. In June 1963, the Boston NAACP had led a "Stay Out for Freedom Day." Some 8,000 students boycotted their classes, attending instead "freedom schools," which were set up in homes, churches, and other neighborhood institutions. In February 1964, the Boston NAACP called again for a "Stay Out for Freedom Day." The idea for another school boycott, while in defiance of the threats and injunctions by the Boston school committee, won the support of black community organizations. The Boston NAACP proclaimed boldly in its literature: "We cannot emphasize too strongly that our children will be staying out for education, and not against it. … We support the Freedom 'Stay Out' so that our children may meaningfully 'Stay-In.'" On February 26, 1964, nearly 20,000 students in the city boycotted their classes. Thus, Black Bostonians came to the March on Washington to reaffirm their ongoing commitment and militant position of defying school board orders, disrupting school board meetings, and holding school strikes.[10]

Some 2,500 persons came from the Chicago area, one even on roller skates. CORE members figured prominently among the Chicago delegates. Like Boston, issues of school desegregation preoccupied much of their civil rights activism. In the months preceding the March, a coalition of civil rights organizations and black working-class neighborhood groups had called for a citywide boycott in protest against mobile classrooms that were set up hastily to address overcrowded facilities, in lieu of integration.

On July 10, 1963, the Chicago CORE launched a week-long sit-in at the Board of Education, and, by the following October, marshaled tremendous support for a boycott. On October 22, 1963, approximately 250,000 students stayed out of Chicago schools for the day.[11]

Activists also came from the West Coast. After picketing an all-white housing complex in Torrance, California, just a day earlier, a group of 87 black and white Californians flew to Washington. Black residents of Seattle, Washington, had been fighting for open housing since the 1950s. Although Seattle was represented at the March, a number of leaders from this city used the same day to call attention to their own protest. One thousand demonstrators in Seattle thus marched for fair housing on August 28, 1963, as a way to emphasize their unity of spirit with the national event.[12]

However, not all the demonstrators at the March on Washington favored integration. Some came to promote new, all-black agendas. Distributing leaflets among the crowd at the March were representatives of the Freedom Now Party, a short-lived but early advocate of a separate black political party—ideologically linked to international struggles against colonialism and distant from either the Democratic or Republican political agendas.[13] Actor Ossie Davis and SNCC workers John Lewis and Cleveland Sellers expressed their surprise at running into Malcolm X in Washington on the day of the March. Taylor Branch notes that Malcolm came alone, and that "he held court for passing demonstrators, mostly students." Branch even posits that Malcolm was among the demonstrators that day—"a faceless dot in the crowd."[14] Nor were all the Southern marchers nonviolent in their beliefs. Outspoken civil rights leader Gloria Richardson from Cambridge, Maryland was present. In June 1963, Richardson had led a militant struggle of sit-ins that resulted in mass arrests, when black Marylanders resorted to armed self-defense in the face of white mobs. Indeed, Malcolm X praised Richardson, who sometimes carried a gun. An article on the Cambridge Movement under her leadership noted: "No one really talks seriously about practicing nonviolence in Cambridge."[15] Even at the March on Washington, some Southern blacks carried placards that expressed a tone more militant than the platform speakers would have wanted. The group from Americus and Albany, Georgia, for example, challenged the legitimacy of the law and the role of the state in administering laws by asking the rhetorical question, "What is a state without justice but a robber band enlarged?"[16]

It is not surprising, then, that such sentiments, already existing in the South and by Southerners in exile like Robert Williams in Cuba, would spring up in 1964 in organized form, specifically the Deacons of Defense in Bogalusa, Louisiana. Charles Sims, founder of the Deacons, stated in 1965: "Martin Luther King and me have never seen eye to eye. He has never been to Bogalusa. If we didn't have the Deacons here there is no telling how many killings there would have been. We stand guard here in the Negro Quarters. We are the defense team."[17] The Deacons existed alongside the nonviolent movement, functioning as esteemed protectors.

In the late 1990s, scholars came increasingly to question static and bifurcated regional images—generalizations that equated the Southern movement with racial desegregation and the belief in nonviolence and the Northern movement with Black Power and violence. Recent publications and doctoral dissertations point to the range of ideological persuasions, competing goals, racially integrated coalitions, and black separatist agendas that informed communities in every region of the United States in the 1950s and 1960s. This growing body of research proves that there was never a monolithic politics of place; no singular strategy in time. George Lipsitz's wonderful book, *A Life in the Struggle* (1988), is perhaps the earliest to articulate the fluid nature of the black freedom struggle. Through the life of rank-and-file activist Ivory Perry, Lipsitz portrays the black freedom struggle across regions and decades from a grassroots perspective. A migrant from rural Arkansas, Perry's move to St. Louis in the 1950s reflected the burgeoning urbanization and ghettoization of blacks in the years between 1940 and 1970. In the 1950s, he demonstrated against discriminatory hiring practices in banks and against segregated schools, theaters, and restaurants. He grew more militant, as did other working-class protesters, adapting more disruptive strategies, e.g., stopping traffic, marching and chanting through department stores, and blocking entrances to banks.[18] His activism in CORE in the 1960s took him south— to Selma and Bogalusa (where he admired the Deacons of Defense)—but it also took him north to the open housing campaigns in the suburbs of Chicago. In the 1970s and 1980s, Perry, still an activist in St. Louis, joined in community mobilizing efforts for equality in housing, employment, and health care.[19]

Quintard Taylor, in a 1995 article on the civil rights movement in Seattle, argued that "distinctly local agendas" constituted an integral part of the national movement to transform American race relations in the 1950s and 1960s. His important work on the movement in Seattle during this time period reveals a rapidly growing black population in search of jobs and freedom. Attracted to Seattle's fast growing economy due to the Boeing Aircraft Company, blacks soon found themselves embroiled in the fight against job bias, housing discrimination, and de facto school segregation.[20]

Thus, *Freedom North* makes an important contribution toward filling the gaps in our knowledge of the struggle outside the South during the 1950s, 1960s, and 1970s. Most important, this book constitutes part of an emergent revisionism of civil rights history, positing a movement broader in time and place. This new interpretation links the North and South, and finds within each region the coexistence and interaction of nonviolent resistance and armed self-defense, interracial coalitions and all-black organizations, and the quest for full inclusion in America and identification with uniquely black cultural traditions.

Notes

1. John Lewis with Michael D'Orso, *Walking with the Wind: A Memoir of the Movement* (New York: Simon & Schuster, 1998), 218-228; Taylor Branch, *Pillar of Fire: America in the King Years, 1963–1965* (New York: Simon & Schuster, 1998), 131; David J. Garrow, *Bearing the Cross: Martin Luther King, Jr., and the Southern Christian Leadership Conference* (New York: W. Morrow, 1986), 282–283.
2. For an excellent historiographical analysis of the early scholarship, see Steven F. Lawson, "Freedom Then, Freedom Now: The Historiography of the Civil Rights Movement," *American Historical Review* 96 (April 1991): 456–471.
3. Aldon D. Morris, *The Origins of the Civil Rights Movement: Black Communities Organizing for Change* (New York: Free Press, 1984); Doug McAdam, *Political Process and the Development of Black Insurgency, 1930–1970* (Chicago: University of Chicago Press, 1982); Charles Payne, *I've Got the Light of Freedom: The Organizing Tradition and the Mississippi Freedom Struggle* (Berkeley: University of California Press, 1995); Clayborne Carson, "Civil Rights Reform and the Black Freedom Struggle," in Charles W. Eagles, ed., *The Civil Rights Movement in America* (Jackson: University of Mississippi Press, 1986), Clayborne Carson, *In Struggle: SNCC and the Black Awakening of the 1960s* (Cambridge: Harvard University Press, 1981); John Dittmer, *Local People: The Struggle for Civil Rights in Mississippi* (Urbana: University of Illinois Press, 1994); Adam Fairclough, *Race & Democracy: The Civil Rights Struggle in Louisiana, 1915–1972* (Athens: University of Georgia Press, 1995).
4. Chana Kai Lee, *For Freedom's Sake: The Life of Fannie Lou Hamer* (Urbana: University of Illinois Press, 1999); Bettye Collier-Thomas and V. P. Franklin, eds., *Sisters in the Struggle: African American Women in the Civil Rights-Black Power Movement* (New York: New York University Press, 2001); Vicki L. Crawford, Jacqueline Anne Rouse, and Barbara Woods, eds., *Women in the Civil Rights Movement: Trailblazers and Torchbearers, 1941–1965* (Brooklyn: Carlson Publishing, 1990); Kay Mills, *This Little Light of Mine: The Life of Fannie Lou Hamer* (New York: Dutton, 1993); Belinda Robnett, *How Long? How Long: African-American Women in the Struggle for Civil Rights* (New York: Oxford

University Press, 1997); Cynthia Griggs Fleming, *Soon We Will Not Cry: The Liberation of Ruby Doris Smith Robinson* (Lanham, MD: Rowman & Littlefield, 1998).

5. See photographs of the marchers in *New York Times,* August 29, 1963, 18.
6. Leon H, Sullivan, *Build Brother Build* (Philadelphia: Macrae Smith Company, 1969), 70–77.
7. "Marchers Sing and Voice Hope on Way to Washington Rally," *New York Times,* August 29, 1963, 19.
8. "Young and Old Make Bus Trip for March," *Washington Post,* August 29, 1963, D-15.
9. "Chicagoan Skates Here for March," *Washington Post,* August 28, 1963, A-6.
10. Henry Hampton and Steve Fayer, *Voices of Freedom* (New York: Bantam Books, 1990), 588–591; Amy C. Offner, " 'Too Late for Pleading': Black Boston and the Struggle for School Desegregation, 1963–1976," Unpublished senior honors thesis, Harvard University, Cambridge, MA, 2001, 16, 21.
11. Ledger Smith, a professional roller skater, skated from Chicago to D.C. in ten days. See "Chicagoans Plan Continuing Civil Rights Rallies in Washington," *Chicago Tribune,* August 29, 1963; "Chicagoan Skates Here for March," *Washington Post,* August 28, 1963, A-6; for the boycott, see James R. Ralph, Jr., *Northern Protest: Martin Luther King, Jr., Chicago, and the Civil Rights Movement* (Cambridge: Harvard University Press, 1993), 13–22.
12. "Marchers Sing and Voice Hope," 19; Quintard Taylor, "The Civil Rights Movement in the American West: Black Protest in Seattle, 1960–1970," *Journal of Negro History* 80 (winter 1995): 6.
13. For discussion of the Freedom Now Party and an illuminating discussion of black radicalism during the early 1960s, see Peniel E. Joseph, "Waiting Till the Midnight Hour: Reconceptualizing the Heroic Period of the Civil Rights Movement, 1954–1965," in *Souls: A Critical Journal of Black Politics, Culture, and Society* 2 (spring 2000): 6–17; also see Timothy B. Tyson, "Robert F. Williams, 'Black Power,' and the Roots of the African-American Freedom Struggle," *Journal of American History* 85 (September 1998): 540–570.
14. Branch, *Pillar of Fire,* 131; Hampton, *Voices of Freedom,* 162–164.
15. Sharon Harley, "'Chronicle of a Death Foretold': Gloria Richardson, the Cambridge Movement and the Radical Black Activist Tradition," in Collier-Thomas and Franklin, eds., *Sisters in the Struggle,* 186–190.
16. "One Note of Bitterness," *New York Times,* August 29, 1963, 17.
17. *Baton Rouge State Times,* July 19, 1965, 1, quoted in George Lipsitz, *A Life in the Struggle: Ivory Perry and the Culture of Opposition* (Philadelphia: Temple University Press, 1988), 96; Fairclough, *Race & Democracy,* 340–343; Timothy B. Tyson, *Radio Free Dixie: Robert F. Williams and the Roots of Black Power* (Chapel Hill: University of North Carolina Press, 1999).
18. Lipsitz, *Life in the Struggle,* 13–14.
19. Ibid., 76–78.
20. Taylor, "The Civil Rights Movement in the American West," 1–14.

Introduction

Jeanne Theoharis[1]

[Martin Luther King, Jr., and the Southern Christian Leadership
Conference's campaign in] Chicago was the first and only real attempt by
the Civil Rights Movement to mount a major campaign of nonviolent
direct action in the North.

Adam Fairclough, Better Day Coming: Blacks and Equality[2]

The spontaneous urban uprisings of 1968 ended an era of black struggle, for unlike earlier rebellions involving SNCC and Southern blacks,
they dissipated quickly when confronted by powerful institutions.

*Clayborne Carson, In Struggle: SNCC and the Black Awakening of the
1960s*[3]

* * *

Detroit, Michigan, 1941—Thousands of blacks, part of the all-black
March on Washington Movement, hold work stoppages and demonstrations to expand job opportunities for black male and female workers
in Detroit's auto and defense industries.

New York, New York, 1958—A group of Harlem mothers refuse to send
their children to school to protest segregated and unequal conditions and
are brought to trial.

New York, New York, 1960—In a speech to the Urban League, Martin
Luther King, Jr., declares, "The racial issue that we confront in America is
not a sectional but a national problem. ... There is a pressing need for
a liberalism in the North that is truly liberal, that firmly believes in integration in its own community as well as in the deep South. There is need for the
type of liberal who not only rises up with righteous indignation when
a Negro is lynched in Mississippi, but will be equally incensed when a Negro
is denied the right to live in his neighborhood, or join his professional
association or secure a top position in his business."

Boston, Massachusetts, 1963—Hundreds of parents jam two School Committee meetings, lead sit-ins, commit civil disobedience, and rally—10,000 strong—to protest segregation in Boston's public schools.

Detroit, Michigan, 1963—Thousands walk for freedom to protest racial discrimination and police brutality. King addresses the crowd, declaring it "gigantic" and a "magnificent new militancy."

New York, New York, 1964—464,361 students boycott New York's public schools on February 3 to demand a plan and timetable for comprehensive desegregation of the city's schools—the biggest civil rights demonstration to date in the history of the United States, eclipsing the numbers of the 1963 March on Washington.

Newark, New Jersey, 1974—Puerto Ricans rebel on Labor Day over police brutality. Thousands of African Americans and Puerto Ricans protest Mayor Gibson's decision to declare martial law.

Boston, Massachusetts, 1975—Over 15,000 people march in support of desegregation to counter a year of violent resistance to court-ordered desegregation.

Tens of thousands of people were active in freedom movements of varying ideologies outside of the South from the 1940s to the 1980s. Yet, while scholars have sought to complicate the historiography of the black freedom struggle in recent years, the dominant civil rights story remains that of a nonviolent movement born in the South during the 1950s that emerged triumphant in the early 1960s but then was derailed by the twin forces of Black Power and white backlash when it sought to move North after 1965. The narrative of the civil rights movement, then, continues to rest on a series of dichotomies: between South and North, nonviolence and Black Power militancy, de facto and de jure segregation, and the movement before 1965 and after. In history textbooks, college classrooms, films, and popular celebration, African American protest movements in the North appear as ancillary and subsequent to the "real" movement in the South. Because racism is southernized in popular versions of American history and political discourse, the main battle is believed to be in the South. Following this logic, the movement fittingly and exclusively emerges there.

Foregrounding the South has constricted popular understandings of race and racism in the United States during and after WWII—making it seem as if the South was the only part of the country that needed a movement, as if blacks in the rest of the country only became energized to fight after their Southern brothers and sisters did, as if Southern racism was more malignant than the strains found in the rest of the country, as if social activism produced substantive change only in the South. As Evelyn Brooks Higginbotham points out in her analysis of the March on Washington in the Foreword, where we look determines what we see. These paradigms make it difficult to account for the decisive spread of the Ku Klux Klan and other racial violence out of the South into the rest of the country in the 1920s. They miss the systems of racial caste and power—pervasive and entrenched across the North—that denied people of color equitable education, safe policing, real job opportunities, a responsive city government, regular sanitation services, quality health care, and due process under the law. Northern segregation operated somewhat differently than Southern. Public spaces—bathrooms, trains, movie theaters, and lunch counters— were not legally separated for blacks and whites in the North. But schools, housing, and jobs operated on a strict racial hierarchy with whites at the top and blacks at the bottom. And many public spaces, while not explicitly marked "for whites only," practiced that just the same. By shielding Northern segregation and the economic and social disfranchisement of people of color from full examination, these formulations naturalize the Northern racial order as *not* a racial system like the South's but one operating on class and culture with racial discrimination as a byproduct.

Moreover, they require ignoring local leaders like Mae Mallory in New York, Ruth Batson in Boston, and Reverend Al Cleage in Detroit, all of whom organized against school inequalities in the North. They miss the breakfast programs and gang truces built by the Chicago Black Panther Party, the campaign against lead paint and for adequate sanitation and health services organized by the Young Lords Party, the movement to open up credit and access to decent goods for welfare recipients led by the National Welfare Rights Organization (NWRO), and the drive to elect independent black politicians carried out by residents in Newark, Chicago, and Oakland. Ultimately, they take a national struggle challenging the politics and economics of race in the United States and pigeonhole it as a heroic triumph over Southern backwardness between 1954 and 1965.

Since scholars first began writing the history of the civil rights movement in the late 1960s, black activism in the urban Northeast, Midwest, and West has largely been cast as secondary to the real struggle taking place in the South. Work on Martin Luther King, Jr., often juxtaposes the successes he and the Southern Christian Leadership Congress (SCLC) had in the South with the difficulty they encountered in Chicago when they tried to take the movement North.[4] However, these analyses miss the similarities between SCLC's "failures" in Albany, Georgia, and those in Chicago, as the movements in both cities ran aground on broken promises by city leadership and indifference by the federal government and nation at large. The fact that some black Chicagoans abandoned nonviolence is not new either, since King had encountered this in both Albany and Birmingham. Similarly, long before Birmingham acquired the name Bombingham, blacks in Chicago suffered hundreds of bombing attacks as they crossed the color line and moved into "white neighborhoods." August Meier's and Elliot Rudwick's 1973 study of the Congress of Racial Equality (CORE) treats CORE's development of the strategy of nonviolent protest in Northern cities during the 1940s largely as a prehistory to the Southern movement.[5] It dismisses the efforts of CORE's Northern chapters to use nonviolent direct action against employment and housing discrimination as inappropriate to racial conditions in the North.

Even ground-breaking scholarship such as Charles Payne's and John Dittmer's studies of Mississippi that elaborate Ella Baker's pivotal leadership and organizing philosophy treat her Northern activism as background for the pivotal role she plays in Southern struggles.[6] Work on school inequalities that extends to the North, such as James Patterson's recent exploration of *Brown* v. *Board of Education,* does so by establishing rigid chronologies, maintaining the erroneous notion that activism around schools was virtually nonexistent in the 1950s and early 1960s in the North.[7] Yet, as Kenneth Clark helped prepare the briefs for the *Brown* v. *Board* case in the early 1950s, he, along with Ella Baker, joined with local activists to organize against school segregation in New York and criticized the NAACP for overwhelmingly focusing its efforts on the South. And Tom Sugrue's seminal study of the ways the politics of race determined the economic, spatial, and social configuration of postwar Detroit does not treat black activism as central to that process.[8] Yet community activists from the March on Washington Movement to the Walk for Freedom to the organization of the League of Revolutionary Black Workers contested—and indeed reshaped—the city.

In more recent years, the vast majority of historical work on black activism in the urban North has focused on the ideological and organizational development of Black Power and other forms of black radicalism.[9] Centered primarily on the biographies of well-known movement leaders, the historiography of Black Power has tended to ignore the local political and economic context for black radicalism, the grassroots activists that nurtured it, and the impact of the radical challenge on the landscape of Northern cities.[10] Other recent studies of racial politics in the postwar urban North have either ascribed Northern protest solely to the influence of Martin Luther King and other Southern leaders or focused primarily on the causes of white backlash against racial reform. In these formulations, the various freedom struggles that emerge outside of the South not only become peripheral to the "Movement" but the geographical particularities of the Northeast, West, and Midwest get clouded. "The North" sometimes refs to northeastern cities while other times stands in as a larger term for the rest of the country (as we will use it here).

The historical connotations of black freedom in the "promised land" (runaway slaves, the Harlem Renaissance, and black migration during the two world wars) and the "backward" nature attached to Southern racism have made it difficult to focus on Northern injustice and the movements that emerged there for racial change.[11] Yet, as the pieces in this collection show, a fuller inclusion of Northern activism within the postwar freedom narrative challenges the notion that the movement went from civil rights to Black Power, that Black Power caused the decline of the movement, that self-defense was new to the movement in the 1960s, and that well-organized nonviolent movements were not as prevalent or successful across the North as they were in the South from 1940 to 1980. These essays decisively move the story away from charismatic male leadership, show that the movement for full citizenship extended far beyond voting rights, link the struggle for civil rights to economics, reveal the role the media played in discounting Northern struggles, and challenge underclass theory that denies structure as a crucial determinant in the experience of Northern blacks.

This book brings together new work on black social movements outside of the South to detail these individual local struggles and to rethink the nature and place of race in recent American history. Many of these stories are unfamiliar. Others have been told only in a sectarian context. Convinced that these movements demand the rigorous and thoughtful treatment that other twentieth-century social movements have been accorded, these authors take the tools of historical scholarship to demystify groups such as the US organization and the Modern Black Convention Movement and activists such as the Reverend Al Cleage and Fred Hampton, and to reconstruct the narrative of postwar black liberation struggles. By placing these freedom initiatives in a dialectical relationship with conditions and developments in the South throughout the course of the movement, we present a different picture of the racial terrain of the United States during and after WWII. We are not questioning the premise that activism in the South inspired activism in the North or that the racial terrain of the South differed from the North; rather, we maintain that activism in the North also inspired activism in the South. These battles are symbiotic—North and South, East and West.

While WWII helped lay the foundation for the civil rights movement and discredit biological theories of race, postwar America was an increasingly racialized place. The industrial build-up needed for the war, the mechanization of Southern agriculture, and Operation Bootstrap had spurred Black and Puerto Rican migration to Northern cities while veterans' loans and

Federal Housing Administration policy encouraged white migration to the suburbs and fortified white enclaves within cities. African Americans and Puerto Ricans found their housing options limited, and GIs of color had difficulty accessing their housing benefits. Those sections of the city open to nonwhite people received fewer loans for home ownership and improvement, and white violence erupted when people of color moved into "white neighborhoods" or sent their children to "white schools." Public services in nonwhite sections of the city were significantly inferior, and urban renewal razed many historically black and Latino neighborhoods, displacing families and further overcrowding nonwhite neighborhoods.

An increasingly elaborate educational system developed in the North in the postwar period to ensure racial inequality and segregation in resources, hiring, administration, and school upkeep that cannot be merely attributed to residential segregation. The schools that nonwhite students were sent to were significantly disadvantaged in resources, curriculum, and personnel compared to those of their white counterparts— and many students, white and black, traveled farther to school than they would otherwise need to in order to maintain this segregation. The GI Bill (the most successful affirmative action program of the twentieth century) opened up college education and the middle class to a generation of working-class white men, but these opportunities were largely denied to men of color and women of all races. A shifting industrial base in most Northern cities combined with the lack of access people of color had to many public jobs (like teaching, police and fire departments, and many levels of city government) made unemployment and poverty increasingly common.

Northern freedom struggles challenged the racialized political economy of postwar cities like the Southern civil rights movement did. Yet, while the Montgomery Bus Boycott, a disruptive urban protest, is now seen as an inspiring fight for public citizenship, welfare recipients demonstrating against Sears or New York residents taking over Lincoln Hospital to protest unsanitary conditions are not given this moral power. In part, this is due to the emergence of popular and scholarly theories of the "underclass," which have linked black migration to Northern cities with the development of a pathological psychology in the black community.[12] Thus, urbanization is tied to the disintegration of the black family—and, by extension, the black community—as urban blacks, particularly black women, are often pictured as non-virtuous and non-righteous. In much of this literature, the problems Northern blacks faced were now largely due to their own values and culture, and not the structures of society and the aforementioned changes in American cities. Even scholars who have looked at the economic and political structures of cities still locate the potential for change in black self-help strategies more than social protest.[13] As the Moynihan report demonstrated, black women were seen as too controlling and aggressive, and black men as too emasculated and absent—further obscuring the possibility of Northern activism and placing the burden of change on the structure of the black family itself.

These theoretical formulations are tied to racialized ideas of place, work, and progress. Because rural blacks are seen as emblematic of long-suffering struggle, and urban blacks as pathological (divorced from the kin and culture of Southern black life), the narrative of the movement's demise when it migrates North is self-justifying. In a troubling tautology, a sharecropper can occupy a place of dignity in the American imagination that a welfare mother cannot; thus, the activism of welfare mothers disappears from view because they cannot hold this place of American hero and symbol of national progress. The story cannot be a story because it fits no category. Yet, an examination of these Northern struggles fundamentally critiques underclass theory and the liberal frame that has come to envelope the civil rights movement. These essays show that black communities in the North, far from being in disarray and plagued by dysfunction, waged a protracted fight for justice and equity but constantly had to contend with theories and policies that blamed them for their condition.

Outlining how many of these freedom struggles, whether in the North or South, challenged the very premises of democracy and capitalism, these authors disrupt a teleology of American democracy that has incorporated the Southern civil rights movement into American history by stripping it of its radical critique. The fight for desegregated public facilities—particularly schools—was always a fight for resources because segregation itself was a tool of economic control and resource distribution. Segregation meant that blacks subsidized finer schools and regular sanitation, accessible city government, better public transportation, and a wide array of public services for whites. It was taxation without representation, and thus the lunch counter and the bus and the schoolroom were never just about a seat but always about gaining full citizenship and economic equity. Since the denial of political power was crucial to circumscribing black economic power, the fight for voting rights was seen as inseparable—and indeed a prerequisite—for economic empowerment. At the grassroots, economics were not divorceable from civil rights (for black activists or white segregationists), even if historians and politicians in recent decades have begun to split them.

The vision of a Southern-dominated movement, then, comes in part from a civil rights narrative that is focused on the campaign to secure voting rights, rather than detailing the broad challenge to political, social, and economic white power. Accordingly, the story is complete when the Voting Rights Act is passed in 1965. This treatment of voting rights dichotomizes the North and South in problematic ways, obscuring the issues of voter registration and political control that became crucial battlegrounds in the North as well. The vote was not completely absent in the South nor fully accessible in the North. Political access was never as simple as "one man, one vote" in the South or the North as political machines in many Northern cities precluded political power and access for blacks, and many black Northerners were thwarted in their efforts to register to vote.

This work demonstrates the geographical specificity of these struggles—Detroit is not Boston is not Newark—and, at the same time, the national impact of these Northern fights. The work here focuses on seven cities—New York, Newark, Boston, Chicago, Detroit, Oakland, and Los Angeles—and two national organizations largely, though not exclusively, based in the North—the NWRO and the Nation of Islam. These pieces show the distinctive forms of U.S. racism, the variety of tactics that community members used to attack these inequalities, and the prevalence of reformist and nationalist thinking in the 1940s, 1950s, 1960s, and 1970s. Three essays on Detroit and Oakland reveal the early roots of black nationalism, locating them within black labor struggles and Christian liberation theology. Beth Bates's study of the March on Washington Movement in Detroit, an explicitly all-black movement that dropped the politics of civility to press for jobs and justice, shows the organizational base of black nationalism in the 1940s. Examining the often-overlooked Christian roots of black nationalism, Angela Dillard takes up the work of Reverend Albert B. Cleage, Jr., to establish links between Cleage's nationalism and his decision to rename his church the Shrine of the Black Madonna with older patterns of radicalism in Detroit. Robert Self traces the political activism of Oakland's black community from the labor organizing of the Brotherhood of Sleeping Car Porters to the electoral strategies of the Black Panther Party.

Struggles for school desegregation and equality in the 1950s and 1960s reveal that Northern school struggles did not lag behind the Southern movement and challenge the accuracy of terming Northern segregation de facto. Adina Back tells the story of the school boycott and legal battles of the "Harlem Nine," school desegregation activists in New York in the late 1950s who were arrested and tried for keeping their children out of the city's segregated schools. Disrupting the ways Boston's school desegregation has become a story of working-class white resistance to "busing," Jeanne Theoharis traces the 25-year struggle that black community members waged for educational equity in the city's schools.

These movements had different ideological approaches to the issues of gender, citizenship and American capitalism. The Nation of Islam and the NWRO provide contrasting examples of how black people—and black women in particular—constructed strategies for protection and self-reliance in the late 1960s. Felicia Kornbluh's essay on the NWRO shows that the organization's consumer protests were rooted in a campaign to demand their rights as Americans and mothers to provide decent food, clothes, and shelter for their children. Ula Taylor examines the reasons, more secular than religious, that many people joined the Nation of Islam after Malcolm X's death in 1965, given the variety of black nationalist organizations to choose from and the Nation of Islam's gender traditionalism.

Radical, often nationalist, movements carried on the work of black liberation through grassroots mobilization and organized protest in the 1960s and 1970s. Jon Rice examines the development of the Illinois Black Panther Party on Chicago's West Side to demonstrate the ways the Party built a revolutionary (not nationalist) group dedicated to meeting community needs and building cross-racial alliances across the city. Challenging the notion that cultural nationalism lacked a political basis, Scot Brown's essay focuses on the US Organization and their involvement in the Freedom City Campaign, the Black Congress, and anti-Vietnam War resistance. Komozi Woodard looks at Amiri Baraka and the local base of the Modern Black Convention Movement that emerged after the 1967 rebellion in Newark. Through an examination of the Young Lords Party in New York, Johanna Fernandez shows how their actions exposed the crisis of sanitation, health, and lead poisoning in New York and successfully pressured the city to take action on these issues.

As these pieces demonstrate, the civil rights movement was profoundly local, yet it transformed the character of the nation. Many of these struggles were urban; thus, these authors scrutinize the politics of place, the histories of migration, the racialized ways that each city developed, the constellation of city services that were or were not available, and the particular machine politics at work in each city. This local history illuminates the multifaceted character of racial privilege and racial injustice. Housing and public services, for instance, became crucial sites of struggle in cities, somewhat different battlegrounds than are seen in the South. These essays also show that the movement had victories in the North as well as the South—that these Northern battlefields were not immune to social protest, as studies of SCLC too often imply, but could be changed through protest and community pressure. The Young Lords forced New York City to take on landlords over the issue of lead paint; the survival programs that the Panthers built—particularly the breakfast program—pushed the federal government to do the same.

These essays also present a more complex picture of the nature of racism in America. By picturing the South as the past and the North as the present, racism is often viewed as a redneck phenomenon of long ago—individualized in the persons of Bull Connor and Byron de la Beckwith. That Northern and Southern racism often came cloaked in middle-class clothes and disguised in civilized language (about standards and crime and the rights of the individual) does not fit with images of fire hoses and police dogs, church bombings, and bold proclamations defending segregation "now and forever." American racism was not only a phenomenon of the working class but had a supple base in the middle class. That racism was imbedded in structures and not just about individual hatred is often missed in the Montgomery-to-Selma story. Part of the power of the Young Lords and the Black Panthers was to make visible the structures that discriminated against people of color. Pulling trash into the street, liberating tuberculosis trucks and garbage brooms, exposing the city's reluctance to provide adequate medical services for poor people, and organizing police patrols were ways to highlight and challenge the inequality of public services.

Arguing that white backlash in the North must be viewed through the same analytical lens as white resistance in the South, this collection decisively challenges the notion that white opposition to civil rights emerges in the North in the latter half of the 1960s. In terms of local struggles, white resistance to civil rights was ongoing and virulent from WWII on (and certainly before). As exemplified in schools struggles in New York and Boston, many Northern whites vociferously opposed change in their own backyards in 1946 and 1956, as well as 1966—but this resistance (which Martin Luther King notes in the opening chronology) is obscured by the journalistic and subsequent historical focus on the South. This raises a historiographic question: If resistance does not undermine the righteousness of the struggle in the South, then why does it in the North? Why does racial violence look different in the South? These essays challenge the idea of dichotomizing Northern de facto segregation with Southern de jure segregation. Such distinctions do not adequately foreground the structural roots and institutional sanction that segregation had in the North and the elaborate methods that city governments, school boards, local and state politicians, and courts devised to protect it. The housing and school segregation that was endemic in Northern and Western cities like Chicago and Newark did not just happen, nor was it the result of private housing choices but maintained and reinforced by the political and legal structures of the state.

The civil rights movement was indeed a national movement—and the social changes produced were the result of struggles happening throughout the country, not just the South. The essays in this volume raise critical questions of chronology, expanding, as other scholars have begun to do, the periodization of the movement beyond the 1954 to 1965 time span. The black freedom movement had its roots and branches in the 1930s and 1940s. This activism was not merely a dress rehearsal but a crucial birthplace and battleground for the mass movement that flowered in the 1960s. Similarly, just as Southern activists took up the task of enforcing the *Brown* v. *Board* decision, so too did Northern blacks in the 1950s, 1960s, and 1970s.

Moreover, the movements' organized challenges to racial injustice extend well past 1965. Indeed, this new scholarship suggests that post-1968 struggles were not anarchic, spontaneous outpourings of anger but well-organized social protest. Black nationalism was not episodic or emotional, as it is often pictured, but developed within a series of initiatives and groups like the Black Panther Party, the Young Lords Party, the Congress of African Peoples, and US, which pushed city and state governments to provide equitable public services to communities of color, promoted the election of blacks to city government, and inspired profound interest in African and African American history, literature, and culture within the black community. Ideologically, theologically, and strategically rooted, nationalism was not just born out of anger and was often continuous with struggles in the 1930s through the 1960s. In many of these cities, there was not a tremendous gap between civil rights and Black Power—in fact, it was often the same work as black activists (and even their white allies) moved between these ideologies.

Black struggles also became struggles that linked people of color—challenging the ways people of color had been pitted against each other in the United States as well as the ways the second-class status of nonwhiteness was conferred on Latinos and Asian Americans as well as African Americans, albeit with certain differences. Still, blackness was not a unitary—or necessarily unifying—concept as class and cultural differences between South Side and West Side Chicagoans or within Detroit's religious and labor community make clear. Antiracist work often led to anticolonialist politics as activists made connections between black struggles in the United States and the Vietnam War, the neocolonial status of Puerto Rico, apartheid in South Africa, and the newly independent nations of Africa. Groups like US saw reclaiming the African heritage of American blacks as a cornerstone to political autonomy for black people. Yet, these connections to Africa were also contested and, at times, rejected, as the Nation of Islam's banning of African dress and hairstyle illustrates.

These essays complicate prevalent understandings of the nature of militancy, challenging the analytical distinctions made between Christianity as passive and the Nation of Islam as militant, between desegregation as politically acceptable and separation as not. They argue that criticisms of movement violence were not always critiques of actual physical violence but instead condemnations of the movement's embrace of disruptive protest strategies and a refusal to work within a politics of civility. Groups were often accused of violence or, conversely, of political naiveté when they began to disrupt the workings of the state. The NWRO's "un-civil" tactics drew the scorn and trepidation of many liberal whites and blacks. And, yet, while the radical imagination may have been more enamored with armed black men in berets than angry black women picketing welfare offices, the NWRO's core philosophy that welfare was an American right provided as stark and frightening a repudiation of capitalism and American democracy as the Black Panther Party did. The fight against segregation in New York, Boston, Detroit, and Newark required decades of civil disobedience and disruption, guerrilla tactics, and community mobilization. And it was bitterly resisted. Indeed, while the movements to build independent black schools or for community control encountered fierce opposition, it was often desegregation that prompted the most sustained, politically systematic, and violent white resistance. Just as Black Power was not a new phenomenon in the mid-1960s, desegregation was not irrelevant by then.

Yet many journalists at the time claimed it so, citing increasing white opposition to and black dismissal of desegregation by the later 1960s, without investigating the substance of these claims. The historiography of Northern movements, and lack thereof, has been decisively influenced by these media portrayals. Since the national media were also the Northern media, the ways these movements were covered—many times negatively or not at all—has shaped the ways we now picture Northern struggles. Media-savvy groups like SCLC and SNCC realized that they needed to capture national media attention because local (Southern) media often shared the same political, social, or economic interests of those who opposed the movement. This became more difficult in Northern cities like Chicago, New York, Washington, and Boston, where the local media were the national media, often sharing economic, social, and political positions at odds with many of these movements. The coverage of Boston's desegregation as a story of white resistance or of the Black Panthers as gun-toting thugs certainly has contributed to many of the historical silences around these groups. The media-conscious Young Lords were able to garner some sympathetic news coverage that proved crucial in their lead paint campaign but was not sufficient to save them from historical obscurity.

The media's proclivity for charismatic male leaders also meant that they missed or misunderstood many of the struggles organized by women. Highlighting the grassroots organizing that took place throughout the country and the central role African American women played in many of those struggles, these essays show the long histories of political organization in these communities, particularly among women. As in the South, women led civil rights organizing in the Northeast, Midwest, and West, often doing much of the day-to-day work. Yet, despite this organizing, the visible leadership was often male. These essays force us to rethink the masculinization of black nationalism and the ways that this has obscured many aspects of Black Power movements. Women were not just sitting in the background in these meetings but doing organizing, often pushing these groups towards grassroots mobilization and away from charismatic leadership. Yet, even as many of these groups empowered women, they still held rigid views of the roles women could and could not play. Militant black activism, however, did not preclude an emerging women's consciousness nor was it necessarily oppositional to feminism. Indeed, black women were struggling through and contesting gender issues and female subordination within these organizations. The problem lies more with the definition of what is considered the women's movement and what is left out of this history—with defining feminism as an ideology born in the white women's community and not in tandem with groups like the Young Lords, the NWRO, and the Black Panther Party—with a definition of women's liberation that does not include safe health care, quality schools, and a living wage for women and their families.

Freedom North begins during WWII, as protest at home during the war was as formative to the movement as the experiences of black soldiers overseas, and continues through the 1970s. Given space constraints, the book could not span the 1980s and 1990s, despite the presence of organized racial protest movements in these decades. The 11 essays in this volume have been arranged roughly chronologically. To organize them by region or theme risked the kind of simplification that this book set out to critique. There was as much difference as commonalty within region (and certainly three essays could not possibly do justice to an entire region) while no piece spoke to just one or two themes. This book is only a beginning of the story. From Cairo, Illinois, to Cambridge, Maryland, to Milwaukee, Wisconsin, to Seattle, Washington, many battles have not been detailed here. Nor have the many multiracial, multiethnic mobilizations, from the student strikes and building takeovers at universities like San Francisco State, to the Poor People's encampment on the mall in Washington, D.C., to the formation of the Combahee River Collective, been explored. As they fill out new details on the rich variety of struggles outside the South and prompt a rethinking of the binaries of much civil rights scholarship, these essays raise as many questions of chronology, ideology, and local detail as they answer. They show how much more work is needed on these local movements before more sweeping histories of the black liberation struggle can be written.

The limited treatment of Northern struggles not only constricts our historical memory but also impoverishes our understanding of the present. If the movement is understood to be Southern and not national, to be focused on the vote as opposed to political power, if segregation is marked by "for colored only" signs and eliminated by the Civil Rights Act, then it has accomplished its goals. But if movements crisscrossed the country attacking the economic, social, political, and cultural structures and belief systems of racial hierarchy, then they made significant gains but are far from over. The erasure of Northern activism not only justifies the present social order but makes it seem as if social change is not possible against the racial inequities we face today. As the gains of the movement have come under attack, only a clear understanding of the past—of the histories of these struggles and what they were fighting for and against—will allow us to see what should be done in the future.

Notes

1. Ideas are born in dialogue. I would like to thank Matthew Countryman, Paisley Currah, Scott Dexter, Johanna Fernandez, Debbie Gershenowitz, Alejandra Marchevsky, Corey Robin, and especially Komozi Woodard for their careful insights and thought-provoking editorial suggestions.
2. Adam Fairclough, *Better Day Coming* (New York: Viking, 2001).
3. Clayborne Carson, *In Struggle: SNCC and the Black Awakening of the 1960s* (Cambridge: Harvard University Press, 1981).
4. See Taylor Branch, *Parting the Waters* (New York: Simon and Schuster, 1988); *Pillar of Fire* (New York: Simon & Schuster, 1998); James Cone, *Martin and Malcolm and America: A Dream or a Nightmare* (New York: Orbis, 1991); Robert Weisbrot, *Freedom Bound* (New York: Penguin, 1990); and David Garrow, *Bearing the Cross* (William Morrow & Company, 1986).
5. August Meier and Elliot Rudwick, *CORE: A Study of the Civil Rights Movement* (New York: Oxford University Press, 1973).
6. John Dittmer, *Local People* (Urbana: University of Illinois, 1994); Charles Payne, *I've Got the Light of Freedom* (Berkeley: University of California Press, 1995).
7. James Patterson, Brown v. *Board of Education: A Civil Rights Milestone and Its Troubled Legacy* (New York: Oxford University Press, 2001).

8. Tom Sugrue, *The Origins of the Urban Crisis* (Princeton: Princeton University Press, 1996).

9. See, for instance, William Van DeBurg, *New Day in Babylon: The Black Power Movement and American Culture,* 1965–1975 (Chicago: University of Chicago Press, 1992), who explicitly starts his far-reaching study of Black Power in 1965.

10. A comprehensive history of the Black Panther Party has yet to be written. While two excellent anthologies have recently been published, *The Black Panther Party Reconsidered* and *Liberation, Imagination and the Black Panther Party,* these works, because of their essay format and thematic organization, have not focused as closely on the politics of place and the specific workings of the local chapters. Charles Jones, ed., *The Black Panther Party Reconsidered* (Baltimore: Black World Press, 1998); Kathleen Cleaver and George Katsiaficas, eds., *Liberation, Imagination and the Black Panther Party: A New Look at the Panthers and their Legacy* (New York: Routledge, 2001).

11. This differentiating of Northern and Southern racism—and the construction of the South as backward—has a history back to the Revolution. Numerous scholars of antebellum and Reconstruction America have shown the ways racial ideology, segregation, and inequity have their own roots in the North and were never just a product of a backward agrarian South.

12. Nicholas Lemann's *The Promised Land* (New York: Knopf, 1991) is a contemporary example of this problematic history, but these theories have roots in the work of earlier sociologists like E. Franklin Frazier and Oscar Lewis.

13. William Julius Wilson's work, *The Truly Disadvantaged* (Chicago: University of Chicago Press, 1987), exhibits this contradiction—discussing structure while still subscribing to a behavioralist analysis. See Alejandra Marchevsky and Jeanne Theoharis, "Welfare Reform, Globalization, and the Racialization of Entitlement," *American Studies* 41:2/3 (Summer/Fall 2000): 235–265 for a more extended critique of underclass theory.

Chapter 1

"Double V for Victory" Mobilizes Black Detroit, 1941–1946

Beth T. Bates

Less than two months after the Japanese bombed Pearl Harbor, plunging the United States into WWII, African Americans launched a highly organized "Double V for Victory" campaign in black communities across the United States. African Americans in Detroit were in the vanguard of this national effort, which utilized a "Double V" to symbolize the need to fight for victory over fascism abroad and second-class citizenship on the home front. Scholars have noted the great strides that African Americans made during WWII. The literature credits the strong demand for labor, which opened up job opportunities for African Americans as the nation prepared for and then fought in the war, as one reason for economic and social progress.[1] The legitimacy and visibility of the black freedom struggle moved higher on the nation's agenda as the rhetoric of patriotic egalitarianism, engendering a vibrant sense of entitlement among African Americans, emerged from the cry for victory over fascism abroad, which permeated the air.[2]

While these factors are important, it is questionable just how great the strides would have been had African Americans not pushed for inclusion from below. Often it was the initiative of black workers that was decisive, turning the war effort into an opportunity for making inroads into war industries. The federal government did not hand Executive Order #8802, which prohibited discrimination in defense industries and agencies of the federal government, to black America. Black activists *demanded* that President Roosevelt issue an executive order declaring fair employment practices as the standard in all defense operations throughout the land. Finally, while African Americans may have drawn inspiration from victory over fascism in Germany, they utilized the patriotic rhetoric calling for victory for democracy in Europe to carry forward what A. Philip Randolph, head of the Brotherhood of Sleeping Car Porters (BSCP), called the "unfinished task of emancipation."[3] Citizenship discourse had been central to ongoing black freedom struggles since the 1860s.

To understand the forward progress that African Americans made during the war, we must step back. The dramatic shift that placed the African American freedom struggle on the national map during WWII grew out of previous struggles and the spirit of the March on Washington, which carried a politics of self-determination and independence from white control to the shop floor. African Americans began mobilizing against exclusion from war industries on the home front months before the United States entered the war. During the spring of 1941, African American workers helped usher in the United Auto Workers (UAW) at Ford and in the process laid the foundation for challenging the racial status quo in the auto workers' union, within the automobile industry, and within the larger community. Community-wide networks, formed during the campaign to organize black workers at Ford, served as springboards for the ensuing challenge against the racial status quo. The simultaneous national call for a March on Washington, issued during the spring of 1941, added fuel to the effort.

A. Philip Randolph organized thousands of black Americans in 1941 for a March on Washington to demand jobs in rapidly expanding defense industries. Faced with the prospect of 100,000 angry black Americans descending on segregated Washington, Roosevelt issued Executive Order #8802 and created a Fair Employment Practices Commission (FEPC) to implement the order. African Americans praised the executive order, calling it a new Emancipation and the "beginning of our economic freedom." Randolph called off the march when the executive order was issued, but kept the March on Washington Movement (MOWM) intact to act as a watchdog over the FEPC and to mobilize local activism for citizenship rights. The MOWM did not die in cities like Detroit after the executive order was issued from the Oval Office and was fused with the "Double V for Victory" campaign in the winter of 1942, further strengthening the challenge against job discrimination. While black Detroit used the patriotic call for war against fascism as a vehicle to energize and validate the "Double V" campaign, the impulse for this giant step came from the 1930s when the push for greater opportunity accelerated considerably in Detroit.[4]

The foundation was laid through initiatives at the local level operating outside the orbit of mainstream black organizations, such as the National

Association for the Advancement of Colored People (NAACP) and National Urban League (NUL). On one level, African American workers employed by the Ford Motor Company, the single largest employer of black workers in Detroit, enjoyed some of the better jobs available to blacks. Henry Ford's paternalism was legendary and extended throughout the black community. He had cooperating ministers announce job openings from the pulpit, he supported the town of Inkster for black Ford employees, and he invited Marion Anderson and other famous African Americans to Detroit for the cultural enrichment of the black community.[5]

Nevertheless, voices from a new crowd of black activists, frustrated with barriers to equal economic opportunity and impatient with the slow rate of reform espoused by the NAACP, grew louder during the 1930s. Desiring substantive change in the racial status quo, they departed from the gradual, legal approach that had been the hallmark of the NAACP, which committed its resources to making appeals in courts on a case-by-case basis and agitated by compiling facts and deluging government officials with information. The new crowd challenged the old guard in the NAACP, spearheaded the formation of the National Negro Congress (NNC), and mobilized the larger community by making demands backed by collective organization.[6] In order to address pressing civil rights issues, Snow Grigsby, a black postal worker, and Reverend William H. Peck, pastor of Detroit's second oldest and second largest black church, Bethel A.M.E., organized the Detroit Civil Rights Committee (CRC) in 1933. The independent organization was designed to mobilize black Detroiters around economic issues, an area where Grigsby, as a member of the NAACP's executive committee, felt the local branch moved too slowly when it moved at all.[7] The CRC lasted for close to ten years, during which time it challenged racist hiring practices of the Detroit Board of Education, the Post Office, the Fire Department, and the Detroit Edison Company. Shortly after Grigsby and Peck began the CRC, they were joined by the Reverend Charles A. Hill, minister of the popular Hartford Avenue Baptist Church, who also was a member of both the CRC and the NAACP.[8]

By 1936, protest networks organized under Grigsby's CRC began working with C. LeBron Simmons, a lawyer, and labor organizers Joseph Billups, Horace Sheffield, and Mason Hodges in the NNC. The NNC's agenda reflected the interests of this new crowd that rejected the racial status quo—including Ford's paternalism—prevailing in Detroit.[9] The NNC, like the CRC, was organized locally to meet the needs not addressed by the local NAACP, which was viewed as out of touch with workers' concerns and not interested in challenging paternalistic labor relations at Ford Motor Company. When A. Philip Randolph came to Detroit to organize black workers as president of the NNC in 1938, major black churches refused to let him speak about union issues from the pulpit for fear of reprisals from Henry Ford. One exception was the Reverend Peck's Bethel Church, which opened its doors despite pressure to keep Randolph from speaking.[10] The NNC played a "definite role in raising the aspiration levels of Negroes, of making them feel that they could make their way in this democratic society," according to Geraldine Bledsoe, a black board member of the Detroit Urban League, who, by the late 1930s attended NNC meetings. Bledsoe argued that the NNC taught black Detroiters that they "had to be vigorous and uncompromising and demanding in order to find their place."[11]

Young people were finding their place in the Youth Division of the local branch of the NAACP. Under the leadership of Gloster Current, who was personally encouraged by Charles Houston, the NAACP's chief legal strategist, the Youth Division was connected to the local branch in name only. Black youth collaborated with the NNC and its campaign to free imprisoned labor activist Angelo Herndon, a black Communist sentenced to 18 years in prison for speaking out for the rights of black workers in Atlanta. While the branch NAACP president, Dr. James McClendon, ignored the case, the black community largely supported the plight of Herndon. The local NNC urged black auto workers to join the UAW, talking with black workers and developing community-wide networks of black union activists.[12]

Still, recruiting was not easy in a community that had depended on recommendations from ministers for getting jobs with Ford Motor Company at its River Rouge plant near Detroit. Years later, C. LeBron Simmons recalled that the NNC, together with the Civil Rights Congress, was in the forefront of organizations "who took the initiative, rather than waiting to see what the government officials were going to do. We started getting people moving in the direction for change." The NNC, along with the CRC, broke new ground by combining labor and civil rights issues in its campaign for the advancement of black Detroiters, "rather than following the same old pattern that had been staked out before."[13] To aid the progressives in their struggle, the Nat Turner Club, headed by Joseph Billups, was formed in Detroit in the 1930s to educate citizens about democratic rights by organizing around unemployment, evictions, and industrial unionism. Organized and shaped by the left-wing, new-crowd activists, the Nat Turner Club laid the foundation for black caucuses that emerged within the UAW during WWII.[14]

In April 1941, African Americans played a significant role in organizing black workers at the River Rouge plant in Detroit for the UAW-Congress of Industrial Organization (CIO). By then, the NNC networks had expanded to include the Reverend Horace White, who spoke for organized labor from the pulpit of Plymouth Congregational Church. The network also gained the support of the *Michigan Chronicle* and Robert Evans, Snow Grigsby, and the Reverends Charles Hill and Horace White. When black leaders in the local NAACP chapter held out against the union movement during the strike against Ford in April 1941, Walter White, executive secretary of the national NAACP, flew into Detroit to try to persuade the local chapter to back the workers' movement. White, sensing that the Ford strike went beyond union representation, declared from the loudspeaker of a union sound truck that "Negro Ford workers ... cannot afford to rely on the personal kindness of any individual when what the workers want is justice." White defended his controversial support of the UAW's strike by explaining to local NAACP leaders that an alliance between the black community and the union movement represented "the new order of things."[15]

The new order was in place before the United States entered WWII. As the *Chicago Defender* warned shortly before Pearl Harbor, "We are not exaggerating when we say that the American Negro is damned tired of spilling his blood for empty promises of better days."[16] Once the United States officially entered the war, Randolph and MOWM organizers linked the war for democracy in Europe and Asia to the war for democracy on the home front with the slogan, "Winning Democracy for the Negro is Winning the War for Democracy." The phrase resonated with black Americans who understood they were now, as philosopher Alaine Locke noted, "a touchstone the world over of our democratic integrity."[17] Building on the "Double V for Victory" campaign, initiated by the *Pittsburgh Courier,* Randolph announced plans "to stage a series of giant protest meetings ... 'to win the democratic rights for Negroes now during the war.' "[18] By the summer of 1942, the MOWM, waving the banner of the "Double V for Victory," basked in the success of the series of large rallies that it had organized in major cities to champion full citizenship rights.

With the intentional exclusion of whites from participation in the MOWM, a politics of black self-determination rose to the fore. The all-black tactic was designed not so much to keep out the Communists, as some have suggested, or to borrow from Marcus Garvey.[19] Randolph used black nationalism as a tool to shatter barriers—social, economic, political—that barred African Americans from full participation in American society. When Randolph resigned as president of the NNC in the spring of 1940, he blasted the Communist Party for violating the independence of black Americans by its alliance with the Soviet Union, which was then a partner with Hitler. He also warned black Americans of the problems inherent in dependence on white financial support of their organizations. For Randolph, the motivation for excluding white participation grew out of his preoccupation with removing the stigma of second-class status from black Americans. Although Randolph severed his ties with the NNC, black activists in Detroit had no trouble working closely with the Communists in the NNC while supporting the MOWM. Randolph hoped the MOWM would be not just a national organization but the means to form local networks, where the experience of building the MOWM at the local level would be in the hands of African Americans.[20] To avoid situations in which white Americans could impose boundaries in interracial strategy sessions as a way to control the decision-making process, black Americans had to formulate their own tactics and agenda based on the interests of the black community; they had to be free from the politics of civility that tried to channel dissent away from protest and toward moderation. By examining activities inspired and supported by the MOWM and the "Double V" campaign in Detroit, we can trace the emergence of the spirit and philosophy embodied in the "March Movement," which framed the direction of black protest politics in Detroit during the war.

MOWM taught black community activists the importance of using mass demonstrations as a tool to challenge existing power relations. Black workers drew from the march formula to demand changes in race relations, particularly within the CIO. When industrial management, government, or union officials dragged their feet over issues involving discrimination in workplaces, black workers expressed their impatience by initiating wildcat strikes and work stoppages, applying the lessons inspired by the politics of MOWM to break down barriers to equal economic opportunity on the shop floor.

Before the ink was dry on Executive Order #8802, black workers at Dodge Truck and Dodge Main in Detroit took matters into their own hands. They protested the transfer of white workers only from foundries at Dodge to defense production jobs at the Chrysler tank arsenal. Key issues were restricting black workers to unskilled jobs and locking them out of training programs (funded by federal tax dollars) to which white unskilled and semiskilled workers had easy access. Robert Weaver, a member of the Labor Division of the National Defense Advisory Commission, documented hundreds of cases of industrialists hiring out-of-town white workers rather than employing local black workers. Seventy-five percent of defense jobs required trained workers. "The greatest needs for workers," as Weaver pointed out, "were concentrated in the very occupations in which colored men had not been used and where often there were the strongest resistances to their training and employment." Thus, gaining access to training programs to learn new job skills was a necessity if black Americans were to work in the arsenals for democracy in significant numbers.[21]

The situation in Detroit is illustrative because the city was one of the most important arsenals during WWII.[22] Despite the presence of a few black workers in skilled positions at Ford Motor Company where, in 1941, approximately 12,000 black workers made up over 12 percent of the labor force, the majority of black employees at Ford worked in foundries, as "general laborers," or as janitors. The A. C. Spark Plug Company in Detroit employed 23 black men and women as janitors out of its 3,500 workers; Vickers, Incorporated, employed about 90 black janitors and stock handlers among its 3,000 employees. During the spring of 1941, Chrysler hired approximately 1,850 black workers who constituted about 2.5 percent of the total labor force in its Detroit plants. Of this total, 1,400 were foundry workers and janitors in the Dodge Motor Division. At the same time, about 4 percent of the 10,000 workers at Packard Motor Car Company were blacks, also employed primarily in the foundry. At Hudson Motor Company, approximately 225 unskilled blacks were counted among its 12,200 workers.[23]

Conversion to war production entailed changes in production, with implications for the occupational future of black workers. The majority of automobile firms needed to reduce drastically the number of foundry jobs, the one area of the auto factory where black workers were dominant. Black workers understood that they would either enter general production jobs along with other foundry workers or be reassigned to traditional dead-end jobs. Generally, management resisted introducing black workers on assembly lines because they alleged that white workers would not accept them. Although a few firms honored the government policy against discrimination in defense employment, it was clear to black workers that they must seize the opportunities for upgrading to higher-paid and skilled jobs.[24] At times, their challenge to the occupational status quo forced a face-off between the rank-and-file and union officials, which led to walkouts, mass demonstrations, work stoppages, and wildcat strikes, as black workers relied on direct action to first secure, and then maintain, new positions in industry.[25]

In July of 1941, black workers at Dodge Truck in Detroit walked out of work when neither their union nor management would transfer them to the assembly line; and in August, black workers at Dodge Main staged two more work stoppages demanding transfer to defense jobs at Chrysler. Both management and local union officials insisted that only management could make transfer decisions. Black workers had stopped work when their grievance was dismissed, which led to an official investigation of racial bias by the Federal Office of Production Management (OPM), to which the Fair Employment Practices Committee (FEPC) was attached. Although black workers continued working in the Dodge foundry, the investigation persuaded the international leadership of the UAW that they ought to pressure the local union to follow the governmental edict lest the UAW-CIO lose support within the black community.[26]

Black workers threatened a third walkout at Dodge when white janitors were transferred to skilled work at Chrysler, despite the fact that black janitors with more seniority were barred from such jobs. Again, the OPM intervened and set up a meeting between labor and management to discuss the matter. Although management and the international union blamed the local union, neither was willing to take bold action. Nevertheless, black workers from Dodge were eventually upgraded from Dodge Main to defense work at the Chrysler tank arsenal. In these instances, the pattern of restricting black workers to unskilled and foundry work was broken because black workers were willing to challenge a prerogative—transfers and upgrading—that management had claimed was its own. Generally, only after black workers acted did the UAW international union representatives, at the behest of black staff members, according to Weaver, admit "the need for firmer control over locals which did not exhaust established grievance machinery set up for such a purpose."[27]

A similar pattern unfolded at the Packard Motor Company's main plant in Detroit. After officials of UAW Local 190 at Packard largely dismissed complaints about FEPC violations, Arthur Perry, Christopher C. Alston, and Tom January, three black unionists, appealed to R. J. Thomas, president of the UAW, to "put teeth" in an agreement that there would be no discrimination against black workers in transferring from non-defense to defense production. Perry, Alston, and January acted after 250 white workers staged a sit-down strike to protest the transfer of two black metal polishers to skilled defense production in September 1941. Management asked the two metal polishers to return to their civilian jobs until the local union could settle the matter. The local union delayed acting on the matter; even when the international union intervened, the local continued to procrastinate. Finally, Local 190 told management that the metal polishers should be transferred to skilled work. At that point, the company refused to issue the transfers because they believed such action would arouse white workers. The situation settled into what *Fortune* magazine called "a wrestling match" between the government, the union, and the company "over two American citizens' rights to contribute their skill to the production of tanks." After six months of negotiations by Thomas and representatives from the FEPC, black workers were placed back on the tank production lines at Packard.[28]

Although relations between black and white workers at Packard remained contested for the next three years, the situation revealed a pattern that repeated itself in many plants, with black workers using wildcat strikes and work stoppages to gain an expanded foothold in the workplace and white workers responding by staging "hate strikes." Some managers quietly encouraged the white hate-strikers, and the Ku Klux Klan used what historian George Lipsitz has described as both "covert and overt mobilization inside the local union."[29] Moreover, August Meier and Elliot Rudwick, authors of *Black Detroit and the Rise of the UAW*, have called C. E. Weiss, industrial relations manager at Packard, "probably the most unabashedly bigoted executive in the industry ... [who] constantly [mouthed] racist cliches." Packard officials encouraged hate strikes and resistance to black upgrading while the leadership of Local 190 split over how to proceed, giving black workers a "runaround" when they made complaints.[30] By utilizing the wildcat strike—banned by every union leader—and operating outside of legitimate channels for negotiating labor grievances, African Americans put into practice MOWM's belief that only "mass action by Negroes" would secure meaningful economic rights of citizenship. As Randolph said, black Americans "must take the lead in fighting their own battles—they cannot expect whites to do it for them."[31]

During the winter and spring of 1942, African American workers expanded their protests to housing when they joined forces with a network in the black community demanding that the federal government uphold its commitment to house black Detroiters at the Sojourner Truth Housing Project.[32] The Reverend Horace White, a leader of the Sojourner Truth Citizens Committee, also led the MOWM local in Detroit. Although White limited membership in the MOWM to black Detroiters to ensure, as a MOWM directive put it, "against whites ... dominating ... in an unhealthy way,"[33] after the Sojourner Project was organized, he welcomed the cooperation of white groups and individuals who wished to *follow* the black agenda. The alliance included a few leaders from traditional black advancement organizations and the UAW. Shelton Tappes, Horace Sheffield, and Joseph Billups, veteran black organizers at the River Rouge plant, joined with Simmons and the Reverends White and Hill to orchestrate direct action against the government's exclusion of black citizens from the Sojourner Project, using strategies they had learned during the 1930s. In February 1942, these new-crowd leaders organized daily picketing of City Hall and the Detroit Housing Commission and sent thousands of postcards to President Roosevelt protesting the restriction of the Sojourner Project to white residents. When negotiations stalled, several members of the Sojourner Truth Citizens Committee—against the advice of NAACP lawyers—arrived in Washington and threatened to bring 10,000 additional black American protestors to the Capitol. At that point, the federal government reversed its previous actions and opened the Sojourner Project to black residents.[34] The message to the larger white community was that the new-crowd black worker and citizen was not going to accept the racial status quo, even when the power reinforcing local housing patterns was that of the federal government. By April, militant pressure from the black community had forced the government to keep the housing project open to African Americans.[35]

When the MOWM held a national policy conference in Detroit in September 1942, it reaffirmed limiting membership to African Americans.[36] Randolph told the Detroit Policy Conference that collective organization among black Americans must come from within the black community to be effective. Although black Americans are highly organized, traditional black "organizations are not built to deal with and manipulate the mechanics of power. ... They don't seek to transform the socio-economic racial milieu," which was the ultimate aim of the MOWM through its "action program."[37] The all-black directive was about power—how to get it and how to keep it. When Randolph issued the call for a massive protest march on Washington during the spring of 1941, he told his fellow African Americans, "Be not dismayed" for "you possess power, great power. Our problem is to hitch it up for action" on a "gigantic scale." During the Detroit Policy Conference, Randolph reminded his audience, "We want the full works of citizenship with no reservations. We will accept nothing less."[38]

Although the NAACP had cooperated with MOWM in 1941, by the fall of 1942 the all-black directive worried more moderate leaders like Walter White and Roy Wilkins because, they argued, it flew in the face of the larger goal of complete integration. Randolph, too, supported complete integration in the long run but believed that black Americans had to formulate their own strategies and tactics for achieving that goal. At the same time, white labor leaders were increasingly uncomfortable with MOWM's politics of black self-determination, referred to as "march behavior," which entailed not only shutting out white advice and suggestions but also the control implicit in accepting direction from whites. "Inevitably," Randolph told the Detroit Policy Conference, the expectation that whites will lead intrudes in "mixed organizations that are supposed to be in the interests of the Negro."[39] As the black rank and file continued its push for immediate access to new jobs created by the demand for war material, new-crowd leaders working within the structure of organized labor felt pressure from union officials whose interests diverged from those of the rank and file. We can perhaps best appreciate the complicated nature of the relationship that emerged between black activists and liberal labor leaders by examining two figures from that time: Walter Hardin and R. J. Thomas.

One year before the Detroit MOWM Policy Conference, in response to wildcat strikes and direct action by black workers on the shop floor, R. J. Thomas created the Inter-Racial Committee, appointed six black UAW international staff members to the committee, and chose Walter Hardin, one of the UAW's first black organizers and the first black representative on the UAW's international staff, as chair of the committee.[40] But by the summer of 1943, Thomas abolished the committee and adopted a more moderate stance in terms of black rights within the union and plant.[41] Why did Thomas's attitude change?

Between 1941 and 1943, the Inter-Racial Committee may have deflected and contained factional disputes within the UAW, particularly between the left-leaning George Addes wing, which included Communists who placed black rights high on their agenda, and the Walter P. Reuther group, which appealed to more conservative interests within the union. Both factions supported the Inter-Racial Committee and competed for black political support. Thus, in the early 1940s, civil rights issues, as Robert Korstad and Nelson Lichtenstein note, were high on the agenda of white UAW officials. But the committee enjoyed very little independence, and Hardin was not able to execute substantive remedies, which may have added to the frustrations felt by many in the black rank and file.[42]

Black activists responded by taking matters into their own hands and expanding their struggle to include jobs not just for black men but also for black women. Inspired by the "Double V for Victory" campaign, victory committees were organized by black workers to organize and bring pressure on the "International and insist on ... Constitutional rights as UAW members," as Sheldon Tappes, recording secretary of Ford Local 600, recalled. Tappes claimed that just about every active black working in a UAW plant was involved in victory committees, which focused on aiding the war by producing for the war against fascism and realizing economic rights of citizenship.[43] While the MOWM and the "Double V" campaigns may have appeared symbolic, the spirit they unleashed frustrated local union officials who had to contend with the activism inspired by these campaigns operating through networks beyond the union's control. Murray Body, Chrysler, Plymouth, and Packard all had victory committees that ostensibly served to aid the war effort but were also designed to realize the "potential of the Negro" in the workplace and within the union, to "safeguard ... seniority rights, promotions on the union staff as well as on the job."[44]

The victory committees were "a pressure group upon the UAW leadership." Loosely organized, they nevertheless met regularly and "actually went into the local union meetings as a caucus, to fight for their rights."[45] Through the victory committees, we see black workers taking charge outside the formal structure of the union in order to better safeguard their rights. The victory committees laid the foundation for the Metropolitan Labor Council, which was formally founded in 1943 as a means to bring together black union workers from several plants throughout Detroit so they could "concentrate the force of these groups. ... They could then apply to the International and insist on their constitutional rights as UAW members."[46]

During this same period, Hardin felt increasingly unable to fight individual grievances or resolve crisis situations from within the UAW and announced that he wanted to quit his "job with the UAW-CIO and go back into the shop unless some of the Negro's labor problems are solved."[47] As a member of the UAW's Inter-Racial Committee, he was, as Meier and Rudwick note, "powerless to fight individual grievances or resolve crisis situations."[48]

During the spring of 1943, the situation at Packard came apart at the seams. Black workers, frustrated with the glacial pace of change, took direct action on the shop floor and into the streets.[49] But in the process, the strategy again challenged the traditional relationship between labor union management and black workers. With Packard continuing to proceed very slowly in upgrading black workers to production line work, Walter Hardin turned to the Citizens Committee for Jobs in War Industry, a militant protest network established by the Reverend Charles Hill, to mobilize a march and mass rally at Cadillac Square in Detroit in April 1943. More than 10,000 black and white citizens protested continuing discrimination in war plants and listened to speeches by NAACP head McClendon, Reverend Hill, and Walter Reuther, UAW vice president. An important goal of the march was to "focus attention on the large number of Negro women available for war jobs." Protesters included great numbers of women carrying signs that read, "Hire Negro Women!" "Democracy Begins at Home," and "We Die Together, Let's Work and Live Together."[50] A "Cadillac Charter," drafted by joint efforts of the UAW Inter-Racial Committee and the Labor Committee of the Detroit NAACP, declared allegiance to seven "Articles of Democracy," including an article declaring "that all industry participating in the war effort treat all labor alike, regardless of race, color, creed, religion, or national origin, in hiring, upgrading and training of men and women, fully observing Executive Order 8802."[51]

By publicizing the commitment of the black community to job equality and the spirit and principles inscribed in Executive Order #8802, the demonstration at Cadillac Square placed Hardin in an increasingly uneasy position both within the UAW and within traditional leadership circles in the NAACP. His attempt to connect the Inter-Racial Committee with black community activism—with white hostility to black upgrading and the hiring of black women workers swirling in the background—appeared to operate at cross-purposes with the union's agenda, despite Reuther's ostensible endorsement of the rally. In addition, old-guard leaders in the Detroit branch of the NAACP, who felt slighted when Hardin organized the Cadillac Square protest march without their advice, disapproved of the rally. Hardin resigned in frustration from his NAACP position shortly after the demonstration.[52]

A month later, as union officials were attempting to reign in grassroots activities, the situation at Packard escalated. White women had walked off the job several times during the spring to protest the hiring of three black females trained to work drill presses.[53] In May, after the company upgraded three black men to the aircraft assembly line, several hundred white workers walked out and would not agree to return until the union local removed the black workers. The union proposed settling the matter by calling a mass meeting. The majority of black workers interpreted the union's decision as indecisiveness, which led black union steward Christopher Alston to call a walkout. Since the majority of black workers were in the foundry, this action closed the foundry for three days. At this point, management, government, and the union had to appeal directly to the black insurgents to get the foundry moving again. Black workers finally returned, but only after the three men were restored to their jobs. White workers then retaliated by walking off the job, and the black workers were removed from the aircraft assembly line again.[54] Before the protest was settled, over 25,000 white workers walked out, which shut down the entire plant. The War Labor Board ordered Packard workers back to work and simultaneously suspended 30 black and white ringleaders. Colonel George E. Strong, a government contract compliance officer called in by Thomas to settle the strike, told Christopher Alston, who was 31 years old with dependents, that if he did not modify his position, he would be drafted.[55] In the wake of the Packard strike, Colonel Strong delivered on his promise: Alston was fired and inducted into the army. The message to black community activists was clear: Fighting for democracy at home could land one in the midst of the war abroad.

Thomas intervened to encourage government agencies to take decisive action against Packard, which he then vigorously supported. As Meier and Rudwick suggest, from the perspective of the black community, Thomas successfully settled the strike, when he announced that the union would not tolerate white racism and would expel those who did not comply with the government's order. Although Thomas's prestige with black community leaders may have increased, Sheldon Tappes recalled many years later that during 1943, Thomas no longer identified with the "left wing group."[56] The Packard situation highlighted the difficulties that union officials faced when trying to address the concerns of various constituencies within the UAW.

By June of 1943, the patience of Thomas and Reuther had apparently worn thin with "march behavior" exhibited by black rank-and-file activists who, rather than follow union procedure, took matters into their own hands, using the language of protest politics. Operating beyond the boundaries of conventional union politics, such behavior demonstrated contempt for union authority. But it also made a mockery of the no-strike pledge agreement between union leadership and the government, which placed UAW leaders Thomas and Reuther in the position of curbing workers' insurgency in exchange for a "modified union shop" contract and dues checkoff.[57] Thomas and Walter Reuther apparently rationalized this awkward position between the interests of workers and those of management and government by claiming that only by demanding a policy of self-restraint regarding work stoppages could the union be spared assault from the right.[58]

Finally, the no-strike pledge, which by the middle of 1943 was threatening to wreak havoc within the UAW, placed union officials in a tricky position. Thomas and Reuther learned to tread carefully through the thickets of this issue since large numbers of both black and white members of the rank and file agreed that the strike was a worker's ultimate weapon. Reuther, who "played his cards with ... finesse," according to Nelson Lichtenstein, viewed maintenance of the no-strike pledge in terms of political tactics. While he straddled the issues, he understood the importance of remaining in the good graces of Washington. The issue was complicated by the Communist Party at the local level, which advocated a no-strike policy in theory but maintained a good relationship with black radicals by scoring points on civil rights and support for a black seat on the UAW executive board—something Reuther denounced. Although the Popular Front's support for the no-strike pledge suggested that victory over fascism must precede further advancement of black civil rights, black radicals in UAW Local 600 seemed to notice the party's identification with civil rights issues more than its allegiance to Moscow.[59]

Hardin remained a staff member of the UAW-CIO for one more year, but his relationship with Thomas deteriorated during the months between the Cadillac Square demonstration in April and the wildcat strikes of late May. Thomas dissolved the Inter-Racial Committee in June 1943, and Hardin was dismissed from the international staff in 1944.[60] Although Thomas did not say why he dissolved the Inter-Racial Committee, Dominic Capeci argues that UAW officers feared an autonomous interracial body that was capable of "outstepping their gradualism and alienating their constituencies."[61] Gradualism had inspired direct action by black workers, who were frustrated over the slow gains they had made on the production line, but aggressive action, or "march behavior," was linked to the MOWM.[62]

"March behavior" was apparently on the minds of Thomas and Reuther. A NAACP memo claimed that Thomas and Reuther were concerned because black workers in Detroit, who were inspired by the spirit of the "March on Washington," were in a position to "close down three or four shops." Work stoppages and wildcat strikes, they believed, would tear "down whatever work they have done to get Negroes into the shops" and hurt the UAW.[63] The problem with the MOWM, according to the UAW leadership, was that it "intensifies the wrong type of racial consciousness."[64] They did not like either the MOWM all-black policy or its militant approach to winning fair employment practices. In an effort to control the situation, the UAW leaders decided to tell Randolph "that he has got to tone it down and make it interracial."[65]

The Detroit Race Riot of June 20, 1943, which left 34 people dead, dampened the militant spirit of many new-crowd activists. A study of the riot by the Governor's Committee cited the demands for equality made by black radical agitators among the factors that led to the violent upheaval.[66] The militant "assertiveness" of black Americans engendered a backlash from portions of the white community in Detroit and throughout the nation. Many incidents centered on white fears of black economic competition. A group of black citizens was driven from a Louisiana town that had set up a welding school for black workers. Those who opposed the school did not want "the colored folk to learn to be anything but sharecroppers and servants."[67] As a *New Republic* article put it, throughout the South a black man in uniform symbolized someone "not knowing his place." The situation encouraged many white Americans to increase their efforts to keep black Americans in "their place."[68] After the Detroit Race Riot, black Americans were increasingly suspected of disloyalty for not toeing the line and controlling their resentment, leading some to declare that "the more they get the more they want."[69] The response to white intransigence was for "mature, tough-minded, thinking Negroes,"—the new crowd—to intensify their resolve to fight against second-class citizenship by asserting their rights as Americans. While white Americans were quick to call the new aggressiveness revolutionary, few may have noted, as a contemporary journalist did, that the battle was not "against the Constitution" but the "great mass of legal and extra-legal Jim Crow practices that have shut him off from many rights that the Constitution grants him."[70] Nevertheless, black demands for equal rights were often portrayed as the behavior of "uppity, out of line Negroes."[71]

In the short run, Thomas and Reuther's attempt to control the insurgency of black workers failed. Wildcat strikes and work stoppages continued to plague production at Packard and other factories.[72] When black foundry workers staged a walkout in November 1943 to protest lack of transfers, Packard quickly upgraded 200 workers by the end of the month; by the end of 1943, Packard had transferred nearly 500 out of the foundry to production jobs previously held only by white workers. Militancy paid off.[73] Black workers helped shape the aggressive democratic spirit that emerged from the war among the rank and file and "made militancy on civil rights the sine qua non of serious political leadership in the UAW" by the end of the war, as Korstad and Lichtenstein argue.[74]

These shop-floor gains were sometimes transitory as several scholars have recently shown.[75] By early 1944, the UAW executive board decided to abandon what they called "the kid-glove tactics of yesterday," suspend local union leaders who defended wildcat strikers, and place their locals under an international administratorship.[76] A large turnover of black UAW organizers and staff shifted their allegiance to the Reuther camp after his successful quest for control of the UAW in 1946. Walter Hardin, who had regained a position on the UAW staff, was ousted once again, along with George Crockett, John Conyers, Sr., and Coleman Young, all new-crowd activists who had been instrumental in organizing black workers and citizens of Detroit in support of the UAW. Although Reuther endorsed civil rights—he was a member of the NAACP board of directors in the late 1940s and the UAW contributed considerable amounts of money to the organization—he structured his relationships with the black community around a politics of civility. Simultaneously, the top leadership in the NAACP increasingly fought the war for first-class citizenship in the courts.[77]

Nevertheless, the pattern established during the war on the home front to secure jobs and break down occupational barriers to better jobs rewarded new-crowd tactics that challenged arrangements of the racial status quo and the politics of civility. Changes and improvements did occur. As Robert Weaver argued, much of what happened between 1940 and 1945 represented a departure from older practices, resulting in greater industrial and occupational diversification than had occurred for black workers in the preceding 75 years. It was the first chance many had to perform basic skilled and semiskilled jobs in a wide range of industries and plants, and it gave black and white workers an opportunity to work alongside each other on the "basis of industrial equality."[78] When black working-class activists seized the "window of opportunity" that the war presented for assaulting Jim Crow both within the union and within the community, their efforts mobilized the larger community and politicized the home front by pushing the issue of black self-determination to a deeper level, carrying forward strategies pioneered by the new crowd during the 1930s.[79]

Although recession, seniority struggles, and layoffs weakened the activism of the black working class in the aftermath of WWII, the seeds planted by black activists in the 1930s and cultivated during the war bore fruit. Despite the bureaucratization and appropriation of the Fair Practices Department after Walter Reuther successfully rose to the presidency of the UAW, the elimination of militant black activists from staff positions within the UAW, the force of Taft-Hartley, and the power of anti-Communist propaganda to silence challenges to the status quo, networks formed during the 1930s, which fostered the activism during the war, did not die. As early as 1949, plans were laid by black activists within UAW Local 600 for the creation of the National Negro Labor Council (NNLC) in the early 1950s. Many of those who came of age during WWII in Detroit carried the struggle for full democratic rights, imbued by a politics of black self-determination, to other arenas. George Crockett used his legal expertise to win election as judge in the Recorders Court in 1966 and later as congressman, representing the Detroit area. James Boggs, an autoworker at Chrysler, took note of the contradictions exposed during WWII, utilized that knowledge to arm himself, and launched his career as a black intellectual and community activist. John Conyers, Jr., became Detroit's second black congressman in 1964. Coleman Young became mayor of Detroit in 1973. Quill Pettway, a member of Local 600 and one of the first blacks to gain entrance to the elite corps of tool and die workers at Ford's Rouge River plant, maintains that although many of the organizations failed to achieve, success in the short run, the process of struggle kept networks intact. In 1956, although the NNLC was in shambles and the power of Local 600 was considerably diluted, several workers from the black caucus at the River Rouge plant collected money to fly Rosa Parks up to Detroit to talk to the local about the Montgomery Bus Boycott, unleashing cooperation and support between northern and southern civil rights struggles.[80]

The Detroit story during WWII suggests that activists mobilized through the MOWM and the "Double V for Victory" campaign posed a problem in the eyes of the dominant culture when they followed a different drummer by insisting on setting their own agenda to fight for their rights. The politics of self-determination was part of a larger, long-term goal to remove vestiges of inferior status embedded in a system that was still coming to terms with accepting black Americans as first-class citizens. The legacy of this period was its contribution to building networks that relied on independent, collective mass action to checkmate the dominant culture's ability to keep African Americans in an inferior place.

Notes

1. Robert Weaver, *Negro Labor: A National Problem* (New York: Harcourt, Brace, and Company, 1946); Nelson Lichtenstein, "Class Politics and the State during World War Two," *International Labor and Working-Class History* 58 (Fall 2000); George Lipsitz, *Rainbow at Midnight: Labor and Culture in the 1940s* (Urbana: University of Illinois Press, 1994); August Meier and Elliott Rudwick, *Black Detroit and the Rise of the UAW* (New York: Oxford University Press, 1979); Michael Honey, *Southern Labor and Black Civil Rights: Organizing Memphis Workers* (Urbana: University of Illinois Press, 1993); Roger Horowitz, *"Negro and White, Unite and Fight!": A Social History of Industrial Unionism in Meatpacking, 1930–1990* (Urbana: University of Illinois Press, 1997); Robert Korstad and Nelson Lichtenstein, "Opportunities Found and Lost: Labor, Radicals, and the Early Civil Rights Movement," *Journal of American History* 75 (December 1988): 786–811.
2. Lichtenstein, "Class Politics and the State," 269.
3. A. Philip Randolph, "The Indictment," *Messenger* 8:4 (April 1926): 114.
4. For more on black workers fighting for economic rights of citizenship, see Beth Tompkins Bates, *Pullman Porters and the Rise of Protest Politics in Black America, 1925–1945* (Chapel Hill: University of North Carolina Press, 2001).
5. Meier and Rudwick, *Black Detroit*, 6–10.
6. For a more detailed analysis of the emergence of a new crowd within the black community, see Beth Tompkins Bates, "A New Crowd Challenges the Agenda of the Old Guard in the NAACP, 1933–1941," *American Historical Review* 102:2 (April 1997): 340–377. Strategies and approaches utilized by the new crowd did not drop out of the sky. They had roots in the history of African American communities. The new crowd and their approach to racial reform was new in relation to the direction and approach of the NAACP, which had been the standard bearer for challenging the racial status quo.
7. Snow Grigsby interview, Archives of Labor and Urban Affairs of Wayne State University, Reuther Library, Detroit (hereafter cited as ALUA), 3, 4.
8. Grigsby interview, ALUA, 6.
9. For example, a report of Daisy E. Lampkin's activities as field secretary of the NAACP between October 1 and November 30, 1938, finds her addressing a NNC forum in Baltimore October 7, 1938, I-C-69; Lampkin to Walter White, December 27, 1938, I-C-69, NAACP Papers. Robin Kelley noted a similar correlation in Birmingham, Alabama, between increased militancy on the part of the local chapter and increased popularity of the NAACP. See "Hamer n' Hoe: Black Radicalism and the Communist Party in Alabama, 1929–1941" (Ph.D. diss., University of California, Los Angeles, 1987), 522–523.
10. Interview with C. LeBron Simmons, president of Detroit chapter of the NNC, 2, Box 33.15, Series VI, Nat Ganley Collection, ALUA.
11. Geraldine Bledsoe, interviewed by Norman McRae, 1970, ALUA, 6.
12. For more on Angelo Herndon's case, see Harvard Sitkoff, *A New Deal for Blacks: The Emergence of Civil Rights as a National Issue: The Depression*

Decade (New York: Oxford University Press, 1978), 150, 151. For more on the black community in Detroit, see Bates, "A New Crowd Challenges the Agenda of the Old Guard," 373–374.

13. Interview with C. Lebron Simmons, 9, 10, Folder 15, Box 33, Nat Ganley Collection, ALUA; Meier and Rudwick, *Black Detroit*, 6–10; and interview by Norman McRae, with C. LeBron Simmons, 1969, 3–5, "Blacks in the Labor Movement," Oral History Transcripts, ALUA.

14. Interview with Joseph Billups by Herbert Hill, 1967, in Detroit, used by permission of Herbert Hill, 3, 5, "Blacks in the Labor Movement," Oral History Transcripts, ALUA.

15. Walter White to A. J. Muste, April 15, 1941, NAACP file: Ford Strike; quote is from notes by Walter White, from Ford Strike, n.d., file: Ford Strike, II-A-333, NAACP Papers.

16. Sitkoff, *A New Deal for Blacks*, 324

17. Editorial, *Black Worker*, April 1942, 4; Alaine Locke, "The Unfinished Business of Democracy," *Survey Graphic* 31:11 (November 1942), 458.

18. "March on Washington Movement Plans Giant Meeting," *Black Worker*, March 1942, 4.

19. For keeping out the Communists, see Sitkoff, *A New Deal for Blacks*, 315; John Sengstacke's column, *Chicago Defender*, January 18, 1941. For borrowing from Garvey, see Paula F. Pfeffer, *A. Philip Randolph, Pioneer of the Civil Rights Movement* (Baton Rouge: Louisiana State University Press, 1990), 58. For more on the politics of the all-black strategy adopted by MOWM, see Bates, *Pullman Porters*, 148–174.

20. Sitkoff, *A New Deal for Blacks*, 112; for Randolph's resignation from the NNC and his warning to black people of the dangers of depending on whites, see Komozi Woodard, *A Nation within a Nation: Amiri Baraka (LeRoi Jones) and Black Power Politics* (Chapel Hill: University of North Carolina Press), 29–30; for black activists working with the Communists while supporting the MOWM, see Angela Denise Dillard, "From the Reverend Charles A. Hill to the Reverend Albert B. Cleage, Jr.: Change and Continuity in the Patterns of Civil Rights Mobilizations in Detroit" (Ph.D. diss., University of Michigan, 1995), 133.

21. My analysis on the economic situation of black workers during WWII would not be possible without the scholarship of Robert C. Weaver, whose *Negro Labor* provides the foundation for much of what follows. Robert Weaver, *Negro Labor*, 65; Patricia Sullivan, *Days of Hope: Race and Democracy in the New Deal Era* (Chapel Hill: University of North Carolina Press, 1996), 135.

22. Thomas J. Sugrue, *The Origins of the Urban Crisis: Race and Inequality in Postwar Detroit* (Princeton: Princeton University Press, 1996), 17–31.

23. Weaver, *Negro Labor*, 60–65.

24. Weaver, *Negro Labor*, 64.

25. Lipsitz, *Rainbow at Midnight*, 73.

26. Meier and Rudwick, *Black Detroit*, 120–124.

27. Ibid., 122, 123; Lipsitz, *Rainbow at Midnight*, 74; Weaver, *Negro Labor*, 68, 69.

28. For the quote from *Fortune,* see Meier and Rudwick, *Black Detroit,* 127; for petition from Perry, Alston, and January, see To Inter-Racial Committee, UAW-CIO from Perry, Alston, and January, November 13, 1941, UAW War Policy Collection, ALUA. See also larger discussion on Packard, in Meier and Rudwick, *Black Detroit,* 125–136, and Dominic J. Capeci, *Race Relations in Wartime Detroit: The Sojourner Truth Housing Controversy of 1942* (Philadelphia: Temple University Press, 1984) 70–74.

29. Lipsitz, *Rainbow at Midnight,* 75.

30. Meier and Rudwick, *Black Detroit,* 165–166.

31. "March on Washington Movement: What Do We Stand For?" pamphlet, 2, 3, Box 26, A. Philip Randolph Papers, Library of Congress, Washington, D.C.

32. Meier and Rudwick, *Black Detroit,* 183.

33. "March on Washington Movement; What Do We Stand For?," 3.

34. Capeci, *Race Relations in Wartime Detroit,* 85–87; Dillard, "From the Reverend Charles A. Hill to the Reverend Albert B. Cleage, Jr.," 150–156; Meier and Rudwick, *Black Detroit,* 176–180.

35. For Sojourner Truth Project controversy, see Meier and Rudwick, *Black Detroit,* 176–184; for composition of the Sojourner Truth Citizens Committee, see Capeci, *Race Relations in Wartime Detroit,* 83, 84; for forces arrayed against black occupancy, see Korstad and Lichtenstein, "Opportunities Found and Lost," 797; Sugrue, *Origins of the Urban Crisis,* 72–75.

36. "MOWM: What Do We Stand For!," Box 26, A. Philip Randolph Papers, Library of Congress, Washington, D.C.

37. A. Philip Randolph, "Address to the Policy Conference," 8, Detroit, II-A-417, NAACP Papers.

38. "Keynote Address to the Policy Conference of the March on Washington Movement," A. Philip Randolph, 5 (September 26, 27, 1942), Detroit, II-A-417, NAACP Papers.

39. Randolph, "Keynote Address to Policy Conference of MOWM," 6.

40. Minutes, UAW International Executive Board (IEB) meeting, September 16, 1941, UAW IEB Meetings Collection, Box 2; "UAW-CIO Board Demands Negro Discrimination End," clipping from newspaper, October 1, 1941, UAW International Activities Vertical File Collection, Box 72; Herbert Hill interview of Sheldon Tappes, 51, "Blacks in the Labor Movement," ALUA; Meier and Rudwick, *Black Detroit,* 40, 41, 121–123; Capeci, *Race Relations in Wartime Detroit,* 68.

41. Sheldon Tappes noted that during 1943, Thomas was no longer part of the "left wing group." Herbert Hill interview with Sheldon Tappes, "Blacks in the Labor Movement," no. 1, part 2, 58, ALUA.

42. Capeci, *Race Relations in Wartime Detroit,* 68-69; Korstad and Lichtenstein, "Opportunities Found and Lost," 799.

43. Hill interview with Joseph Billups, 11, 12.

44. Ibid., 11.

45. Hill interview with Sheldon Tappes and Joseph Billups, 11.

46. Ibid.
47. For quote, see Meier and Rudwick, *Black Detroit,* 164.
48. Quote is cited in Meier and Rudwick, *Black Detroit,* 164 (from *Michigan Chronicle,* March 27, 1943).
49. Lipsitz, *Rainbow at Midnight,* 89, 90; quote found in Lipsitz, p. 90, from *Michigan Chronicle,* April 17, 1943.
50. Meier and Rudwick, *Black Detroit,* 113–115, 163, 164; C. L. R. James, *Fighting Racism,* 235; "Forward With Action" (Annual Report, 1943, of Detroit Branch of NAACP), especially 20, 21, 37, Branch Files: Detroit, II-C-87, NAACP Papers, Library of Congress.
51. "The Cadillac Charter," Branch File: Detroit, II-C-86, NAACP Papers.
52. Meier and Rudwick, *Black Detroit,* 164, 212, 213. By the summer of 1943, R. J. Thomas pleaded, as Nelson Lichtenstein points out, "for an end to wildcat strikes" as pressure mounted to control factions within the union and black workers insurgency even as Thomas and Reuther struggled to maintain its compact with the government to uphold the no-strike pledge. See Nelson Lichtenstein, *Walter Reuther: the Most Dangerous Man in Detroit* (Urbana: University of Illinois Press, 1995), 211, 212.
53. Meier and Rudwick, *Black Detroit,* 166.
54. For the Packard uprising of late spring 1943, see the excellent analysis in Meier and Rudwick, *Black Detroit,* 165–174.
55. For Strong's threat to induct Alston into the army, see interview by author with Marti Alston, December 11, 1999, Detroit, Michigan. Strong's threat to Alston was a dramatic contrast from his previous role as an interventionist who helped expand black economic opportunity (see Meier and Rudwick, *Black Detroit,* 158). The link between the war production and workers insurgency was underscored by the presence of military officers in uniform in all war production plants. Scholar Martin Glaberman notes that military officers regularly intervened in strikes and potential strikes. See Martin Glaberman, *Wartime Strikes: The Struggle Against the No-Strike Pledge in the UAW During World War II* (Detroit: Bewick/ed, 1980), 49.
56. For more on the relationship between R. J. Thomas, Colonel Strong, and the Packard strike, see Meier and Rudwick, *Black Detroit,* 165–172. For Sheldon Tappes on R. J. Thomas, see Hill interview with Sheldon Tappes, no. 1, part 2, 58, ALUA.
57. Nelson Lichtenstein, "Defending the No-Strike Pledge: CIO Politics During World War II," in *Workers' Struggles, Past and Present: A "Radical America" Reader,* James Green, ed. (Philadelphia: Temple University Press, 1983), 272.
58. Ibid., 276.
59. Lichtenstein, *Walter Reuther,* 211–214; Korstad and Lichtenstein, "Opportunities Found and Lost," 797.
60. For the "increasingly strained" relationship between Hardin and Thomas and the dissolution of the Inter-Racial Committee see, Meier and Rudwick, *Black Detroit,* 117, 118, 212, 213.

61. Capeci, *Race Relations in Wartime Detroit,* 68–69.

62. See Leslie Perry to Walter White, May 4, 1943, "MOWC General," II-A-416, NAACP Papers.

63. Lichtenstein, "Defending the No-Strike Pledge," 272.

64. Perry to White, May 4, 1943, "MOWC General."

65. Ibid.

66. Wynn, *The Afro-American and the Second World War,* 70; Harvard Sitkoff, "The Detroit Race Riot of 1943," *Michigan History* 53:3 (1969): 199–204; Charles S. Johnson, "News Summary of National Events and Trends In Race Relations," August 1943, prepared for Julius Rosenwald Fund, 4, 17–21; File: Rosenwald Fund, II-A-513, NAACP Papers.

67. These two incidents are related in Harvard Sitkoff, "Racial Militancy and Interracial Violence in the Second World War," *Journal of American History* 58:3 (December 1971): 672.

68. "Negroes in the Armed Forces," *New Republic* 109 (October 18, 1943): 542–543.

69. Harvard Sitkoff, "Racial Militancy," 669, 670.

70. Sancton, "Something's Happened to the Negro," *New Republic* 108:6 (February 8, 1943), first quote, 178; second quote, 176.

71. Sitkoff, "Racial Militancy," 673.

72. Finally, there were many exceptions to the Packard pattern. When Briggs Manufacturing Company, Kelsey-Hayes Wheel Company, and Consolidated Brass Company initiated programs of upgrading black workers to higher-paying defense jobs, no trouble erupted. Weaver attributes the difference to the firm stand that both management and labor took in expediting the transfers. Another incident, at the Chrysler Corporation, reinforces this reasoning. Chrysler ordered all loaders and boxers at Dodge transferred to defense work at the Chrysler Highland Park plant, and management declared that the transfers would take place despite rumors of a white workers' hate strike. Management was backed by both the local and international union. When a stoppage did occur, union representatives told "management to fire all workers who refused to return to their jobs." One day after the transfer, management said all was well (see Weaver, *Negro Labor,* 71). The situation of upgrading was nevertheless volatile and filled with uncertainty. Even at plants where hate strikes had been resolved in favor of black workers, hiring black workers could set off new eruptions from white workers. At the Briggs's Mack Avenue plant in Detroit, a hate strike followed the placement of black women on an assembly line despite its history of amicable relations between black and white workers. But Emil Mazey, the white president of Local 212, promptly terminated the walkout by whites when he directed the UAW plant chairman to let the strikers know that if they stayed out, the union would back the company in firing them. Within ten minutes, "everyone returned to work." In this instance, Mazey was able to draw upon his record as someone who meant what he said. In 1938 he was the first white union officer to hire a black secretary for a local union office. When the white secretaries objected, Mazey told them they would be fired if they did not treat

the black women as equals. They complied. (This analysis draws from the work of Meier and Rudwick, *Black Detroit,* 42, 162, 163.)

73. Meier and Rudwick, *Black Detroit,* 173; Glaberman, *Wartime Strikes,* 51–60.

74. Lipsitz, *Rainbow at Midnight,* 92, 99; For transfer of black workers out of the Packard foundry, see Meier and Rudwick, *Black Detroit,* 173; quote from Korstad and Lichtenstein, "Opportunities Found and Lost," 799.

75. William H. Harris, *The Harder We Run: Black Workers Since the Civil War* (New York: Oxford University Press, 1982), chapters 5 and 6; Korstad and Lichtenstein, "Opportunities Found and Lost," 786–811; Honey, *Southern Labor and Black Civil Rights;* Michael Honey, "Industrial Unionism and Racial Justice in Memphis," in *Organized Labor in the Twentieth Century South,* Robert Zieger, ed. (Knoxville: University of Tennessee Press, 1991).

76. Quote is from Lichtenstein, "Defending the No-Strike Pledge," 276.

77. Meier and Rudwick, *Black Detroit,* 212, 213; Korstad and Lichtenstein, "Opportunities Found and Lost," 800, 806, 807.

78. Weaver, *Negro Labor,* 78, 79.

79. This argument is cited in Karen Tucker Anderson, "Last Hired, First Fired: Black Women Workers during World War II," *Journal of American History* 69:1 (June 1983): 95. See also discussion of this topic by Lipsitz, *Rainbow at Midnight,* 338.

80. Interview with Quill Pettway, February 3, 2001, conducted by author, L. Todd Duncan, and Kathryne Lindberg, February 3, 2001, Department of Africana Studies, Wayne State University.

Chapter 2

The World of the Illinois Panthers

Jon Rice

The political and social conditions of 1960s Chicago helped establish a Black Panther movement that was unique to that city. Based on the ideology of the Black Panther Party in Oakland, the Party was a response to the local politics of Chicago, the Cook County Democratic Party, and the perceived failure of the Chicago Freedom Movement (CFM) that preceded it. A year after the murder of Chicago Panther leader Fred Hampton by Chicago police officers, thousands of high school students staged walkouts, protesting his murder at over a dozen high schools.[1] Their activities were the result of Panther cadres in most black high schools in the city that grew out of the organizing the party had done in the city. The Chicago Panthers manifested a spirit of intense optimism, practicality, and sincerity that was startling and refreshing to the students. It promoted interethnic coalitions and took pragmatic steps to achieve them. It was integrationist in its ultimate goal—a society without racism—and rather cool to the idea of Pan-African unity. The Black Panther Party's ideologies and activities in Chicago, then, differed significantly from popular perceptions of the Party both then and today.

The West Side Ghetto

Chicago's West Side ghetto was expanding in the 1960s. Southern migrants from Mississippi, Arkansas, and Louisiana were joined on the West Side by poor black Chicagoans, who had been pushed out of their South Side homes by urban renewal. In the period from 1941 to 1965, Chicago displaced

160,000 poor blacks (and 40,000 whites) from their homes to make way for urban renewal and expressway construction. Of these displaced people, 3,100 were provided with public housing.[2] Consequently, the West Side communities of North Lawndale, the Near West Side, and East and West Garfield experienced dramatic population growth. Between 1950 and 1960, North Lawndale's population grew from 100,000 to 125,000 and from 13 percent black to 91 percent black. Sixty-two percent of these black people were from the South.[3] In the 1960s, West Garfield's population increased from 45,000 to 48,000, changing from almost all white to entirely black. Similar demographic shifts occurred in East Garfield and the Near West Side.[4]

Housing on the black West Side was deteriorating and overpriced, largely due to the machinations of local realtors. Realtors encouraged white owners to flee incoming blacks and sell their homes at low prices. Black buyers often had to double up with other families to purchase a house.[5] With real estate profits averaging 70 percent, both black and white realtors profited from the manipulation of racial prejudice; some encouraged this fear and prejudice by paying poor black mothers and children to walk through these changing neighborhoods. Chicago banks refused to make loans in areas that were racially changing, so black home buyers not only paid more for their homes but also purchased homes via contract, without equity.[6] These bank policies also meant that home improvements did not get financed in black communities, except through loan sharks. Black families, hemmed in by segregation, paid more in home costs and in rent, due to this artificial housing scarcity created by segregation.[7]

Rigid segregation and gerrymandered school districts denied blacks open enrollment in community schools and meant the city's black schools held two shifts a day. Decreased garbage pickup and increased population on the West Side also meant that the rat population outnumbered the human population. North Lawndale, or Lawndale, as its residents called it, had some of the worst housing in the city by 1960; and, by 1960, it also had the highest percentage of people on welfare (31 percent)[8] and the highest crime rate in the city. To aggravate matters, Chicago police were assigned to its Fillmore District as punishment for misconduct elsewhere.[9] Documented cases of police abuses were common in the *Chicago Defender* in the 1950s and 1960s. Abusive language, arbitrary arrests, searches without provocation, torturing of arrestees, refusal to assist people in distress, and laxness in arresting certain criminals were the most common complaints. These complaints were met consistently with denials of *any* wrongdoing by police and elected officials.[10] In Chicago, in the 1960s, the local Democratic Party controlled key positions in the police department.[11] Since police jobs required an alderman's endorsement, aldermen tended to stick by police. From the black West Sider's perspective, the white Democrats ruled, with the police as their enforcement.[12]

West Siders were not only oppressed by the worst policing but were segregated from black South Siders, through screening renters and high rents.[13] However, the scarcity of financial and real estate possibilities even on the South Side split up families as well as the community. A minority of black South Siders had moved to the southern extremity of that ghetto—the Chatham neighborhood—and found some financial success by servicing the black poor as their school teachers, funeral directors, barbers, and postmen. Thus, the South Side had a range of incomes much broader than that on the West Side.[14] This class diversity also became a class divide, as some black South Siders enjoyed the benefits of political power denied black West Siders and many poor South Siders. This inhibited community-wide activism on the South Side.

Chicago's newer, more powerless ghetto, the West Side, had a spirit of militancy greater than the South Side in the 1960s. In the period 1965-1968, there were three major black riots in Chicago, all occurring exclusively on the West Side. The Deacons for Defense and Justice (also chartered with the National Rifle Association [NRA] as the National Negro Rifle Association), formed on the West Side in 1965. Over 200 residents allied themselves with local youth clubs and armed themselves to protect black citizens from police violence and harassment.[15] They sent food to civil rights marchers in the South and organized against local store owners who discriminated against black people. There was no comparable organization on the South Side. The Contract Buyers League, a community protest group that spanned both black ghettoes, split into West Side and South Side factions over the South Siders' perception of West Siders as too militant.[16]

Traditional West Side Politics

In the 1960s, the vote on the West Side was relatively meaningless, tied as it was to a Democratic precinct captain's favors. Failure to vote Democratic could cost a citizen a job, rejection of a needed license, intense inspection by city building inspectors, or other municipal punishment. West Side precinct captains knew how a citizen voted because they generally accompanied voters into the voting booth.[17] The Democratic political machine in the early 1960s controlled the West Side wards (often known as "plantation wards") with an iron hand and was inclined to use petty violence to keep black people away from independent politics. As historian Alphine Jefferson argues, "If there ever was a colonial set-up, the West Side was it. Men work for the city ... if they don't do as they're told, they lose their jobs."[18]

West Side black political activists began the push to take control of their communities in the late 1950s and early 1960s. Local white aldermen were well entrenched, however, and known as the West Side bloc, a cadre of white politicians and gangsters who ran the 24th, 25th, 27th, 29th, and 28th wards.[19] Although all five wards were majority black, "Izzy" Horowitz (Jewish), ran the 24th; Italian Vito Marzullo ran the 25th; Irishman Edward Quigley ran the 27th; Bernie Neinstein (Jewish) ran the 29th, and Italian Joseph Jambrone ran the 28th.[20] Racism filtered down through the ranks. Of some 63 precincts in the all-black 24th Ward in 1960, 59 had white precinct captains.[21] The West Side bloc politicians could not keep these black people unrepresented for long, and they knew it. They needed to select black successors who would follow orders, so they picked Benjamin Lewis, who was elected to run the 24th Ward.[22] On the surface, Lewis appeared to be a pliant tool but he did things for the community that evidenced an independent mind. Political activist Richard Barnett was convinced that Lewis's loyalty to the machine was a ruse. He believed it was Lewis who prevented high-rise housing projects in the ward, insisted on garbage collections twice a week, and fought the idea of double-shifted schools.[23] Lewis also challenged the Elrod insurance business, run by former ward committeeman Arthur Elrod's family, by setting up his own insurance business there. The politics of this money-making venture illustrate the "corruption-is-normal" mindset of Chicago in the 1960s. The ward committeeman controlled the issuing of liquor licenses. Since liquor store owners needed a license, the committeeman usually created an insurance company to pressure the store owner to buy his insurance in exchange for a license.[24] Arthur Elrod, the previous committeeman, had an insurance monopoly on this practice in Lewis's ward until Lewis set up his business.[25] All in all, Ben Lewis made a number of moves that did not go along with the West Side bloc.

On February 27, 1963, the West Side's first black alderman, Ben Lewis, was shot execution style (three 0.32 caliber bullets in the back of his head) while he was handcuffed on the floor. He had not put up a struggle, according to newspaper reports. The lone Republican alderman in the Chicago City Council, John Hoellen, identified the likely culprits as the police/politician linkage of the West Side bloc and called for an investigation.[26] Not a single black alderman (and there were six from the South Side) supported the investigation. The city's daily newspapers alluded to Lewis's love affairs and gambling but when the police investigator found clues that a police officer might have been involved, the three detectives were dropped from the case.[27] Whether the West Side bloc had Ben Lewis killed or not will probably never be known. The perception among black activists in his community is that Lewis's independence and commitment to the black community got him killed.[28] It is out of such perceptions that carrying weapons, independent politics, and even revolution are legitimized. Chicago politics had worked so well at excluding West Side black citizens that many of them moved from trying to get into the system to overthrowing it.

The Chicago Freedom Movement

On July 10, 1966, approximately 60,000 people gathered in Chicago's Soldier Field to hear Dr. Martin Luther King, Jr.[29] Black political activists from Chicago had gone south to help civil rights efforts, helping to topple the wall of Jim Crow in the South. Now Dr. King had come north to participate in the desegregation of Chicago.[30] There was an air of hope present. The Andrew McPherson Quartet was playing "John Brown's Body" when more than 50 teenagers burst onto the playing field of the stadium, with a large, red flag. They were shouting something, probably "Mighty Blackstone!" or "Stone Love!" in reference to the Blackstone Rangers, for these teenagers represented the largest gang in Chicago at that time. The interruption stopped Dr. King from entering as the boys circled the field on the run. The crowd, largely middle-class, did not like this disruption from these poor black boys. The gang wanted to be a part of the civil rights movement, as a recognized institution.[31] But the crowd at the rally did not seem to think so. "Call the police!" many people yelled, and more people cheered that idea.[32] The police never came, and the gang eventually charged into the upper east side of the stadium and let the rally continue.

This is how the CFM was born. Moral and law-abiding, the CFM supported civil disobedience where the law transgressed "right" and "wrong"— and that was the point at which it would clash with the city police, who tended to be both arrogant and racially biased. Generally speaking, police had no sympathy with the civil rights movement and tended to see disorder, whether caused by demonstrators or gangsters, as criminal.[33] "Respectable Negroes" in Chicago had, for decades, tried to distance themselves from the poorer, rougher black people and prove their worthiness to "white" America. The police, however, tended to view all blacks as criminals.

The community leaders who organized the CFM—which began with the July rally and the posting of 50 demands on the door at City Hall that same day—had a fairly good idea of what created the conditions of a black ghetto. Through their 50 demands, leaders directed grievances at real estate brokers, banks, the Federal Housing Authority (FHA), the Democratic Party, the Chicago Board of Education, and the local trade unions.[34] They indicated that the profit from the dual housing market, bolstered by the policies of banks, the FHA, the local political machine, and the manipulation of the prejudices of white homeowners worked together to produce the conditions of the ghetto[35] and a segregated, unequal school system. The factors that tied these interests together were economic profit and political control of the poor.[36] The consequences were an unhealthy living environment for the poor and an immense waste of lives and money for society as a whole.[37]

Dr. King understood that in Chicago the law did not confine his movement and race did not necessarily define the oppressor. At the rally, he declared:

> We will be sadly mistaken if we think freedom is some lavish dish that the federal government will pass out on a silver platter. ... This day we must decide to fill up the jails of Chicago if necessary in order to end slums ... We must make it clear that we will purge Chicago of every politician, *whether he be Negro or white*, who feels that he owns the Negro vote.[38]

For example, a West Side summit that took place the previous year between Mayor Richard Daley and several West Side community leaders had failed to produce action on *any* of the West Siders' grievances: (1) resignation of precinct captains who did not live in the community; (2) a civilian review board on police brutality, (3) a local voice in federally funded programs; (4) equal job opportunities in city jobs; (5) city influence over bank loan policies, and (6) community influence in community schools. Mayor Daley ignored all of the demands—except to lecture West Side leaders on the suggestion that Chicago police needed a review board.[39] Among the followers of the West Side community leaders who were rebuffed by Mayor Daley were Jewel Cook and Lamar Brooks, both young men who would become founding members of the Illinois Black Panthers.

Moreover, many black municipal leaders did not think race issues were a problem in Chicago. When black and white CFM activists in the movement received assistance from the Southern Christian Leadership Conference (SCLC) in 1966, Chicago's black South Side Congressman William Dawson labeled King an unwanted "outside agitator." "Desegregation isn't needed here," Congressman Dawson said. The Chicago NAACP echoed Dawson, calling Dr. King "intemperate."[40]

Nevertheless, Dr. King came, led the march from the Soldier Field rally to City Hall, and personally posted the CFM's 50 demands. Following that action, the CFM's first protest activity was a nonviolent march against realtors in the all-white Gage Park community. They had previously sent an integrated group of home buyers to see if both races would be shown the same list of available homes. They were not.[41]

Actions like the Soldier Field rally and the Gage Park protest reflected the CFM's faith in nonviolent civil disobedience. The CFM attracted young idealistic college-educated people, black and white, who had witnessed the desegregation of the South, either first hand or on television. Activists such as David Finke, of the American Friends, and Patricia Berg, of the Student Woodlawn Area Project, believed that they could attack prejudice with love and that segregationists could be won over through the courage of nonviolence.[42] Solving the problems of the black ghetto, young activists believed, meant erasing the ghetto itself. Open housing in Chicago, therefore, was a step in the process of creating a color-blind society.

Some older, more politically sophisticated activists had a pragmatic attitude toward nonviolence. Bob Lucas of the Congress of Racial Equality (CORE), for example, believed the mere presence of open-housing marchers in these segregated white communities would provoke a violent response from local whites whose blatant racism would embarrass Chicago's Democratic Party. Lucas hoped that if violence ensued, it would force the Cook County Democratic Party to the bargaining table in order to preserve its tenuous foundation—an alliance of a variety of white ethnics, generally desirous of segregation, and black people, most of whom longed for the end of ghettoization. The mood among West Side young people was more in line with Bob Lucas than with young idealists like Pat Burg and David Finke. By 1966, West Side youth were skeptical of King's nonviolent tactics[43] and had apparently reached the threshold of what they were willing to tolerate. This was demonstrated by a riot on the West Side on July 12, 1966—ostensibly the result of a scuffle between police and black teens over a fire hydrant. The teens opened the hydrant to give children relief from the stifling heat, who had no swimming pool available to them because three of the four pools in the immediate vicinity were not open to blacks.[44] In the scuffle, the police clubbed five youths bloody, which aggravated the tension in the community. The next day, when a police official lectured the youth on their unlawful behavior (opening the hydrant), the neighborhood of East Garfield erupted, fire bombing white-owned stores and pelting police cars with rocks. The police were unable to contain the violence, and the National Guard was called in. Once calm was established 24 hours later, the police reentered the neighborhood and shot up several homes in retaliation.[45] "We could have stopped this rioting the first day by laying out two of those guys with [our] guns," a police officer claimed.[46] His answer to social problems rested in his holster. The riot not only reflected black Chicago's skepticism with Dr. King's nonviolent approach, it also gave white residents of Gage Park reason to be apprehensive about black people marching on their community primarily because the news media portrayed the riot as irrational violence, confirming the white ethnic image of blacks as a violent, criminal people.[47]

Two weeks later, on July 30, 1966, over 350 open-housing marchers assembled at the New Friendship Baptist Church in Englewood. The group included blacks, whites, priests, nuns, ministers, and members of the Blackstone Rangers gang (who served as parade marshals and were sworn to practice nonviolence.) Dr. King and two flag bearers—one carrying the American flag and the other a brown flag with an "End the Slums" motto—led the march.[48] They marched into Gage Park through a mob of angry whites, many of whom jeered and hurled insults at them. Believing the safety of their neighborhood and its property value was at stake, the crowd of whites then attacked the marchers with bricks, bottles, and firecrackers, reserving particular violence for the nuns and priests. Many of the attackers, Slavic Catholics, saw Irish Catholic clergy participation in integration as cynical and primarily at their expense. Discovering some of the cars the marchers had used to get to Gage Park, attackers turned them over, hacked open the gas tanks, and tossed in lighted matches. Amid the chaos, the marchers found their police protection disappearing and faced the mob's fury alone.[49]

The Blackstone Rangers were the marchers' sole defense, leaping into the air to catch rocks, bottles, and bricks with baseball gloves.[50] Meanwhile, community leader "Ma" Houston prayed, "Oh Lord, you see that boy in the plaid shirt with the brick? Tell him to put that brick down Lord! You see that man with the cherry bomb? Tell him not to throw it, Lord!"[51] Once back in the Englewood community, the marchers reassembled, carrying many wounded and some unconscious people. The floor of the church was red with blood[52] but the movement was not over. The racist town of Cicero, just west of Chicago, would be the next stage for an open-housing march.

Before the march into Cicero could take place, Daley and four CFM leaders, including Dr. King, held a summit meeting. The march had become the national embarrassment that Lynch and his colleagues had hoped would jar the local Democratic Party and threaten Daley's control over the black community. Daley put forth an agreement that promised to end segregation and improve housing in Chicago but offered no means of enforcing its goals. Instead of taking the offer back to the CFM rank and file, the four leaders agreed to it, without consulting fellow leaders. This antagonized leaders of CORE, Student Nonviolent Coordinating Committee (SNCC), and the West Side Organization; many of their youthful followers felt betrayed.[53]

The West Side Organization, SNCC, and CORE repudiated the agreement and called for the march into Cicero,[54] but this time with no commitment to nonviolence. The march occurred on September 7, 1966, just weeks after black teen Jerome Huey had been beaten to death by white teens for job hunting in Cicero. Approximately 290 marchers—almost all of them black—traded jeers, catcalls, and bricks with several hundred hecklers, while the Illinois National Guard looked on. In spite of the National Guard, the two crowds managed to have a fight at the end of the march. Nonviolent civil disobedience had seemingly failed in Chicago.

King himself later admitted that the agreement was a serious error,[55] as the only behavior it changed was that of the marchers. They stopped demonstrating and gave up the only weapon blacks had to ameliorate the conditions of the ghetto.[56] Yet, a more open housing market did develop over the next two decades. Though progress was not apparent at the time, segregation by race, enforced by the arson bomb and un-prosecuted white violence, began to disappear in Chicago.

The Limits of Nonviolence

The CFM of 1965–67 showed black Chicago activists that the Cook County Democratic Party clearly blocked their access to political and economic power. They would have to fight to get a reallocation of power, and the question for politically active black youth in 1968 was how to get that power.

The answer had some important historical roots. Following extreme violence in Albany, Georgia, and McComb County, Mississippi, as they tried to register blacks to vote, SNCC members armed themselves when they worked in Lowndes County, Alabama, in 1966. They formed an independent political party that appeared on the ballot in the symbol of a black panther. The local people referred to the organization as the Black Panther Party.

Meanwhile, in Oakland, California, a young man named Huey P. Newton was working to create a political party for black people that was committed to self-defense and changing the conditions of urban black ghettos. Newton read Malcolm X and, following Malcolm's exhortations to study historical revolutions throughout the world, immersed himself in the writings of Frantz Fanon, Mao Tse-Tung, and Vladimir Lenin. Newton drew on these thinkers to create his own vision of a radical worldwide movement of politicized poor, black youth.

On April 4, 1968, Dr. Martin Luther King was killed in Memphis, and Chicago's West Side went up in flames. Mayor Richard Daley issued his famous "shoot to kill" order, and some nine black people were killed in that riot.[57] Two months later, SNCC members Bobby Rush, Bob Brown, and a few other SNCC activists began touring local city college campuses, looking for recruits to form a branch of the Black Panther Party in Chicago.[58]

Fred Hampton

Fast-talking, personable, and an ambitious young man, Fred Hampton wanted to be a lawyer and a fighter for his people.[59] Like Huey Newton, he was an avid reader. Unlike Newton, however, Hampton consciously worked at making himself into a persuasive and compelling speaker, studying the speeches of Malcolm X and Dr. King.[60] Like Newton, Fred Hampton had little or no fear of physical confrontations, although he was more inclined to persuasion. He was what the Chicago Panthers needed, an articulate fighter. The members of the Illinois Black Panther Party were largely street warriors who were not easily led but were in need of a courageous, intelligent leadership that could harness their anger and their ambitions and use personal charm to smooth their roughness.

Hampton was fascinated with political activism. He had joined the Maywood branch of the NAACP in 1966 and became president of its West Suburban Youth Council.[61] Residents of Maywood who knew Hampton in his pre-Panther days describe him as a remarkable young man. In 1966, he defused a potential riot in Maywood by leading 500 angry young people on a nonviolent march to protest the neighborhood's all-white swimming pool. White Maywoodians enlisted Hampton to talk with white students about their racism, and he let them see their actions through a black perspective. The white students ended up admitting their own prejudice.[62]

Lennie Eggleston, a young man from the Los Angeles Panthers, won Hampton over to the philosophy of the Black Panther Party.[63] In 1968, Eggleston, touring Chicago on speaking engagements for the Panthers, met and talked with Hampton at great length.[64] Before talking with Lennie Eggleston, Hampton considered himself a black nationalist and regarded racial unity as fundamental and poor whites as natural adversaries. In the discussion, Eggleston agreed with Hampton that poor whites were racist but asserted that black people should not let others define who was and who was not an ally. Eggleston explained that black people, although a poor minority, still had the power to define their own reality and could use class solidarity as a tool to unite the poor and revolutionize America. Eggleston's argument was low-key, patient, and persistent, and it won Hampton over. The idea of redefining and uniting poor people resonated with Hampton's Maywood experiences. By the end of their discussions, Fred Hampton agreed that a movement that transcended race was revolutionary and original. It was a creative idea, particularly considering that it came from black youth in the ghettoes of America. Hampton envisioned a revolution of the poor, composed of warriors from all the "tribes" uniting to fight the dominant power structure.[65]

Weeks after Dr. King was assassinated, black activist Phil Cohran, formerly a leader of the now defunct CFM, held a black leadership conference in Chicago. Fred Hampton electrified a rally of several hundred young people at the Afro-Arts Theater. He stressed that nonviolence as a tactic was fine but it was time for armed self-defense.[66] Bobby Rush was at the rally looking for a dynamic speaker, while Hampton, buoyed by his recent discussions with Lennie Eggleston, was looking for a Black Panther Party chapter to join. The match was made. At the same time, another Black Panther Party was forming in the East Garfield area. Led by Drew Ferguson and Jewel Cook, they were younger members of the Deacons for Defense and Justice, and local young adults, some from the Vice Lords street gang. In August, they held a rally at the Senate Theater. About 20 SNCC-formed Panthers attended the rally, led by Bobby Rush and Bob Brown, both formerly active in the CFM.[67] The two groups met that afternoon and decided to merge.[68]

The West Side had a significant influence on the ethos of the Illinois Black Panther Party. The community was home to thousands of Southern-born and Southern-raised Chicagoans, who retained their Southern ways of community solidarity, morality, and kinship ties. The Panthers, mainly from the neighborhood, brought these values with them when they went out into the streets to recruit members. In pool halls, taverns, nightclubs and playgrounds, they talked about respecting black women, staying in school, and revolution.[69]

The language they used, however, did not come from the Bible, or the law book but from *The Quotations from Chairman Mao Tse-tung*. Mao and the Chinese Communists had defeated foreign imperialism and became guides for the Panthers, at least in terms of revolutionary phraseology. Mao's advice was cast in easy phrases: "All power to the People; The spirit of man is greater than Man's technology; The masses are the real heroes; The people, and the people alone, are the motive force in the making of world history." These words emboldened Panthers as they patrolled the streets of the West Side. It was not uncommon for Panthers to stop a woman from selling her body, lecture her, interfere with her trade, threaten her pimp, order drug dealers off the streets, and beat them up if they did not heed a warning.[70] This behavior corresponded with Southern values, so every time the Panthers went out they came back with new recruits.

As local community leader Nancy Jefferson said, "The Black Panthers were like the old-time men. They were not afraid to put somebody straight."[71] Mrs. Jefferson, Director of the Mid-West Community Council, 25 years senior to the average Panther, not only admired their spirit and their self-respect but also saw them as having the character that was lacking in many of the area's young people. Other residents, like 19-year-old Joe Shaw, joined the Panthers because they were his "homeboys" doing right.[72] Shaw, like scores of local young adults, did not know a lot about socialism, or Mao or Fanon but he felt that the Panthers' hearts were in the right place.[73]

Panther Party Structure

The Black Panther Party headquarters in Oakland, California, was organized, like the Chinese Communist Party, with no single leader but rather a central committee. Branch chapters, including the Illinois chapter, followed that same organization but their offices reflected the Oakland headquarters' supremacy by labeling the local officers as deputy officers. While the Oakland Panther Party had a minister of defense, the Illinois chapter had a deputy minister of defense, who was Bobby Rush.

The Illinois Deputy Central Committee consisted of a deputy chairman, Fred Hampton, who acted as the spokesperson for the Central Committee. There were also deputy ministers of defense, education, information, culture, finance, and labor. These ministers made decisions for the organization jointly. They included Lamar Brooks, the Deputy Minister of Education, and Yvonne King, Deputy Minister of Labor. In 1968 there were three field lieutenants, Jewel Cook, Bobby Lee, and Joan Gray. Each deputy minister was responsible for a cadre of individual Party members. Every Party member had a job to perform, although all shared in two basic tasks: (1) Selling the *Black Panther Community News* every day, and (2) Helping with the Free Breakfast for Children programs organized that year. Members voted on all decisions and could appeal a decision but had to obey the decision until the appeal was made. Discipline was physical. If a Party member was late for a meeting or failed to carry out an assignment, it meant a slap in the face for the women and a hard kick in the behind for the men. According to Yvonne King, who took one hard slap in the face, physical punishment was effective. She said it made the Black Panther Party the most reliable organization she ever worked in.[74] Since discipline was evenhanded and determined by popularly elected leaders, it did not hurt morale.[75]

In its first three or four months the Illinois Panther Party's growth was phenomenal, expanding from some 40 original members to well over 300, not to mention the unofficial members of runaway adolescents who left home to be "like the Panthers," as one put it, "one hundred percent for the people!"[76] Many Party members had not expected this sudden popularity. It was, however, strictly local. The great majority of people in Chicago did not know who they were, and those that heard about them through the media assumed they were some sort of new gang. People who were not from the neighborhood, such as South Siders, often confused the Panthers and the Blackstone Rangers.

Black Chicago and the Panther Style

In 1968, male and female blacks activists wore Afros as a hairstyle and a political statement. In contrast to the processing oils and acids that blacks used to make their hair straighten and glisten, the idea was that black people no longer had to strive to act white. Whether wearing a process was acting white is another issue but it was perceived as such by those who wore "Naturals." One of the most common words heard up and down the streets of the black ghetto was "mothafuckah." The Panthers expropriated the expression, punctuating their statements with it: "We ain't bullshitting we muthafuckin' revolutionaries, mothafuckah!"

Panthers also incorporated expressions from Chairman Mao and the Communist Party members, such as "Political power comes from the barrel of a gun!; The spirit of man is greater than Man's technology!; and Dare to Struggle, dare to win." Panthers also began to call the police "the pigs" instead of the current slang term "the man." Calling for their death with the expression "Off the Pigs!" let the Panthers directly challenge the macho style of the police. Implicit in the Panther style was an appreciation of poor black culture, which did not imitate white America but was nevertheless distinctly American. All over black Chicago, people stopped "slapping five" (hitting each other's open hand) and began "giving the fist." The fist had originally meant "Black Power!" but for the Panthers, it became "All Power to the People!" "All Power to the People!" which gave people a rush.[77] The spirit was empowering; when one became a Panther one wanted to serve the people. Pimps stopped pimping to serve the people, and gang-bangers quit their gangs to join the Panthers. This optimism challenged the power structure that treated the poor and the nonwhite as second-class citizens. The Illinois Black Panther Party was an expression of the spirit of grass-roots empowerment that had rid the South of de facto segregation.

Class and the Black Panthers

The Black Panther Party's ultimate goal, as its Chicago spokesperson Fred Hampton saw it, resembled Dr. King's, which was to end racial and class oppression. He explained:

> We never negated the fact that there was racism in America but we said that the by-product, what comes off of capitalism, that happens to be racism. That capitalism comes first and next is racism. ... [W]hen they brought slaves over here, it was to make money. So first the idea came that we want to make money, then slaves came in order to make that money. That means that capitalism had to, through historical fact, racism had to come from capitalism. It had to be capitalism first and racism was a by-product of that .[78]

Black Panther political theory was influenced by Mao, Fanon, and Marx and altered to fit black Chicagoan realities. In the early months of 1969, the Illinois Black Panther Party met and attempted to build alliances with five youth groups from different racial, ethnic, and class backgrounds. For 50 years, segregation, social mores, and Democratic politics had precluded this type of alliance building. Segregation was accepted behavior, politically expedient and profitable to realtors, landlords, and politicians. The Panthers ignored the social mores of segregation, armed with their belief in the rightness of their cause and the transformative power of class unity. The groups that the Panthers met with included the Black P Stone Nation, the South Side gang formerly know as the Blackstone Rangers; the Students for a Democratic Society, a revolutionary political organization of white college students; the Young Lords, a Puerto Rican gang, which, like the P Stone Nation, was developing a social conscience;[79] a gang of young, white Appalachian migrants called the Young Patriots; and a club of young greasers from the Logan Square area called Rising Up Angry.

The Black Panther Party's work with the Black P Stone Nation set the wheels in motion for an alliance to form. The Blackstone Rangers, who changed their name to the Black P Stone Nation in 1968, were involved in city politics by 1965. With urging from the Reverend Jesse Jackson, the gang fought to get black men into the all-white trade unions and helped Jackson block construction sites on the South Side. Burly, white workers had earlier run Reverend Jackson and his protesters off of a site, and they returned with the P Stone members, who chased the unionized construction workers from the site with bats, pipes and bricks.[80]

Scores of P Stones then went with Reverend Jackson to a construction site at the University of Illinois at Chicago, and when Reverend Jackson decided to back off from a confrontation, the Stones blocked him from leaving, forcing him to complete the action.[81] Although he had invited the gang into the movement, they were not under Jackson's control. The Illinois Black Panther Party viewed this political activity as a sign of a potential ally.

In January 1969, the P Stone Nation (based on the South Side) and Black Panther Party (based mainly on the West Side) held an impromptu meeting, precipitated by the shooting of a member of the Panther Party selling *The Black Panther Community News* in the Woodlawn neighborhood, which was P Stone Nation "Territory."[82] The Panthers used the incident to take 30 armed Panthers over to the P Stone Nation headquarters. Jeff Fort, an unusually charismatic leader of the Stones, greeted his visitors by summoning (via walkie-talkie) about 100 teens armed with new carbines, pistols, and shotguns. Fort was known for his ability to get his young followers to commit brazen acts of lethal violence, even when he carried out his commands over the phone from jail. These recorded "hits" would be his undoing in later years but as of 1969, he may have been the most independent leader of the black poor in Chicago.[83] Fort did not impress the Panthers, however, who, armed with a cause they believed in, were convinced they were as tough as, or tougher than, any South Sider.

The Panther leaders called for an end to gang violence, the right to sell their newspaper anywhere in the city, and that the P Stone Nation join the Black Panther Party and take up socialism and revolution.[84] The Stones were out to make money, not to share it, and socialism sounded like a sharing process to them.[85] Still, they believed that the Illinois Panther Party was sincere and respected the fact that the Panthers had acknowledged them.[86]

The Rainbow Coalition

The Panthers who went south with Hampton to talk with the Stones were warriors—young men like Jewel Cook, formerly of the Deacons for Defense and Justice; Drew Ferguson, a redeemed member of the conservative Vice Lords gang; and Vietnam War veterans Willie Calvin and Henry English. When they looked the Stones in the eye and said, "Stop killing other black folks," their sincerity and strength were obvious.[87] The Illinois Panthers also had a cadre of intellectuals—Fred Hampton, Bob Brown, Bobby Lee, Joan and Michael McCarty, Joan Gray, Yvonne King, Kassandra Watson, Gregory Garrett, and Lynn French.[88]

These warrior intellectuals spurred the establishment of the Rainbow Coalition, as Hampton named it (a good ten years ahead of Reverend Jesse Jackson's coalition of the same name). The Panthers' Rainbow Coalition was a defining event in the history of black Chicago, a political coalition that respected ethnic communities of all kinds led by poor, black youth. It was the base upon which Harold Washington put together a coalition that won the mayoral election in 1983. In the same month that Fred Hampton's group went to pay a visit to the Black P Stone Nation, Panther Field Lieutenant Bobby Lee went to Uptown, a poor white neighborhood, to discuss a coalition between the Illinois Black Panther Party and the Young Patriots.[89] The Young Patriots were immigrants from the coal mines of West Virginia and Tennessee who were struggling to better their community and were proud of their Southern heritage. One might not expect these two historic antagonists—poor Southern whites and poor Southern blacks—to get along. However, by that spring of 1969, the Young Patriots were running a Free Breakfast for Children program, modeled after the Panther Party program.[90] About that same time, a group of white youths from the Logan Square area drove over to the heart of the black West Side to meet the Panthers. These youths had heard of the Party, formed their own organization, and sought guidance from the Panthers. In the spirit of class solidarity, they called themselves Rising Up Angry. They had their own newspaper, *Rising Up Angry*, which imitated the Panther paper but used the street vernacular of the white North Side. Rising Up Angry's first trip to Panther headquarters caught the attention of the local police who did not know what to make of a gang of whites coming en masse to this poor black ghetto. Immediately after their meeting with the Panthers, the police arrested them all and took them to the Fillmore District Police Station for questioning. Like the Panthers, Rising Up Angry visited pool halls, parks, and taverns, talking to people about the need for revolution and class solidarity across racial and ethnic lines.[91]

The Illinois Black Panther Party significantly influenced Rising Up Angry, the Young Patriots, and the Young Lords, a Puerto Rican gang that reorganized as an activist group to save their community from displacement by gentrification.[92] Without these shared goals and tactics, it is doubtful that the Rainbow Coalition would have succeeded. The Rainbow Coalition demonstrates that the Panthers recognized that different minorities could unite along class lines to fight oppression. We don't fight fire with fire, Hampton believed, and we don't fight white racism with black racism—we fight racism with class solidarity. Solidarity had its limits however. The Illinois Panthers were determined that they could work with anybody—except the police.

Women and the Gender Issue

As the spring of 1969 began, the Illinois Panther Party increased in size and effectiveness. Membership reached about 1,000, and Panthers expanded their reach into other neighborhoods, including middle-class, working-class, black, and Latino enclaves.[93] Panther women were key to this growth beyond the West Side. Women like Joan Gray, Stephanie Grant, Yvonne King, Joan McCarty, and Lynn French were personable and attractive, which helped them relate to people in middle-class and poor settings. They were responsible for distributing the *Black Panther Community News* from the airport to its several distribution centers, for staffing the free medical center, and for ensuring that the numerous fund-raisers were effective and entertaining. Lynn French had been a SNCC activist, until "it played out," and became a Panther because she "did not accept the limitations of class, race and gender" that society placed on people. French maintains that she was not forced to defer to men in the Illinois Panther Party nor did she experience or hear of sexual harassment. "Not in Chicago. We [women] would not accept it."[94] Other Party members admit, however, that there was an element of male chauvinism that came with the social environment. Ahmad Rahmad of the Illinois chapter remembers that it was in the Illinois Panther Party where he "first took orders from a woman who wasn't my mother."[95]

Perhaps women's most important contribution and role in the Illinois Black Panther Party was in the Free Breakfast for Children program, which opened at the Better Boys Foundation on Pulaski Avenue near 16th Street in April 1969. The Better Boys Foundation had initially resisted the Panthers because they did not want a revolutionary organization's program in their midst. However, the Illinois Panthers, largely local people, used persuasion and threats to get the agency to agree.[96] If the Better Boys Foundation, which was run by people not from the West Side, wanted to be a part of the West Side, it needed to cooperate with the Panthers. Free breakfast for children was an idea from the Oakland Panther headquarters, based on a survey of the black community there. But the need for warm breakfasts for Chicago children was just as real.[97] Having enough to eat, the Panthers maintained, was a right every American child should have. The program had good attendance and was supported locally, despite police harassment; and it was good public relations for the Panthers.

The Illinois Panthers then searched for more community centers willing to give them the chance to feed local children. The local Protestant churches, many of them beholden to the Democratic Party, uniformly turned them down. Yet, some Catholic churches welcomed the Panther free breakfast programs. For example, the white priests at St. Dominic's, in the Cabrini-Green Housing Project, allowed the Panthers the use of their church for movies, forums, and rallies. These Catholic priests appreciated the idea of kids getting food and young adults serving children, so they ignored the Panthers politics.[98]

When the Illinois Panthers sought food donations, it was the local black businessmen who most often responded. These were the kind of business-men the Panthers labeled in classes as "pork-chop capitalists." However, the children at a Panther-run breakfast site often drank Joe Louis milk and ate Parker House sausages.[99] (Both Joe Louis and Parker House were black-owned companies.) Two members of the Party also worked for Oscar Meyer, where the black foreman gave them surplus meat.[100]

By the end of May 1969, the Chicago Panthers had expanded their pro-gram to six more sites on the West and South Sides and were feeding breakfast to approximately 4,000 children daily, while having them recite joyously "Power to the people! Free Huey!"[101] The Panthers accomplished this without any government money. The Free Breakfast for Children pro-gram lasted about six years—as long as the Illinois Panther Party existed. Two of their other service programs outlived the Party—free busing to prisons (for family visits) and free medical care.[102]

Conclusion

The Illinois Panthers were Chicago-born and streetwise. Their "gut" sense worked well in their own neighborhood but could they harness Chicago politics before Chicago politics destroyed them? They were most assuredly handicapped for having very little knowledge of the history of the black communities on the South and West Sides. Moreover, by exuberantly advo-cating the violent overthrow of the U.S. government, they were inviting the federal government to attempt to destroy them. The Panthers were some-what unaware of the federal government's tactics and strategies when it came to radicals. At least one of the chapter's core members was an FBI informant who set up Fred Hampton to be murdered by Chicago police in 1969 and helped sabotage their alliance with the P. Stone Rangers.

From the office's opening in September 1968 through 1974, when the office and the Panthers shut down, the Party's core membership, perhaps 30 members, labored 16 hours or more a day, seven days a week by the summer of 1969. They worked, ate, and slept with the Panther Party's ten-point program on their minds—and how to take the program to the peo-ple. Fewer and fewer Panthers held jobs, which became too time-consuming, and the Panthers instead relied on their ability to get donations.[103] Illinois Deputy Minister of Defense Bobby Rush later esti-mated that the Illinois Panther Party took in about $1,000 a day (the financial records they kept were destroyed by police and FBI, or lost). Rush estimated that about 60 percent of this money was used to fund their Free

Breakfast for Children Program or the People's Free Medical Clinic. The remainder of the money went for rent, food, and utilities.[104]

While other black nationalist groups criticized the Panthers for their coalition building, the Panthers considered themselves pragmatics. Making alliances with Appalachian whites, Puerto Ricans, black gangs, and white college students was practical.[105] The emphasis on Africanisms by other black groups at the time seemed superfluous and impractical as far as the Black Panther Party was concerned. Hampton explained:

> We don't care if niggahs wear dashikis. You understand? That's not gonna mean anything in the final analysis. ... When they come in here with tanks, you come out with dashikis and nothing but dashikis, ... you're in the wrong place at the wrong time, with the wrong people. ... They say, niggah, how come your name ain't changed. ... Changing your name is not gonna change our set of arrangements.[106]

The Panthers embodied an attitude of self-respect, which perhaps included elements of West African culture but came from their current way of life. Back home was not Africa. It was Louisiana, Mississippi, and Arkansas. The Panthers were more familiar with the Puerto Ricans across the block than with Africans 5,000 miles away. Poor folks could not afford to go to Africa but they could cross the street. And those people across the street could vote and make a political difference.[107]

The Chicago Panthers' optimism was a product of their culture, despite the Party's ideology, which was rooted in socialism. Socialism may have been a foreign concept but it sounded like sharing to them, so they accepted it. Community members looked into a Panther's eyes, listened to the tone of his voice, and judged his/her actions in regard to what he or she said. That is, when the neighborhood accepted intellectuals like Fred Hampton and Lynn French, it was not because of their intellect, or the sophistication of their message but because Hampton, French, and the others appeared to be sincere. Leaders expressed the same views as migrant Southern Black West Siders did.[108] Excluded from Chicago politics and strongly in touch with their Southern roots, the Panthers moved with the best their community had to offer: courage, intelligence, and pragmatism.

Notes

1. *Chicago Sun-Times,* December 5, 1970.
2. Peter Knauss, *Chicago: A One-Party State* (Chicago: University of Illinois at Chicago Press, 1974), 20.

3. Alphine Jefferson, "Housing Discrimination and Community Response in North Lawndale (Chicago), Illinois 1948–1968" (Ph.D. Diss., Duke University, 1979), 66–67.

4. J. Kittigawa and E. Tauber, *Local Community Factbook for the Chicago Metropolitan Area, 1980* (Chicago: University of Chicago Press, 1982), 70, 74 79, 82.

5. Jefferson, 79; see also Arnold Hirsch, *Making the Second Ghetto, Race and Housing in Chicago, 1940–1960* (Chicago: University of Chicago Press, 1983), 29.

6. Jefferson, 80–84; Hirsch, 33.

7. Jefferson, 72.

8. Ibid., 12–19.

9. Interviews of former Chicago Police Department Superintendents Leroy Martin (December 1994) and Richard Brzcezek (April 1996). The statement was originally made to me by founding member of the Afro-American Patrolmen's League Howard Saffold, in an interview I did with him in 1983 while writing for the *Chicago Defender* but both superintendents agreed that this was the unofficial policy.

10. *The Chicago Daily Defender,* March 5–13, 1958; a series of articles on police brutality in the black community.

11. William Roemer, *Man Against the Mob* (New York: Ivy Books, 1989), 211.

.   Interviews with Edward Crawford, April 1982; Richard Barnett, August 1989; Ila Daggart, Janaury 1981; Bernetta Howell Barnett, April 1994; and Gale Cincotta, July 1995. Unless otherwise cited, I conducted all of the interviews.

13. Jefferson, 73.

14. Census of Population and Housing, Nineteenth U.S. Census (Washington D.C.: Chamber of Commerce, U.S. Government Printing Office), Census Tracts, Chicago Standard Metropolitan Statistical Area.

15. Edward "Fats" Crawford Interview, July 1982. Crawford's version of why the Deacons were formed and by whom is corroborated by interviews with Congressman Danny Davis, aldermanic candidate for the 29th Ward in 1996, Floyd Thomas, and 29th Ward precinct Captain Harry Reese. Crawford was killed in an "accident" that indicated foul play on the part of the police officers who arrested him on a DUI charge.

16. Jefferson, 220–233.

17. "Democratic Voting West-Side Style," *Chicago Sun-Times,* November 11, 1968.

18. Jefferson, 67. Echoed by Richard Barnett, Bernetta Howell Barnett, and Danny Davis.

19. David Fremon, *Chicago Politics Ward by Ward* (Indiana University Press, 1988), 179–181.

20. William Grimshaw, *Bitter Fruit, Black Politics and the Chicago Machine,* 1931–1991 (Chicago: University of Chicago Press, 1992), 119–121; also the Richard Barnett interview, 1989, 21. Richard Barnett interview, August 1986.

22. Bernard Neinstein reportedly said, "The last thing I need is a smart nigger!" According to Richard Barnett, 1986, Neinstein sponsored Benjamin Lewis, a black man who spoke Yiddish and called him Mr. Neinstein, while Bernie Neinstein called him "Ben."

23. Richard Barnett interview, August 1986.
24. Thomas Millea, *Ghetto Fever* (New York: Bruce Publishing, 1968), 95–96.
25. Congressman Danny Davis interview, April 1994.
26. *Muhammad Speaks*, April 1, 1963. This was the official newspaper of the Nation of Islam under Elijah Muhammad. The paper had exceptional quality of writing and journalism and was reportedly written and edited by former black members of the Illinois Communist Party.
27. "Recorder Hunted in Lewis Slaying, Believed Killer's Voices Were on Tape," *Chicago Sun-Times*, March 4, 1963.
28. Every black political activist I interviewed in Chicago—Robert Lucas, Danny Davis, Bernetta Howell Barnett, Richard Barnett, Harry Reese, Joseph Shaw, Bennett Johnson—held this perception of Lewis's death.
29. Interview of activist-musician Phil Cohran, August 1982.
30. Interview of political activist Bennett Johnson, founder of the League of Negro Voters, and Herman Gilbert, activist and author of *The Negotiations*, July 11, 1992.
31. Phil Cohran interview.
32. Ibid.
33. Jerome Skolnick, *The Politics of Protest* (New York: Simon and Schuster, 1969), 263–266
34. Alan Anderson and George Pickering, *Confronting the Color Line: The Broken Promises of the Civil Rights Movement in Chicago* (Athens: University of Georgia Press, 1986), 208–209.
35. Hirsch, 257–259, 263–275.
36. Grimshaw 96–97; Hirsch 129, 274–275.
37. Jefferson, 250–258.
38. Manning Marable, "Black Power in Chicago," *The Review of Radical Economics* 17 (1985): 171.
39. Anderson and Pickering, 210.
40. Marable, 165, 173.
41. Anderson and Pickering, 210–212.
42. Interviews of activist David Finke, of the American Friends and participant in the Open Housing Marches in Marquette Park, Chicago, April 11, 1984, and Patricia Burg, former president of Chicago SNCC, August 14, 1994.
43. Anderson and Pickering, 209.
44. Millea, 38–39.
45. Ibid., 39–42.
46. Anderson and Pickering, 213.
47. Ibid., 214–215.
48. Ibid., 226–229.
49. David Finke interview.
50. Ibid.
51. Ibid.
52. Ibid.

53. Millea, 79–81.

54. Anderson and Pickering, 200.

55. James Ralph, *Northern Protest, Martin Luther King, Chicago and the Civil Rights Movement* (Cambridge: Harvard College Fellows, 1993), 196.

56. Knauss, 50–53.

57. Len O'Connor, *Clout, Mayor Daley and His City* (New York: Avon Books, 1975), 203. O'Connor quotes Daley as saying, "I told (Police Supt.) Conlisk to issue an order to police to shoot to maim or cripple any looters, and to shoot arsonists on sight."

58. Interview of Bobby Rush, April 10, 1982.

59. Interview of Akua Ngeri, formerly Deborah Johnson, girlfriend of Fred Hampton and mother of his child, on July 12, 1988.

60. Akua Ngeri interview.

61. Interview of Joan Elbert, President of Lutheran Human Relations Association of Maywood, Illinois, February 1981. Mrs. Elbert was a neighbor of the Hampton family and knew them for several years as Fred Hampton grew up.

62. Joan Elbert interview.

63. "Bunchy" Carter was a Los Angeles gang-banger turned Panther and leader of the L.A. Panthers until killed by Ron Karenga's US organization. Karenga excused the murder by saying, "We were duped by the FBI."

64. Joan Elbert interview.

65. Ibid.

66. Phil Cohran interview.

67. Interviews of Jewel Cook, Lamar Brooks, and Cleveland Cook, all former members of the Illinois Black Panther Party, August 11, 1982.

68. Interviews of former Illinois Panthers Lamar Brooks, Henry English, Bobby Rush, and Jewel Cook.

69. Interviews of former Illinois Panthers, Lamar Brooks, Henry English, Bobby Rush, Yvonne King and Jewel Cook.

70. Ibid. When they told me this story, their faces were proud.

71. Interview of Mrs. Nancy Jefferson, President of Mid-West Community Council and Civilian Review Board for the Chicago police, June 3, 1981.

72. Interview of former Illinois Panther Joseph Shaw, May 14, 1995.

73. Shaw interview.

74. Interview of former Minister of Labor, Illinois Black Panther Party, Yvonne King, April 6, 1982.

75. Summary of Illinois Panthers interviews. There were no contradictions.

76. Lamar Brooks interview.

77. Film *The Murder of Fred Hampton,* produced in 1970, Howard Auk and Michael Gray, producers. Gray went on to make *The China Syndrome* in Hollywood.

78. *Vita Wa Watu, A New African Theoretical Journal* 11 (August 1987). From Hampton's speech "It's a Class Struggle Goddamit!" delivered at Northern Illinois University, DeKalb, Illinois, September 1969.

79. Interview of Carlos Flores, former member of the Young Lords, a youth group of the Humboldt Park area, Chicago, September 1996. Flores explained how the Panthers influenced the Young Lords into political action.

80. Interviews of Henry English and Phil Cohran. Also see James Fry, *Locked Out Americans, a Memoir* (New York: Harper and Row, 1974), a story of a minister who worked with the Blackstone Rangers in the late 1960s.

81. Interviews of Jewel Cook, Henry English, and Phil Cohran.

82. Former Illinois Panthers Willie Calvin and Henry English, interviewed in Chicago on June 12, 1981.

83. Interview of Marianne Jackson, an attorney for one of the Blackstone Rangers/El Rukins Main 21; held in Chicago on April 4, 1994.

84. Brief for Plaintiff-Appellants Anderson, Bell, Lark, Satchell, Truelock, No. 77-1698, appeals from the U.S. District Court for the Northern District of Illinois, Eastern Division, Appeal no. 70-C-1384. J. Sam Perry, Judge, 15–18. This is the legal appeal following the acquittal of a suit filed against the raiding police officers in the killing of Fred Hampton, 21, Deputy Chairman of the Illinois Black Panther Party. This document uses extensive facts from the FBI's own documents gathered by their informant within the Panther Party, and the correspondence between them, the Chicago Police Department, and the Cook County Illinois State's Attorney's office, and so is a shorthand account of the federal government's involvement in the death of Hampton. The lawyers for the Panthers won the appeal, and the families of the deceased received over one million dollars.

85. Interview of attorney James Montgomery, who defended Blackstone Ranger leader Jeff Fort in the killing of police officer James Alfano, August, 1970. Both Attorney Montgomery and Attorney Marianne Jackson emphasized that the Rangers were motivated by one quest, the desire to make money.

86. James Montgomery interview; also the fact that Jeff Fort was a pallbearer at Fred Hampton's funeral.

87. The nearly 30 Panthers I interviewed were all still dedicated to the ideals they had espoused 15 years earlier, when the Party existed. I would describe them as hard, dedicated men, tinged with frustration at the failure of the revolution they had attempted. At the same time, with a few exceptions, they were leading stable and productive lives and still are.

88. I had met them previously when I was 22 and teaching in the Illinois Department of Corrections and they were Party members. What I remember is their intensity and their intellectual knowledge of Fanon and other writers.

89. Film *American Revolution II,* produced by Michael Gray, 1972. The film documents Panther Bobby Lee's work in the poor white community of Uptown (Chicago) in 1969.

90. Interview of Reverend John Auer, United Methodist Church of Rogers Park, whose church hosted the Young Lords' Free Breakfast for Children program.

91. Interview of Rick James, founder of Rising Up Angry, in Chicago, April 11, 1996.

92. Interviews of Carlos Flores, Rick James, Joan Auk, and Reverend John Auer.

93. Bobby Rush interview.

94. Interview of former Illinois Panther Lynn French. French was responsible for distribution of the newspaper, and was also punched and kicked by Chicago police on December 5, 1969, in a raid that got very little attention, following the raid that killed Fred Hampton.

95. Interview of Ahmad Rahman, former member of the Illinois Panther Party, at the Organization of American Historian's Convention in 1996.

96. Interview of Lamar Brooks and Henry English; also interview of Eugene Perkins, Director of the Better Boys Foundation, June 1982.

97. Huey P. Newton, "War Against the Panther: A Study of Repression in America" (Ph.D. diss., University of California, Santa Cruz, 1980), 38.

98. Interview of Father Paul, at St. Dominic's Catholic Church, August 1981.

99. Interviews of Jewel and Cleveland Cook.

100. Interview of Willie Calvin, former member of Illinois Black Panther Party, April 12, 1982.

101. The children singing revolutionary songs while being served breakfast at a Chicago site are documented in the film *The Murder of Fred Hampton*.

102. Interview of Gregory Garrett, who ran the Free Busing to Prisons Program while the Panther Party existed and a few years after the Party disbanded; also interview of former Illinois Panther Joan McCarty, who helped with both programs, again after the Party folded, August 1995.

103. Interview of Yvonne King, July, 1983.

104. Interview of Bobby Rush, April 2, 1983.

105. Huey P. Newton, *To Die for the People: The Writings of Huey P. Newton* (n.p.:Writers and Readers Publishing Company, 1973), 45–49.

106. Hampton speech, *Vita Wa Watu*, 23.

107. Nancy Jefferson interview.

108. Jewel Cook interview.

Chapter 3

Exposing the "Whole Segregation Myth": The Harlem Nine and New York City's School Desegregation Battles

Adina Back

"We will go to jail and rot there, if necessary, but our children will not go to Jr. High Schools 136, 139, or 120," asserted Mrs. Viola Waddy.[1] Mrs. Waddy was part of a group of African American mothers who had been keeping their children out of three Harlem junior high schools since the beginning of the 1958 school year. The black press dubbed the group the "Little Rock Nine of Harlem," an honorific title that favorably compared the women to the "Little Rock Nine" in Arkansas, the group of high school students whose integration efforts had made national headlines the prior year.[2] Harlem's "Nine" claimed that their sons and daughters were not receiving an equal education in these Northern segregated schools.

These boycotting parents were brought to court by the New York City Board of Education in December 1958. They were charged with illegally keeping their children out of school. Their cases were heard before two different judges who issued opposing verdicts: Four of the mothers were found guilty in Judge Nathaniel Kaplan's courtroom for violating New York State's law on compulsory education. Less than two weeks later, two other boycotting African American mothers were found innocent of similar charges in Judge Justine Polier's courtroom. In a landmark legal victory, Judge Polier charged the New York City Board of Education with offering inferior educations to the city's black children.

This essay tells the story of New York City's postwar school integration activists, focusing closely on the school boycott and legal battles of the "Harlem Nine." Their protests are linked to the Northern civil rights movement and the battles to desegregate the New York City schools. Two themes emerge from these intertwined stories of female and civil rights activism: First, this 1950s story reveals that the Northern struggles did not lag behind the Southern movement but happened concurrently. In other words, these school battles shift the traditional periodization of the Northern civil rights movement, which has generally focused on the 1960s and the Black Power movement.

Popular and scholarly accounts of school integration battles have generally followed the federal legal and legislative battles that have assumed that de jure and de facto segregation were distinct systems requiring separate dismantling. Therefore, attention to Northern conflicts related to equal educational opportunities has often been linked to legal cases that explicitly ruled on de facto segregation in the early 1970s.[3] In New York City specifically, the highly publicized confrontations of the late 1960s around the issue of decentralization and community control in the Ocean Hill-Brownsville school district came to represent New York's civil rights movement.[4] Yet for New York's black residents—those who had been in the North for generations as well as new migrants from the South—racial equality in the city's public schools was also a Northern issue that took on heightened urgency in the 1950s. When we tell the history from the experience of parents who were on the front lines in the North in the 1950s, how does our understanding of postwar civil rights struggles change?

The prominence of women as parent activists in this period of supposed female passivity, the second theme, links the reperiodization of the Northern civil rights movement with the ongoing project of reinterpreting the history of women and gender in postwar America.[5] The protesting African American mothers articulated their concerns through a variety of discourses that offer insights into women's political culture of the 1950s. While they often suggested that their demands were natural, emanating from nurturing maternal instincts, their assertions were not limited to a "motherist" rhetoric.[6] Like women activists in the South, their claim to equal rights was also driven by a deep understanding of black women's social and economic status and their desire to see their children have other options. They were motivated by shared and individual histories of racial discrimination, gender inequality, and economic exploitation. And they demonstrated that "motherwork" in the black community bridged the boundaries between public and private and revealed that motherhood was hardly a monolithic identity.[7] The mother activists expanded their arguments with references to the national civil rights movement that was erupting around them and boldly asserted that they too deserved "a fair share of the pie."[8]

Judge Justine Polier's decision in favor of the boycotting parents explicitly linked the Northern and Southern struggles for civil rights. Polier's ruling, drawn extensively from the case built by Paul Zuber, the parents' attorney, was premised on precedent-setting civil rights cases. The paradox of her ruling, however, was that though she referenced legal cases that challenged de jure segregation in the South in order to prove that Harlem's black schoolchildren were not receiving an equal education, she did not indict the Board of Education with practicing de facto segregation. It was the parent activists who challenged the very definition of de facto segregation by exposing the ways in which de facto style segregation was protected and insured by the state.

New York City was a whirlpool of competing ideologies and political agendas in which race was only beginning to emerge as an important force. The varied responses of white parents, Board of Education administrators, leaders, teachers, and the mayor reveal the complicated nature of race relations in New York in the postwar decades. The city's white communities denounced any association with a blatantly racist South. Recalling the television coverage of Southern black students being attacked for attempting to integrate Central High, they were quick to assert that New York City was not Little Rock, Arkansas. White parents expressed concern that they not be seen as racist while laying claim to their neighborhoods and asserting their rights as citizens and taxpayers.

Black communities like Harlem were bubbling with political activity ranging from the Democratic Party-style politics of Congressman Adam Clayton Powell, Jr., and Manhattan Borough President Hulan Jack to the growing presence of the Nation of Islam and its nationalist orientation. Harlem intellectuals and artists were actively embracing anticolonial struggles in Africa and defining their struggles in relation to these international independence movements. And blacks throughout the city were reading Jackie Robinson's responses to civil rights struggles around the country in his *New York Amsterdam News* columns.[9] Yet New York's blacks still wielded little economic and political clout when it came to the city's power base.

Mayor Robert F. Wagner, a Democrat, whose three terms in office spanned this period of school integration battles, paid limited attention to the concerns of New York's blacks. Borrowing the language of intergroup relations, with its emphasis on intergroup statesmanship that social scientists made popular during the war, he created a commission of religious and ethnic leaders who were mandated to resolve the city's racial and ethnic problems in the spirit of "unity."[10] The Commission on Intergroup

Relations (COIR) in fact shaped few policy decisions. The mayor's political base was not the city's African Americans, and so he did not fear the threats from local NAACP leaders that he would lose black votes if he failed to intervene, for example, in a school integration conflict in Brooklyn's Bedford-Stuyvesant.[11]

The Board of Education, however, could not so easily dismiss parent activists from the city's black communities. And the activists persistently pursued both the board's lay leadership and its paid administrators. These differing responses offer useful insights into New York's postwar racial culture. Both bureaucratic imperatives and ideological racism motivated the superintendent and his deputies who opposed integration efforts. At the simplest level, school administrators needed to protect their turf and defend their actions and policies.[12] School Superintendents William Jansen and his successor, John Theobald, masked their objections to integration proposals in their advocacy of the "neighborhood school" policy.[13] In contrast, the lay leaders (who were selected by the mayor) were far more likely to support efforts to study the issue of school integration while embracing the liberal racial ideology being advanced in the postwar period that pathologized the black family.[14]

Employing the language of "cultural deprivation" in describing their black and Puerto Rican students, the majority of the city's 40,000 public school teachers were also invested in maintaining the status quo. The teachers used phrases like "problem children" and "difficult schools"—the accepted educational and sociological terminology of the day—to discuss the city's African American and Puerto Rican schoolchildren. In public testimony, their characterizations of these "problem children" ranged from frankly racist descriptions of "primitive children" to more subtle descriptions of children coming from "culturally deprived homes" and suffering "cultural handicaps."[15] Their racial attitudes were informed, in part, by the desire to protect their working conditions and workplaces. Organized into dozens of small associations and unions (without collective bargaining power), most of the teachers' groups opposed desegregation recommendations that threatened to force them into schools with predominantly black and Puerto Rican students. From their perspective, they had the most to lose by desegregating the schools.[16]

Those who actively and passively resisted implementing a program to integrate the school system—Mayor Wagner, Board of Education administrators and lay leaders, the school system's teachers, and the city's middle-class and working-class white parents—did not speak in a unified voice on this issue. However, the combined impact of Northern-style liberal racism, ethnic solidarity, and class fear created a formidable obstacle to desegregating New York City's public schools in the 1950s and 1960s.

* * *

Harlem parents had complained about the poor quality of the schools in their community for over two decades. In the aftermath of the 1935 Harlem Riot, Mayor Fiorella LaGuardia's Commission on Conditions in Harlem confirmed these grievances: The schools were antiquated (no new schools had been built in Harlem for over 20 years), poorly equipped, overcrowded, and staffed with too many substitute and inexperienced teachers.[17] It was to this report that Kenneth Clark, the African American psychologist, referred 20 years later when he claimed that in the interim, conditions in Harlem schools had only deteriorated.[18] In February 1954, Clark characterized the prior two decades as "a stage of educational decline" for African American students in the city's schools and called for a study of these conditions.[19]

High level administrators within the Board of Education attacked Clark's analysis, which he issued three months before the landmark Supreme Court decision *Brown* v. *Board of Education*. The attacks ranged from outright rejection of Clark's characterization of the schools as segregated to attempts to discredit Clark himself by insinuating that he had Communist affiliations as a supporter of the radical Teachers Union.[20]

Try as they might and did, the Board of Education could not readily dismiss Clark's charges. He was backed by the Intergroup Committee of New York's Public Schools, a broad and vocal coalition of 28 organizations.[21] Shortly thereafter, the Supreme Court's *Brown* v. *Board of Education* decision, issued in May 1954, gave national prominence to an issue that board administrators may have hoped would just go away. And certainly Clark's important role in the Supreme Court decision made it far more difficult for the board to discredit him. Equally important, Clark's rather mild call for a study was supported by a powerful sympathizer, Arthur Levitt, the President of the Board of Education.

Dr. Clark succeeded in getting the board's attention only after the *Brown* decision. However, Clark had been attending to the interrelated issues of New York's troubled youth and the impact of school segregation on New York's schoolchildren since the mid-1940s. Kenneth and Mamie Clark, two young psychologists, opened the Northside Center for Child Development in 1946. Based in Harlem, the center offered a range of mental health services to the community's underserved troubled youth. Developing black youth's self-esteem was a central concern of the Clarks. It was this issue of self-esteem that was pivotal in Kenneth Clark's testimony in the *Brown* case as he argued that segregation stigmatized and damaged black children. At Northside in New York City, the Clarks and their staff developed a model for building self-esteem that employed "psychological counseling in part to heal the injuries of racism in a largely segregated city."[22] The Clarks also set about to address the structural causes of racism by attacking New York City's segregated school system.

School Superintendent William Jansen finally agreed to support Clark's call for a study that was entitled "The Status of the Public School Education of Negro and Puerto Rican Children in New York City." The study was to be conducted by the Public Education Association, an independent organization. However, maintaining his view that segregation did not exist in the New York City schools, Superintendent Jansen demanded that the researchers use the word "separation" instead of "segregation" in their report. Segregation, he insisted, was what they had in the South, not in the North.

The board also decided, as advised by its Public Relations Department, to "show good faith" and set up its own committee to evaluate the findings of the Public Education Association's report.[23] Thus the Commission on Integration was founded. The two most divisive issues that the Commission on Integration addressed were zoning, which dealt with the configuration of neighborhood boundaries for defining local school zones, and teacher assignments, which addressed the contentious issue of how to staff the predominantly black and Puerto Rican schools. It was these two issues that were hotly debated at the commission's January 1957 public hearing.

At the public hearing, Mrs. Mae Mallory, who later became one of the "Harlem Nine," accused the New York City school system of being as much of a "Jim Crow" system as the one she experienced in Macon, Georgia, where she grew up.[24] She could not have used more provocative language as far as the Board of Education was concerned. The guiding principle for Superintendent Jansen as he participated in the commission's work was a deep-seated and seemingly intractable race blindness. His refusal to recognize the impact of race conflicted with NAACP leader Ella Baker's demand for a census of the city's student population. By January 1958, Ella Baker would be heading to Atlanta to work with the Southern Christian Leadership Conference and eventually with the Student Nonviolent Coordinating Committee. Though widely known for her leadership in the Southern civil rights movement, Baker, in fact, lived most of her adult life in New York City and, from 1946 to 1958, devoted much of her attention to the issue of school segregation in New York.[25] Both she and Superintendent Jansen served on the Commission on Integration. Their disagreements reflected a fundamental difference— her insistence and his unwillingness to name race as a critical force in the shaping of educational opportunities for New York City's schoolchildren.

Race was at the heart of the matter for those parents who opposed the commission's recommendations. The issue of race surfaced in the avoidance of the issue in the testimony of one white working-class parent who expressed the views of many in her letter to the president of the board. She wrote, "There is no segregation in N.Y. City public schools, so why integration?"[26] Others addressed the issue of race explicitly by simply stating, "We don't want our children integrated with Blacks."[27] Some parents, fearing their loss of control, identified the problem in terms of race and warned the Board of Education, "Do not let the Negro politicians and spellbinders mislead you."[28] And another parent did not mince his words as he expanded on stated and unstated prejudices. He said, "Clean up the Jungle Homes and you won't have Blackboard Jungle Children; sending them to other schools won't change their stripes."[29]

The vehement, sometimes vitriolic responses of white parents from around the city confirmed the suspicions of black parents who testified that their children were not receiving an equal education—a fact that had been determined by the Public Education Association's report. At the 1957 public hearing, Naomi Clark, a black PTA president, described the inferior part-time education that her children were receiving due to an overcrowded school:

> May I give you a picture of an antiquated school which has 43 classrooms and 51 classes. This is one of the overcrowded schools in the Bedford-Stuyvesant area. … I am the mother of three children. One goes to school from 8:30 to 12:30, the other two from 11:30 to 3:30. This part-time is a hardship on children and parents alike.[30]

William Delmar, a Harlem parent, described the contrasting educational experiences of his 15-year-old son in a mostly white school and his 13-year-old daughter in a 100 percent black school:

> We notice the difference in the content of the curriculum, in its quality and the amount of enrichment. … We notice the difference in the quality of guidance. In the mixed school, guidance counselors try to be imaginative, to be in guidance with the aspirations and potentialities of the students. In my daughter's school, guidance is limited to channeling children to be [beauticians] or nurse's aides.

He linked these unequal educational conditions directly to the teachers' situation. In his daughter's school, 52 percent of the teachers were substitutes. As he noted, "competent teachers refuse to come or stay in the school."[31]

While the Commission on Integration's public hearing in the winter of 1957 revealed a good deal about school conditions and parents' attitudes and fears, it yielded few concrete changes or improvements. For many African American parents, the board's pace and concern was far too slow and half-hearted. In an attempt to exert greater pressure on the board, parents joined forces and created Parents in Action Against Education Discrimination, a coalition of organizations that included local chapters of the NAACP, the Negro Teachers Association, Harlem's Parents Committee for Better Education, Jamaica School Improvement Council, and the 369th Veterans Association. Parents in Action, believing that integration was the only way to insure that their children would receive an equal education, escalated their organizing throughout the summer of 1957.[32]

Parents in Action met with Mayor Wagner on the day he hosted a reception for Althea Gibson, the African American Wimbledon champion. The irony of airing their grievances on that particular day was not lost on the parents as they tried to hold the mayor accountable on the issue of educational discrimination in New York City.[33] Quick to remind Wagner of his role in appointing the school superintendent, they cited Superintendent Jansen's failure to provide experienced teachers to the schools that their children attended and to act on the integration reports in general and called for Jansen's retirement.[34] While making little impact on the mayor, Parents in Action continued organizing throughout the summer. The coalition called upon parents to listen to a weekly radio show on WLIB devoted to the issue of educational discrimination, write their complaints to the Board of Education, and sign a petition. Seasoned organizers like Ella Baker helped run weekly parent workshops where, according to Baker, the parents "became aware that they had certain rights."[35] The activities of the summer culminated in a picket and rally at City Hall in the beginning of the new school year.[36]

On the heels of the fall rally, one group of Harlem parents formed the Junior High School Coordinating Committee around a campaign for "Freedom of Choice of Junior High Schools" and began planning a school boycott for the following school year.[37] The committee was composed of a mixed-income group of parents who resided in Harlem's middle-class projects, the Riverton Development, and the lower-income Lincoln Projects across the street.[38] Children from both projects were zoned for local Junior High Schools (JHS) 120, 136, and 139. The committee demanded that the children of Harlem be allowed to attend junior high schools outside of Harlem so that they "can have the opportunity to receive *all* the education that is being given on the best standard possible." This was something they did not believe was possible in the Harlem junior high schools.[39]

The Junior High School Coordinating Committee had well-developed analyses about why Harlem children were receiving inferior educations. They recounted how as parents, Board of Education officials had told them that their children were culturally deprived. Once so designated, the schools they attended were branded as "X" or "difficult" schools; lower standards were then applied to the schools. The Coordinating Committee backed their analysis with statistics about JHS 120, 136, and 139, the three junior high schools in Harlem that parents had chosen to boycott. They claimed that teachers referred 40 percent of the student body in these junior high schools to trade and vocational high schools and recommended less than 20 percent of the students for specialized high schools with college-bound tracks. Furthermore, they argued, while teacher shortages were a citywide problem, the shortages were 20 percent higher in the Harlem junior high schools than in all-white or predominantly white enrollment schools.[40] Mirroring the arguments made by leading integrationists like Kenneth Clark, the Coordinating Committee spoke passionately of the damage done to all students—black and white—in segregated schools.

A year later, in the fall of 1958, the Harlem parents began a school boycott. The parents of 15 Harlem children zoned to attend JHS 120, 136, and 139 kept their children home.[41] By the time the boycott was in full gear, the participating parents were primarily from the low-income Lincoln Projects. As Barbara Zuber, Paul Zuber's wife, described, "Their philosophy is, what have we got to lose when you are on the basement floor of humanity in terms of educational opportunities."[42] With truly nothing to lose, Carrie Haynes, a spokeswoman for the boycotting Harlem parents, described the growing frustration, "Conference upon conference has procured nothing. We're going to see this through to the bitter end [even] if it goes to the Supreme Court."[43]

The Harlem parents did not get to the Supreme Court with their boycott; however, their case ultimately made it to the city's Domestic Relations Court. Initially the boycotting parents, with the assistance of their attorney Paul Zuber, addressed the illegality of keeping their children out of school by organizing private tutoring sessions. Reverend Eugene Callendar, minister at the Mid-Harlem Community Parish on Seventh Avenue and 122nd Street, was sympathetic to the grievances of the Harlem parents and offered his church as a site for the students' classes. For over a month the children were taught English, mathematics, social studies, world events, music, French, and art appreciation by five licensed teachers, as well as by Paul and Barbara Zuber.[44]

By mid-October, the boycotting parents realized that the Board of Education was duly impressed with the tutorial classes they were running and was going to leave them alone. Recognizing the irony of the situation, they decided to end the private tutoring. Knowing that they now defied the compulsory education law, the parents hoped to force the Board of Education to act on their grievances by filing a claim against the city for $1 million. The claim accused the city of "sinister and discriminatory purpose in the perpetuation of racial segregation in five school districts in Harlem;" it named Superintendent Theobald, Mayor Wagner, the Board of Education, and the Board of Estimates as the defendants.[45]

The parents succeeded in prompting several responses from the Board of Education. A couple of days after the claim against the city was filed, Theobald requested that the State Education Department conduct a study of the three junior high schools in Harlem that the parents were boycotting. Theobald asserted that the parents' protest had not influenced him to request the state study but did play a part in determining which schools would be selected for the study. Though he attempted to downplay the ongoing school boycott, the boycotting parents declared a victory in their two-year-long battle.[46]

The Board of Education also responded by summoning the Harlem parents to appear before the Domestic Relations Court "for failure to comply with the provisions of the compulsory education law."[47] For the boycotting parents, the court summons also proved to be a victory, though not initially. Judge Nathaniel Kaplan, who found four of the parents guilty of violating the state's law on compulsory school attendance, tried six of the nine parents.[48] However, less than two weeks later, Judge Justine Polier, who was hearing the case of two of the parents in her courtroom, dismissed the charges against them.

In this landmark decision, Polier concurred with the boycotting parents that the children who attended the junior high schools in Harlem were receiving "inferior educational opportunities in those schools by reason of racial discrimination."[49] While agreeing with the defendants that de facto segregation existed in the junior high schools of New York City, Polier did not find evidence that de facto segregation was a consequence of any wrongdoing on the part of the Board of Education. However, citing the testimony of expert witness Dr. Kenneth Clark, she agreed that regardless of whether segregation is a result of governmental action or private housing segregation the separation of children by race disables equal educational opportunities.

The black press and community groups hailed the ruling as the first Northern decision against de facto segregation in public schools.[50] Polier did not charge the board with causing segregation; she charged it with the results of segregation. However, in basing her decision on pre- and post-*Brown* cases that Zuber, the parents' attorney, cited, she argued that the

North could no longer hide behind de facto segregation as an excuse for inferior educational facilities. Polier referred, for example, to a recent case in Virginia, *Dobbins v. Commonwealth of Virginia* (Va. 1957) in which the Supreme Court of Appeals of Virginia overturned the lower court's conviction of black parents for refusing to send their children to a racially segregated school on grounds that the school was segregated and inferior. The Virginia Supreme Court argued that compulsory education laws, "cannot be applied as a coercive means to require a citizen to forego or relinquish his Constitutional rights." The judge admonished the New York City Board of Education for suggesting "that the courts of this State be less solicitous of the rights of its citizens."[51] In general, she chided the Board of Education for having "done substantially nothing to rectify a situation it should never have allowed to develop," more than four years after *Brown* and eight years after the Supreme Court's ruling in *Sweatt v. Painter*.[52]

The focus of Polier's ruling in favor of the parents was on the damaging aspects of segregated education, and she held the Board of Education responsible for these inferior educational facilities. Most specifically, she blamed the board for allowing discrimination in teacher assignment that resulted in less qualified teachers being assigned to the schools in which black and Puerto Rican children predominated. Explaining that the Board of Education is legally responsible for assigning teachers, she linked the board's actions—or inaction—to Southern-style racial discrimination, stating:

> The Board of Education of the City of New York can no more disclaim responsibility for what has occurred in this matter than the State of South Carolina could avoid responsibility for a Jim Crow State Democratic party which the State did everything possible to render "private" in character and operation.[53]

Polier based her conclusions about the board's discriminatory practices on the recent Board of Education figures, showing that as of September 1958, the average percentage of teacher vacancies was 49.5 percent in schools with over 85 percent black and Puerto Rican (X schools, as they were euphemistically called in the Public Education Association's 1955 study).[54] The city's Y schools (those with over 85 percent white students) had an average of 29.6 percent teacher vacancies. What this meant for students attending the junior high schools being boycotted in Harlem was best relayed by Alfred Nussbaum, the principal of JHS 136.[55]

Nussbaum testified at the hearing that of the 85 teachers in his school, less than half were regularly licensed. Forty-three teaching positions were filled by substitutes, and often the substitutes were filling positions in subject areas that they were not trained to teach. For example, 9 of the 11 math teachers in his school were not licensed to teach that subject. Only three of the six teachers in the Science Department were licensed to teach science. (One of the science substitute teachers was licensed as a substitute social studies teacher; a second substitute was licensed to teach first through sixth grades but not junior high school.) In addition, the heads of the science and art departments were not licensed to teach those subjects, and one of the assistant principals was not licensed as an assistant principal. Under questioning by Justice Polier, Nussbaum granted that the curriculum at his school was as good as any "subject school" but not necessarily as good as the curriculum in integrated or all-white schools.[56] It was on the issue of teacher staffing that Polier repeatedly criticized the New York City Board of Education for being in violation of U.S. law, going back as far as the 1896 *Plessy* v. *Ferguson* Supreme Court decision that sanctioned segregation but at least required "equal facilities."

Perhaps, most importantly, Justice Polier approached this case not from the narrow perspective of whether the parents had violated the law but from the broader perspective of what she called "institutional racism."[57] As she wrote in *The Matter of Skipwith and Rector* decision, "The Board of Education contends that one arm of the state—this court—must blindly enforce the unconstitutional denial of constitutional rights by another arm of this state—the Board of Education."[58]

Judge Polier's ruling was a powerful vindication for the Harlem parents of their experiences in the junior high schools that they were boycotting. Furthermore, the court hearing itself served to support the community's historic and ongoing complaints that their children were not receiving an equal education. Her ruling also helped embolden the four mothers who were convicted by Judge Kaplan for violating the state's compulsory school law. On the eve of their sentencing, which could include a ten-day jail term, they declared: "We are packing our tooth brushes and bags and we will present ourselves before Judge Kaplan for jail sentencing. We will go to jail and rot there, if necessary, but our children will not go to Jr. High Schools 136, 139, or 120."[59]

On the heels of Judge Polier's dismissal of the charges against two of the parents, the four convicted mothers asked Judge Kaplan to reopen their case and dismiss the charges filed against them by the Board of Education.[60] Ultimately, Judge Kaplan announced that he would take no action against the four mothers, and they escaped punishment.[61] The leniency they were granted was also directly related to an interim solution that was reached between the "Harlem Nine" and the Board of Education. The agreement, negotiated between Zuber and Superintendent Theobald, with the assistance of the mayor's COIR, represented a compromise on both sides. The children would not return to the schools for which they had been zoned, nor would they be admitted to the schools that their parents requested. Instead they would be sent to a school that Superintendent Theobald chose, JHS 43. This school was also based in Harlem but it had a pilot project that offered special guidance services and a cultural program sponsored by the College Entrance Examination Board and the National Scholarship Services for Negro Students.[62]

Both the Board of Education and the parents considered the solution an interim one as they awaited the outcome of a couple of court cases. Much to the chagrin of the Harlem parents, the Board of Education had appealed the Polier decision.[63] Concurrently, the parents were waiting on a $1 million civil suit they had filed against the city for the "alleged injustice suffered by the children in segregated schools."[64]

The very fact that the board initiated (though ultimately dropped) an appeal of the Polier decision served to unite many in Harlem against it.[65] Shortly after the board announced its intent to appeal the decision, the Empire State Baptist Convention, representing 350,000 Baptists, called for the removal of every board member, with the exception of Baptist board member Dr. Gardner Taylor, the one black board member. Forming an emergency committee on the Harlem School Crisis, the convention's leadership threatened a mass march on City Hall if Mayor Wagner did not replace the board. Their only stipulation, according to Reverend George Lawrence, the emergency committee's chairman, was that if the board rescinded its decision to appeal the Polier decision, then they would not lead "a City Hall pilgrimage."[66] Board of Education member Taylor, president of the Protestant Council and pastor of the Concord Baptist Church, called upon his congregation of more than 8,000 members to contribute $1,000 to help cover the expenses of fighting the board's appeal.[67] Explaining that the congregation made a yearly donation to the United Negro College Fund, he said that this year the funds collected would "be used to conduct New York's Jim Crow School fight."[68]

The Harlem Neighborhoods Association (HNA), a coalition of Harlem civic and social organizations, also protested the board's appeal. As they argued, an appeal would "increase the gap separating the Board of Education from our community."[69] Within Harlem's political arena, two state legislators, Senator James L. Watson and Assemblyman Lloyd E. Dickens, both Harlem Democrats, responded to the board's appeal by sponsoring a resolution that called for a joint legislative committee, with subpoena power, to study the school segregation issue in New York City.[70]

The public outcry demonstrated that many in Harlem were deeply offended by the implications of the board's decision to appeal Judge Polier's verdict. The board's action confirmed many African Americans'

long-held suspicions that, as Dr. Taylor put it, "The city of New York is saying to underprivileged Negro and Puerto Rican children just this: You
can't go to schools that are equal, you can't have equal opportunities
here."[71] And in the process of confirming suspicions, the city's black parents and community leaders saw their protests as linked to similar struggles in the South. "Wittingly or unwittingly the board erased the last line
of differences between Little Rock and New York," concluded Dr. Taylor.[72]

Southern civil rights struggles like the Little Rock, Arkansas, school integration battles featured prominently on the front pages of the *New York
Amsterdam News*. The editors juxtaposed photos of mob action in Little
Rock with headlines reminding readers, "Don't Forget, N.Y. Has Its Own
School Problem" and a photo of a Harlem mother registering her daughter
in the local school. The caption under the photo stated: "While [the]
nation's eyes [are] focused on attempts by Negro children to enter all-white
schools for the first time in the South, little Gertrude Jenkins undergoes the
same experience right here in New York City. Here she registers at 100 percent segregated Public School 194."[73] The 1959 New Year's Day cartoon
depicted an African American toddler aiming a shotgun at three crows,
"Jimcros" [sic], that represented the Little Rock Board of Education, the
Norfolk Board of Education, and the New York City Board of Education.[74]

If being cast in relation to nationally televised Southern battles gave
greater weight and importance to this Northern fight, then being linked to
Southern civil rights leaders served a similar function for the Northern
women boycotters. The Harlem mothers were compared to Daisy Bates in
Little Rock, Rosa Parks in Montgomery, Autherine Lucy in Tuscaloosa,
Irene Morgan in Virginia, and Ada Sipuel in Oklahoma and celebrated in
the sisterhood of Southern women activists.[75] Being associated to these
Southern heroes helped ensure their respectability at least within the black
community as they publicly asserted their rights. *New York Amsterdam
News* editor James Hicks had been noting the importance of Southern
women civil rights activists for several years before paying attention to
local parent activism. In one particularly explicit editorial, Hicks offered a
chronology of women challenging segregation in the South and concluded: "The hand that rocks the cradle is shaking up this country of ours
in the fight for civil rights!"[76]

These Southern activists were represented as mothers regardless of their
maternal status. Their political value and moral authority rested in the fact
that they were, at least symbolically, "cradle rockers." In painting this image,
Hicks was mirroring the portrayals of black women in the national media.
Jacqueline Jones noted in her study of *Ebony* that the black magazine,
which had the largest circulation in the postwar period, regularly featured

accomplished black women who defied prejudice and challenged bigotry. While acknowledging the reality that many black women had to work outside of the home, the magazine consistently presented portraits of women who successfully combined careers with motherhood. At the same time, the magazine also celebrated those women who were able to take advantage of their husband's postwar higher wages and stay at home. As one editorial announced, "Goodbye Mammy, Hello Mom."[77]

Constructing an image of respectable black women as good mothers—in the North and South—was in keeping with popular culture's depictions of America's postwar (and laid-off) happy housewives. In the black community, however, this representation of motherhood was also a response to a political struggle in which motherhood was the battlefield over which the rights and legitimacy of black families were being fought.[78] Analyzing the black family—its social structure, psychology, and history—proved to be fertile territory for postwar liberal and conservative social scientists to explore. The implications of their theories were critical as they affected legal decisions and public policy. Building on the writings of E. Franklin Frazier and Gunnar Myrdal, social theorists focused on the "matriarchal" family structure to characterize the black family as pathological. African American mothers came under the scrutiny of social scientists who essentially blamed these supposedly dominant women for the failures of black men and the "cultural deprivation" of black children. As social scientists shifted the focus on racial inferiority from biological determinism to cultural pathology, advancing an image of good mothers was one response to the cultural wars of the 1950s.[79]

The portrayal of Harlem's women activists in the local black press suggests that the black community looked to their maternal roles to provide leadership. The women were saluted as "courageous mothers" whose resistance became the copy for headlines: "Striking School Moms Say ... 'We'd Rather Go To Jail.' "[80] Equally important was the presentation of these women as regular, normal mothers—just like white mothers—who want the best for their children. Hence, an article subtitled one section "Mothers Comments" and included simple and universal comments by a group of Brooklyn boycotting mothers, such as, "I want to see that he [ten-year-old Harold] gets a better education" and "I want her [ten-year-old Deborah] to attend a good school."[81]

As they were represented to the black community, it was black women's maternal roles that gave them credibility and authority to step into the public sphere. Often it was Amsterdam News editor Hicks who would appeal to the "moms" to join the demonstrations at City Hall: "But don't go alone. See to it that your minister goes and as many people from your church as possible."[82] Hicks, who the year before was attacked while covering the "Little Rock Nine"'s attempts to integrate Central High School, placed Harlem's "moms" in their domestic space in his informal "chat" with them and depicted them as responsible mothers, caring for their children the way good mothers do:

> Hi Mom,—May I come in a minute? Thanks. No, I won't sit down. I know you're busy getting the kids ready for school and I hate to bother you. But it was so important that I thought I'd better drop in and tell you about it. It's about the schools, Mom, and I know you're interested, that's why I came. You go ahead with your ironing and I'll try to be as brief as possible.[83]

These mothers were good mothers, not only in their private domain but also in their public roles as workers. Contrary to popular depictions of America's women returning to the home after WWII, black female participation in the labor force remained steady after the war and increased for white women. By 1950, one-third of all black wives worked outside of the home compared to one-quarter of all married women. African American women continued to find work in the lowest paying sector of the economy, with almost half of all black women employed in domestic work.[84] Their work lives, therefore, had to be presented as yet another aspect of what made them good and responsible mothers. As Hicks reminded readers in another editorial, these mothers who worry about the ways in which the minds of their children have "been subtly, but systematically twisted, stunted and warped by a school system" are the ones who also stand "over a hot stove eight hours in someone's kitchen."[85]

The maternalist representation enhanced the status of black activists as respectable mothers and women. The maternalist argument, however, advanced on behalf of the boycotting mothers, was also a restricting one that was premised on a belief in male superiority and did not allow women to claim leadership positions.[86] For ultimately, though these women were saluted as courageous by the local black press, it was equally apparent that their cause would only succeed with the leadership of black male lawyers and civil rights leaders. In his "chat" with the "moms," Hicks put it quite clearly:

> Things have been happening in this school business since I talked with you last time, Mom. In the first place, you and your child have at last some support—some real support, Mom. You're not fighting alone, anymore. A young lawyer by the name of Paul Zuber has filed suit against the schools. And you know what else—I saved this until the last, Mom, because I knew you'd be tickled to hear it—you know what else? Thurgood Marshall has stepped into the picture on the side of the young lawyer.[87]

The black press authenticated the power of the mothers by linking it to real, male power. And the leaders were not only male but also educated. They were the professional class of lawyers, ministers, psychologists, and journalists within New York's black community. Their professional status suggests that the lines of division within the community were embedded in both class differences as well as traditional gender roles. Hicks's description of the gendered and class divisions within New York City's community of civil rights activists simply mirrored the divisions operating in the civil rights movement as a whole as public power was taken by male leaders in the North and South.[88]

Not only did a maternalist identity offer little power, the activists themselves did not necessarily embrace it. As Mae Mallory explained, her role in the movement for equal educational opportunities did not stem from a moral authority embedded in her maternal role. Quite to the contrary, she was motivated by a powerful desire to ensure that her daughter not be defined by her gender and race and relegated to the bottom of the social and economic ladder as a black woman. "I wanted both my children to get the best possible public education that they could," asserted Mrs. Mallory, "because I wanted to break the cycle of women doing days work or factory work."[89] She shared the belief of her Southern sisters from Montgomery's Women's Political Council that "a woman's duties do not end in the home, church or classroom."[90] Their sense of entitlement extended beyond the boundaries of class, race, and gender as they described their activism as the struggle for human rights.

How do we assess the impact of these mothers who were on the front lines of the school integration battles? In the short run they were successful in drawing the Board of Education's attention to their issues, and the board offered piecemeal solutions to individual black families. When black mothers demanded equal educational opportunities for their children in Harlem's segregated schools, they brought attention to an issue generally seen as the exclusive domain of the segregated South. The school boycott and Polier decision underscored, as Mae Mallory put it, the "whole segregation myth" in New York City. In other words, the boundaries between de jure and de facto segregation, between the North and the South, were blurred as the mothers called attention to inferior educational opportunities in the city's black schools, and Judge Polier admonished the Board of Education for having administered this inequality in the wake of *Brown*.

The "Harlem Nine" provided a model of neighborhood school boycotts that would be replicated in black and Puerto Rican neighborhoods over the next decade and a half. Like the "Harlem Nine," future parent boycotters would experience first hand the intransigence of the Board of Education.

Steeped in its institutional machinations that, in many cases, related to racial politics and in some cases had nothing to do with race, it would prove to be a very difficult system to change. Black parents would continue to experience the limitations of their political power and legal rights when it came to the city's power structure. Conversely, they would be radically affected by the changing demographics of the city that had everything to do with race and class, as the city lost a significant share of its tax base in the flurry of white flight. Finally, as political activists, the parent boycotters would continue to be confined by maternal identities that limited their power and the possibilities of the movement.

Notes

1. "Defy Court's Order in School Boycott," *New York Amsterdam News,* December 13, 1958.
2. "Parents Close Special School," *New York Amsterdam News,* October 18, 1958. In the fall of 1957, nine African American school children attempted to integrate Central High School in Little Rock, Arkansas. The mobs of white residents who attempted to block the students from entering the school became a national and international story, as did Governor Orval Faubus's use of the Arkansas National Guard to achieve the same purpose. Though President Eisenhower called in U.S. paratroopers to protect the nine students, and in June 1958 the first black student graduated from Central High, the struggle continued through the fall of 1958 when Governor Faubus closed all of the public high schools in Little Rock. The schools were not reopened until August 1959, when the Supreme Court ruled that the closing was unconstitutional. See Daisy Bates, *The Long Shadow of Little Rock: A Memoir* (New York: David McKay Co., 1962); Henry Hampton and Steve Fayer, *Voices of Freedom* (New York: Bantam, 1990), 36–52; and Taylor Branch, *Parting the Waters: America in the King Years, 1954–1963* (New York: Simon and Schuster, 1988), 222–225.
3. The literature on Northern (and Western) struggles for equal educational opportunities generally picks up the story with the Supreme Court's 1973 challenge to de facto segregation (*Keyes* v. *Denver School District No. 1*) and the court-ordered school busing cases of the early 1970s. Boston's busing war has received a fair amount of attention (see Jeanne Theoharis's critical analysis of this literature in this volume). Other examples include Gregory S. Jacobs's study of Columbus, Ohio's 1977 court-ordered school desegregation case, *Getting Around Brown: Desegregation, Development, and the Columbus Public Schools* (Columbus: Ohio State University Press, 1998); George R. Metcalf, *From Little Rock to Boston: The History of School Desegregation* (Westport: Greenwood Press, 1983); several essays in *Dismantling Desegregation: The Quiet Reversal of Brown* v. *Board of Education,* Gary Orfield, Susan E. Eaton and the Harvard Project on School Desegregation, eds. (New York: The New Press, 1996), including "Still Separate, Still Unequal," by Susan E. Eaton, Joseph Feldman,

and Edward Kirby, and "Segregated Housing and School Resegregation," by Gary Orfield. The recent publication of James T. Patterson's *Brown v. Board of Education: A Civil Rights Milestone and Its Troubled Legacy* (New York: Oxford University Press, 2001) and ensuing debate about the court's, the civil rights attorneys', and the historians' attention to Northern school segregation underscores that this remains a contentious historical and contemporary issue. See Lewis M. Steel's review of Patterson's book and letters to the editor in *The Nation,* February 5, 2001, and April 30, 2001.

4. The media coverage of the Ocean Hill-Brownsville conflict specifically and the Northern civil rights movement in general focused on the militancy of the black community leadership's demand for community control. Journalist Daniel Schorr has talked about the ways in which reporters were directed to focus on violent aspects of the movement. See interview with Schorr, *Bridges and Boundaries: African Americans and American Jews,* exhibition video, "The Civil Rights Movement," (produced by the Jewish Museum, New York, 1992). For references to various partisan accounts and scholarly interpretations of the Ocean Hill-Brownsville episode and a discussion of the conflict's 1950s context, see Adina Back, "Blacks, Jews and the Struggle to Integrate Brooklyn's Junior High School 258: A Cold War Story," *Journal of American Ethnic History* 20 (winter 2001): 38–69.

5. Joanne Meyerowitz's anthology has been pivotal in challenging traditional depictions of women in the 1950s. *Not June Cleaver: Women and Gender in Postwar America, 1945–1960* (Philadelphia: Temple University Press, 1994).

6. Annelise Orleck, Alexis Jetter, and Diana Taylor use the term "motherist" to describe the activism of mothers, which may include but is not necessarily limited to a maternal rhetoric. *The Politics of Motherhood: Activist Voices from Left to Right* (Hanover, N.H.: University Press of New England, 1997), Introduction. See also Kathleen Blee, ed., *No Middle Ground: Women and Radical Protest* (New York: New York University Press, 1998); Evelyn Glenn, Grace Chang, and Linda Rennie Forcey, eds., *Mothering: Ideology, Experience, and Agency* (Routledge: New York, 1994); and Molly Ladd-Taylor and Laurie Umansky, eds., *"Bad" Mothers: The Politics of Blame in Twentieth Century America* (New York: New York University Press, 1998).

7. In offering a black feminist theory of motherhood, Patricia Hill Collins has coined the term "motherwork" to argue that the rigid distinctions between public and private posited in feminist theorizing about motherhood are not applicable for understanding racial ethnic women's experiences and histories of motherhood. "Shifting the Center: Race, Class and Feminist Theorizing About Motherhood," in Glenn, Chang, and Forcey, eds., *Mothering: Ideology, Experience, and Agency,* 47–48.

8. Author interview with Mrs. Mae Mallory, January 30, 2000, Brooklyn, N.Y.

9. Charles Green and Basil Wilson, *The Struggle for Black Empowerment in New York City* (New York: McGraw Hill, 1989); "2000 at Moslem Feast in Harlem," *New York Amsterdam News,* July 20, 1957; Robin D. G. Kelley, "House Negroes

on the Loose: Malcolm X and the Black Bourgeoisie," 16 (essay, author's personal possession); and Kelley and Betsy Esch, "Black Like Mao: Red China and Black Revolution," 2–5 (essay, author's personal possession).

10. Remarks by Mayor Wagner at Dinner of the Urban League, February 15, 1954. Robert F. Wagner Papers, New York City Municipal Archives (hereafter referred to as the Wagner Papers), B.59, F.685. See Stuart Svonkin, *Jews Against Prejudice: American Jews and the Fight for Civil Liberties* (New York: Columbia University Press, 1977) for a discussion of the intergroup relations field.

11. "Brooklyn Pupils Shifted in Integration Program," *Herald Tribune,* October 30, 1956.

12. David Rogers offers a comprehensive analysis of the bureaucratic structure and functions of the Board of Education during this period. *110 Livingston Street: Politics and Bureaucracy in the New York City Schools* (New York: Random House, 1968).

13. Though Jansen and Theobald both embraced the "neighborhood school" policy, Theobald was not as unequivocally opposed to integration as was his predecessor. Having served as Mayor Wagner's deputy mayor before being appointed to be Superintendent of Schools, Theobald brought to the position political skills and an intellectual understanding of the issue that Jansen never had. See Rogers, *110 Livingston Street.* Diane Ravitch also discusses the differences between the two superintendents, though our conclusions about Theobald's commitment to school integration differ. *The Great School Wars: A History of New York City Public Schools* (New York: Basic Books, 1974), chapter 23.

14. The work of E. Franklin Frazier, *The Negro Family in the United States* (Chicago: University of Chicago Press, 1939), and Gunnar Myrdal, *An American Dilemma: The Negro Problem and Modern Democracy* (New York: Harper and Brothers, 1944), strongly influenced postwar policymakers. As historian Regina Kunzel has noted, however, they were less inclined to focus on the aspects of Frazier's analysis that indicted racism. Regina Kunzel, "White Neurosis, Black Pathology: Constructing Out-of-Wedlock Pregnancy in Wartime and Postwar United States," in Meyerowitz, *Not June Cleaver,* 320. See Michael Katz, *The "Underclass" Debate: Views from History* (Princeton: Princeton University Press, 1993), 3–23, for a useful historical overview of the pathologizing of the "underclass."

15. The testimony of various teacher organizations at the public hearing held by the Board of Education's Commission on Integration in January 1957 offers insights into teachers' attitudes about race. See Adina Back, "Up South in New York: The 1950s School Desegregation Struggle " (Ph.D. Diss., New York University, 1997), chapter 3.

16. Ibid. Only the small, radical Teachers Union and the even smaller Negro Teachers Association organized vigorously on behalf of school integration.

17. Report of the Sub-Committee on Education and Recreation of the City-Wide Citizens' Committee on Harlem and Recommendations of the Sub-Committee on Education and Recreation, Supplemental to the Report of April

1942 (personal collection); Mark Naison, *Communists in Harlem During the Depression* (New York: Grove Press, 1983), 215.

18. "Segregated Schools in New York City," speech by Dr. Kenneth B. Clark, April 24, 1954 at "Children Apart" Conference. United Parents Association Archives, Special Collections, Milbank Memorial Library, Teachers College Columbia University (hereafter referred to as UPA Collection), S.10, F.52.

19. Speech by Kenneth B. Clark, Urban League of Greater New York, Negro History Week-Brotherhood Month Dinner, February 12 and 15, 1954, pp. 1–2. UPA Collection, S.10, F.52.

20. Letter to William Jansen from Clare C. Baldwin, Assistant Superintendent, May 12, 1954, 2–3. Board of Education Collection (hereafter B/E Collection), S.456, F.2C.

21. The Intergroup Committee included organizations like American Jewish Congress, Citizens Committee on Children, NAACP, Public Education Association, and United Parents Association.

22. Gerald Markowitz and David Rosner, *Children, Race and Power: Kenneth and Mamie Clark's Northside Center* (Charlottesville: University Press of Virginia, 1996), 23.

23. Letter to William Jansen from Paul W. Aron, Public Relations Assistant, November 22, 1954. B/E Collection, S.456, F.2C.

24. Testimony by Mrs. Mallory (Speaker #38) from PTA of Public School 10, Manhattan, at the B/E Public Hearing, January 17, 1957. B/E Collection, S.261, B.2, F.14.

25. Joanne Grant, *Ella Baker: Freedom Bound* (New York: John Wiley & Sons, 1998), chapter 5. According to Grant, Baker was critical of the New York City branch of the NAACP for paying little attention to "problems in its own backyard." Curiously, Baker's biographers also pay little attention to her leadership in the Northern civil rights movement, though biographer Barbara Ransby describes that moving to Atlanta to work with SCLC was a difficult decision for Baker to make as she was "deeply involved" in the local struggles for educational equality. Barbara Ransby, "Ella J. Baker and the Black Radical Tradition" (Ph.D. Diss., University of Michigan, 1996), 199–200. Baker's organizing skills and philosophy, well honed in the North, suggest links between Northern and Southern civil rights activities worth exploring more fully. Historians' inattention to pre-1960s Northern civil rights activism is demonstrated again in Kenneth B. Clark's oral history interview conducted for the Oral History Collection of Columbia University. In this extensive interview, which was conducted over the course of *14 sessions* between 1976 and 1985, the oral historian never once asked Clark about his involvement with New York City's school integration movement.

26. Letter to Charles Silver from Mrs. Henry C. Kolin, February 21, 1957, B/E Collection, S.261, B.1, F.10.

27. Letter to the New York City Board of Education from O'Neil and Nillson, n.d., B/E Collection, S.261, B.1, F.10.

28. Letters to Charles Silver from Samuel Atkin, March 23, 1957, and Wesley Baker, January 29, 1957. B/E Collection, S.261, B.1, F.10.

29. Letter to Board of Education from Raymond M. Chaitin, January 19, 1957, B/E Collection, S.261, B.1, F.9.

30. Testimony by Naomi Clark (Speaker #48), President of the PTA of PS 129, Brooklyn, B/E Public Hearing, January 17, 1957, B/E Collection, S.261, B.2, F.14.

31. Comments to Charles Silver, members of the board, Mr. Jansen from William Delmar, President of the PTA of PS 136, Manhattan, n.d., B/E Collection, S.261, B.1, F.8.

32. "Parents Rap School Jim Crow: Air Protests Before Mayor," *New York Amsterdam News,* July 20, 1957. Letter to Mayor Robert F. Wagner from Ella Baker, Paul B. Zuber, and Richard Parrish, June 28, 1957. National Association for the Advancement of Colored People, the Collections of the Manuscript Division, the Library of Congress. (Hereafter referred to as NAACP). II, F: "Ella Baker." Their strategy for achieving integration included calling for a construction moratorium on new schools in sites that would only intensify segregation and transferring all junior high school students from schools with predominantly black enrollments to junior high schools in other districts. As they monitored the actions of the board, the parents accused it of a variety of abuses: They charged the district superintendent with establishing the summer school remedial reading program in a school closest to the area's white communities and farthest from the black neighborhoods, and they accused the board of intending to send the newest teachers with the lowest passing grades to the Harlem schools.

33. Report of Education Committee to the Executive Committee of the New York Branch, NAACP, by Ella Baker, July 9, 1957. NAACP, II, F: "Ella Baker." Gibson was the first African American to be honored by New York with a ticker tape ceremony. See coverage in *New York Amsterdam News,* July 20, 1957.

34. Parents in Action Against Educational Discrimination, leaflet, "Jansen Must Go!" July 1957. NAACP, Ella Baker File. "Parents Rap School Jim Crow: Air Protests Before Mayor," *New York Amsterdam News,* July 20, 1957.

35. Ellen Cantarow, "Ella Baker—Organizing for Civil Rights," in *Moving the Mountain: Women Working for Social Change,* Ellen Cantarow and Susan O'Malley, eds. (Old Westbury: The Feminist Press, 1980), 68.

36. "Parents Picket City Hall Over Integration Delay," *The New York Times,* September 20, 1957; and "Don't Forget, N.Y. Has Its Own School Problem," *New York Amsterdam News,* September 28, 1957. *The New York Times* claimed that 200 parents attended the picket, and *New York Amsterdam News* offered the figure of 500 parents.

37. Parents in Action Against Educational Discrimination, leaflet, "Your Committee Had Things to Report ... So Please Be Present October 10 [1957]. ... " NAACP II, F: "Ella Baker."

38. The Riverton Development was built by the Metropolitan Life Insurance Company in response to the company's exclusionary policies in its Stuyvesant

town development. Kenneth Clark, *Dark Ghetto: Dilemmas of Social Power* (Hanover, N.H.: Wesleyan University Press, 1965), 57.

39. Letter to Rose Russell from Carrie E. Haynes, Chairman, Junior High School Coordinating Committee Supporting 9 Parents of Harlem, and Ruby Sims, President of the PTA JHS133, January 31, 1959. The Teachers Union of the City of New York records. Labor-Management Documentation Center, Cornell University. (hereafter referred to as the TU Collection) 5015, 45–49.

40. Ibid., 1.

41. Letter to Rose Russell from Carrie E. Haynes; "21 Negro Pupils Are Kept Home on Charge of Segregation Here," *The New York Times,* September 9, 1958, 1; "Harlem Parents Still on Strike," *New York Amsterdam News,* September 20, 1958. Six of the 21 boycotting students were from Brooklyn. The Brooklyn boycott was resolved within several days as the new school superintendent, John Theobald, agreed to admit the boycotting students to a better-integrated school than the one for which they had originally been zoned. The Board of Education characterized this rezoning as part of a general rezoning plan that they had been intending to effect later in the school year. "Brooklyn School Dispute Settled When Negroes Accept Rezoning," *The New York Times,* September 16, 1958. "Brooklyn Parents Seeking Showdown on JimCro [*sic*] Schools," *New York Amsterdam News,* September 13, 1958; "Brooklyn Parents in School Victory," *New York Amsterdam News,* September 20, 1958.

42. Author interview with Barbara Zuber, Troy, N.Y., July 16, 2001.

43. "21 Negro Pupils Still Kept home," *The New York Times,* September 10, 1958. Carrie Haynes personally experienced the benefits of being part of the larger community of civil rights activists. When the city nearly evicted her from her Lincoln Project home, Bayard Rustin, acting executive director of In Friendship, the organization formed by Rustin, Ella Baker, Philip Randolph, and Stanley Levinson to raise funds for Southern integration activists, literally stopped the eviction with a loan from In Friendship. "Community Halts Woman's Eviction," *New York Amsterdam News,* October 4, 1958.

44. "Harlem Parents in Plea to State," *The New York Times,* September 17, 1958; "Harlem's Boycott Classes," *New York Amsterdam News,* September 20, 1958; "School Boycott Rests with Theobald," *New York Amsterdam News,* October 11, 1958.

45. "School Boycott Rests with Theobald," *New York Amsterdam News,* October 11, 1958; "Parents Close Special School," *New York Amsterdam News,* October 18, 1958; and "Harlem Parents File for Million," *The New York Times,* October 29, 1958. This was not the first time that African American parents brought a suit against the Board of Education. In fact, Mae Mallory, one of the parents on whose behalf the 1958 suit was filed, had filed a suit against the Board of Education the year before. In that suit, Mallory attacked the school zoning laws as unconstitutional and sought to compel the board to permit her daughter to attend a junior high school outside of her school district. That same fall, Mrs. William Robinson, a Bronx parent, filed a similar suit. "Negro

Sues City on School Zoning," *The New York Times,* July 18, 1957; "More Parents File School Suits," *New York Amsterdam News,* July 27, 1957; and "2D School Suit Filed," *The New York Times,* August 1, 1957.

46. "State to Probe JHS in Harlem," *New York Amsterdam News,* November 8, 1958; and "State Will Study 3 Harlem Schools," *The New York Times,* October 30, 1958.

47. "6 Mothers Summoned," *The New York Times,* November 12, 1958.

48. "4 Mothers Guilty in School Boycott," *The New York Times,* December 4, 1958. Kaplan heard three other cases and adjourned one of them until a further hearing; dismissed another on a technicality; and in the third case, the mother was placed on parole because she had returned her child to public school.

49. Judge Polier Ruling, Domestic Relations Court of the City of New York, Schlesinger Library, Radcliffe Institute, MC413 Justine Polier Collection, B21, F247, 28, December 15, 1958. "2 Harlem Schools Called Inferior as Court Frees Two in Boycott," *The New York Times,* December 16, 1958; and "Court Finds Bias in Harlem Schools," *New York Amsterdam News,* December 20, 1958.

50. Justine Wise Polier, *Juvenile Justice in Double Jeopardy: The Distanced Community and Vengeful Retribution* (Hillsdale, N.J.: Lawrence Erlbaum Associates, 1989), 152.

51. Polier Ruling, 13.

52. Ibid., 25. The Supreme Court ruled that Heman Sweatt be admitted to the University of Texas Law School, as there were no equal facilities in Texas for African Americans wanting to go to law school.

53. Ibid., 26.

54. "The Status of the Public School Education of Negro and Puerto Rican Children in New York City," presented to the Board of Education Commission on Education, prepared by the Public Education Association assisted by the New York University Research Center for Human Relations, October 1955. TU Collection, 45-1. The postwar vocabulary in New York for "deserving" (white) and "non-deserving" (nonwhite) students ranged from the impersonal notations of "X" and "Y" to references to "problem" schools, "difficult" schools, and "subject" schools.

55. Ibid., 21–22.

56. Ibid., pp. 19–20; *New York Amsterdam News,* November 15, 1958.

57. Polier, *Juvenile Justice in Double Jeopardy,* 151. Polier described the criticism she received after the ruling, especially from the higher judicial hierarchy, like state Supreme Court judges who "showed anxiety about a Juvenile Court judge acting as either a citizen or a judge to protect constitutional rights." On the other hand, Polier had the support of Thurgood Marshall (then Director of the NAACP's National Education and Defense Fund), who called after her decision and said that the fund would take the case if it were appealed (page 9). Polier also described the volumes of hate mail she received, including the last vituperative letter she received, 14 years after the decision, in which the person wrote: "People like you are the real criminals—not the stupid black and white niggers who are wrecking a once great City and nation. They are

doing what scum like you have taught them to do—take an aggressive violent stance or demand their alleged rights. May you rot in hell" (page 152).

58. "2 Harlem Schools Called Inferior as Court Frees Two in Boycott," *The New York Times*, December 16, 1958.

59. "Defy Court's Order in School Boycott," *New York Amsterdam News*, December 13, 1958.

60. "Boycott Parents Want New Trial," *New York Amsterdam News*, December 27, 1958. Other concerned parents were also emboldened by the Polier decision. Shortly after her ruling, another group of Harlem parents visited JHS 52 (on Academy Street and Broadway) and requested, to no avail, that their children be allowed to register there. As they explained, "The parents based their request upon their constitutional rights and on Justice Polier's recent decision." Telephone message to the Teachers Union from Carrie Haynes. TU Collection 5015, 45–49.

61. "Harlem Parents to Gain Leniency," *The New York Times*, February 12, 1959; and "4 Negro Mothers Freed in Boycott," *The New York Times*, February 19, 1959.

62. "Harlem Talks Bid for School Peace," *The New York Times*, January 30, 1959; "School Boycott End Foreseen in Harlem," *The New York Times*, February 8, 1959; "Pact is Reached on Harlem Schools," *The New York Times*, February 11, 1959; and "A Joint Statement" by John Theobald and Paul Zuber, February 10, 1959. B/E Collection, IV/A/3, B.22, F.3.
Some of the parents had tried unsuccessfully to enroll their children in Inwood Junior High School, an integrated school in Washington Heights. "Boycott Parents to Sue on Schools," *New York Amsterdam News*, January 10, 1958.

63. Theobald and Zuber, "A Joint Statement"; James L. Hicks (columnist), "Wasting Time," and editorial, "Why Not Act," *New York Amsterdam News*, January 3, 1959; "Dr. Taylor Raps N.Y. School Board," *New York Amsterdam News*, January 10, 1959; and Board of Education, "Statement Released at Press Conference," January 13, 1959. B/E Collection, IV/A/3, B.22, F.3; and "City Plans Appeal in School Boycott," *The New York Times*, January 14, 1959.

64. "Pact is Reached on Harlem Schools," *The New York Times*, February 11, 1959; "Negro Parents Act To Sue City Schools," *The New York Times*, January 6, 1959; and "Boycott Parents to Sue on Schools," *New York Amsterdam News*, January 10, 1959.

65. Polier, *Juvenile Justice in Double Jeopardy*, 152.

66. "School Board Appeal Enrages Baptists," *New York Amsterdam News*, January 24, 1959. The Empire State Baptist Convention included all of the Baptists in New York State who attended some 340 churches. The Baptists represented the largest denomination of African American Protestants. See Clarence Taylor, *The Black Churches of Brooklyn* (New York: Columbia University Press, 1994), 236–238.

67. The next year, Reverend Taylor, one of Martin Luther King's closest friends, was part of an insurgent group that included King and that tried unsuccessfully to get Taylor elected to the presidency of the National Baptist Convention (NBC). Their goal was to bring the NBC into the forefront of the civil rights

movement. See Taylor Branch, *Parting the Waters,* 227, 335–336. See also Shirlee Taylor Haizlip, *The Sweeter the Juice: A Family Memoir in Black and White* (New York: Simon and Schuster, 1995), 197–198.

68. "School Board Appeal Enrages Baptists," *New York Amsterdam News,* January 24, 1959.

69. Letter to Teachers Union from Milton Yale, Executive Secretary, HNA, March 4, 1959. TU Collection, 5015, 45–11. Until the late 1950s, the HNA was called the Central Harlem Council for Community Planning. It was founded in 1934 and was under the umbrella of the Welfare Council of New York City.

70. "Dickens, Watson Will Ask State Probe of School Integration," *New York Amsterdam News,* January 24, 1959; "2 Bid State Study City School 'Bias,'" *The New York Times,* January 28, 1959.

71. "2 Bid State Study City School 'Bias,'" *The New York Times,* January 28, 1959

72. "City Plans Appeal in School Boycott," *The New York Times,* January 14, 1959.

73. Front page photo, *New York Amsterdam News,* September 14, 1957. "Don't Forget, N.Y. Has Its Own School Problem," *New York Amsterdam News,* September 28, 1957.

74. Cartoon, "Knot-Hole Gang," *New York Amsterdam News,* January 3, 1959.

75. "The Message," *New York Amsterdam News,* July 27, 1957. See Vicki Crawford, Jacqueline Anne Rouse, and Barbara Woods, *Women in the Civil Rights Movement: Trailblazers & Torchbearers, 1941–1965* (Bloomington: Indiana University Press, 1990) for the best compilation to date on civil rights women activists.

76. "A Woman's World," *New York Amsterdam News,* May 5, 1956. As I note in "Blacks, Jews and the Struggle to Integrate Brooklyn's Junior High School 258," (63, n. 42), initially there was no coverage of local school integration struggles in the *Amsterdam News.*

77. Jacqueline Jones, *Labor of Love, Labor of Sorrow: Black Women, Work, and the Family from Slavery to the Present* (New York: Basic Books, 1985), 268–274. Joanne Meyerowitz's study of women's magazines in the postwar decade concurs with Jones's analysis and offers a general corrective to Betty Friedan's monolithic characterization of America's postwar housebound women. See Meyerowitz, "Beyond the Feminine Mystique: A Reassessment of Postwar Mass Culture, 1946–1958" in Meyerowitz, *Not June Cleaver,* 229–262.

78. Ruth Feldstein makes a powerful argument for looking at motherhood as a battleground on which the meaning of respectability and rights was fought in the race wars of the civil rights movement. Ruth Feldstein, "'I Wanted the Whole World to See': Race, Gender, and Constructions of Motherhood in the Death of Emmett Till," in Meyerowitz, *Not June Cleaver,* 263–303.

79. Many scholars have written about the emergence of a postwar theory of black family pathology. In addition to works cited in note 14, other works that focus especially on the gendered aspects of these theories and their impact on black women include Paula Giddings, *When and Where I Enter: The Impact of Black Women on Race and Sex in America* (New York: Bantam Books, 1984), chapter 14; Patricia Morton, *Disfigured Images: The Historical Assault on Afro-American*

Women (New York: Greenwood Press, 1991), chapter 6; and Rickie Solinger, *Wake Up Little Susie: Single Pregnancy and Race Before Roe v. Wade* (New York: Routledge, 1992), chapter 2.

80. *New York Amsterdam News,* December 13, 1958; "Wasting Time," January 3, 1959.

81. "Brooklyn Parents Seeking Showdown," September 13, 1958.

82. "City Hall Date," *New York Amsterdam News,* September 9, 1957.

83. Ibid.

84. Jones, *Labor of Love, Labor of Sorrow,* 260–269.

85. "We're Sick Too," *New York Amsterdam News,* November 22, 1958.

86. Hicks explicitly asserted this in one editorial in which he described himself as a man who "believes in the superiority of the male," *New York Amsterdam News,* May 5, 1956.

87. "City Hall Date," *New York Amsterdam News,* September 9, 1957.

88. Belinda Robnett probes the meanings and forms of black women's leadership in the Southern civil rights movement in which leaders like Ella Baker and Septima Clark described being excluded from the formal network of male religious leaders. *How Long? How Long?: African American Women in the Struggle for Civil Rights* (New York: Oxford University Press, 1997). Fannie Lou Hamer's biographer, Chana Kai Lee, describes the ways in which Hamer was discriminated against by NAACP male leadership, who considered her an inappropriate leader as a poor, uneducated woman. According to Lee, Hamer had a sharp analysis of class divisions and hierarchy within the civil rights movement. *For Freedom's Sake: The Life of Fannie Lou Hamer* (Urbana: University of Illinois Press, 1999). For other discussions of women's roles, see Vicki L. Crawford, Jacqueline Anne Rouse, and Barbara Woods, eds., *Women in the Civil Rights Movement: Trailblazers & Torchbearers, 1941–1965* (Bloomington: Indiana University Press, 1993).

89. Author interview with Mrs. Mae Mallory, Brooklyn, N.Y., January 30, 2000.

90. Jo Ann Gibson Robinson, *The Montgomery Bus Boycott and the Women Who Started It: The Memoir of Jo Ann Gibson Robinson* (Knoxville: The University of Tennessee Press, 1987), 172.

Chapter 4

"Negro Leadership and Negro Money": African American Political Organizing in Oakland before the Panthers

Robert O. Self

The historiography and much of the social science theorizing about the post-WWII black freedom struggle draw on the Southern experience. Indeed, the Southern civil rights movement has been rendered so normative as *the* paradigmatic postwar freedom struggle in the United States that historical surveys like the American Social History Project's *Who Built America?* make little mention of the North and West, outside of a brief discussion of Black Power, and offer no framework in which to understand the Northern and Pacific Coast dimensions of African American politics and social movements. The collection of readings edited by Jonathan Birnbaum and Clarence Taylor, *Civil Rights Since 1787: A Reader on the Black Struggle,* includes a section entitled "The North Has Problems Too," an opaque reference to the North's status as a secondary site of struggle. Attention to the South is richly deserved, but an over-reliance on the Southern story has shaped national understandings of black politics and given them a spurious twist: As triumphant civil rights supposedly "moved North" after 1965, the movement foundered on the shores of urban rebellions and black nationalism, and whites withdrew critical support in ever larger numbers. North and South have come to represent the binary histories that we tell about black liberation politics in the second half of the twentieth century. The South is "the movement." The North is the foil.

The South is nonviolent. The North is violent. The South is normative; the North, an aberration.[1]

This is changing, as a generation of scholars, including many contributors to this volume, rewrites the history of postwar African American social movements and politics in the North and West. Emerging from this recent work is a richer, deeper, and necessarily more complicated story in which historians see Northern and Pacific Coast cities not as places where civil rights organizing stalled or failed but as places where the postwar black freedom movement took unique forms and trajectories, where African American politics overlapped with the racialized logic of urban industrial and postindustrial capitalism, and where a dynamic black political culture nurtured multiple strategies and ideologies of resistance, accommodation, and liberation. These places deserve to be understood as more than derivative of, or the denouement to, the central and putatively normative Southern movement. Collapsing African American politics into such a narrative flattens twentieth-century U.S. history and shoehorns one of the world's most complicated indictments of mid-century Western modernity into the banal demand for a lunch counter seat. This is not to suggest that Northern and Western African American history should be disconnected from Southern history—far from it. Such a gesture would do little justice to the three million black migrants who came to the cities of the North and West from the South between 1940 and 1965 and remade the nation's neighborhoods, electorate, and laws. Rather, it is to argue that we must connect the building of African American political capacity and social organizing to the longer sweep of Northern and Western urban history, urban political culture, and political economy. And in doing so, we must rethink paradigms of the field beyond the triumphalist Southern story and the declensional Northern one.[2]

Oakland, California, provides an excellent vantage from which to launch such an effort. Best known as the birthplace of the Black Panther Party in 1966 and as a national fulcrum of black radicalism throughout the late 1960s, Oakland is less remembered as a major seat of African American influence in California politics beginning in the late 1940s and as the home of an extensive tradition of black social advocacy and organizing in the 1950s. The generation of black activists before the Panthers developed strategies, alliances, and sources of power that profoundly shaped the political terrain of race in both the East Bay and California as a whole. Recovering the story of that generation, men and women who achieved none of the national media exposure and fame of the Panthers and faced little of the state-sponsored harassment and investigations allow us to appreciate both the surprising continuities as well as the jarring divergences between the activists of the 1940s and 1950s and those of the

1960s and 1970s. Understanding these antecedents, as well as broader patterns of African American political organizing in Oakland and California in the decades before 1966, brings into focus a neglected chapter in the black freedom struggle and helps to confirm a trajectory of African American struggle that depends neither on the traditional markers of the Southern movement nor on the conflation of violence, protest, and nationalism that hampers thorough understandings of Black Power. The postwar black freedom movement in the East Bay featured a fluid political environment in which philosophies and strategies competed with one another, interpenetrated, and overlapped. Above all, in the decades after WWII, civil rights in Oakland stood less for *civil* rights than for economic rights, the foundation on which American liberalism had rested since the 1930s.

Before turning our attention to Oakland, a caveat is in order. California's postwar racial landscape stands out as more complicated than that in many Northern states because of the legacy of anti-Asian movements, ongoing Filipino immigration, wartime imprisonment of Japanese and Japanese Americans, and the state's relationship with ethnic Mexicans and the borderland region. It is not my intention to overlook the very real complexities of racial and national community formation beyond the traditional black-white paradigm or to insist that African American politics in the state occurred in some sort of vacuum in which *white* and *black* were entirely unproblematic, finite, and knowable terms. Much of the best work on California is now taking on the challenge of understanding racial formation and postwar issues of liberation precisely in terms of the complicated geography of color and race within the state. The triangular patterns of racial formation and contention among whites/Anglos, African Americans, and ethnic Mexicans in postwar California, in particular, deserve greater attention and research. Nonetheless, for the purposes of this essay I have bracketed those concerns in order to address more specifically patterns of African American politics.[3]

African American Oakland at Mid-Century

The center of African American social life and politics in San Francisco's East Bay was West Oakland. A compact neighborhood of tree-lined streets, Victorian "two-flats," apartments, workers' cottages, single-occupancy hotels, and scattered bungalows, West Oakland lay nestled between the downtown business district and the warehouses, rail yards, and factories of Oakland's port and industrial flatlands. Prior to WWII, West Oakland offered inexpensive housing mainly to three groups of workers: working-class European-American refugees from San Francisco's 1906 earthquake and fire, immigrants from Southern and Eastern Europe, and African American workers employed by the Southern Pacific Railroad, the Pullman Company, and Oakland's numerous other freight yards and warehouses. In the 1930s, 60 percent of African American income in Oakland came from the railroads. "At one time around here, it's all they had was cooks and waiters, Red Caps and things," West Oakland resident Royal Towns recalled. But paychecks were only part of the story. West Oakland stood at the axis of the West Coast's black railroad working-class culture, nurtured and sustained by employees of the Pullman Company and the Southern Pacific. African American railroad workers nourished a variety of institutions with their time and money, including the Brotherhood of Sleeping Car Porters (BSCP), the city's two oldest African American churches, the Alameda County NAACP, fraternal and civic associations, women's clubs and auxiliaries, DeFremery Recreation Center (an important focal point of community organization, youth entertainment, and athletics), and substantial black commercial and professional districts. The Brotherhood's West Coast headquarters was located in West Oakland, where C. L. Dellums, a close working partner of A. Philip Randolph and one of California's most important black leaders, lived and worked.[4]

The Brotherhood fostered a rich organizational and social tradition that extended beyond pure trade unionism and linked West Oakland to other black communities nationwide. Pullman porters returning to Oakland after sometimes weeks of absence brought with them black newspapers from Chicago, Los Angeles, New York, and occasionally even Atlanta, New Orleans, and Birmingham. Paul Cobb, who became an influential grassroots organizer in West Oakland in the 1960s, remembers Pullman Porters bringing newspapers, especially the *Chicago Defender,* into his grandfather's grocery store near the Southern Pacific tracks. As a young man, he marveled at the stories from faraway black communities, narratives of black life and politics, and black-white relations that became the foundation of his early political education. His father, Roosevelt, was a longshoreman in Harry Bridges' International Longshoremen's and Warehousemen's Union (ILWU) and a local community activist. In places like Cobb's corner store, Brotherhood members joined black ILWU, Marine Cooks and Stewards Union (MCSU), and Dining Car Cooks and Waiters Union members in a cosmopolitan laborite culture that blended politics, trade unionism, and human rights. Dellums and other "railroad men," along with dock and maritime workers, were among the most visible public figures in Oakland's dynamic prewar African American neighborhoods.[5]

African Americans in West Oakland developed a unique geographic relationship to work. In ways largely untrue of the vast industrial cities of Chicago and Detroit, black workers in mid-century Oakland did not have to travel long distances through hostile white neighborhoods to reach jobs crucial to the community. The docks, the tracks, and West Oakland's small factories lay within easy walking distance or a short streetcar ride of the majority of African American homes. Of greater importance for the laboring elite of West Oakland's African American working class—the sleeping car porters, dining car waiters, and merchant marine cooks—work took them out of West Oakland and even outside California (an opposite trajectory applied to longshoremen, who came into contact in Oakland with ship workers from around the world). Despite the vicious racism that confined black workers to the worst and most menial jobs, the experience of labor for this small but important working-class elite was a cosmopolitan one. They came into contact with the larger world and in many ways brought that world back to Oakland in the form of the newspapers, described by Cobb, as well as informal reportage and storytelling by returning train and ship workers. This dual experience, of immediate spatial confinement in West Oakland and of expansive connections to and exchanges with a much larger world, became the foundation of black Oakland's working-class culture.[6]

Racism was an everyday reality in the local labor movement, but a handful of unions in the East Bay exerted positive influences on black employment and culture. Two progressive, Congress of Industrial Organization (CIO)-affiliated unions joined the BSCP and Dining Car, Cooks, and Waiters union (both American Federation of Labor[AFL]) in the 1940s as strongholds of African American trade union membership in Oakland and San Francisco: the ILWU and the MCSU. Between 1934 and 1937, the era of the brutal Pacific Coast dock wars, these unions forged an intense solidarity, and Harry Bridges and white radicals of both Communist and syndicalist persuasion, along with black union leaders, turned this solidarity into a force for racial equality. African American workers made up one-fourth and one-third of the membership of the ILWU and MCSU, respectively, by the early fifties, and an important black leadership cadre developed within each union. Neither union earned a perfect record regarding racial matters—job upgrading in the late 1940s and 1950s, in particular, seemed to favor white workers—but the importance of the Bay Area locals of the ILWU and MCSU to shop-floor racial equality and civil rights has been well established. More open to radicalism than the anti-communist Brotherhood, they nonetheless joined the BSCP at the center of the Bay Area's African American trade union culture and remained an influential force in all of the region's mid-century black communities.[7]

WWII transformed few places in the East Bay as dramatically as West Oakland. Tens of thousands of African American migrants from the Southern states, recruited by major defense contractors and the federal government, settled in the flatlands of West Oakland. Housing discrimination in white neighborhoods in Oakland and in the nearby cities of Albany, El Cerrito, Alameda, and San Leandro crowded these black migrants into established African American districts. In subdivided flats, apartments, and hotels overbooked and bursting, these newly arrived workers made the best of cramped conditions. As the war progressed and increasing numbers of black migrants arrived, West Oakland's European descendants took advantage of white-only wartime public housing or the equally restricted working-class housing projects built by private developers in satellite suburban communities. Still, West Oakland boomed. By the middle years of the war, African American West Oakland was thriving on the income of its thousands of new black residents, who found work in the region's famous shipyards and other war-related factories. West Oakland's established prewar working and professional classes benefited as well. Seventh Street's commercial district flourished with black-owned businesses and professional offices, Slim Jenkins's jazz club on Seventh and Wood streets headlined a famous (now legendary) nightclub scene; women's clubs, churches, and fraternal lodges thrived; and the district developed a special sense of transplanted community as Southern migrants from the same towns and even neighborhoods in the "near South" states of Texas, Arkansas, Oklahoma, and Louisiana settled close to one another. A new African American community took shape in West Oakland during the war years, planted suddenly and somewhat precariously among the deeper roots of Oakland's prewar black railroad culture.[8]

In urban African American communities nationwide, from Chicago's South Side to Detroit's Paradise Valley, North Philadelphia to West Oakland, a great deal was at stake in the 1940s. The war brought racial liberalism from the margins of political discourse to the center of the nation's wartime anti-fascism. Racial liberalism held that American democracy was incomplete so long as Jim Crow laws separated the races in the South and a combination of legal restrictions and common practice kept black people from jobs and neighborhoods in the North. Racial liberals at mid-century—led by whites and blacks in the NAACP, the Congress of Racial Equality (CORE), and the Popular Front—believed that new laws (prohibiting lynching and police brutality and guaranteeing equal employment and housing opportunity), along with appeals to the hearts and minds of whites, would ultimately ensure African Americans' full integration into American life. Their model was European immigrants, whose acceptance into mainstream culture was widely celebrated in the 1940s. If African Americans could translate the national rhetorical commitment to racial equality fostered by the war against fascism into real gains in employment, housing, and urban quality of life, the unfulfilled promises of Reconstruction in the agricultural South might be realized in the postwar industrial North. In the "Double V for Victory" campaign, black communities across the nation called for victory over racism in Europe and victory over racism at home. The *Chicago Defender* declared that "the Negro is damned tired of spilling his blood for empty promises of better days." America must "bomb the color line," the paper demanded during the war.[9]

How sincere the nation, its white citizens, and institutions were in this newfound racial liberalism remained an open and heated question in African American households throughout the country. But the issue at stake in those households was not simply or only the defeat of Jim Crow. Mid-century black communities embraced multiple political crosscurrents, from ideologies of racial uplift and integrationism to Garveyite nationalism and black capitalism to workplace-based black power (as in the BSCP) and, especially in the East Bay, radical laborite socialism and communism. These crosscurrents produced a lively and productive debate over the future of African American neighborhoods and the cities in which they were situated. This rich political tradition belies a facile integration/separation or civil rights/Black Power dichotomy in black politics, which are inadequate frameworks for understanding the range of African American responses to the changing face of urban life either before or after 1945.[10]

Few African American women encountered unions in their places of employment, but women shaped Oakland's postwar African American working-class community in other critical ways. Migrant women transplanted Southern folk and family traditions to their Oakland neighborhoods. They constructed informal bonds across the community, reciprocal relationships of exchange and mutual dependence that provided newly arrived families with essential goods and services: from childcare and weddings to health care, jobs, food, and shelter. This kind of face-to-face social networking, an essential feature of rural Southern African American tradition, gave West Oakland's bustling streets and neighborhoods a sense of safety and familiarity while quietly holding families and homes together. Moreover, women's social networking often translated into politics. In churches, the NAACP, the East Bay Parent-Teacher Associations, the East Bay Democratic Club, and numerous other community, civil rights, and political organizations and institutions, migrant women, as well as their more established counterparts, brought a hard-working, aggressive advocacy to East Bay political culture. In the early 1960s, African American women led fights against redevelopment in West Oakland. Black women's labor, too, sustained the community. In an era when few black men outside of the laboring elite were permitted to hold positions that paid a family wage, women performed an untold range of jobs: in the service sector, as domestics, in factory work, and in informal labor, such as laundering, babysitting, taking in and cooking for boarders, in addition to raising children and providing for a home. African American women added important elements of both formal and informal work and politics to the more male-centered trade union culture in Oakland's growing black community.[11]

California's version of segregation meant that African American workers in nearly every sector of the local economy faced job ceilings. Census figures suggest that WWII offered African American migrants only a tenuous foothold in the local job market, with most finding postwar work in semi-skilled and unskilled jobs and in the service sector. The thousands of African American men and women recruited to work in the wartime shipyards found the conversion to civilian production especially difficult. Sixty percent of African American men in 1950 found work as blue-collar laborers, machine operatives, or in back-of-the-house service work. African American women found that their wartime employment in the shipyards did not easily translate into postwar opportunities beyond the familiar household service. Half of all black women workers labored in 1950 as private domestics or in other kinds of service work. Groups like the NAACP and the Urban League continued to fight discrimination in employment in the late 1940s and early 1950s, but progress was often slow and incremental. African American workers, especially men, made substantial inroads in one area of employment, federal government and civil service jobs, that would remain a foundation of black opportunity in the postwar decades. The Oakland Army Base, the U.S. Naval Supply Station, and the Naval Air Station at Alameda took on large numbers of black workers during the war and kept them. While not entirely free of discrimination in job assignments and pay, these military installations, all three located in or near West Oakland, acted as something of a community bulwark against the more pervasive bias in the private sector and the large-scale postwar layoffs in shipbuilding.[12]

Workplace segregation provided the most obvious example of regional Jim Crow practices, but a more general, widely observed, social separation of the races defined a variety of settings. Signs announcing "We Refuse Service to Negroes" sat in the windows of many hotels, bars, and restaurants, particularly in the areas of downtown closest to West Oakland and in cities like Albany and San Leandro, which remained closed to African Americans. Oakland's educational system, relatively integrated prior to the war, emerged in the late 1940s on a steep path toward almost complete segregation. Parts of the East Bay escaped these hardening racial lines, especially areas in Berkeley and North Oakland, where churches, schools, and civic organizations continued to bring some black and white residents together; but this was confined largely to the established middle and professional classes. Recent working-class migrants, black and white, tended to live in monoracial worlds. Despite the reality of racial separation, many in Oakland's white community perceived black migrants as intruding on what one local observer called "the old and peaceful understanding between the Negro and the white in Oakland." The dramatic wartime expansion of West Oakland's African American community disrupted the mind-set of many people in Oakland's established white working- and middle-class districts and set the stage for a series of conflicts in the late 1940s and 1950s over jobs, neighborhoods, and public space.[13]

"Keep Mississippi Out of California": Postwar Liberalism in the Golden State

Between the end of WWII and the 1960s, African Americans worked to extend racial liberalism into the industrial and residential communities that Californians produced in the postwar years. The attempt raised crucial questions. Could the class-based New Deal liberalism of the 1930s be expanded to encompass more systematic racial equality, especially economic equality, and could social justice be realized through trade unionism? What, indeed, were the appropriate vehicles for changing racial politics in the mid-century United States? Each of these questions was contested nationwide in the 1940s: from the March on Washington Movement and the 1944 Declaration of Negro Voters to the conservative 1946 Congress, from hundreds of local Fair Employment Practices Commission (FEPC) battles and white hate strikes during the war to the widespread postwar strike wave and A. Philip Randolph's proposed African American boycott of the U.S. military, and ultimately to local politics in cities like Philadelphia, Baltimore, Detroit, Los Angeles, and Oakland. The attempt to answer these questions in California led black leaders and the state's burgeoning black electorate to form a political alliance with organized labor in the 1940s, which by the late fifties had elected a liberal governor, Edmund G. "Pat" Brown, and Democratic state assembly majorities. This coalition made California a national testing ground for extensions of the welfare state through *state* rather than federal initiative—for example, the creation of the nation's most extensive and accessible system of public higher education, equal employment and housing laws, and the establishment of generous workers' health, unemployment, and safety programs. African Americans benefited unevenly from such programs, and labor proved to be a fickle ally in local politics and on the shop floor. But the combination of African American migrants, who poured into the state by the tens of thousands between 1942 and the 1960s, and organized labor solidified a liberal-left electoral bloc that placed California ahead of the national curve in its embrace of postwar New Deal-style liberalism.[14]

That liberalism promised a broad social wage for the American working class—including old age pensions, a welfare safety net, and the right to organize trade unions—and, in its most progressive version, a more democratic distribution of social resources for African Americans. As he looked back over the first two postwar decades in 1965, Oakland NAACP Chairman Clinton White explained California's liberal dream in human terms. "These fine young men, Negro men, Spanish-speaking young men. Think of them," he asked an African American and ethnic Mexican audience in West Oakland's McClymonds High School. As parents, he continued, "you looked forward to the day that here in the United States, and even more so in the state of California, you looked forward to the day" when your son "could say that he was a union member, and that he could make between four and five and six hundred dollars a month." Those same workers, White explained, could "take what their earnings are ... save them up ... go down and get a loan, because the federal government would back it up ... buy a home and raise other children." Both union membership and home ownership enjoyed government protections. In the end, with a reliable, well-paying job and a decent home, the "Negro and Spanish speaking young men" could "walk the earth with dignity." Here was postwar liberalism refined to its essence. When White asked his audience to recall their dreams for their children, it was no abstract set of rights he implored them to conjure, but the concrete ambitions of a generation raised on the cautious but sustained faith that government protections, union wages, and a strong economy could be leveraged with the right pressure into upward mobility and a more secure future for succeeding generations of African Americans. In mid-century California the state government appeared the strongest and most likely ally in the securing of that future.[15]

The background of black participation in California's postwar liberal moment and the sources and strategies of African American organizing date back to the 1930s, when black voters nationwide began leaving the Republican Party en masse for the Roosevelt-led Democrats. In Oakland

and San Francisco, the key years were the 1940s, when wartime migration gave the Bay Area's black population political clout for the first time. There, black radicals and liberals alike mobilized behind Roosevelt's wartime FEPC, forged ties with solidly Democratic constituencies in Northern California—organized labor, progressive churches, and liberal white professionals—and began to campaign for fair employment and housing ordinances at the city level in Berkeley, Oakland, and San Francisco. By the late 1940s, Bay Area African Americans helped to anchor California's liberal political coalition. Organizationally, a constellation of groups held the alliance in place behind a common vision: dramatically improved working-class opportunity achieved through legal reform, especially fair housing and employment laws, and strong labor laws. These groups included the NAACP, CORE, the California Federation of Labor (AFL), the CIO, Jewish Labor Committee, the California Ministerial Alliance, Democratic Clubs of California, and a variety of other religious organizations. Only the voices of black and white radicals, who had been purged from liberal-labor coalitions in the wake of McCarthyism, were missing from the coalition.[16]

For African Americans, the alliance represented more than a mere electoral partnership. Two objectives underlay black coalition politics: forcing Jim Crow hiring practices out of private industry and opening the housing market to black buyers, both in older cities like San Francisco, Oakland, and Los Angeles and in the emerging suburban periphery. California had, as did the nation, dual labor and housing markets throughout the first half of the century. The racial and national complexity of the West—where Americans and immigrants of Mexican, Chinese, Japanese, and Filipino background lived and worked alongside European immigrants and native-born Euro-Americans—made California's color line variegated. This was little consolation to black migrants, however, who found that segregation in the Golden State rivaled that anywhere in the country. "There's very little difference between the segregation here in California and the blatant things that go on in the South," Oakland fireman Arthur Patterson told an interviewer. Robert Edwards, a dining car waiter working out of Oakland in the forties and fifties recalled the work environment being "highly Jim Crowed. They just did not believe in promoting blacks to any positions of authority. [And] they had special places for the black passengers to eat. They were always served behind the curtain."[17]

African American activists in Southern and Northern California had been pressing for legal guarantees of job and housing equality since the 1930s. The wartime FEPC, along with Popular Front politics, gave crucial momentum to these efforts in the forties. But postwar red scares and the subsequent fracturing of the left cut them prematurely short. A decade of intensive lobbying, coalition-building, and community mobilization followed; and in the decisive year of 1958, African American voters joined organized labor to defeat an anti-union right-to-work statewide ballot initiative, elect Pat Brown, and give 60 percent of all statewide offices to Democrats. On the strength of this tide the state had both fair employment and fair housing laws by 1963. "Labor and NAACP branches supplied over ninety percent of the money" for fair employment lobbying, Dellums recalled of the crucial generational alliance between the New Deal labor movement and black activists.[18]

These statewide victories were made possible by political strategies at the grassroots, and here we may turn to Oakland for an illustration. Democratic Party strength in California was rebuilt in the 1950s after the red scares by what James Q. Wilson called "amateurs" who created a network of Democratic clubs throughout the state. In Oakland and Berkeley, African Americans stood in the forefront in this process. D. G. Gibson, a political strategist, former railroad dining car waiter, and business entrepreneur, established the East Bay Democratic Club in the late 1940s. Two groups joined Gibson in the formation of the club, one of the most important African American organizations anywhere in the West: black leaders from the city's railroad and dockside working class and a self-conscious group of black professionals, including lawyers, social workers, ministers, and civil servants. Dellums, who built and then led the West Coast BSCP, and Evalio Grillo, a Cuban-born social worker, proved especially important. The East Bay Democratic Club forged alliances with progressive CIO and AFL labor and liberal professionals in Oakland and Berkeley to elect Byron Rumford, an African American pharmacist, to the state assembly in 1948. Rumford went on to sponsor and win passage of both the Fair Employment (1959) and Fair Housing (1963) laws and served in the assembly for nearly two decades. Dellums emerged as one of the state's most visible and indefatigable advocates of equal employment, serving on the state's inaugural Fair Employment Practices Commission after years of advocacy and coalition-building, in addition to his duties with the Brotherhood. Under the guidance of D. G. Gibson, the East Bay Democratic Club dominated a political territory in which state assembly district boundaries in Berkeley and Oakland neatly tracked the remarkable growth of the East Bay's African American population in the working-class flatlands adjacent to the bay. In the closest thing to a ward possible under California election laws, the seventeenth assembly district in the Oakland-Berkeley flatlands, under the leadership of the East Bay Democratic Club, became a crucial and enduring lever of East Bay African American power.[19]

Gibson's handling of the 1948 campaign demonstrated the kind of political acumen that he would bring to East Bay black politics. Faced with a possibly debilitating glut of candidates in the Democratic primary for state assembly, including multiple choices on the liberal left, Gibson held a series of meetings with both black and white brokers. Among whites, labor remained the key ally. But AFL leaders did not want an African American candidate in 1948 and had "centered its efforts at the time on a Caucasian," according to Rumford's memoirs. Meeting with CIO officials, whom he believed would be more open to a black candidate, Gibson pressed for either Rumford or Tom Berkeley, an attorney, former track star, and fellow traveler. The bourgeois Rumford was less attractive to radicals within the CIO; however, Gibson convinced enough CIO regulars that *any* black candidate would constitute a radical step so when Berkeley declined to run, Rumford emerged as the favorite. Among African Americans, Gibson worked through ministers and Dellums's "railroad men" to form a Black Caucus, which selected a single black candidate, Rumford, in order not to divide the black vote. With Dellums working African American unions for campaign funds and volunteers, Gibson focused on unifying the black vote and bringing enough white labor and liberal professionals in North Oakland and South Berkeley into the coalition to secure Rumford's victory by an astonishing 35,000 votes. According to Rumford and other contemporary observers, without Gibson's behind-the-scenes organizing, there would have been little chance to elect an African American from the Seventeenth Assembly District in 1948. "D. G. Gibson may very well be the father of all of us who are now active in the black political arena," former Assembly leader and San Francisco Mayor Willie Brown said.[20]

We have seen how West Oakland's working-class African American politics developed out of the neighborhood's railroad and dockside employment. Within the city's black middle class, a second major political project, one whose influence would extend far into the 1970s, also evolved in the postwar years. Shortly after Gibson founded the East Bay Democratic Club, a group of African American attorneys, educators, ministers, and social work professionals established the Men of Tomorrow, an organization dedicated to community service. Their explicit mission was to "serve society through fellowship," but members worked diligently in other areas as well, especially in courting the business and civic connections necessary to win political office, open professional positions in the East Bay to blacks, and garner African American appointments to local judgeships and the district attorney's office. Dominated by Southern men who had migrated to Oakland from Arkansas and Louisiana before and during the war, the Men of Tomorrow outwardly embodied the racial liberalism and racial uplift of the period—the notion that middle-class African Americans were responsible for raising the cultural level and political consciousness of the working class. Though later critics charged that the organization was too accommodating to whites and too concerned with the public image of black professionals, the Men of Tomorrow produced African American city councilmen in both Berkeley and Oakland, as well as judges, school board members, two mayors, and numerous city officials who adhered to a wide variety of political positions in the left-leaning Bay Area political culture. Middle-class leaders helped to make the Men of Tomorrow the community face of the East Bay Democratic Club.[21]

The East Bay Democratic Club advanced a racial project that straddled African American political traditions. Rumford was a thoroughly bourgeois figure whose racial liberalism inclined him to believe in middle-class integration, racial uplift, and a race-blind society achieved through legislation. For both Gibson and Dellums, on the other hand, liberalism was linked to the labor movement, working-class advancement, and a distinct proto-nationalism. Dellums, the Randolph laborite, and Gibson, the former dining car waiter and economic and political entrepreneur, shared some of the assumptions of 1940s racial liberalism, but they emerged and drew their authority from all-black organizations that rejected the paternalism of racial uplift. Both emphasized self-help and the power of an organized working class advancing its own and its *race's* broader interests. The Brotherhood and other African American railroad unions were mid-century America's black power institutions—built "with Negro leadership and Negro money," as Dellums put it—places where creative leaders and shop-floor solidarity transformed discrimination and the concentration of black workers into confined economic and political leverage. "Negroes will have to pay for their own organization," Dellums declared, "their own fights, by their own funds as well as their own energy." Determined to build an influential black institution, Dellums also believed that "the Negro will never come into his own until he is a complete, total part of the mainstream of American life." In his life and politics, Dellums consistently held black power in one hand and integration in the other.[22]

Attempts to mix integrationist ideals with black-only organizations were not unique to Oakland in this period. The black church was the most visible and influential institution that nurtured both integrationist aims and intraracial solidarity, combining the spirit of full participation in the dominant white society with the ethos of African American separateness, power, mission, and nationalism. African American urban politics in cities like New York and Chicago had, since the 1930s, functioned as some combination of intraracial power and extraracial alliances with and appeals to whites. There is no need to romanticize figures like Adam Clayton Powell and William Levi Dawson in order to see that they operated in multiple racial worlds with overlapping strategies vis-à-vis whites. To many black activists in the 1940s and 1950s, there was little contradiction in such multiple strategies. Or, if there was a contradiction, it lay, as Dellums insisted, in mainstream white American society and not in African American politics. Segregation had enforced black separatism. Political action thus required the instrumental use of separate institutions to leverage power. At the same time, ideologies of racial liberalism encouraged the belief that American society was not *irredeemably* racist and thus could potentially welcome African Americans on African American terms. In ways common to black politics across the North and West, African Americans in Oakland fought against Jim Crow even as they built separate lives and institutions within its boundaries.[23]

Dellums's and Gibson's alliances with whites were not based on pleas to liberals or on anything resembling the "beloved community" invoked by sixties civil rights figures. Their influence came from horse-trading votes, the mechanics of power. "D.G. organized the black vote for the first time so that the black vote meant something," former Oakland NAACP chairman William Patterson remembered. "They got people to buy in and subscribe to it. If we give you our vote on this, then you got to help us do that." Neither Dellums nor Gibson would have conceived of their politics within the nationalist framework articulated by subsequent Black Power figures like Malcolm X, Stokely Carmichael, Eldridge Cleaver, and Huey Newton. But their fusion of integration, strategic alliances with whites, and the nurturing of all-black institutions and economic networks again points to the inadequacy of an integration/separation model for understanding black politics. The conjunction of racial liberalism and a laborite version of black power and proto-nationalism, though occasionally at odds, sustained the East Bay Democratic club for decades and established a model of African American politics that would influence nationalists and radicals in Oakland a generation later.[24]

The East Bay Democratic Club's strategies and successes also depended on a political geography that presented both opportunities and obstacles as black activists searched for leverage at different scales of electoral power. The boundaries of African American residence in the East Bay encompassed assembly and congressional districts in Berkeley and Oakland but a relatively small percentage of the total land area of Oakland. As a result, Gibson's East Bay Democratic Club had far more success in the 1950s and 1960s running candidates for state and federal offices than electing city council members in Oakland. Progressive-era reforms mandating citywide balloting for city council positions prevented any single district from controlling an elected seat. No Democratic machine capable of incorporating, or co-opting, black votes existed in Oakland. And in any case, the legal leverage that racial liberals sought to destroy Jim Crow existed in the state assembly and federal Congress, not local government. The spatial logic of American political institutions—the scale at which various powers are held and administered—compelled black leaders in Oakland to look beyond the local political landscape. Such questions of scale were as important to Northern black politics as they were, in the question of "state's rights," in the South. The East Bay Democratic Club's electoral strategies thus reflected both a debilitating fact of local politics *and* a deliberate strategic shift in the scale of political engagement. Rumford's election and Gibson's rise represented important new possibilities for the legislation of racial equality at the state level.[25]

The possibilities reached symbolic fruition in the election year of 1958, when the state NAACP mobilized black voters with the slogan "Keep Mississippi Out of California." That year, the political agenda of the California right included passing an anti-labor, right-to-work ballot measure and defeating fair employment legislation in the state assembly. African American activists fought back. The California NAACP encouraged black voters to "fight sharecropper wages" and warned them that "the enemies of decent FEPC laws are the sponsors of 'right-to-work' laws." On the cover of an NAACP pamphlet that year, an employer clad in suit and tie whipped a kneeling "California Worker" with a "Right-to-Work" lash. A Nazi insignia and the states "Tennessee," "Arkansas," "Texas," "Alabama," "Georgia," and others from the South leapt from the whip. Encouraging their members to "expose the fake 'right-to-work' plot of the enemies of FEPC," the NAACP pamphlet called on the state's African American voters to reject Proposition 18, the offending measure. Franklin Williams, Regional Secretary of the NAACP, warned voters that "California minorities will suffer a severe blow if a destructive 'right-to-work' law were enacted to handcuff and straightjacket organized labor." The 1958 campaign cemented the electoral partnership between African Americans and labor, as black and white workers joined to send Proposition 18 down to defeat and sweep Democrats statewide into office.[26]

C. L. Dellums and Byron Rumford believed that with the electoral victory of 1958 and the subsequent legislative achievements of 1959 and 1963, they *had* kept Mississippi out of California. The passage of fair employment and housing laws represented nearly 30 years of activism and political organizing. Looking backward from the late 1960s, critics of the NAACP's and other groups' legal strategies of racial reform would argue that these efforts suffered from a naive faith in legal remedies and whites and an incomplete understanding of the deeply racist nature of American society. Such critics were right in an elemental way, but the sixties generation benefited from hindsight, having witnessed the failure of equal employment and housing to prevent the rise of widespread and concentrated poverty in black communities and having watched as whites increasingly withdrew their support for racial equality over the course of the 1960s. Things looked vastly different, and more hopeful, in 1958, and to discount the achievements of the Dellums generation is to give that backward gaze too much authority. The African American architects of liberal racial policy in California—many of whom emerged from the Oakland-Berkeley political hothouse nurtured by the East Bay Democratic Club and the progressive wing, in both AFL and CIO, of the labor movement—looked instead forward, heartened by their alliance with the state's strong labor movement. To build that alliance, Dellums and other black activists had for a decade practiced delicate coalition politics: operating in white-dominated coalitions from a position of strength in all-black institutions.

Liberal reform nonetheless proved only marginally effective in bringing social equality to black communities in California. Liberalism neither anticipated nor could resolve according to its own precepts the structural and spatial legacies of racial exclusion in urban America and the reactionary white racial politics at the heart of the New Deal coalition. California's postwar liberal movement came to end in 1964–65, split by three overlapping developments that widened existing political fault lines. First, deep opposition among employers, combined with the weakness of grievance procedures in the state's fair employment law, forced proponents of racial equality to turn to affirmative action. The shift to affirmative action in both rhetoric and practice in the early 1960s inaugurated a long period during which whites increasingly resisted efforts to achieve social equality and fell away from the liberal coalition. Second, against this background, in 1964, California voters repealed the state's Fair Housing law with Proposition 14. In the same 1964 election in which Lyndon Johnson claimed 60 percent of the California vote, two-thirds of the state's voters favored the fair housing repeal, an overwhelming rejection of a core liberal promise. Proposition 14 represented the widespread defection of working-class whites from the liberal coalition when their perceived material interests, elevated to "property rights," were threatened. Finally, the rebellion in Watts in 1965 destroyed lives, property, and optimism, as people who had been relegated to the margins of postwar economic prosperity and political life engaged in a combination of street theater, guerilla politics, and mob violence. Watts laid bare the formation of the "second ghetto" and the culpability of liberals, who had either contributed to or ignored its rise. All three events exposed existing contradictions within postwar liberalism, contradictions embedded within American political culture since the 1930s.[27]

From War on Poverty to Urban Plantation

Histories of post-1965 Black Power have long treated this complicated movement in terms of charismatic figures and ideological pronouncements that represented a distinct, even fatal, break with the civil rights movement. The bitter splits within the Student Nonviolent Coordinating Committee (SNCC) and the simultaneous rise of the Black Panther Party in the mid 1960s typically provide the evidence for such a full and fundamental schism. As Matthew Countryman has argued, however, historians and popular critics alike have devoted far less attention to the evolution of Black Power politics out of earlier liberal efforts, have downplayed the extraordinarily effective grassroots organizing undertaken in the name of Black Power, and have relied on the "revolutionary turn" of a small segment of the movement to marginalize a much broader and more diverse set of strategies and analyses. It is possible to follow continuities between the liberal generation of African American activists and the Black Power generation without downplaying the very real differences between the two. Indeed, following the continuities, as I have argued elsewhere, helps to contextualize the emergence of Black Power within the longer sweep of urban history and political economy in the twentieth century. Such an effort provides an important counternarrative to accounts of Black Power as an emotional, rhetorical, and ultimately marginal and self-destructive political phenomenon.[28]

In the years between 1965 and 1972, two broad groups in Oakland were drawn to Black Power: liberal reformers from the East Bay Democratic Club involved in the War on Poverty and grassroots organizers and activists in West Oakland. Each brought a different set of expectations and life experiences to Black Power, and each group theorized and acted on Black Power in distinct ways. But most important, in each case, calls for Black Power emerged as a tactical and philosophical development arising out of earlier efforts. And in each case, the model of black politics established by D. G. Gibson, Byron Rumford, and C. L. Dellums in the 1940s served as both inspiration and blueprint. Finally, their efforts anticipated the Black Panther Party's political campaigns of 1973 and 1974. Black Power was an extraordinarily broad ideological and political umbrella under which various cultural and radical nationalisms competed for rhetorical and intellectual leadership. But the politics fought out underneath that broad umbrella were nonetheless fierce and combative, pregnant with future implications, and linked in crucial ways to mid-century African American precedents.[29]

Middle-class leaders from the East Bay Democratic Club and the Men of Tomorrow were early advocates of social programs in Oakland that culminated in the War on Poverty in 1965. By then, as much as one-third of Oakland residents lived at or near poverty. Federal, state, and private foundation efforts designed to mitigate, as Oakland's city manager put it, "the people problems of the city," dramatically reengaged African American communities in local and municipal issues. Beginning in the late 1950s, juvenile delinquency programs, civic councils dealing with neighborhood racial transition, and early Ford Foundation grants to invest in educational and occupational services for poor working-class black neighborhoods created a network of bureaucratic and community sites where the meaning of race and opportunity in the city were contested and debated. The federal War on Poverty, which officially came to the city in 1965, intensified these ongoing efforts. Superior Court Judge Lionel Wilson, chairman of Oakland's poverty board and an activist in the East Bay Democratic Club, told local reporters that "Oakland is the first city in the nation to put planning for human development on par with physical and economic planning." Between 1965 and 1968, the federal Office of Economic Opportunity (the principal War on Poverty agency), Manpower Development and Training programs, the Economic Development Administration (EDA), and dozens of other federal initiatives brought tens of thousands of dollars to Oakland and legions of programs designed to attack the city's worsening poverty. "What we do here," Clinton White, another East Bay Democratic Club member said, "will lay a foundation, set a pattern, a precedent for national action, for metropolitan areas throughout this great nation as they struggle to breathe new life into the tangled and dying cities." The city's established professional black leadership embraced the War on Poverty as an extension of the fair employment and housing efforts of the previous decade. Removing the barriers that obstructed exits to the ghetto remained their overwhelming priority. New federal antipoverty efforts seemed a logical extension of the freedom movement to include the most marginalized segment of the African American community.[30]

Over time, however, the failure of these programs to ameliorate Oakland's unemployment crisis convinced a growing number of African American antipoverty activists and administrators of the need for a black "power base." Liberal hopes that federal antipoverty and employment programs would create real avenues out of poor neighborhoods yielded increasingly to calls for Black Power. Poverty programs ran into two principal roadblocks. First, they provided much-needed services to poor people, but not concrete jobs, what nearly every observer of Oakland in this period saw as the city's most pressing need. Second, programs that did include provisions for concrete jobs ran up against employer and union resistance. Percy Moore, executive director of the city's poverty program, argued in early 1968 that "the present problem isn't lack of jobs. The problem is the way jobs are distributed across the community." Moore's solution was to create an African American-controlled agency, funded by the federal government, that could negotiate from a position of strength with employers and unions. Donald McCullum, an early War on Poverty advocate and member of both the East Bay Democratic Club and the Men of Tomorrow, joined Moore in seeking a concrete form of Black Power. "The only thing that will be understood by business is the same with the unions, a power base," McCullum told an audience of the city's antipoverty activists in 1968. Moore and McCullum embodied a set of ideological and strategic shifts that in the late sixties transformed Oakland's antipoverty programs and ultimately the city's political culture.[31]

Moore and McCullum did not invent their politics from whole cloth. Indeed, they had come somewhat late to the notion of a black urban power base. African American activists in key major Northern cities had been advancing since the 1950s a variety of political projects that drew in creative ways on the conditions of the "second ghetto" to articulate new calls for power. The National Negro Labor Council in the early 1950s, the Nation of Islam and Malcolm X in the middle and late 1950s, and the Organization of Afro-American Unity in the early 1960s, among a number of other groups, had begun to conceive of urban black communities as the vanguard of nationalist politics and a natural site of artistic and cultural forms of black pride and expression. SNCC had famously turned to Black Power in 1966. And locally, African American professors at Merritt College in Oakland had organized a strong black studies program by the early 1960s, their students studying and practicing a variety of cultural and political nationalist politics. At the University of California at Berkeley, the Afro-American Association and its law-student leader Don Warden made black power and cultural nationalism an important presence on the state's premier university campus. By the early 1960s, Warden had a popular local radio show in which he fused Afro-centrism with calls for greater local control and political power in black communities. And the Black Panther Party had become, since its founding in late 1966, a touchstone of black power in Oakland. Moore and McCullum, then, drew on a discourse and set of ideological frameworks already well established in African American intellectual and activists circles both nationally and in the East Bay.[32]

Middle-class leaders in Oakland's War on Poverty bureaucracy turned to Black Power for an additional reason. They felt pressure and came under attack from community organizers, the second important group in Oakland to embrace calls for an African American power base. These men and women lived primarily in West and North Oakland and had witnessed a decade of profound changes to their neighborhoods. The transformation of West Oakland especially, the city's oldest and most densely African American neighborhood, engaged black Oakland around local issues of property and jobs between 1955 and 1965. The changes came from multiple directions. Large-scale redevelopment projects prompted home owners to organize to protect their homes from destruction and their property from purchase under eminent domain laws. Others labored both within and outside of the city's Redevelopment Agency to ensure that displaced residents could afford to live in the "redeveloped" neighborhoods. Activists organized mass protests against the enormous BART (Bay Area Rapid Transit) construction project that failed to employ African American workers. New interstate highways cut dramatic swaths through the neighborhood, destroying homes and displacing residents. In all, West Oakland lost between 7,000 and 9,000 housing units in the first six years of the 1960s. At the same time, few of the construction projects employed black workers in large numbers or in anything more than unskilled positions. Finally, the extraordinary modernization of the Port of Oakland, which became the nation's busiest in the 1970s, had failed to bring economic revitalization to its nearest neighbor, West Oakland. These transformations and massive interventions from institutions outside of the neighborhood stirred a new generation of African American activists, who sought to return power and decision-making to the local community through Black Power.[33]

"The time has come for a declaration of independence in Oakland," West Oakland community organizer Paul Cobb declared in 1968. "We live on an urban plantation. We have to plan our liberation." To Cobb and others involved in grassroots activism in West Oakland in the second half of the 1960s, both the "bourgeois" black leadership class and city government needed to yield influence to what John Ditmer has called "local people." West Oakland organizers had begun to understand the black predicament through theories of internal colonialism, adapted to metropolitan America, which argued that African American neighborhoods were exploited by an absent white society living in suburban communities. "The Port has over $100 million cash flow annually," Cobb told reporters, "but 78% of the people who work for the Port don't live in Oakland." Cobb and his colleagues in West Oakland's grassroots movement embraced an analysis of black communities that was inspired by Black Power ideologies of national liberation, but tactically they took a page from D. G. Gibson's book on coalition building. With the formation of the Black Caucus in 1968, under the leadership of Cobb, West Oakland activists created a second East Bay Democratic Club, an all-black organization that would bargain with city government and local political parties, horse-trading votes and interests. Cobb, himself, ran for Oakland City Council in 1971, calling for community control of the port and a broad affirmative action program that would rebuild the city's African American working class. He lost the election, but the coalition of voters that he put together, which included large numbers of white Oaklanders, would come to play a pivotal role in the city in the coming half decade, including the campaigns of the Black Panther Party in 1973 and 1974 and the successive mayoral run of Lionel Wilson in 1977.[34]

The economic fate of postwar American cities was intimately intertwined with federal policy and the political culture of liberalism. By the 1950s, New Deal liberalism had been fully incorporated into the growth economics of the cold war, in which the modernist faith in abundance guided urban policy. New alignments of capital within metropolitan space—neighborhoods, downtown urban cores, and suburban districts—drove a massive reorganization of cities. Capital mobility industrialized the suburbs, and services replaced blue collar industry as the mainspring of central city employment. Federal housing programs reconstructed the home mortgage market, channeling billions of dollars into the suburban construction industry. Federal-local partnerships produced new freeway systems that cut through older urban districts, and redevelopment and renewal programs reorganized urban space in older central cities. These forces remade cities and neighborhoods. Mid-sixties federal antipoverty programs had foundered against intransigent municipal governments and trade unions and the stubborn legacies of Jim Crow in the private economy. At the same time, nearby all-white suburban enclaves industrialized, exercised new power in regional and countywide governing boards, and seemed to siphon both tax revenue and private capital away from older core cities. In California, Proposition 13, the nation's first and most extensive property tax limitation measure, passed a statewide vote less than a year after Lionel Wilson was elected mayor of Oakland in 1977. The "tax revolt," as it became known, further limited the power of central cities vis-à-vis their suburban neighbors. This was the political economic terrain inherited by black political leaders across the nation in the 1970s. The whole of metropolitan development since WWII had largely worked against the economic interests of black communities. In this context, Wilson and others like him faced a series of crises, rather than an extended period of prosperity from which to build a successful and transformative new urban political terrain.[35]

It is beyond the scope of the present essay to assess the causes and consequences of Black Power's incorporation into municipal politics in places like Oakland. I have done so elsewhere, and there are provocative alternatives in the existing literature. In particular, Adolph Reed has argued that incorporation on a variety of political fronts, coupled with the ideological weakness of Black Power political thought, spelled a quick end to the black radical moment of the late 1960s and early 1970s. These debates and arguments aside, what is striking about Oakland in this period is the extent to which that Black Power moment made possible the political objectives that Oakland's black leaders had articulated in the 1940s. Despite a seemingly radical break with the liberal "civil rights" generation, Black Power in the East Bay eventually took a form that closely corresponded to those earlier efforts—coalitions with whites from a position of strength in all-black organizations, belief in the importance of political power, cross-class alliances within the black community, and a coupling of uplift and self-help. I am not suggesting that the East Bay Democratic Club and the Black Caucus, or the Black Panther Party, were the same thing. Distinct ideological, generational, and tactical differences marked each as unique. In particular, Black Power organizations in Oakland placed far more emphasis on community organizing than had the earlier generation—and this is not to mention the guns, rhetoric, and internationalism of the Panthers. Nevertheless, a continuum runs between the 1940s/1950s efforts and those of the 1960s and 1970s, one that cannot be simply or easily divided into two opposing, even contradictory, segments. In the end, black migrants to California after 1945 joined with labor and progressive whites in a statewide political coalition that, despite its peaks and valleys and strains, survived for nearly 40 years and remade politics in the state, as well as its major cities, including Oakland, Berkeley, San Francisco, and Los Angeles.[36]

It is now commonplace to talk about the postwar United States in terms of urban decline and crisis. We possess an extensive popular and academic vocabulary to describe the features of post-1945 urban transformation: the racialization and deindustrialization of cities, suburban growth, urban decline, the weakening of unions and working-class consciousness, the increasing mobility of capital, and the rise of a politics focused on private property. That these processes victimized African American communities in the North and Pacific Coast more than white communities has been established. But there is a pressing need to move beyond the trope of the black ghetto and the paradigm of crisis and to theorize how African American communities responded—in creative, productive, and at times even disastrous ways—to the structural changes brought on by migration and metropolitan reorganization. In short, there is a pressing need to place the dynamics of African American political organizing and political ideology between the 1940s and the 1970s in the broader context of American urban and political history. Looking at how the various spaces and political cultures of urban America were produced in the postwar decades in places like Oakland is one way to do this. Oakland—and Los Angeles, Chicago, Detroit, Philadelphia, etc.—offers a vantage from which to rethink not only the inherited wisdom about the relationship between the southern movement and the North and West but to assess the antecedents to Black Power ideology in the black activism of the 1940s and 1950s. Examining African American politics through urban history suggests that the civil rights/Black Power dichotomization of movement activism may no longer yield interesting or useful questions. It may, in fact, obscure as much as it purports to reveal.[37]

Notes

The author would like to thank Matthew Countryman, Thomas Sugrue, Scott Kurashige, Earl Lewis, James Gregory, Richard White, Mark Brilliant, Peniel Joseph, Wendell Pritchett, Roberta Gold, Martha Biondi, the Michigan Society of Fellows, and the History Department and Urban Studies Program at the University of Wisconsin, Milwaukee.

1. American Social History Project, *Who Built America? Working People and the Nation's Economy, Politics, Culture, and Society* (New York: Pantheon, 1992); Jonathan Birnbaum and Clarence Taylor, *Civil Rights Since 1787: A Reader on the Black Struggle* (New York: New York University Press, 2000). See, among many others, Harvard Sitkoff, *The Struggle for Black Equality, 1954–1980* (New York: Hill and Wang, 1981); Alan J. Matusow, *The Unraveling of America: A History of Liberalism in the 1960s* (New York: Harper and Row, 1984); Jack M. Bloom, *Class, Race, and the Civil Rights Movement* (Bloomington: Indiana University Press, 1987); John Dittmer, *Local People: The Struggle for Civil Rights in Mississippi* (Urbana: University of Illinois Press, 1994); John Egerton, *Speak Now Against the Day: The Generation Before the Civil Rights Movement in the South* (Chapel Hill: University of North Carolina Press, 1995); Charles M. Payne, *I've Got the Light of Freedom: The Organizing Tradition and the Mississippi Freedom Struggle* (Berkeley: University of California Press, 1995); Patricia Sullivan, *Days of Hope: Race and Democracy in the New Deal Era* (Chapel Hill: University of North Carolina Press, 1996).

2. For examples of recent work, see William Van DeBurg, *New Day in Babylon: The Black Power Movement and American Culture, 1965–1975* (Chicago: University of Chicago Press, 1992); William J. Grimshaw, *Bitter Fruit: Black Politics and the Chicago Machine, 1931–1991* (Chicago: University of Chicago Press, 1992);

Gretchen Lemke-Santangelo, *Abiding Courage: African American Migrant Women and the East Bay Community* (Chapel Hill: University of North Carolina Press, 1996); Kenneth Goings and Raymond A. Mohl, eds., *The New African American Urban History* (Thousand Oaks, Calif.: Sage Publications, 1996); Gerald Horne, *The Fire This Time: The Watts Uprising and the 1960s* (New York: Da Capo Press, 1997); Roger Horowitz, *"Negro and White, Unite and Fight": A Social History of Industrial Unionism in Meatpacking, 1930–90* (Urbana: University of Illinois Press, 1997); Charles E. Jones, ed., *The Black Panther Party Reconsidered* (Baltimore: Black Classic Press, 1998); Quintard Taylor, *In Search of the Racial Frontier: African Americans in the American West, 1528–1990* (New York: Norton, 1998); Komozi Woodard, *A Nation Within a Nation: Amiri Baraka (LeRoi Jones) and Black Power Politics* (Chapel Hill: University of North Carolina Press, 1999); Beth Tompkins Bates, *Pullman Porters and the Rise of Protest Politics in Black America, 1925–1945* (Chapel Hill: University of North Carolina Press, 2001); Eric Arnesen, *Brotherhoods of Color: Black Railroad Workers and the Struggle for Equality* (Cambridge, Mass.: Harvard University Press, 2001); Wendell Pritchett, *Brownsville, Brooklyn: Blacks, Jews, and the Changing Face of the Ghetto* (Chicago: University of Chicago Press, 2002); Robert Self, *American Babylon: Class, Race, and Power in Oakland and the East Bay, 1945–1978* (Princeton: Princeton University Press, 2003); Martha Biondi, *To Stand and Fight: The Struggle for African American Rights in Postwar New York City* (Cambridge, Mass.: Harvard University Press, 2003); Andrew Wiese, *Places of Our Own: African American Suburbanization Since 1916* (Chicago: University of Chicago Press, 2003); Adam Green, "Selling the Race: Cultural Production and Notions of Community in Black Chicago, 1940–1955" (Ph.D. diss., Yale University, 1998); Rhonda Williams, "Living Just Enough in the City: Change and Activism in Baltimore's Public Housing, 1940–1980" (Ph.D. diss., University of Pennsylvania, 1998); Matthew Countryman, "Civil Rights and Black Power in Philadelphia, 1945–1971" (Ph.D. diss., Duke University, 1999). For another call to rethink post-1945 African American history, see Kevin Gaines, "The Historiography of the Struggle for Black Equality Since 1945," in *A Companion to Post-1945 America,* Roy Rosenzweig and Jean-Christophe Agnew, eds. (Cambridge, Mass.: Blackwell, 2002).

3. See George Sánchez, *Becoming Mexican American: Ethnicity, Culture, and Identity in Chicano Los Angeles, 1900–1945* (New York: Oxford University Press, 1993); Tomás Almaguer, *Racial Fault Lines: The Historical Origins of White Supremacy in California* (Berkeley: University of California Press, 1994); David G. Gutierrez, *Walls and Mirrors: Mexican Americans, Mexican Immigrants, and the Politics of Ethnicity* (Berkeley: University of California Press, 1995); Shirley Jennifer Lim, "Girls Just Wanna Have Fun: The Politics Of Asian-American Women's Public Culture, 1930–1960" (Ph.D. diss., UCLA, 1998); Eduardo Obregon Pagan, "Sleepy Lagoon: The Politics Of Youth And Race In Wartime Los Angeles, 1940–1945" (Ph.D. diss., Princeton University, 1996); Scott Kurashige "Transforming Los Angeles: Black and Japanese American Struggles for Racial Equality in the 20th Century" (Ph.D. diss., UCLA, 2000).

4. Interview with Royal Towns, conducted by Sonoma State University Anthropological Studies Center (ASC) for the Cypress Freeway Replacement Project, CALTRANS, District 4, transcript held by Anthropological Studies Center, p. 4 (hereafter ASC Oral History).

5. Oral history interview with Manuel Fernandes by Bill Jersey of Quest Productions and/or Marjorie Dobkin for the documentary film *Crossroads: A Story of West Oakland,* prepared for the Cypress Freeway Replacement Project, CALTRANS, District 4, Oakland, 1995, 20–37 (hereafter West Oakland Oral History), oral history Interview with Tom Nash, West Oakland Oral History, 178–185, oral history interview with Vivian Bowie, West Oakland Oral History; interviews with Royal Towns and Arthur Patterson, ASC Oral History. See also, Paul Cobb, interview with author, August 20, 1997, Oakland, Calif.; Joe Johnson, interview with author, August 21, 1997, Oakland, California; Marilyn Johnson, *The Second Gold Rush: Oakland and the East Bay in World War II* (Berkeley: University of California Press, 1993), 97–103. For a broader study of the importance of trade union solidarity among African American railroad workers, see Arnesen, *Brotherhoods of Color.*

6. Interviews with Royal Towns, Arthur Patterson, Cleophus Williams, Clarence Oldwine, Norman Joseph Bradley, and Willie B. Jackson, ASC Oral History.

7. Fred Stripp, "The Treatment of Negro-American Workers by the AFL and CIO in the San Francisco Bay Area," *Social Forces* 28 (March 1950): 330–332; Albert Broussard, *Black San Francisco: The Struggle for Racial Equality in the West, 1900–1954,* 156–157; Bruce Nelson, *Workers on the Waterfront: Seamen, Longshoremen, and Unionism in the 1930s* (Urbana: University of Illinois Press, 1988); Bruce Nelson, "Class, Race, and Democracy in the CIO: The 'New' Labor History Meets the 'Wages of Whiteness,'" *International Review of Social History* 41 (1996): 351–374; Joe Johnson, interview with author; Paul Cobb, interview with author; interview with Royal Towns, ASC Oral History.

8. Johnson, *The Second Gold Rush,* 83-111; Lemke-Santangelo, *Abiding Courage;* West Oakland Oral History, 224–232, 261–263, 394–398, 431–440; Paul Groth and Marta Gutman, "Workers' Houses in West Oakland," in *Sights and Sounds: Essays in Celebration of West Oakland,* Suzanne Stewart and Mary Praetzellis, eds. (Rohnert Park, Calif.: Anthropological Studies Center, Sonoma State University Academic Foundation, 1997), Paul Groth, "A Profile of Work in West Oakland in 1952," in Stewart and Praetzellis, *Sights and Sounds.* For additional treatments of African Americans in the Bay Area during WWII, see Cy Record, "Willie Stokes at the Golden Gate," *Crisis* (June 1949): 175–179; Charles Johnson, *Negro War Workers in San Francisco, A Local Self-Survey* (San Francisco: n.p., 944); Joseph James, "Profiles, San Francisco," *Journal of Educational Sociology* (November 1945): 166–178.

9. The *Chicago Defender* quoted in Ronald Takaki, *Double Victory: A Multicultural History of America in World War II* (New York: Little, Brown and Company, 2000). On the "Double V" campaign, see Richard Dalfiume, *Fighting on Two Fronts: Desegregation of the Armed Forces, 1939–1953* (Columbia: University of Missouri Press, 1969), Beth Bailey and David Farber, "The 'Double-V'

Campaign and World War II Hawaii: African Americans, Racial Ideology, and Federal Power," *Journal of Social History* 26 (summer 1993). For an analysis of how these two tendencies within mid-century racial liberalism diverged into distinct approaches to black politics in the 1950s, see Thomas J. Sugrue, "Breaking Through: The Troubled Origins of Affirmative Action in the Workplace," *Color Lines: Affirmative Action, Immigration, and Civil Rights Options for America* (Chicago: University of Chicago Press, 2001), 31–52.

10. On the multiple political crosscurrents and debates within African American communities in the first half of the century, one that is critical of the class dimensions of uplift ideology in particular, see Kevin Gaines, *Uplifting the Race: Black Leadership, Politics, and Culture in the Twentieth Century* (Chapel Hill: University of North Carolina Press, 1996); for an account of mid-century black politics that stresses everyday forms of resistance and cultural politics, see Robin D. G. Kelley, *Race Rebels: Culture, Politics, and the Black Working Class* (New York: Free Press, 1994). See also Manning Marable, *Race, Reform, and Rebellion: The Second Reconstruction in Black America* (Jackson: University of Mississippi Press, 1991); Earl Lewis, *In Their Own Interest: Race, Class, and Power in Twentieth-Century Norfolk, Virginia* (Berkeley: University of California Press, 1991); Jervis Anderson, *This Was Harlem: A Cultural Portrait, 1900–1950* (New York: Farrar, Straus, & Giroux, 1981); Eric Arnesen, *Waterfront Workers of New Orleans: Race, Class, and Politics, 1863–1923* (New York: Oxford University Press, 1991). For a perspective on African American internationalists in the United States in this period, see Penny M. Von Eshen, *Race Against Empire: Black Americans and Anticolonialism, 1937–1957* (Ithaca: Cornell University Press, 1997), and Nikhil Singh, *Black Is a Country: Politics and Theory in the Long Civil Rights Era* (Cambridge, Mass.: Harvard University Press, 2003).

11. Lemke-Santangelo, *Abiding Courage;* Jacqueline Jones, *Labor and Love, Labor of Sorrow: Black Women, Work, and the Family From Slavery to the Present* (New York: Basic Books, 1985); Elizabeth Clark-Lewis, *Living In, Living Out: African American Domestics and the Great Migration* (New York: Kodansha International, 1994).

12. Broussard, *Black San Francisco,* 207; interview with Cleophus Williams, ASC Oral History.

13. "What Tensions Exist Between Groups in the Local Community?" "What Courses of Action are Needed to Achieve the Essentials of Good Human Relations in the Local Community?" "Are the Rights of All Secure in the Local Community?" (Oakland Institute on Human Relations, Seminar Reports, November 13, 1946, mimeographed); East Bay Conference on Human Relations, August 27, 1949, California Federation of Civic Unity Collection, Carton 1, The Bancroft Library, University of California, Berkeley.

14. On California liberalism, see James Q. Wilson, *The Amateur Democrat* (Chicago: University of Chicago Press, 1962); Philip Taft, *Labor Politics American Style: The California Federation of Labor* (Cambridge, Mass.: Harvard University Press, 1984); Peter Iverson, "A Half-Century of Conflict: The Rise and Fall of Liberalism in California Politics, 1943–1993," in *Politics in the*

Postwar American West, Richard Lowitt, ed. (Norman: University of Oklahoma Press, 1995); Gayle B. Montgomery and James W. Johnson, *One Step From the White House: The Rise and Fall of Senator William F. Knowland* (Berkeley: University of California Press, 1998); Matthew Dallek, *The Right Moment: Ronald Reagan's First Victory and the Decisive Turning Point in American Politics* (New York: The Free Press, 2000). Needless to say, we should not regress into nostalgia for California's liberal age. Far too many contradictions lay at its heart. But neither should we dismiss its accomplishments nor overlook the potential that it represented in the 1950s. For works that explore the transfiguration of liberalism by the cold war, see Mary L. Dudziak, *Cold War Civil Rights: Race and the Image of American Democracy* (Princeton: Princeton University Press, 2000); Roger Lotchin, *Fortress California, 1910–1961: From Warfare to Welfare* (New York: Oxford University Press, 1992).

15. Clinton White, from a speech at McClymonds High School in West Oakland, 1965, broadcast on KPFA Radio, Berkeley, "Oakland—The Next Watts," Tape BB1289, Pacifica Radio Archives, North Hollywood, California. The inclusion of "Spanish-speaking" in White's address was a concession to the enormous growth in the ethnic Mexican population of Oakland in the early 1960s. Though liberals, both black and white, included references to "Spanish-speaking" people in public addresses, civil rights work continued to focus almost exclusively on the situation of African Americans. For the larger story of California's multiracial/national postwar civil rights battles, see Gutierrez, *Walls and Mirrors;* Kurashige, "Transforming Los Angeles."

16. The left-liberal politics of the 1940s in the Bay Area are more complicated than I have space here to explore. For a more detailed account, see Self, *American Babylon.*

17. Interviews with Arthur Patterson and Robert Edwards, ASC Oral History.

18. *C. L. Dellums: International President of the Brotherhood of Sleeping Car Porters and Civil Rights Leader, An Interview Conducted by Joyce Henderson* (Berkeley: University of California Regional Oral History Office, 1973), 128 (hereafter Dellums Oral History). Fair employment and housing laws in California were modeled on New York State's. For this story, see Biondi, *To Stand and Fight.*

19. Ron Dellums, who served in the U.S. Congress from 1971 until 1998, representing the Oakland-Berkeley flatlands, was the nephew of C. L. Dellums. See his memoir, *Lying Down with the Lions: A Public Life from the Streets of Oakland to the Halls of Power,* with H. Lee Halterman (Boston: Beacon, 2000). C. L. Dellums became International President of the BSCP in 1968 upon the death of Randolph.

20. Rumford and Brown, quoted in "D.G. Gibson: A Black Who Led the People and Built the Democratic Party in the East Bay," in *Experiment and Change in Berkeley: Essays on City Politics, 1950–1975,* Harriet Nathan and Stanley Scott, eds. (Berkeley: Institute of Governmental Studies, University of California, Berkeley, 1978), 12, 24.

21. Men of Tomorrow Collection, African American Museum and Library at Oakland; author interview with Norvel Smith, March 1, 1999, Oakland, California.

22. Dellums Oral History, 51; Letter to A. Philip Randolph from Dellums, May 13, 1940, C. L. Dellums Collection, Bancroft, Carton 4; Oral History interviews with Manuel Fernandes, Tom Nash, and Vivian Bowie, West Oakland Oral History; interviews with Royal Towns and Arthur Patterson, ASC Oral History. See also Paul Cobb, interview with author; Joe Johnson, interview with author; Johnson, *The Second Gold Rush*, 97–103.

23. Charles Hamilton, *Adam Clayton Powell, Jr.: The Political Biography of an American Dilemma* (New York: Atheneum, 1991); Aldon Morris, *The Origins of the Civil Rights Movement: Black Communities Organizing for Change* (New York: Free Press, 1984); Biondi, *To Stand and Fight.*

24. Author interview with William Patterson, September 3, 1997, Oakland, California. See also Cary D. Wintz, ed., *African American Political Thought, 1890–1930: Washington, DuBois, Garvey, and Randolph* (Armonk, N.Y.: M. E. Sharpe, 1996). For a discussion of racial projects in the late twentieth-century United States, see Michael Omi and Howard Winant, *Racial Formations in the United States: From the 1960s to the 1990s* (New York: Routledge, 1994).

25. Harriet Nathan and Stanley Scott, eds., *Experiment and Change in Berkeley: Essays on City Politics, 1950–1975* (Berkeley: Institute of Governmental Studies, 1978).

26. NAACP pamphlet, "Keep Mississippi Out of California," Clipping File, Box 162, William F. Knowland Collection, The Bancroft Library, University of California, Berkeley.

27. Horne, *The Fire This Time.*

28. See the Introduction to this volume. See also Robert Self, "'To Plan Our Liberation': Black Power and the Politics of Place in Oakland, California, 1965–1977," *Journal of Urban History* 26 (September 2000): 759–792.

29. For the purposes of this essay, I am lumping rather than splitting the landscape of Black Power and black nationalism. The very real differences between various kinds of nationalism and debates over the relative inclusiveness of the term "black power" can be followed more profitably elsewhere. See Robin D. G. Kelley, *Race Rebels: Culture, Politics, and the Black Working Class* (New York: The Free Press, 1994); Timothy B. Tyson, *Radio Free Dixie: Robert F. Williams and the Roots of Black Power* (Chapel Hill: University of North Carolina Press, 1999); Peniel E. Joseph, "Black Liberation Without Apology: Reconceptualizing the Black Power Movement," *The Black Scholar* 31/3-4 (fall/winter 2001), 2–19; Woodard, *A Nation Within a Nation;* Clayborne Carson, *In Struggle: SNCC and the Black Awakening of the 1960s* (Cambridge, Mass.: Harvard University Press, 1981); Nikhil Singh, *Black Is a Country;* Biondi, *To Stand and Fight.*

30. This emphasis on community organizing has a deep history in social science and policy literature, a briefer one in historical literature. See Sheldon Danziger and Daniel H. Weinberg, eds., *Fighting Poverty: What Works and What Doesn't* (Cambridge, Mass.: Harvard University Press, 1986); Thomas F. Jackson, "The

State, the Movement, and the Poor: The War on Poverty and Political Mobilization in the 1960s," in *The "Underclass" Debate,* Michael Katz, ed., (Princeton: Princeton University Press, 1993); Gareth Davies, *From Opportunity to Entitlement: The Transformation and Decline of Great Society Liberalism* (Lawrence: University Press of Kansas, 1996).

31. Clinton White, from a speech at McClymonds High School in West Oakland, 1965, broadcast on KPFA Radio, Berkeley, "Oakland—The Next Watts," Tape BB1289, Pacifica Radio Archives; Moore and McCullum, quoted in the *Oakland Tribune,* March 28, 1968.

32. Marable, *Race, Reform and Rebellion;* Woodard, *A Nation Within a Nation;* Rod Bush, *We Are Not What We Seem: Black Nationalism and Class Struggle in the American Century* (New York: New York University Press, 1999); Von Eshen, *Race Against Empire.* This brief description does not do justice to the trajectory of black nationalist and Black Power thought across the middle of the century. For a more detailed account, see the essay by Peniel Joseph "Black Liberation Without Apology" and Singh, *Black Is a Country.*

33. The reengineering of West Oakland from 1959 through the late 1960s can be followed in a variety of local periodicals, including the *California Voice, Flatlands,* the *Black Panther,* and the *Oakland Post.* See also Louise Resnikoff, "The EDA in Oakland: An Evaluation (Berkeley: University of California Oakland Project, 1969, mimeographed); William L. Nicholls, *Poverty and Poverty Programs in Oakland* (Berkeley: Survey Research Center, 1967); *Oakland's Formula for the Future* (Oakland: Oakland City Planning Commission, 1957); *General Neighborhood Renewal Plan* (Oakland: Oakland City Planning Department, October 1958).

34. Oakland *Tribune,* June 20 and July 2 and 3, 1968, January 31, April 18, 1971; *California Voice,* December 18, 1970; *People's World,* April 17, 1971.

35. Barry Bluestone and Bennett Harrison, *The Deindustrialization of America: Plant Closings, Community Abandonment, and the Dismantling of Basic Industry* (New York: Basic Books, 1982); Richard M. Bernard and Bradley R. Rice, eds., *Sunbelt Cities: Politics and Growth Since World War II* (Austin: University of Texas Press, 1983); Michael Wallace and Joyce Rothschild, eds., *Deindustrialization and the Restructuring of American Industry* (Greenwich, Conn.: JAI Press, 1988); Bruce Schulman, *From Cotton Belt to Sunbelt: Federal Policy, Economic Development, and the Transformation of the South, 1938–1980* (New York: Oxford University Press, 1991) Ann Markusen, Peter Hall, Scott Campbell, and Sabina Deitrick, *The Rise of the Gunbelt: The Military Remapping of Industrial America* (New York: Oxford University Press, 1991); Jefferson Cowie, *Capital Moves : RCA's Seventy-Year Quest for Cheap Labor* (Ithaca: Cornell University Press, 1999). On the position of cities within the capitalist marketplace, see Paul E. Peterson, *City Limits* (Chicago: University of Chicago Press, 1981), and John H. Mollenkopf, *The Contested City* (Princeton: Princeton University Press, 1983); Richard A. Walker, "Industry Builds the City: The Suburbanization of Manufacturing in the San Francisco Bay Area, 1850–1940" (Department of Geography, photocopy); Greg Hise, *Magnetic Los*

Angeles: Planning the Twentieth-Century Metropolis (Baltimore: Johns Hopkins University Press, 1997). On housing and mortgage markets, see Gail Radford, *Modern Housing for America: Policy Struggles in the New Deal Era* (Chicago: University of Chicago Press, 1996); Gwendolyn Wright, *Building the Dream: A Social History of Housing in America* (Cambridge, Mass.: MIT Press, 1981); David Freund, "Making it Home: Race, Development, and the Politics of Place in Suburban Detroit, 1940–1967" (Ph. D. diss., University of Michigan, 1999).

36. Adolph Reed, Jr., *Stirrings in the Jug: Black Politics in the Post-Segregation Era* (Minneapolis: University of Minnesota Press, 1999). For a systematic study and typology of black incorporation into municipal politics from the perspective of political science, see Rufus P. Browning, Dale Rogers Marshall, and David H. Tabb, *Protest Is Not Enough: The Struggle of Blacks and Hispanics for Equality in Urban Politics* (Berkeley: University of California Press, 1984). Also see Self, *American Babylon.*

37. In addition to this anthology, see the special issue of *Black Scholar* (fall 2001) devoted to Black Power, edited by Peniel Joseph.

Chapter 5

"I'd Rather Go to School in the South": How Boston's School Desegregation Complicates the Civil Rights Paradigm[1]

Jeanne Theoharis

They seem to think we're animals or something. They just don't want us to be able to get the kind of education they've already got.

—*Margie, a black student who desegregated South Boston High on September 12, 1974*

I'd rather go to school in the South.

—*Cynthia , another black student who desegregated South Boston High and had a brick thrown at her head*

From Mississippi to Massachusetts, unequal schooling was a crucial battleground of the black freedom struggles that followed WWII. Understood as one of the primary ways that a racial caste system was perpetuated in America, civil rights activists across the nation saw schools as the front line for racial justice. Analyzing school struggles outside of the South, then, is a critical site for exploring and expanding the civil rights narrative. Indeed, the nature of school segregation and the variety of tactics community members used to challenge it reveal the commonalties between the racial landscapes of Northern and Southern cities and the struggles to change them across the United States. At the same time, the particular ways that Northern segregation operated and the tools whites used to defend it meant that Northern activists had to prove that segregation actually existed, was harmful, and was enacted deliberately by the state. Because Northern segregation was not usually defended as segregation, scholars have often marginalized these civil rights struggles for educational equality, casting white resistance more sympathetically as a movement against busing to protect neighborhood schools. Within this paradigm, it becomes nearly impossible to understand how a black teenager living in Boston in 1974 would wish to be going to school in the South. Moreover, the ways that Boston's desegregation was framed and is now historicized has contributed to a public sense (both conservative and liberal) that the costs of school desegregation, particularly in the urban North, were simply too high.

Attacking the ways the school system funneled black students into poorly funded, under-equipped, overcrowded schools, community members in Boston fought to equalize education in the city in the 1960s and 1970s.[2] After a decade and a half of sustained black activism around education, the black community, through the National Association for the Advancement of Colored People (NAACP), filed a federal desegregation suit against the school system. In June 1974, Federal Judge W. Arthur Garrity ordered Boston Public School system (BPS) to begin desegregation. As the school district unwillingly began a plan for school desegregation, Boston became the site of one of the latest, most publicized, and most violent battles for school desegregation in the nation's history, as many whites took to the streets and kept their children home. Television publicized white fear, hatred, and violent resistance against desegregation to the nation, shattering Boston's reputation as the "cradle of democracy." It decisively revealed that school desegregation was neither just an issue facing the South nor a strategy that had outlived its usefulness in breaking down racially inequitable public institutions. It also showed the power blacks and their white allies had gained through organizing to pressure the city to give black students the same access and resources it had long reserved for white students and to hire black teachers in every school in the city.

Boston's school desegregation has not garnered the kind of scholarly attention that many events of the civil rights movement have. In part, this stems from the fact that Boston's movement challenges many prevailing popular assumptions about postwar black freedom struggles: namely, that it did not take place in the South during the 1950s and 1960s. Such views too often focus on segregation as a Southern problem, desegregation as a Southern solution, and the civil rights movement as a Southern movement. De jure segregation in the South is contrasted with de facto in the North, foregrounding the role of the state in perpetuating racial hierarchies in the South and downplaying them in the North. Thus, by implying that Northern segregation was not furthered by the political and legal structures of the state, African American protest movements in the urban North appear as ancillary to the "real" movement in the South, requiring different tactics and aimed at different targets. Southern politicians' willingness to embrace segregation publicly and Northern politicians' reluctance to embrace segregation rhetorically, while acting to preserve it in practice, has mistakenly been construed as proof that segregation was more robust and more protected in the South. This historical focus on the South makes Northern school segregation appear to be solely the function of private housing decisions made by individual white families and, thus, beyond the reach of political or judicial interventions, when in fact government policies, at both the federal and local level, clearly reinforced and extended residential and public school segregation in the urban North. Overlooking movements in the North, then, both naturalizes the racial order in these cities and makes it increasingly difficult to see the ways it could be and was changed.

Accounts that do take up Northern movements usually do so to trace how the movement moved from South to North, to show how tactics that worked in the South were less successful in the North, and to argue that blacks in the North had rejected integration by the mid-1960s in favor of nationalist strategies.[3] Adam Fairclough encapsulates this thinking best when he writes that his survey of the black quest for equality in the twentieth-century, *Better Day Coming*, focuses on the South because "the South evolved particular forms of racial domination that set it apart from the rest of the nation, making it the main focus of black campaigns against discrimination and oppression."[4] There is a certain tautology here; scholars focus their inquiry on the South and then because there is less scholarship on the North, justify studying the South because there is more to study. *Eyes on the Prize* provides probably the most interesting and nuanced epic account of postwar black freedom struggles to date, detailing a number of Northern movements, including Boston's desegregation, yet still reifies a South-to-North, heroism-to-backlash view of the movement. Much of the variety of efforts of Boston's black community during the 1950s, 1960s, and 1970s were left out of the series.

According to this reasoning, then, as black communities radicalized in the 1960s, they came to see desegregation as irrelevant and too compromising to address the profound social and economic inequalities blacks faced. Contrary to these views, Boston's struggle was a Northern movement for educational equity and school desegregation that succeeded through black organizing efforts to eliminate acute school segregation and expand racial equity in resources and hiring in the city for a time.[5] Black Boston's struggle for educational justice culminated in a federal desegregation suit; while not all blacks in the city supported this, by and large the community saw desegregation as a last resort to secure equal resources for the majority of black children in the city.[6]

Accounts of Boston's desegregation have focused primarily on white resistance to desegregation, ignoring the 25 years of organizing prior to Judge Garrity's decision and the many whites who did not oppose it.[7] While devoting ample space to white parents and their organized resistance, many authors brush over the well-coordinated, decades-long struggle that black parents went through to address racial inequalities in Boston's public schools.[8] Thus, this essay seeks to accomplish two related goals. It begins to document the struggles blacks waged, led largely by women, from the early 1950s through Garrity's decision in 1974 to address educational injustice within the city and to press the city to protect and provide for their children during desegregation. In doing this, it challenges the prevailing views that dichotomize segregation as de facto in the North and de jure in the South and that portray white resistance in Boston as a working-class movement against "busing."

These struggles for educational justice in Boston complicate the prevalent dichotomy made between integrationist and Black Power strategies. Activists in Boston strategically worked within and outside the system in their struggles with the city, finding a common enemy in Boston's School Committee. Much more than black children sitting next to white children in school, the movement to end segregation sought a fundamental transformation of the economic, political, and social landscape of the city[9]—to ensure, as organizer Ruth Batson explained, that "there was no place where black people can't go."[10] Freedom House founder Muriel Snowden elaborated.

Black children "were not going to have a chance unless there is this kind of equity. There's got to be educational equity and what it takes, there are two kinds of things. It takes something to bring them to the point where they start at the beginning line, unencumbered. Then, there are those who are at the point that need to be showed that they don't get tripped up or rabbit punched or something along the way."[11]

Thus, self-determination, equity, and access to jobs—crucial ideological goals of black nationalist struggles in the 1960s and 1970s—were at the heart of the movement for desegregation in Boston. Desegregation was not the only strategy pursued but one that activists kept returning to, even into the 1970s, as a way to open up educational opportunities for all black students in the city and jobs for black teachers in every school in the city.

Beginning in the early 1950s, before the *Brown* decision, a group of parents, led by political activist Ruth Batson, organized around the educational disparities within BPS. Born to politically active, Garvey-supporting West Indian parents, Batson grew up in the Roxbury section of Boston. Married at 19, Batson had three daughters and became very involved in their schools. In 1949, she joined the Parent's Federation, a predominantly white group that focused on the racial inequities and deterioriating quality of Boston's schools; Batson was politicized through her involvement in the Federation and the way the organization was decimated through red-baiting (like many Northern and Southern organizations fighting for racial change in this period). In 1950, she registered a complaint with the school department that black children (including her daughters) were receiving an inferior education.[12] In 1951, seeking systemic change, Batson became the first black person to run for school committee in five decades and lost.[13] In 1956, she ran for Democratic Primary state committeewoman and was elected. She was also active in the NAACP in the 1950s, becoming the first woman president of the New England Regional NAACP in May 1958.

Batson's personal experience and political work laid the groundwork for the movement that emerged in the 1950s and 1960s.[14] After finding out that a white friend's son had science in school but her daughter did not, Batson went to talk to the principal. The principal assured her that her daughter would have science later that year. Sure enough, her daughter soon had a science project to do for school—the only one in class. When Batson went back down to school, the principal flatly denied that her daughter was receiving different work. Realizing a problem, Batson went to the NAACP, but they told her they did not have a committee to deal with the public schools. The next day, however, the NAACP called her back saying that they wanted to form a subcommittee to organize around the issue and asked her to chair it.

From the outset, this committee of parents focused on educational equity and the allocation of resources within the system. They saw first-hand that keeping black students in separate schools was a way for the School Committee to provide an inferior education to them.[15] According to Batson, "We decided that where there were a large number of white students, that's where the care went. That's where the books went. That's where the money went."[16] Their studies revealed that many black schools, including six of the nine black elementary schools, were overcrowded.[17] Of the 13 schools with predominantly black populations, at least 4 had been recommended to be closed because of health and safety reasons, and 8 were in need of repairs to meet present city standards.[18] Per pupil spending averaged $340 for white students but only $240 for black students.[19] The city spent 10 percent less on textbooks, 19 percent less on libraries and 27 percent less on health care for black students than it did for white students. The curriculum at many black schools was outdated and often blatantly racist, and black students were overwhelmingly tracked into manual and vocational classes (and trade high schools) rather than college preparatory ones. Teachers at predominantly black schools were less permanent and often less experienced than those assigned to white schools.

Parents knew that this was a deliberately racialized school system, evidenced by the policy that fed blacks into high school in ninth grade but whites in tenth—and often into different junior high schools before that. As parent activist Ellen Jackson explained, "[Y]ou could live on the same street and have a white neighbor, as I did, and you went to one junior high school and she went to another junior high school. So it was that dual pattern. ... It was not de facto at all."[20] Segregation was also a way to reserve the overwhelming majority of the jobs in the district for whites. The district engaged in racially differential hiring and promotion practices; thus, many schools had no black teachers (blacks made up only 0.5 percent of the city's teachers), and there were no black principals in the system. As community activist Mel King, who would later run unsuccessfully for School Committee, observed, "The teachers were either Irish or Yankee. ... I didn't see my first black teacher until I was in the seventh grade."[21] The NAACP public school subcommittee began its work in the early 1950s and was heartened when the Supreme Court passed its landmark decision in *Brown v. Board of Education,* believing that this would mean significant change in BPS. In the late 1950s, as the national NAACP focused its efforts on the South, Batson and others struggled to press the issue of segregation in Boston's public schools.

In the early 1960s, the Education Committee of the NAACP tried to get the Massachusetts Commission Against Discrimination (MCAD) to recognize segregation in Boston's schools. MCAD refused, claiming that racial segregation was not a problem in the schools. While the existence of public commissions like MCAD seem to attest to a different racial climate in Massachusetts, their unwillingness to investigate institutions like BPS protected the school system's discriminatory practices. Community activists took their case to the School Committee in June 1963. They packed the hearing to report their findings and urge the Committee to makes changes. Another 800 desegregation supporters were turned away and congregated instead in front of City Hall. Batson spoke for the

NAACP. "We are here because the clamor from the community is too anxious to be ignored ... the injustices present in our school system hurt our pride, rob us of our dignity and produce results which are injurious not only to our future, but to that of our city, our commonwealth, and our nation."[22] Organizers expected an ordinary meeting but were met with a lot of press and an intransigent School Committee. According to Batson, "We were insulted. We were told our kids were stupid and this was why they didn't learn. We were completely rejected that night."[23] The biggest issue was the committee's refusal to acknowledge any form of de facto segregation or differential hiring within the schools—that is, they refused to acknowledge any role in maintaining unequal schooling in the city.[24]

To continue the pressure on the School Committee, community leaders turned to direct action, holding school boycotts and sit-ins. The first school boycott occurred a week after the School Committee meeting. Nearly half of the black high school students, approximately 2500 students, participated in the Stay-Out-For-Freedom boycott and attended Freedom Schools.[25] Organizers celebrated the success, calling for more actions.[26] The NAACP was able to get a second one-hour meeting with the School Committee on August 15. This meeting, like the first, was filled with civil rights supporters, once again with many demonstrators out in the street. However, the School Committee ended the meeting after 15 minutes, cutting off Batson's presentation, rather than discussing issues of segregation within the school system.

The NAACP during this period was chaired by long-time political activist Melnea Cass. Born on June 16, 1896, in Richmond, Virginia, she moved to Boston's South End when she was five. In part through the influence of her politically active mother-in-law, Rosa Brown, Cass joined the NAACP, attending meetings with William Monroe Trotter, W. E. B. Du Bois, and A. Phillip Randolph. She was also a member, national vice president, and president of the Northeastern Region of the National Association of Colored Women and one of the charter members of Freedom House. After decades of political activism, Cass, known as the "First Lady of Roxbury," explained the anger many felt around the city's inaction, "It's very frustrating; every time you turn around, you got to have a demonstration, you got to have a law. ... Why have you got to do all these things, to make people understand that you're entitled to these things?"[27] The NAACP under Cass's leadership carried out numerous sit-ins and pickets against the School Committee to highlight the city's recalcitrance. Many were arrested in these actions. "[W]e took it as a very serious thing, and a calamity happening to us as black people, trying to get something done, and couldn't impress anybody."[28]

The NAACP even ran a float with a picture of John F. Kennedy and a banner that read, "From the Fight for Irish Freedom to the Fight for U.S. Equality. NAACP" in the 1964 St. Patrick's Day parade. Their float was pelted with rocks, cherry bombs, bricks, garbage, and food. Thomas Atkins, the executive secretary of the Boston NAACP chapter, compared the violence to "the viciousness of the type you might expect to see in New Orleans or in the back woods of Mississippi. But it happened in Boston and this is where it must be dealt with."[29]

Martin Luther King, Jr., came twice to Boston on the invitation of the Massachusetts Southern Christian Leadership Conference to connect Southern struggles against segregation with those in Boston. He too got nowhere with Boston's School Committee, although his second visit in April of 1965 brought 25,000 people to rally on the Boston Commons. Thus, many of the tactics that characterized the Southern civil rights movement in the early to mid-1960s—sit-ins, boycotts, freedom schools, and civil disobedience—were part of the same arsenal that activists in Boston drew upon in the early to mid-1960s. In Boston, just as in many Southern cities, white politicians tried to discredit the NAACP as "outsiders" and claimed that the real problem was not segregation but the motivation of black children.[30] Unlike their Southern counterparts (whose opposition publicly embraced segregation), however, blacks in Boston struggled to get the issue of segregation recognized—to prove that distinct and harmful racial patterns within the city's schools even existed.

A second boycott of schools was called for on February 26, 1964, coinciding with a nation-wide campaign organized by the Student Nonviolent Coordinating Committee (SNCC) to dramatize issues of segregation in the nation's schools.[31] Drawing somewhere between 22 and 40 percent of all black students and nearly 20,000 people throughout the city, this successful boycott prompted action—at the state level, not with the School Committee.[32] The day after the boycott, Governor Peabody convened a blue-ribbon committee to study discrimination in the schools. The committee's report found that Boston's schools were indeed racially imbalanced (racial imbalance being the more palatable Northern word for segregation) and that such imbalance was harmful to students. The lobbying efforts of the black community and its white allies (one minister, Reverend Vernon Carter, held a 118-day vigil on the steps of the School Committee building[33]) led to the passage of the Racial Imbalance Act in August 1965.[34] Calling on "all school committees to adopt as education objectives the promotion of racial balance and the correction of existing racial imbalance," the act forbade the commonwealth from supporting any school that was more than 50 percent nonwhite (although the act considered majority or all white schools racially balanced). However, a school committee denied funding through the act was given the opportunity to seek judicial review of their situation. Filing suit in 1967, Boston's School Committee challenged the act's legality in court, tried to get it overturned by the state legislature, and used the judicial review as a delaying tactic to avoid obeying the law for nearly a decade.

With legislation proving ineffective in moving the School Committee, parents decided to take matters into their hands and took the lead (rather than the civil rights organizations) to devise new strategies. They were particularly concerned with overcrowding in black schools. This group of parents began to think: "If we take our kids, and we go over to where these schools are, and ... inconvenience some of these people who didn't seem to quite understand and sympathize with our plight. Let them know what it meant to have an overcrowded classroom."[35] They found that there were "plenty of seats" in less crowded "white schools" and "plastered these signs all over," telling parents about the open seats elsewhere in the city. These parents, led by Ellen Jackson, formed the North Dorchester-Roxbury Parent Association, believing that the educational bureaucracy might respond better to a group explicitly made up of parents.[36] Black parents had been systematically excluded from parent organizations within the schools; thus, these parent organizations also made a public claim to advocate for their children as "parents," just as whites in the city did.

Born in Boston on October 29, 1935, Ellen Jackson had grown up in Roxbury, attended Girl's Latin, and had been active as a teenager in the NAACP Youth Council.[37] Like Batson, Jackson had a history of political activism and five kids in BPS. She joined the Northern Student Movement (NSM) over concerns about their education, becoming the parent coordinator of the NSM from 1962 to 1964.[38] Her work in the NSM, advocating for students and parents, led her to found the Parent Association. She explained, "It was because of these many affronts and confrontations with an unheeding school committee and school board that we decided other action was necessary."[39] But the group's attempts to get change from within the school bureaucracy were largely thwarted. The School Committee had initially proposed a double session day for the overcrowded schools in Roxbury. Pressure from parents led the committee to scrap the plan, but it offered no other solutions to remedy overcrowded black schools.

Boston had started an open enrollment policy in 1961 that allowed students to attend any school as long as there were open seats. But the School Committee forbade the use of school funds to bus children to the 7,000 open seats throughout the city.[40] While it was designed to make it possible for black students to attend white schools, numerous barriers erected within the system made it extremely difficult for black families to take advantage of open enrollment. Thus, open enrollment served largely as an administrative shield against charges of racial privilege within the system—and in many ways functioned like "freedom of choice" plans did in the South.

Since the city refused to make it possible for black students to fill those open seats, the Parent Association decided that they would do it themselves. The vast majority of these mothers had been active before in Headstart, school strikes, and tutorial programs like the NSM[41] and thus had experience doing grassroots organizing. They did research to figure out where the open seats were and on the first day of school arranged buses and cars to "open" these schools to black children. According to Jackson, on that first day, a reporter asked her what their initiative was called. She explained, "'Casting our children out to reap,' you know, the benefits, so that they could come home and sow the oats at home. In a sense we were giving them a chance to go out and gain whatever they can, and come back to benefit their community. And I said, 'That's sort of an exodus because we don't mean to stay out there. We're coming back, we're coming home.'"[42]

And so it became Operation Exodus. The Parent Association was able to pay for it only through continuous fund-raising from individuals in the community, the NAACP, and a number of labor unions—and, over the next years, bused black children to vacant seats in many white schools in the city. Open enrollment policy did not ensure welcome for Exodus students. At some of the schools, black students were locked out, segregated into separate classes, or relegated to the back of the classroom. Yet, James Teele, who evaluated the program's effectiveness, found that students in Exodus did make substantial improvement in reading, and most Exodus parents were happy with their children's educational progress over time.[43] The Parent Association believed that if they began busing black students to these open seats, they would shame the school district into complying with the state law and taking over the operation and funding of the buses. They were wrong. The school district never did, despite publicly endorsing the program as part of its attempts to look compliant and racially balanced. Operation Exodus bused 250 students in 1965, 450 in 1966, 600 in 1967, and then decreased to 500 in 1968 (in part because of the formation of another busing program, METCO [Metropolitan Council for Educational Opportunity]).

METCO took a different tactic from Operation Exodus, bringing black students from the city to predominantly white suburbs for school.[44] Ruth Batson became director of METCO while continuing to fight for desegregation within the city. Like Operation Exodus, founders of METCO thought the program would force the city to deal with racial equity issues within the city limits while demonstrating the ways that the city and its suburbs were intricately connected. As Batson explained, "When Metco started ... I thought 'We'll take the kids out and embarrass them [the Boston School Committee]. Then we'll throw the rascals out and bring the kids home.' Nobody expected it to go on and on."[45] By the mid-1970s, with help from the U.S. Office for Education and the Carnegie Corporation, METCO was busing nearly 2,500 students to 38 suburbs.[46] While this was a great expansion from the original 220, it still only affected a small minority of black students (some of the most academically advanced, although organizers consciously picked students with a range of family income and academic ability) and was never an option available to most black children.[47] Batson resented the ways METCO was criticized for taking the "cream of the crop." "Were 220 students all of the cream?"[48]

Parents also created independent black schools—Highland Park Free School, Roxbury Community School, and the New School—to ensure quality education for their children.[49] These derived partly from the Freedom Schools operated during the boycotts, as parents saw the need to set up more permanent separate institutions because the School Committee remained unbending. Rallying around the firing of white teacher Jonathan Kozol, the parent organization, Concerned Gibson Parents, helped form the New School, in 1966, along with the Roxbury Community School. These schools drew middle-class blacks and whites from across Boston and modeled what a quality interracial education could look like. The Highland Park Free School, formed in 1968, drew only black children and had a decidedly more nationalistic focus.[50] But, as with METCO and Operation Exodus, these schools could only serve a small number of Boston's black children. The enrollment in the three schools in 1969 totaled 520 students,[51] which did not provide the system-wide solution many in the community desired.

These educational struggles in Boston complicate the prevalent dichotomy made between reformist and nationalist strategies. Because this struggle was led largely by women, many of whom were mothers, these interconnections have been difficult to see because nationalism has often been cast as the ideological purview of men. While many women came into this activism to improve their children's education, the ideologies that drove their work focused broadly on justice and self-determination for the black community as a whole. They were taking matters into their own hands— whether it was to organize and pay for a bus or to set up an alternative school. And they moved between strategies in an attempt to address the systemic issues of educational inequality. As Ruth Batson declared in 1965, "We intend to fight with every means at our disposal to ensure the future of our children."[52] These acts of self-determination or separation were not at odds with advocating for desegregation. They would do both. Jackson elaborated,

> I don't think I fit any of the labels ... but I do know that I believe, if you know, the history of our project in the sixties, was not to integrate the kids into the Boston public schools. We were really about the business of upgrading the quality of education our kids were getting and we didn't give a damn where it took place. One thing we knew, it was not taking place in Roxbury. ... At that point, the majority of the resources, the real, tangible resources, that we felt made at least a crack, or afforded an opportunity for a dent in the future ... was not going to be found in Roxbury.[53]

Activists in Boston strategically used a range of tactics in their struggles with the School Committee. *The Bay State Banner,* an independent black newspaper founded in 1965 to provide an independent voice for issues important to the black community, made educational issues and the varying ideologies and approaches in the fight with the School Committee a key topic in its coverage.

In the late 1960s and early 1970s, growing frustration among black students led to the creation of the Black Student Federation, the Black Students Alliance, and the Black Student Union. In January and February of 1971, the Black Student Union organized a citywide boycott to protest racial segregation. Demonstrations and strikes erupted at many city high schools as black students asserted their right to wear dashikis and learn the history of black peoples. They had five demands: Recruit black teachers, recruit black guidance counselors, commission an independent study of racial patterns in the city's schools, end harassment of black students, and grant amnesty to all striking students. Their demands reveal how intertwined integrationist and nationalist strategies were. These students fought for the right to wear dashikis and also pressed for a study of racial patterns within the school system and the hiring of more black teachers (clearly aware of the difficulty the community had been having in establishing these concerns with the School Committee). Many of their demands were similar to those that the NAACP had presented to the School Committee in 1963. The Black Educators' Alliance, the organization of black teachers, endorsed the student strikes. Black teachers had also organized a one-day sick-out in 1969, protesting the disproportionately small numbers of black staff in Boston's schools.[54] These "militant" tactics and "nationalist" movements still focused on issues of segregation within BPS.

Ultimately, seeing little other recourse, parents, through the NAACP, sued the School Committee in federal court. According to Cass, who was still active with the NAACP though no longer the president, "We couldn't get the desegregation any other way. ... It was just a suit, brought to open it up and let the court know that we still want it done."[55] When the Racial Imbalance Act passed in 1965, there were 46 imbalanced schools (schools that were more than 50 percent nonwhite) in Boston; by 1970, there were 63.[56] The School Committee's blatant disregard of the law—as well as of the quality of education offered to black students—had left the organization with little option other than a federal lawsuit.[57] In 1973, for example, the School Committee willingly gave up $65 million in state and federal funds rather than desegregate the schools.[58]

On June 21, 1974, Federal Judge W. Arthur Garrity ordered the Boston School Committee to begin desegregation. The movement had created the climate for this decision. As Tahi Mottl argues in her study of Boston, "The Garrity decision was an end product of 'public opinion' created over a decade of conflict."[59] Garrity's meticulous legal findings[60] cited overcrowding and underutilization in Boston's schools, the use of districting to preserve segregation, the creation of a dual system of secondary education, the use of less qualified and lower paid teachers to predominantly black schools, and the restricting of black teachers largely to black schools[61] as *intentional* segregation and cause for legal action.[62] In short, as blacks had argued for decades, this legal decision unequivocally dismantled the idea that racial patterns within Boston's schools had just happened; rather, the segregated nature of Boston's schools had been supported and exacerbated by the political, administrative, and legal structures within the city. Rejecting the School Committee's argument that school segregation resulted from neighborhood segregation and not from their actions,[63] Garrity held that the School Committee had engaged in deliberate segregation and thus it must be eradicated.[64] The plan, beginning the following September, called for 23 of the 65 unbalanced schools to be corrected through busing and for the feeder system, which fed black students into high school in ninth grade and white students in tenth grade, to be eliminated. Despite the popular belief that the judge was forcing his own ideas on the city, Garrity did not come up with Phase 1 of the plan, to be implemented in September, but relied on one that had come out of the litigation around the Racial Imbalance Act in the Massachusetts courts.[65]

The multifaceted social movement that led to this decision is hardly to be found in most accounts of Boston's struggles. Indeed, this struggle was led largely by women such as Ruth Batson, Ellen Jackson, Betty Johnson, Melnea Cass, and Muriel Snowden but most accounts quote men in the few places they acknowledge the black community.[66] The head of the NAACP during Boston's desegregation was former city council member and long-time activist Thomas Atkins. In most of the media coverage of the time, he is the only black person quoted and just sporadically, treated more as a representative of the black community than someone determining the action. The erasure of women, and of black community efforts, more generally, depicts blacks in Boston as recipients of the court's largesse rather than the organizing force that made the court take up the issue in the first place. That this was a grassroots struggle organized largely by local women—with the most charismatic leader being a woman—does not fit with prevalent conceptions of what the black freedom struggle looked like. Even as scholars have begun to foreground the organizing and leadership roles of Southern women activists like Ella Baker, Fannie Lou Hamer, Septima Clark, Diane Nash, and Ruby Doris Smith Robinson, these women still exist alongside Martin Luther King, Jr., Stokely Carmichael, Robert Moses, Julian Bond, and Ralph Abernathy. And thus, lacking these prominent male figures, Boston's movement has a hard time fitting within prevailing movement paradigms.

Accounts of desegregation spend little time on the activities of the black community during this period. Freedom House, referred to as the "Black Pentagon" during desegregation, was central to these efforts.[67] Troubled by the conditions of the neighborhood, Muriel and Otto Snowden began Freedom House in 1950 as a neighborhood improvement association, composed predominantly of middle-class blacks. They started a job preparation workshop for high school students and worked to press for better city services and police protection for Roxbury. Securing its own building in 1952, Freedom House sought to add a community voice on issues of urban renewal and pressure the city to invest in the needs of Roxbury residents.[68] Through this work, Freedom House evolved into a meeting house and community center.[69] In late 1973, the Freedom House Institute on Schools and Education was formed to work with parents and students to oversee the desegregation process.[70] Ellen Jackson became the director of this new project—and helped coordinate efforts within the black community to prepare for desegregation. According to Jackson, "The mood in the black community was one of confusion, concern, and fear because the elected officials during that summer of 1974 ... were very often making statements that this would not happen."[71] Batson, who at that time was working at Boston University as Director of Consultation and Education,[72] developed a program that would train people to work with the kids going to these schools. Funded through the federal government, this program taught individuals from various local groups what to do on the buses, how to deal with white harassment, and how to work with the kids after school.

Freedom House set up a hotline that operated "almost twenty four hours a day," according to Jackson, for parents to call about desegregation.

They received hundreds of calls before school began. Along with the Roxbury Multi-Service Center and the Lena Park Community Development Corporation, they formed a coalition to protect white children being bused into black schools and to support black children going into white schools. Part of their role at Freedom House was to get young people to talk about their anger and to channel their anger away from violence. After school began and violence broke out in the city, parents decided that they could not rely on the city to protect their children and would have to protect them themselves. They formed groups to accompany the buses. Freedom House also protected black students legally: According to Batson, "We would let the parents know that there were people on their side whatever their kid did."[73] Without the support network they established, a support network that had hardly been recognized, the desegregation of BPS would have been even more rocky.

While white violence received much of the media attention, pro-desegregation meetings, rallies, and marches turned out significant support but little mainstream media coverage. Decrying the violence infecting the city, black Communist activist Angela Davis spoke at a packed workshop in October: "The question is not that of busing but a developing trend of racism. There must be social equality for all Americans."[74] The presence of Angela Davis at a pro-desegregation event shows the ways that Boston's desegregation was supported by a broad spectrum of the black community as a necessary step for profound social change. Freedom House also organized an "assembly for justice" in early October, bringing together a coalition of black community groups. On November 30, 1974, Coretta Scott King led a march of 2,500 people, and two weeks later, 12,000 people marched in support of desegregation. The NAACP continued to press the racial issues behind the resistance to desegregation. On May 17, 1975 nearly 40,000 marched to show their public—and organized—support for desegregation. Ellen Jackson explained the need to counter the prevailing view of the city's desegregation, "We wanted to show Boston that there are a number of people who have fought for busing, some for over 20 years. We hoped to express the concerns of many people who have not seen themselves, only seeing the anti-busing demonstrations in the media." Jackson's comment reveals the ways that black organizers struggled to keep the issue of racial justice in the public view and how media attention to white resistance shaped the ways that desegregation would subsequently be understood. Christine Rossell's study of the *Boston Globe* has shown that the media's focus on anti-desegregation whites and desegregation-related conflicts led the public to have an overinflated sense of the costs and problems with desegregation and thus were more likely to oppose it.[75]

Most work on Boston has focused on the white resistance movement that developed in the wake of Garrity's decision. After the court order, Louise Day Hicks, who had left the School Committee for a seat on the city council, began organizing various factions of white parents in hopes of derailing desegregation. She and a group of parents founded a group called Restore Our Alienated Rights (ROAR), which called on white parents to refuse to let their children go to school and held numerous rallies from July to September to demonstrate their resistance to desegregation. These rallies drew the support of the School Committee, many teachers and police officers, and most of the Boston City Council. The boycott, demonstrations, and verbal and physical harassment of pro-desegregation black and white Bostonians continued when school began. The start of school provoked some of the most angry and violent demonstrations against desegregation in the nation's history. Buses were stoned, children attacked, and mobs of whites demonstrated their opposition across the city.

Yet, in contrast to most scholarship on Southern freedom struggles and some research on other Northern cities which also analyze in detail white resistance, most books on Boston's desegregation have been more sympathetic to the actions and perspectives of those whites who resisted "busing."[76] Ronald Formisano characterizes the genre best when he describes the aim of his book, *Boston Against Busing: Race, Class, and Ethnicity in the 1960s and 1970s:* "I have tried to portray organized anti-busing with understanding, and from what is a perspective hitherto unexplored. ... [This book] is not essentially about blacks but about whites."[77] Hardly unexplored, this perspective is shared by most authors who also focus on "understanding" white resistance. Their attempts to excuse white Boston's overtly racialized notions about busing, community, and entitlement—as Ronald Formisano writes, "thousands of decent, moderate whites across the city cannot be said to have been racists"[78]—reflect the problematic assumption that racism did not pervade the Northern consciousness as it did the South's. By de-emphasizing the centrality of race in favor of working-class political alienation in the development of ROAR, these authors obscure the ways race and class were inseparable and how "the wages of whiteness" motivated the actions of anti-desegregation whites.[79] They focus on community control, the preservation of neighborhood schools, the loss of political power in the city, and resistance to outsiders of working-class South Bostonians as the impetus behind this resistance to desegregation—eliding white ethnic working-class alienation with political powerlessness with opposition to desegregation. Thus, this literature naturalizes, rather than investigates, why racism becomes the chosen response for many politically alienated working-class whites.

Long-held stereotypes of black people were at the heart of ROAR's movement. According to one white father, "The question is, Am I going to send my young daughter, who is budding into the flower of womanhood, into Roxbury on a bus?"[80] The black students desegregating South Boston High were met by a mob of whites throwing rocks, bottles, eggs, and rotten tomatoes and yelling "Niggers Go Home."[81] One student, Phyllis Ellison, who attended school that day, explained, "And there were people on the corners holding bananas like we were apes, monkeys. 'Monkeys get out, get them out of our neighborhood. We don't want you in our schools.'"[82] One white mother, Connie Maffei, who chose to send her children to school, explained the violent reaction, "There's a general depressed feeling here that we don't count anymore. Everyone has a feeling it's a black city. Nothing is going our way. Even our husbands are coming home from work saying that every promotion goes to a black, Spanish-speaking or woman."[83]

Most writers on Boston portray white resistance as a working-class phenomenon. Yet, while working-class South Boston received the bulk of media attention, the middle-class neighborhoods known as the High Wards—Hyde Park, Roslindale, and West Roxbury—also experienced significant racial violence. The first race riot at school happened not at South Boston High but at Hyde Park High School on September 19, 1974. In October, black students were chased out of a Roslindale restaurant by a crowd of whites, and two men were arrested for carrying Molotov cocktails outside of Hyde Park High School.[84] With the media focus on South Boston portraying resistance to desegregation as a working-class movement as opposed to one that found support in working-class and middle-class neighborhoods in the city, many whites in South Boston reacted angrily against institutions like the *Boston Globe*. They resented the ways their actions were singled out when resistance was happening throughout the city. The Boston Teacher's Union and the Police Patrolmen's Association committed money to appeal Garrity's decision and adamantly opposed desegregation. Open in their opposition to desegregation, City Council members Louise Day Hicks, Dapper O'Neill, Christopher Ianella, and Patrick McDonough each displayed the letters R-O-A-R in their window to spell the acronym of the anti-desegregation organization and let ROAR use their chambers to meet.[85] ROAR leader Louise Day Hicks was often pictured as working class, even though she herself was an attorney and former teacher, and her father was also an attorney.[86] Thus, to portray white resistance as a working-class movement ignores its middle-class base and minimizes the benefits whites across the city accrued from segregation. Making it a story of the working class takes attention away from the systemic basis and acceptance of racial privilege across the city: The racism becomes parochial rather than ingrained (and thus not a central battleground of the civil rights struggle like Selma or Birmingham).

While opposition to school desegregation was framed as opposition to busing, this issue was largely a smoke screen. The term anti-busing (or forced busing) used by the media and politicians at the time—and picked up wholesale by scholars—is a disingenuous description of the opponents of integration. As civil rights activist Julian Bond pointed out at a rally in Boston in 1974, "It's not the bus, it's us."[87] By 1972, there were few neighborhood schools in Boston. Indeed, by the 1960s, school buses were linked to quality education across the North, and certain kinds of cross-neighborhood mixing were understood as a way to ensure quality education.[88] Thirty thousand Boston students were being bused to school, including 50 percent of all middle schoolers and 85 percent of all high schoolers.[89] In fact, thousands of white students who were not ensconced in all-white neighborhoods were bused past black schools to all white schools—traveling farther in order to maintain these segregated schools.[90] Thus, part of the reason that the desegregation remedy included two-way busing was because busing was already so prevalent in the city. Garrity also argued in his decision that it was the actions of the School Committee—"[t]he harvest of these years of obstruction and of maintenance of segregated schools"—that made busing essential for desegregation.[91] Tellingly, the bulk of the racial harassment and violence of the "anti-busing" movement focused on the high schools, despite the fact that the overwhelming majority of high school students were bused before Garrity's decision. Garrity also directly rejected the School Committee's rhetoric of preserving neighborhood schools. The judge cited extensive busing, open enrollment, magnet schools, citywide schools, and widespread high school feeder programs (all of which were already going on in BPS) as "antithetical" to a neighborhood school system.

To frame resistance as a class-based ethnic movement against busing and for neighborhood schools, then, is to ignore the widespread existence of busing in Boston before desegregation. However, the language of "neighborhood control" and "forced busing" provided a socially acceptable rhetoric to harness many whites' virulent opposition to integration at the time.[92] Evidenced in the election and presidency of Richard Nixon, this covert racial language was proving successful in turning back the progress of the civil rights movement, producing racial results without actually speaking about race. And the labels "anti-busing" and "neighborhood control" have been picked up in problematic ways in the historiography, serving to distinguish Northern resistance to desegregation from Southern.[93] Glossing over the linkages between Northern and Southern opposition deracializes Boston's resistance. Sounding arbitrary and antidemocratic, the phrase "forced busing" turns the issue away from racial equity to pity for the small schoolchildren being forced by a judge to ride hours on a bus. "Neighborhood schools," conversely, brings to mind a close-knit, small-town (if imaginary) America that diverts attention away from who gets to be part of the neighborhood in the first place.

At the same time, most accounts of Boston do not fully investigate whites in the city who did not oppose integration. Many schools, in fact, desegregated peacefully, yet few of these white supporters find their way into books. The ROAR boycott failed in most schools, with 66 percent of students showing up for school. Eithu Greenwood Elementary School, which had been nearly all white, opened its doors to five buses of black children from Mattapan and Dorchester. The principal, Paul Donovan, boarded each bus with a cheery, "Hi you all look handsome and beautiful today."[94] The Jeremiah Burke High School, a formerly black high school, was also desegregated peacefully and with little incident in 1974.[95] Staff and students found it to be an resounding success.[96]

South Boston mother Tracy Amalfitano sent her two boys to school, despite the anger it caused within her South Boston community. "The community basically was talking about kids not being safe going into the minority communities, but because I went in and out every day myself, I knew that they were safe there. ... [M]y concern was that they were safe when they got off, when my older son got off the bus in his own community." Amalfitano's efforts were unsupported by local politicians: "Political leaders were meeting quite routinely with those that boycotted. But for those of us around the city that decided to support the desegregation order, it was very much a lonely place for a long time."[97]

Some whites from South Boston were willing to meet informally with blacks to form an ad hoc biracial council since community opposition had prevented constituting a formal one. One who did was James O'Sullivan, a former opponent of desegregation who found some of the first demonstrations horrifying. "It made me ashamed to be from South Boston, ashamed to be a Catholic."[98] He chose to serve on the Roxbury-South Boston Parents' Biracial Council and faced hate mail and violence from whites as well. ROAR was extremely effective at canvassing neighborhoods, targeting whites who went along with integration.[99] Many white pro-busing mothers would talk and meet in secret, afraid of what their families and friends would do if they found out. One mother explained, "ROAR doesn't represent all white people."[100] While she did not tell her husband about her meetings, she was committed to continuing them. "The Black students face quite a bit of abuse but they have as much right to go to school here as my kids do. ... I can feel what the Black parents are going through now, and I know we have the same concern for our children."[101] Ignoring the views of whites who went along with desegregation naturalizes the racialized notions of ethnicity, entitlement, and neighborhood of the whites who resisted integration. Leaving out white supporters and the reasons that they did go along with desegregation homogenizes white working-class identity and goes far in making it "understandable" that many whites violently opposed integration. Ultimately, then, the history of Boston's desegregation becomes the story of the violence of those who resisted it.

Despite the extensive organizing that led up to Judge Garrity's decision, most authors frame this complex social movement 25 years in the making as the result of a benevolent white judge instead of an organized black community. This was a fight for educational justice—not busing—and desegregation was one of many strategies employed by community activists in their attempts to secure it. By ignoring that it was black people's actions that prompted change within Boston's public schools, many writers downplay the profound racial inequalities in the city's schools and extreme prejudice in the city at large that fueled the push for integration in the first place. The limited treatment of Boston's educational struggles not only constricts our historical memory but also impoverishes our understanding of the present.[102] As Batson herself explained, this has facilitated the backsliding in educational gains in recent years and prevented a continued push for desegregation and real educational equity.[103] "We've gone right back to the 1960s. ... The whole issue of racism has been set aside. This is why all of the setbacks are happening because people are not exercising their right to be indignant."[104] A more thorough examination of Boston's history reveals the inadequacy of terming Northern segregation de facto. Such a characterization does not adequately foreground the institutional and legal sanction that segregation had in the North, and in Boston, in particular.

Blamed for the violence of those who resisted it, Northern school desegregation and Boston's, in particular, has come to be seen as foolhardy, disruptive, and ultimately unnecessary. In contrast, Southern desegregation is viewed as an important and long-overdue movement that is, if anything, made more righteous by the violent backlash against it. Southern activists are remembered for their long and courageous histories in the fight against racial injustice. Boston's black activists, on the other hand, are criticized for their ineffectiveness—for their mistaken and naive desire to get next to white people—or simply ignored.[105] White resistors, conversely, capture the historical record, seen as working-class ethnics denied political power in the city who struggled to preserve their neighborhoods. The fight for school integration in Boston was, ultimately, a fight for racial equity in Boston's public schools; to remember it as a fight against busing is to capitulate to the terms set by anti-desegregationists themselves.

Notes

1. An earlier and different version of this paper was published in the fall 2001 issue of *Radical History Review* (issue 81): 61–93. I would like to thank Adina Back, Matthew Countryman, Paisley Currah, Scott Dexter, Robin Kelley, Earl Lewis, Alejandra Marchevsky, Karen Miller, Komozi Woodard, my students at Brooklyn College, my three University of Michigan UROP research assistants: Jacqueline Woods, Nikkela Byrd, and Robyn Stanton, and my family for their insights, contributions and support of this work.

2. While this paper focuses on school desegregation campaigns in the 1960s and 1970s, black Bostonians have a long history of activism around schools. Blacks petitioned for their own school in 1781, and in 1806 the city agreed to help fund an existing school in the African Meetinghouse. This was rebuilt in 1835 to become the Abiel Smith School. Having trouble sustaining the Smith School, blacks turned to pressuring the city to allow blacks into white schools. In 1855, the legislature passed a bill disallowing racial and religious distinctions for enrolling students in public schools. Emmett Buell, *School Desegregation and Defended Neighborhoods* (Lexington: Lexington Books, 1982), 59–60.

3. Some examples include Robert Weisbrot, *Freedom Bound* (New York: W. W. Norton, 1990), Adam Fairclough, *Better Day Coming* (New York: Viking, 2001), William Chafe, *The Unfinished Journey* (New York: Oxford University Press, 1999), Philip Klinkner, *The Unsteady March* (Chicago: University of Chicago Press, 1999), and the *Eyes on the Prize* documentary television series I and II (Blackside Productions, aired on PBS).

4. Fairclough, xi.

5. According to traditional accounts, part of the successes of the Southern movement came from inducing the support, however tentative, of the federal government. See, for example, Weisbrot's *Freedom Bound*. Given Gerald Ford's public disagreement with Judge Garrity's order for integration, blacks in Boston were up against the intransigence not only of local forces but also of the highest executive in the nation.

6. Despite sustained organizing throughout the 1960s, Boston's desegregation did not happen until 1974–76, a full 20 years after the Supreme Court had overturned segregated schools in the *Brown* v. *Board of Education* decision.

7. Most works portray whites as victims of liberal (suburban) good intention, and these authors see their job as contextualizing white resistance to busing as a class-based ethnic struggle. Such works include Anthony Lukas's *Common Ground* (New York: Alfred A. Knopf, 1985), Alan Lupo's *Liberty's Chosen Home* (Boston: Little, Brown and Company, 1977), George Metcalf's *From Little Rock to Boston* (Westport, Conn.: Greenwood Press, 1983), Ronald Formisano's *Boston Against Busing: Race, Class, and Ethnicity in the 1960s and 1970s* (Chapel Hill: University of North Carolina Press, 1991), and Michael Ross and William Berg's *"I Respectfully Disagree with the Judge's Order": The Boston School Desegregation Controversy* (Washington, D.C.: University Press of America,

1981), which portray blacks largely as passive actors in the drama. Even Steven Taylor's recent book, *Desegregation in Boston and Buffalo: The Influence of Local Leaders* (Albany: State University of New York Press, 1998), which claims to examine the role of local leaders focuses decisively on white resistance.

8. A clear example is James Patterson's recent study of the effects of *Brown* v. *Board of Education:* "Starting in 1973, the struggle consumed the city for many years, generally (as in Little Rock in 1957 and in many other places) pitting working-class whites against wealthier white people—'limousine liberals' to their foes—and some blacks." James Patterson, *Brown v. Board of Education: A Civil Rights Milestone and Its Troubled Legacy* (New York: Oxford University Press, 2001), 173

9. As historian Craig Wilder has written about New York, " Segregation was the initial stride of domination. The Central Brooklyn ghetto allowed white people to hoard social benefits while people of color became the primary consumers of social ills. Its residents underwrote the life chances of those outside its borders." Craig Wilder, *A Covenant with Color* (New York: Columbia University Press, 2000), 216.

10. Ruth Batson, telephone interview by author, 1991.

11. Ruth Hill, ed., *The Black Women Oral History Project* from The Arthur and Elizabeth Schlesinger Library on the History of Women in America (Westport, Conn.: Mechler, 1991), 117.

12. Brian Sheehan, *The Boston School Integration Dispute* (New York: Columbia University Press, 1984), 71–72.

13. Jon Hillson, *The Battle of Boston* (New York: Pathfinder Press, 1977), 65. Tahi Mottl, "Social Conflict and Social Movements: An Exploratory Study of the Black Community of Boston Attempting to Change the Boston Public Schools" (Ph.D. diss., Brandeis University, 1976), 174.

14. In much of the scholarship on Boston, because the lifelong organizing and leadership efforts of black activists are not explored, their actions seem to come out of nowhere.

15. Such widespread segregation was a relatively new phenomenon in Boston. The city's black population had hovered around 3 percent of the city's population until WWII. It was not until after the war that blacks began moving to the city in large numbers. By 1960, blacks made up nearly 10 percent of Boston's population and, by 1970, formed 16.3 percent of the population, an increase from 1940 to 1970 of 354 percent. Thus, while discriminatory treatment had plagued blacks in the city for centuries, it was during the period of 1940–1970 that the Boston School Committee expanded and solidified its system of grossly unequal schools for blacks and whites.

16. Henry Hampton, *Voices of Freedom* (New York: Bantam, 1990), 588–589.

17. One school with a capacity of 690 students had enrolled 1,043, while another with a 300 student limit had 634 students enrolled. "Racism and Busing in Boston: An Editorial Statement" *Radical America* 8.6 (November–December 1974): 11.

18. Ruth Batson, "Statement to the Boston School Committee" in *Eyes on the Prize Civil Rights Reader* (New York: Penguin, 1991), 598.

19. Along with these reports, Jonathan Kozol's award-winning *Death at an Early Age* (Boston: Houghton Mifflin, 1967) amply documented the poor conditions, administrative neglect, and substandard learning environment of black public schools. Kozol shared his classroom, which was actually the auditorium, with another teacher and fourth grade class.

20. Hill, 235.

21. Lupo, 142–143.

22. Batson, "Statement," 597–598.

23. Hampton, 589.

24. Batson concluded, "[W]e found out that this was an issue that was going to give their political careers stability for a long time to come" (Hampton, 589).

25. Ross and Berg, 49.

26. Civil rights leader Noel Day explained, "It is most important that we educate our children in how to participate in a democracy where you must dissent at times" (Sheehan, 65).

27. Hill, 350.

28. Ibid.

29. Lupo, 146–147.

30. This was a popular political message among white voters. Louise Day Hicks was decisively reelected in November 1963 to the School Committee with turnout higher than the previous mayor's election. "The people of Boston have given their answer to the de facto segregation question," she stated (Buell, 64–65).

31. Boston's activists saw their actions as part of the larger freedom struggle unfolding across the nation and wanted their fight to be seen as part of this national civil rights movement. It is interesting how these national campaigns take a back seat in the historiography.

32. Ross and Berg, 49; Sheehan, 70.

33. Carter explained his motivations for beginning a vigil that he vowed to continue until the law had been passed. "I was determined to complete what so many people were working and hoping for. I felt it was now my responsibility since so many were burnt out. ... I walked 21 hours a day and slept 3 hours a day (4 A.M. to 7 A.M.) I succumbed on the 54th day and was taken to St. Elizabeth Hospital for 10 days, then returned to my Vigil to complete the task before me 'Because It is Right.'" Ruth Batson, *A Chronology of the Educational Movement in Boston,* unpublished manuscript in Ruth Batson's papers, 2001-M194, Schlesinger Library, Radcliffe Institute (hereafter referred to as *Chronology*), 204.

34. During 1964, five racial imbalance bills were introduced to the Massachusetts legislature by black representatives from Boston to remedy the situation but were not taken seriously. It was not until a white senator, Beryl Cohen, introduced the sixth bill that racial imbalance became a legislative matter. Cohen had drafted the bill with advice from the NAACP and the Congress of Racial Equality.

35. Hill, 58.
36. According to Tahi Mottl, black parents' organizations emerged as movement bases and organizers in 1964. These include Boardman Parents, Concerned Gibson Parents, Roxbury-North Dorchester Parents Council, Parent Participation Project of the Alternative Schools, and the Change Committee.
37. The militant tactics of the Youth Council (particularly their use of civil disobedience and ties to suspected Communists) angered the national NAACP, and they lost their charter.
38. The NSM was formed in part because black parents were often denied access to home and school associations within BPS.
39. Teele, *Evaluating School Busing: Case Study of Operation Exodus* (New York: Praeger, 1973).
40. U.S. Commission, xiv; Taylor, 43–44.
41. Teele, 8.
42. Hill, 179.
43. Teele, 8, 23.
44. Black activists have been criticized in works like Lupo's *Liberty's Chosen Home* for focusing their efforts solely within the city, another example of how scholars have ignored the larger movement around Boston's desegregation.
45. Nicholas Paleologos, "Wrong Plan and Wrong Place," *The Boston Globe,* July 15, 1988.
46. By 1969, the state legislature took over the funding for METCO, and by 1972, the state was spending $2 million on METCO (Formisano, 38).
47. Buell, 85.
48. Batson, *Chronology,* Addendum 265a, 5.
49. For more in-depth treatment on the free schools, see Jonathan Kozol's *Free Schools* (Boston: Houghton Mifflin, 1972).
50. Mottl, 413–416.
51. Mottl, 491.
52. Hampton, 588.
53. Hill, 234–235.
54. Mottl, 387.
55. Hill, 352. Batson was still the chair of the Education Committee of the NAACP.
56. Mottl, 507.
57. Metcalf, 69; Formisano, 54. The number of racially imbalanced schools in BPS had increased since the act had passed from 46 to 67 percent (Lupo, 149).
58. *Time* (September 23, 1974): 29.
59. Mottl, 575–576.
60. The decision withstood numerous appeals all the way to the Supreme Court and was given a bar association award the next year. Robert Dentler and Marvin Scott, *Schools on Trial: An Inside Account of the Boston Desegregation Case* (Cambridge: ABT Books, 1981), 4.
61. In 81 of Boston's 201 schools, no black teachers had ever been assigned, and an additional 35 had only one black teacher (Metcalf, 201).

62. Despite this careful attention, Garrity was unwilling to look at the role Boston's suburbs played in the educational inequities and segregation black students faced—and would not consider a metro-wide solution.

63. As the Boston Bar Association noted, Garrity "concluded that the School Committee's actions over the past 10 years with respect to segregation in the schools may have helped to create the segregated residential patterns which the School Committee now sought to use in an attempt to justify the segregation found to exist in the schools. Even beyond that, Judge Garrity found that the School Committee 'with awareness of the racial segregation of Boston's neighborhoods, had deliberately incorporated that segregation in the school system.'" John Adkins, James R. McHugh, and Katherine Seay, *Desegregation: The Boston Orders and Their Origin* (Boston Bar Association Committee on Desegregation, August 1975), 22.

64. The Supreme Court had already weighed in on the matter of intentional segregation. For example, in a 1973 Colorado case, they ruled that there did not need to be a state law requiring separate schools for segregation to be intentional and thus a violation of the Equal Protection Clause.

65. As the Boston Bar Association noted, "The Plan which Judge Garrity ordered the School Committee to use as a temporary plan on June 21, 1974, thus was a plan wholly created by Massachusetts state agencies, a plan which the School Committee had been ordered a role in creating, and a plan which the Committee not only had been aware of for some time but also had been under orders to comply with for some time" (Adkins, McHugh, and Seay, 24).

66. Anthony Lukas, George Metcalf, Alan Lupo, Ronald Formisano, and Michael Ross and Alan Berg portray blacks as passive actors and all but deny the existence of black women in the fight.

67. Muriel Snowden had attended Radcliffe College and the New York School of Social Work but the Snowdens moved back to Boston in 1945 where Otto's family had lived for 70 years. The Snowdens chose to send their daughter Gail to a parochial school, St. Mary's. Muriel Snowden explained, "[W]hen we took our child out of the Boston public schools, we did not take ourselves out of the Boston public schools system despite that" (Hill, 62–63).

68. Ibid., 6. Some community members were critical of Freedom House's middle-class leadership and elite focus.

69. Muriel Snowden explained, "Freedom House in a sense represents the efforts of middle class black people to their own. And when I say their own, I mean all black people" (Hill, 68).

70. Hillson, 63.

71. Hampton, 599.

72. Batson was associate professor of psychiatry at Boston University from 1970 to 1986.

73. Batson interview, 1991.

74. *Bay State Banner,* October 10, 1974, 1.

75. Taylor, 85.

76. One of the best analyses of grassroots white resistance movements is Tom Sugrue's *The Origins of the Urban Crisis* (Princeton: Princeton University Press, 1996).

77. Formisano xiii, 4. Indeed this push to "understand" Northern whites' violent reactions diverges sharply with scholarship on the Southern freedom movements. Scholars such as Charles Payne, John Dittmar, Diane McWhorter, Howell Raines, Fred Powledge, and Aldon Morris, while looking carefully at white resistance, never seek the sympathetic understanding that some scholars of Boston have.

78. Formisano, xi.

79. It is interesting how whites in Boston are never called segregationists, while whites in Southern cities who attacked desegregation are. See also David Roediger's *The Wages of Whiteness* (New York: Verso, 1991) for a more extended exposition of how white working-class identity has long rested on ideas of racial superiority and the ways these ideas provide a psychic wage for working-class whites whose class position might make them natural allies with black workers. Michael MacDonald's memoir of growing up in South Boston makes a similar point, "We all were on food stamps but most of the jokes around town were about black people on welfare. The same thing with living in the projects and eating wellie cheese—those were black things." Michael MacDonald, *All Souls: A Family Story from Southie* (New York: Ballantine, 1999), 71.

80. *TIME* (September 23, 1974): 29.

81. "Boston: Echoes of Little Rock," *Newsweek* (September 23, 1974): 48.

82. Hampton, 600–601.

83. Benjamin Taylor, "Kids … the Real Heroes," *Boston Globe*, September 13, 1974.

84. Steven Taylor, 136–137.

85. Ibid., 78.

86. As Michael MacDonald writes, "People said she was from Southie but she didn't look like she'd been through much. Her father was a judge and she lived in a big beachfront house in City Point, but she was okay with us. 'She's the only one sticking up for us,' someone said" (MacDonald, 75).

87. Hillson, 89.

88. As the U.S. Civil Rights Commission observed in 1972, the school bus has been a "friendly figure in the North" for 50 years.

89. Dentler and Scott, 16, 28.

90. Schools were not located in the center of the district but "near the edges of irregular districts" (Taylor, 49).

91. Adkins, McHugh, and Seay, 28.

92. Many scholars focus on this idea of neighborhood schools and opposition to busing without grappling with why before desegregation whites in the city had been comfortable with busing and certain forms of neighborhood mixing.

93. It is worthy of further study how the lexicon used to describe Northern civil rights struggles and Northern racism differs from that describing Southern ones.

94. John Kifner, "Violence Mars Busing in Boston," *New York Times*, September 13, 1974.

95. Students who spoke before the U.S. Commission on Civil Rights gave positive reports on the first year at the Burke. One young black woman explained, "As the year progressed, we talked and we got to understanding, and we found, like, a common ground" (Formisano, 205).

96. In his graduation address, the Burke valedictorian explained, "What struck me the most was that the school was practically new to most of the student body. . . . But everyone opened his friendship to one another. . . . And now, not only can we say that we are proud of the Jeremiah Burke High School, but we can also say that the high school is proud of us" (U.S. Commission, 82).

97. Hampton, 606.

98. Hillson, 106.

99. Indeed, Amalfitano's windows were broken, her car smashed, and her sister's beauty salon destroyed as a result of her public support for desegregation (Taylor, 140).

100. Hillson, 109–110.

101. Ibid.

102. Indeed, I would argue that the ways that Boston's desegregation has been historicized has led not only to negative ideas about, and an abandonment of, desegregation but of a commitment to quality public education in the city in general (outside of the academic magnet schools).

103. Garrity's plan temporarily alleviated some of the worst segregation in BPS (Buell, 157). Building renovations, greater minority parent involvement in schools, and better and more merit-based teacher recruitment were improvements that resulted from desegregation. The case also succeeded in introducing bilingual education in BPS on a widespread level. Finally, there were definite gains in black school performance initially following desegregation (Dentler and Scott, 218). Louise Day Hicks lost her seat on the City Council in 1977, and John O'Bryant became the first black person elected to the school committee in the twentieth century.

104. Batson interview, 1991.

105. As Ruth Batson explained, "Even now when I talk to a lot of people, they say we were wrong in pushing for desegregation. But there was a very practical reason to do it in those days. We knew that there was more money being spent in certain schools, white schools—not all of them, but in certain white schools—than there was being spent in black schools. So therefore, our theory was move our kids into those schools where they're putting all of the resources so that they can get a better education" (Hampton, 590).

Chapter 6

Religion and Radicalism: The Reverend Albert B. Cleage, Jr., and the Rise of Black Christian Nationalism in Detroit

Angela D. Dillard

We went through certain stages getting here. It didn't just happen overnight. ... It took time. A whole lot of people worked for years on this. It's a long way from Dr. King in Montgomery to Twelfth Street [in Detroit].

—*Reverend Albert B. Cleage, Jr.*[1]

On Easter Sunday, 1967, the Reverend Albert B. Cleage, Jr., rechristened Detroit's Central Congregational Church as the Shrine of the Black Madonna, and formally launched his ecumenical Black Christian Nationalism movement. With an overflow crowd and with much fanfare—including the unveiling of a seven-foot painting of the Black Madonna and Christ-child[2]—Cleage dedicated himself and his congregation to the cause of redefining Christianity and bringing the church in line with the political logic of black nationalism. As one of the founders of black theology, his actions were guided, in part, by the notion of a black Christ as a black revolutionary, and of a (new) black church as the cornerstone of a (new) black nation. "We reject the traditional concept of church," Cleage explained:

In its place we will build a Black Liberation movement which derives its basic religious insights from African spirituality, its character from African communalism, and its revolutionary direction from Jesus, the Black Messiah. We will make Black Man's struggle for power and survival. We will build a Black communal society which can protect the minds and bodies of Black men, women and children everywhere.[3]

Calling for community control of institutions in the inner city, as well as for self-determination in economics, politics, and, above all, religion, Cleage and his cohorts offered what they claimed was the only viable alternative to the "moribund" framework of the post-WWII and Southern-based civil rights movement.

The desire to mark a radical break between the movement's Southern, reformist past and its Northern, radical future had been on Cleage's ideological agenda at least since 1963. In that rather tumultuous year, which, as I argue below, was a major turning point in the history of Detroit's movement, Cleage was vocally insisting that "[i]n the North, the Black Revolt of 1963 departed radically from the pattern established in the South." In Northern centers such as Detroit, he continued, a "new kind of 'Black Nationalism' began to emerge," as one disillusioned with integration "began to look for another way—an independent course he could chart and travel alone."[4] And by alone, Cleage meant without the assistance (and, more pointed, the leadership) of whites, since his evolving political theology demanded repentance from those guilty of an overidentification with their "white oppressors." They must declare, Cleage sermonized,

I have been an Uncle Tom and I repent. I have served the interests of my white oppressor all my life because in ignorance I identified with him and wanted to be like him, to be accepted by him, to integrate with him. I loved my oppressor more than I loved myself. I have betrayed my Black brothers and sisters to serve the interests of the oppressor. ...[5]

Along with such demands for cultural and psychological reorientation, in the Reverend Cleage's writings, speeches, and sermons from this period, there is a constant invocation of the radical newness of his project—a language and rhetorical strategy more commonly found among the young. But Cleage's critique was not structured exclusively or even primarily in generational terms. Rather, his call to action was based in what he saw conceived of as a rupture, or major departure, from the patterns established in the past, in general, and from the patterns established in the South, in particular. Foreshadowing one of the most pervasive strains of the movement's historiography (and perhaps mythology), Cleage was a proponent of the proposition that the movement underwent a radical transformation in Northern industrial centers such as Detroit in the second half of the

1960s. Decades later, debates over the nature of this "radicalization" via an embrace of black nationalism and Black Power remain rife within the histories of the movement.[6] Did the black nationalist turn precipitate the destruction of the movement, or did it breathe new life and vigor into the struggle? Was there always an organic link between the Northern and the Southern branches of the movement, or did they develop along separate and distinct lines only to come into conflict with each other in the late 1960s? Was it, in fact, "a long way from Dr. King in Montgomery to Twelfth Street" in the heart of Detroit's burgeoning black ghetto?

In this brief essay, I hope to use the experiences of Reverend Cleage and others to begin to formulate a more nuanced picture of the movement's political and intellectual history—one that, ironically, necessitates a critical evaluation of Cleage's own claim to radical newness as well as his insistence on a North-South divide. The physical distance between Alabama and Detroit might be substantial, but the two locations are bound together—by patterns of migration and travel, by history, by culture, by family ties, and by mutual identification. Further, I want to emphasize Cleage's and Black Christian Nationalism's place in the long history of the Black Freedom movement in America, while foregrounding an indebtedness to the particular history of political and religious radicalism in twentieth-century Detroit. The introduction of "Black Power" into the national movement's public vocabulary may have shocked the nation in 1966, but the ideas implied by the slogan had been percolating in various activist communities in the city for years. Cleage was simply part of a gradual shift in ideas and ideologies that moved from the margins to the center by the late 1960s, and this is one of the reasons I selected him as a focal point for this analysis. Not only was he deeply involved in some of the most exciting developments in Detroit from the early 1960s onward, but he was also schooled, in various ways, by an older generation of ministers, labor unionists, and political militants whose activism structured the movement's earlier phases. Hence, he is an ideal figure to provide at least a thumbnail sketch of intergenerational patterns of both change and continuity within the various "phases" of Detroit's civil rights movement from the 1930s to the 1960s. And, last but certainly not least, Cleage is recommended because of his religious orientation.

As part of the coterie of individuals who embraced Black Power and black nationalism in the mid-to-late 1960s, Cleage's views were not entirely unique. But what makes his contribution notable and compelling was the theological foundations he constructed to substantiate and justify his call for nationalism, cultural separatism, and self-determination. For Cleage, who had previously supported the goals of integration and nonviolence, came to believe that one of the chief problems with King (and, by extension, the Southern-based movement overall) was rooted in political theology. More specifically, he blamed the religious-political perspective tied to the Social Gospel: a product of early twentieth-century religious liberalism that viewed human nature as essentially good and human society as inherently malleable. What was needed to counter this overly optimistic vision of man and society, Cleage insisted, was an infusion of "realism" of the type proffered by neoorthodox theologians such as Reinhold Niebuhr.

At first glance, this may appear to be nothing more than an overly technical theological dispute. Yet, it resonated with the *political* fights that shaped Cleage and his ideas about Black Christian Nationalism. "I read Niebuhr for a time," Cleage explained, "especially as an antidote to the social gospel." For Cleage and others who adopted a similar critique, neoorthodoxy was seen as a "realistic" remedy to the excessive "utopianism" of the Social Gospel. Where the latter held out the possibility that the Kingdom of God could be created on earth, neoorthodoxy depicted this doctrine as an unrealistic conceit. Neoorthodoxy also took exception to the conception of human nature on which much of the Social Gospel was said to be based. Individuals might be able to achieve a morally grounded existence, but morality is impossible as the foundation of the social order. Social change, moreover, is effected not through moral suasion or by God working through history toward perfection, as the old Social Gospel tended to assert, but by organized power meeting organized power. No amount of indulgence in millennial hope could hide the essential fact that the relationships between social groups are based in inequality and coercion, masked by ideology.[7]

There can be no "beloved community," no interracial brotherhood, in a world where social groups clash and individuals create a hell for each other. "This creating hell for each other," Cleage explained with reference to Jean Paul Sartre's *No Exit,* "is terribly true, though people wish to think something else." Hence, for Cleage, who stubbornly chose to ignore the fact that King was also influenced by Niebuhr, King failed to be sufficiently realistic—not only about human nature and society but also about race and race relations. "We've got to make sure the definitions of human nature and society are sound," he argued. "This was the problem of Dr. King. He was not realistic. You can hope for change, but it must be predicated on reality, not what we dream of." Yet Cleage's critique seems in some ways less about King, himself (thus, perhaps, his refusal to credit the complexities of King's theology), than Cleage's derogatory view of King's overly complacent white supporters. To all the "white liberals," who in Cleage's eyes were more enamored with King's dream than with the realities of power, he suggested that they "ought to all go back and read Niebuhr because they react when you say that all whites are part of immoral society."[8]

Although Cleage drew heavily on the work of theologians such as Niebuhr, his vision of Black Christian Nationalism developed at the nexus of academic theology, a rejection of integration and King's beloved community, as well as the shifting circumstances in Detroit and across the nation. While much as been written, both positive and negative, about the advent of Black Power and black nationalism in the mid-to-late 1960s, the generative role of religion remains relatively underexplored. Unlike studies of the movement's Southern centers, the role of religion in developing and maintaining cultures of protests tends not to be accorded the same degree of attention in Northern activist communities. Perhaps this has something to do with the biased view that Northern activism was more "advanced" and "rational," whereas the Southern trends remained more "backward" and "emotional." Such an unsupportable view adds nothing to our understanding of how activism was conducted in locations such as Detroit where, at almost every turn, religion—along with race and labor—was intimately intertwined.

"Detroit has a reputation as a city of good preachers"—so said the Reverend C. L. Franklin, pastor of Detroit's New Bethel Baptist Church for nearly three decades and once a leading figure in the city's civil rights community.[9] By the time Franklin relocated to Detroit in 1954, the city had also amassed a formidable history of political activism among its clergy and members of its religious communities. As many histories of Detroit have at least alluded to, politically engaged ministers were in the forefront of every movement for social change and social justice that structured so much of the city's twentieth-century history: from industrial unionism in the 1930s, to the civil (and economic) rights movement of the 1940s and 1950s, to the rise of Black Power and black nationalism in the 1960s.[10] Detroit was also, it is worth recalling, the birthplace of the Nation of Islam. Even after the shift of its home base to Chicago, the Nation of Islam continued to exert an influence within the city's various communities, and, as I discuss in more detail below, the Nation of Islam's ideology helped to mold Cleage's vision of Black Christian Nationalism.

With this broader historical context very much in mind, I want to suggest that one way of writing religion back into the story is to focus on figures such as Cleage who drew in equal measures on religious perspectives and political and cultural strategies to address the pressing social problems in a local and national arena. That Cleage was a minister with a seminary education matters to the story I want to tell about his life and his activism. That he was raised in Detroit and returned to the city to satisfy his dream of founding his own church is also key. For Cleage was shaped by that distinctive urban industrial center where religion and politics and labor went hand in hand. Moreover, Cleage and Black Christian Nationalism are deeply embedded in a long local (and national) tradition of reconfiguring the black church to render it more politically and socially relevant to the lives and struggles and desires of African Americans. This tradition has not, however, been without moments of tension and conflict.

Laying the Foundation: Religion, Labor, and the Early Civil Rights Movement in Detroit

It is commonly held that the black church is the premiere independent institution created and sustained by African Americans, for African Americans. Yet, at key moments in the history of political radicalism in Detroit, the independence of the church was poignantly questioned and hotly disputed. It is worth briefly reviewing some of these older debates, particularly those to which a young Albert Cleage was witness. Cleage was born in Indianapolis in 1911 and moved with his family to Detroit while still an infant. The first of seven children reared by Dr. Albert B. Cleage, Sr., and wife, Pearl Reed Cleage, Albert, Jr., was drawn to the church from a young age. The prosperous Cleage family attended Plymouth Congregational, pastored by the pro-union and politically active Reverend Horace A. White. In the late 1930s, White was among the few African American clergymen who challenged the "cooperative" relationship between churches and the Ford Motor Company which, since 1918, had provided a major avenue of employment for black men in the company's area plants. One was required to secure a letter of recommendation from one's minister, certifying that the bearer was "upright" and "reliable." In exchange, ministers received gifts and donations from the company and benefited from well-paid congregants able to tithe and support the church.[11]

Although the relationship was beneficial to the company, to ministers, and to their congregants, it nonetheless gave the company a powerful tool of social control. Ministers who supported unionization or who dared to provide pro-union speakers with a platform at their churches were threatened with reprisals, including the ever-present possibility that all members of their congregations who worked at Ford plants would be summarily fired. This form of economic terrorism was hardly inconsequential. The thousands of workers employed in the various Ford plants (River Rouge, Highland Park, and Lincoln Park, especially), plus their families, meant that the welfare of 30,000 to 40,000 individuals, or roughly one-fourth of the black population of Detroit, depended on wages from Ford jobs. As one contemporary observer noted, "There is hardly a Negro church, fraternal body or other organization in which Ford workers are not represented. Scarcely a Negro professional or businessman is completely independent of income derived from Negro employees."[12] It was a situation that compelled White to ask what was swiftly becoming one of the major questions of the day: "Who owns the Negro Church?"

In a 1937 article published in *Christian Century,* White railed:

> In Detroit the people interested to see to it that the Negro stays anti-labor start with the preachers. The one organization through which the Negro ought to feel free to express his hopes and work out his economic salvation cannot help him because the Negro does not own it—it belongs to the same people who own factories. ... The leadership of the Negro people is still in the hands of their clergymen and will be for years to come, and these clergymen are at the moment leading for the industrialists rather than for the welfare of the Negro people.[13]

Such opinions were duly seconded by labor activists and like-minded clergy. In fact, White's question was taken up again and again during the raucous national NAACP meeting held in Detroit in 1937, as the organization debated the merits of endorsing the efforts of the Congress of Industrial Organizations (CIO).

The pro-Ford clergy, which dominated the local NAACP, was incensed, remarking repeatedly as one minister put it, "We can't afford to have Ford close us down."[14] The union and its representatives weighed in, not only on the practical and political dimensions of the dispute but on the religious ones as well. "I come to you tonight representing the poor, the oppressed and the exploited people, both colored and white," proclaimed the United Auto Worker's (UAW) Homer Martin, an ex-Baptist minister turned union organizer. "The elimination of prejudice against the Negro is to me a definite part not only of a wise labor movement ... but a part of Christianity itself."[15] In the convention's aftermath, which did adopt a pro-union position over the howls of protest from the pro-Ford clergy, Roger Wilkins, the NAACP's executive secretary, felt compelled to pen an editorial that read, in part: "The spectacle of poor preachers, ministering to the needs of the poor whose lot from birth to death is to labor for a pittance, rising to frenzied, name-calling defense of a billionaire manufacturer is enough to make the Savior himself weep."[16]

The national NAACP came and went, but local ministers and activists were still confronted with the realities of the Ford-black church alliance; and fighting it became a sort of civil rights issue in and of itself. In this regard, the young Albert Cleage not only benefited from the example of Reverend White, who he idolized, but was also instructed by the example of the Reverend Charles A. Hill, pastor of Hartford Avenue Baptist Church, and perhaps the most active black minister during the "early" phase of the city's civil rights movement. Hill was among the handful of ministers who refused the overtures of the company: "I told them that, when we were building our building, that we were going to do it out of our own pockets so we can be free to take a stand for anything that is right. ... So we did it differently because we did it ourselves."[17] And, like White, Hill used his social and professional position as a minister to critique the status quo and to push for a conjoining of the rights of labor with the rights of African Americans in general.

Echoing the sentiments of Reverend White, Hill believed that the church must play a commanding role in the civil rights battle to unionize Ford—the last holdout after UAW-CIO had conquered General Motors and Chrysler. For Hill, this was not only a political necessity but a spiritual one as well. Though not well-versed in academic theology, Hill was in essence a practitioner of the Social Gospel. Once described as "an old-fashioned Bible-thumping preacher whose only political concern was making things right in the sight of the Lord," he worked enthusiastically with anyone, from unions and labor-based organizations, to Communist "front" groups such as the National Negro Congress, to the NAACP and religious groups, to accomplish this task.[18] More concretely, Hill opened the doors of his church to clandestine union meetings. "If they met in a regular union hall," Hill elaborated, "then some of the spies from Ford would take their automobile license numbers and they lost their jobs. By holding it in a church, it would be difficult for them to prove we were discussing union matters."[19] Hill's religious liberalism and commitment to social justice led him to take many stands over the years, stands that would eventually land him in front of a House Un-American Activities Committee (HUAC) session in 1952. Yet he continued to search for concrete ways to put his faith into action, often working with marginalized activists and for unpopular causes. Despite being labeled as a "Red" and as a "dupe" of the Communist Party, Hill was nonetheless praised for being, as a 1963 article in the *Michigan Chronicle* put it, part of a generation of "Negro leadership that was born of the foggy gloom of the depression years and that later matured into a formidable and militant vanguard of Negro progress."[20]

From this older generation of activists, Cleage (and indeed the entire apparatus of the post-1954 phase of the city's civil rights movement) was presented with examples of the centrality of coalition building, especially with labor activists and unions, as well as with a diverse array of religious and secular individuals and organizations. In particular, Cleage learned, in both word and deed, about the importance of maintaining a truly independent institution; about opening the doors of the church to provide "free spaces" for organizing; about striving to speak in a language able to cross the so-called divide between the religious and the secular; and about the dynamic possibilities of what I have, for lack of a better term, been referring to as political theology.

By contrast, Cleage would, in time, come to reject the theological underpinnings of older generation ministers such as White and Hill. Of the former, he said, "Horace White was essentially social gospel, which had little connection to reality." And while he attended services and meetings at Hill's church and while he admired Hill's "radicalism," he could not abide the older minister's "spiritualism."[21] (Hill, in turn, did not much care for Cleage or his politics, claiming, at one point, "I believe in God power, not Black Power.") But Cleage did embody the fierce dedication and activist spirit of his elders. How he came to embrace black nationalism and reject integration as a strategy for social justice and black freedom is an interesting story in its own right, and one that deserves much more attention than I can herein allot. It is also a story about the personal and political interaction between generations of activists in Detroit and, indeed, between two phases of the city's civil rights movement.

Albert Cleage, Jr., carried his early lessons with him as he continued his more formal education, first as a student in sociology at Wayne State University, during a brief stint at Fisk, and later at Oberlin's seminary school, where he became so enamored of neoorthodox theology. As a caseworker for the Detroit Department of Health between graduating from Wayne and enrolling at Oberlin, Cleage had been discouraged by the "band-aid" approach of city social services and was already viewing the church as an alternative to meet the needs of the poor and the marginal. Ordained in 1943, his early career as a pastor was relatively conventional, however. He passed an uneventful year as pastor of a church in Lexington, Kentucky, before receiving a call to serve as interim copastor of the Fellowship of All Peoples in San Francisco, until Howard Thurman, the noted black theologian, would be free to relieve him. Presumably, Cleage arrived with an open mind about this experiment in interracial worship but soon soured on it. Looking back on his experiences, he denounced the existence of an interracial church as "a monstrosity and an impossibility."[22] There was, he claimed, an artificiality to the style and substance of worship, and a lack of concrete engagement in the problems of the world. He was particularly annoyed by his copastor's avoidance of issues such as the Japanese internment during the war, as well as the treatment of black soldiers and workers. When offered a permanent position, he declined.

Between 1945 and his return to Detroit in 1954, Cleage completed close to two years of course work toward an advanced degree at the University of Southern California film school and eventually secured another pastorate, this time in Springfield, Massachusetts, where he was able to throw himself into various modes of civil rights activism. While regarded in Springfield as an outspoken and even blunt opponent of police brutality, employment discrimination, and racial segregation in housing, there is little to suggest that he was inordinately radical in the context of post-WWII civil rights activism. He was, in fact, fairly popular among his congregants and coworkers. But Cleage wanted to be back in Detroit. When a post opened up at Detroit's St. Mark's United Presbyterian, he leapt at the chance. Unfortunately, Cleage was less than happy with his new church. With high hopes of building a real community church, once again he chafed at the "Sunday piety" of his congregation. Moreover, the Presbyterian hierarchy did all it could to discourage Cleage's activism on the political front. In the end, he led a small group of dissenters out of St. Marks's—"We didn't leave more than two Uncle Tom's sitting in the church building,"[23] Cleage later explained—and formed a new congregation.

Lacking a permanent physical structure, the small congregation held services around Detroit until 1957, when they purchased a building in the Twelfth Street district. For the first time, Cleage was able to build a church from the ground floor. Blending theology, social criticism, and calls to action, during the late 1950s Central Congregational began to attract a large following of young professionals and working-class residents. He also began to attract a core of activists who would become influential in the theory and practice of black nationalist politics in Detroit. Attorney Milton Henry and his brother, Richard (future founder of the separatist Republic of New Africa in the late 1960s), both attended services at Central; as did James and Grace Lee Boggs, local Marxists associated with the Detroit branch of the Socialist Workers Party (SWP) and its various splinter groups; and Edward Vaughn, owner of the city's largest black bookstore. Outside of the church and pulpit, Cleage worked through the other traditionally recognized vehicle of social and political influence in African American communities: the independent press.

In the latter half of 1961, Cleage, along with his siblings and a few friends, launched their own bimonthly newspaper, the *Illustrated News.* Printed on bright pink newsprint and with a (self-proclaimed and potentially exaggerated) free circulation of 35,000, it appeared until 1965. How many persons actually read the family-financed paper is open to dispute, but during its brief existence, the *Illustrated News* was the chief public platform for Cleage and his associates. Cleage penned the majority of articles with frequent contributions from his brother, Dr. Henry Cleage, as well as Milton and Richard Henry. It was an outlet for their emerging black nationalist views and their often virulent criticism of the racial status quo. It also served as a conduit for political organizing around community issues. In the pages of the *Illustrated News,* Cleage was especially critical of the black middle classes and the liberal-labor coalition that dominated African American politics. He took great pains to distance himself from both. Not surprisingly, he reserved special scorn for the clergy. In one article, for example, Cleage insisted, the "Negro church has prospered poorly in the North because it has been unable to relate the gospel of Jesus meaningfully to the everyday problems of an underprivileged people in urban industrial communities." Because it had failed to tap into the authenticity of "the folk," the church could not keep pace with the needs of the community. The church had, therefore, "become lost in a sea of triviality and aimlessness."[24]

Politically, Reverend Cleage focused his dissatisfaction in two major directions: the public school system and the practice of urban renewal—two of the most pressing issues facing the black population in postwar Detroit. The former issue became a particularly important wedge issue between Cleage and the liberal-labor coalition, which had guided the course of civil rights activism in the city since the early 1950s.[25] On a personal level, Cleage recalled being aware of "discriminatory practices of our public schools since I was a student at Northwestern High back in the 1930s."[26] And he did not believe those practices, including mistreatment by white teachers, biased textbooks, inadequate funding, and unequal facilities. Part of the difficulties, of course, had to do with the changing demographics of the city. Between 1962 and 1966 as "white flight" was draining off the city's white middle class, the school population increased by over 11,842 students, well over half of whom were black. Patterns of residential segregation meant that entire districts became predominately African American, and because of the ever-shrinking tax base of homeowners (which determines levels of funding), predominately black schools became increasingly impoverished as well.[27]

The sorry state of many Detroit schools serving the black population was a major impetus in the formation of GOAL, the Group on Advanced Leadership, an all-black organization led by Cleage and Milton and Richard Henry. Founded in 1961, GOAL was designed to be a "chemical catalyst" in the fight against racial discrimination. "A chemical catalyst speeds up the chemical reaction," Richard Henry wrote in the *Illustrated News.* "Similarly we will speed up the fight against bias."[28] Tensions between GOAL and the NAACP over how best to address the conditions in public schools erupted throughout 1962, as Cleage and GOAL turned to what many viewed as an outrageous form of protest. In an unprecedented move, they proceeded to drum up support in opposition to a tax millage increase in property taxes for school funding. Why, Cleage asked, should African American parents vote themselves a tax increase and, in effect, increase funding for a system that mistreats their children?

Cleage's antimillage campaign brought down a storm of criticism for the liberal coalition. "We must decide whether we will follow in the paths of destruction and chaos of Negro extremists," read an article in the *Michigan Chronicle,* the city's major black weekly. "By voting against the millage, we are automatically casting our lot with the lunatic fringe. ... We cannot afford to sacrifice the future of our young by following the foolish counsel of the radical elements in our midst."[29] While members of the black press and the liberal coalition did their best to render Cleage persona non grata, his campaign did have an effect: More than 50,000 black voters changed their votes from yes to no. Ninety-eight percent of all black voters were for a millage increase in 1959; in 1963, more than 40 percent voted against it.[30] Encouraged by this showing, Reverend Cleage and GOAL stepped up efforts to build alliances with others attempting to occupy a space to the left of the NAACP and the liberal-labor coalition. The seemingly radical positions adopted by Cleage, Central Congregational, and GOAL were particularly attractive to younger activists. A report on one group of young, mostly black, radicals noted that "they have a great deal of respect for Reverend Cleage and the leadership of GOAL," and suggested that only Cleage and GOAL could "give them a little discipline."[31]

Cleage and GOAL may not have offered much discipline, but they did offer encouragement. Historian Sidney Fine may be right that many of the new organizations created by younger activists were "flyspecks in terms of posing a threat to the black leadership position occupied by the NAACP."[32] But they were nonetheless important markers of the slow yet steady ideological shifts creating tensions within the city's civil rights movement. In fact, by the late 1960s, this younger generation of activists would have a decisive impact on the course of political mobilizing in Detroit—in the formation of the League of Revolutionary Black Workers, in the sphere of antipoverty and welfare rights organizing, and in other causes relating to black empowerment. In the early 1960s, one of the most dynamic "flyspecks" to appear was UHURU, founded in March 1963 by Luke Tripp, John Watson, Ken Cockrel, and General Baker—all of whom had ties to Reverend Cleage and GOAL. In a sense, UHURU was among the earliest organizational expressions of the diverse intellectual and political trends circulating in radical circles where nonviolence as a strategy and as a philosophy was critiqued and where black nationalism and worldwide revolution was embraced. Many of those involved in small groups such as UHURU had been regular attendees of the SWP's Militant Labor forums. Some had been involved in the Southern struggle, traveling south to work with the Student Nonviolent Coordinating Committee (SNCC) and the Congress of Racial Equality (CORE). Many had been influenced by the writings and examples of Cuban and African revolutionaries and, closer to home, by Robert Williams, Malcolm X, and Albert Cleage.[33]

Few, apparently, saw any ideological or political incongruities in moving from a SWP forum, to attending a talk by Cleage, to traveling to or otherwise supporting the Southern branch of the struggle. Rather, it was a fertile social and political space in which younger activists and older radicals were striving to make connections: between an "old left" and a "new" one, between local, national, and international struggles for justice. "I think Detroit radicalism ran ahead of the national pace," says Dan Georgakas, who went on to chronicle the experiences of his cohort group in his 1975 volume (with Marvin Surkin), *Detroit: I Do Mind Dying:*

> In the early 1960s a group of Black Detroiters went to New York to meet Che Guevara when he was at the United Nations and others were on the first flights made to defy the travel ban to Cuba. All those guys belonged to a broad social circle I was connected with. The Cuban missile crisis drove the last liberalism out of people like myself. I remember attending a lecture by Albert Cleague [*sic*] and going home and thinking we might be dead by morning.[34]

Most of these younger activists were not religious in the conventional sense. For Luke Tripp, one of the founders of UHURU, while still at student at Wayne State, religion was relatively unimportant. "Man, I don't operate out of a religious bag," he told a reporter. "I was baptized a Catholic but now you can say I am a free thinker." "When I was eighteen I left the church," recalled Charleen Johnson, who became heavily involved in community organizing and welfare rights. The church, she felt, contributed to a sense of "powerlessness" in its members' lives, while she was seeking "to overthrow the system."[35] Cleage understood this impulse to leave or to critique the church, and he shared many of the frustrations articulated by younger activists. And, further, he aspired to heal the breach, the disjuncture between religion and radicalism within activist communities in Detroit. In his fights with the NAACP and the liberal-labor coalition, Cleage repeatedly attempted to tap into the potential of younger activists, and they responded in kind.

1963 and the "Black Revolt" in Detroit

Too often, historians of the post-WWII civil rights movement present the "sudden" eruption of calls for "Black Power" in 1966 as *the* key turning point in the movement's evolution (or devolution, depending on one's point of view). Yet, in places such as Detroit, the development of a black nationalist agenda was neither so stark or so sudden. Rather, as early as 1963, fights within and between local activist communities were becoming increasingly frequent, and the events of that year proved to be more decisive. It was a year filled with tensions: some of them based in disputes about what strategies should be pursued, some based in philosophical differences, some based in the dynamics of personality and pride. Nearly all had to do with race and the emergent vision of black nationalism and self-determination. All of these tensions came to a head during the planning of Detroit's "Walk to Freedom March." Held several weeks before the national March on Washington—which so eclipsed the Detroit march that it is rarely ever noted outside of the historiographical literature on Detroit—it was judged to be a success by the media and by many of its participants. Yet its greater historical relevance may have to do with the ways in which it exacerbated numerous fissures and fractures within the local activist community. The religious nature of this internal struggle among local activists was, far from being in any way unusual, perfectly understandable, given the city's and the movement's history.

On the one side of what was increasingly taking on the cast of a religious "holy war" stood Reverend C. L. Franklin, pastor of New Bethel and head of the Detroit Council for Human Rights (DCHR), an organization that had aspired to eclipse the more cautious NAACP. On the other side stood the NAACP itself which, at one point, threatened to boycott the march altogether. Having been repeatedly denounced as "a bunch of Uncle Toms" by Franklin and others within the DCHR, they were in no mood to cooperate. On still another side stood the Reverend Albert B. Cleage.

Initially, Cleage had been fairly close to Franklin. Both had been involved in issuing the original call for a march. Both desired an "unprecedented show of strength" that would stand as a reproach to the previous "disappointing" NAACP-sponsored demonstration in sympathy with the Southern wing of the struggle.[36] Both ministers were, at the beginning, open to a broad coalition. Since the "Walk to Freedom March" was to double as a fund-raiser for the Southern Christian Leadership Conference (SCLC), there was general agreement that King should be invited to lead the procession and to address the postmarch rally at Cobo Hall, a convention center on the city's downtown waterfront. There were hostile disagreements, however, about who the other dignitaries should be. Reverend Cleage, who served on the board of the DCHR, wanted to keep the march as black-led as possible. On this score, he lost. The NAACP was especially keen on the idea of inviting Mayor Jerome Cavanagh and the UAW's Walter Reuther. This proved to be the price exacted for their support, causing Cleage and his supporters to balk that the march did not need to be "legitimated" (and contained) by the white establishment.[37]

There were also disputes among various segments of the black clergy, and the DCHR found itself forced to placate members of one group in particular: the Baptist Minister's Alliance. As it turned out, one member of the alliance was the newly designated Detroit representative of the SCLC and the alliance felt that he, and not Franklin or Cleage, should play the bigger role. They were also reportedly disquieted by the "Negro character" of the planned march, insisting that "local white churches wanted to have a share in raising funds ... and to support future actions toward desegregation." In addition, Franklin and Cleage had already angered members of the alliance by keeping a studied distance from the organization. When Franklin attended one of their meetings to extend an olive branch, the alliance forced him to pay a membership fee before being allowed to speak. Even after he made his case for religious and political solidarity, the alliance not only declined to officially support the march but actively boycotted it.[38] Once again, questions and debates over the proper role and function of the black church rose inevitably to the surface.

In the end, Detroit's "Walk to Freedom March" was not all Franklin, Cleage, and the DCHR had hoped it would be, even though the turnout surprised the organizers and represented an impressive show of solidarity with the Southern wing of the struggle. It seems that no one was quite prepared for the thousands and thousands of mostly black and working-class marchers, dressed in their Sunday best, who created a sea of people washing down the broad avenues of the city. During his address at Cobo Hall, King proclaimed it the "largest and greatest demonstration for freedom ever held in the United States," with numbers far greater than the vast majority of Southern demonstrations. It was, in King's words, a shining example of a "magnificent new militancy" that could be harnessed and magnified into an equally massive March on Washington. At the close of his 48-minute speech, King delivered a longer and richer version of his "Dream sequence," which would become the highlight of the national march two months later. Reverend Cleage also addressed the overflow crowd. As local radical activist James Boggs recalled, "After King finished talking about conditions in the South, Reverend Cleage got up and said that we'd better start looking at conditions in Detroit."[39]

On this last point, if on little else, there was a general sense of agreement, although disputes over strategy, tactics, and philosophy continued to present persistent problems. In the wake of the march, for instance, the DCHR continued its minor war with both the NAACP and the Baptist Minister's Alliance. To make matters worse, ideological differences between the Reverends Cleage and Franklin became increasingly apparent. The final break between the two ministers and, by extension, the left-of-center coalition as a whole, occurred during the DCHR's attempt to harness the momentum of the march by creating a Northern Christian Leadership Conference (NCLC) to serve as a regional counterpart to the SCLC. While significant for reminding us of the transregional nature of the movement, the plans for a NCLC also provide us with an ideal case study of the sorts of ideological, political, and religious struggles inside the local activist community, especially where the issue of black nationalism was concerned.

Originally, the proposed three-day founding convention of the new NCLC was to be open to *any and all* representatives of Northern-based civil rights organizations. Yet, difficulties began to emerge when Franklin categorically rejected Cleage's intention to invite Conrad Lynn and William Worthy, both of whom were charter members of the recently organized Freedom Now Party (FNP), one of that era's most interesting and successful attempts to construct a national, all-black political party.[40] Both also had long-standing ties to the SWP and to Robert Williams, who had been ousted from his post as head of the Monroe, North Carolina, branch of the NAACP for questioning the efficacy of nonviolence and who was then living in Cuba. In addition, Cleage also made the "mistake" of inviting representatives of GOAL and UHURU, as well as representatives from the Nation of Islam, including Minister Malcolm X and his brother, Minister Wilfred X, head of Temple No. 1 in Detroit. Franklin was incensed. He rejected the attendance of anyone associated with "Communists" (Lynn, Worthy) and with "extremists" (Malcolm and Wilfred X). Such promiscuous "mingling" with "communists, black nationalists and persons with criminal records," Franklin maintained, would "only destroy our image."[41]

"Ours is the Christian view and approach," added James Del Rio, another member of the increasingly fractious DCHR. "Those who refuse to turn the other cheek are having their own conference."[42] And, indeed, Cleage resigned in protest from the DCHR and set about coordinating plans for a rival conference—the Grass-Roots Leadership Conference—whose very name was meant to symbolize their separation from and critique of the NCLC. The situation in Detroit was thrown into further chaos when Cleage and his allies decided to hold their conference during the same weekend as the NCLC's. It was no doubt gratifying to Cleage that the

NCLC meeting was widely judged to have been a flop. Even with Adam Clayton Powell addressing the NCLC's main event at Cobo Hall, only a "disappointing 3,000 souls attended." (Cobo Hall seats 15,000.) Further, less than half of the delegates from Northern organizations showed up, and many left the NCLC proceedings to attend the Grass-Roots sessions across town in the Twelfth Street district.[43]

The Grass-Roots Leadership Conference, while well-attended, with estimates ranging from 300 to 400 persons, was itself only a blip on the larger radar of progressive black politics and the rise of a black nationalist agenda. Although generally remembered (if at all) for Minister Malcolm X's now famous "Message to the Grass Roots" speech, it nonetheless serves in retrospect as an important moment in the formation of a new activist coalition with its own distinctive ideology and, moreover, its own distinctive political theology. Cleage, GOAL, and the Grass-Roots organizers went out of their way to smooth over the differences between local and national radicals as well as between Christians and Muslims. The latter was symbolized, as the *Liberator* put it, by "a Christian minister [Cleage] marrying an Islamic invocation into a Christian prayer" during the opening event.[44] Cleage's experiences in organizing and facilitating the conference and his fights with the DCHR, the NCLC, and other moderates also proved to be a crucial step in the evolution of his own political and religious thinking. In fact, it was the planning and implementation of the Grass-Roots Conference that provided much of the substance to Cleage's claim that 1963 represented the beginnings of a "Black Revolt" in places such as Detroit.

From this point on, Cleage had very little that was positive to say about King, SCLC, and most of the Southern branch of the movement—although he did support what he saw as the more radical potential of youth-oriented groups such as SNCC. Working with the FNP and other local and national black organizations also allowed Cleage to keep abreast of various political developments in other regions of the country. As the decade wore on and the civil rights movement increasingly "moved" North, Cleage and other black nationalists in Detroit continued their struggle to redefine both the nature of the movement and the very meaning of "civil rights." For Cleage, this meant not only black nationalism in terms of politics and economics but also in terms of culture and religion. The real difference, Cleage wrote in 1963, was that "Black men began to talk of Black History, Black Art, Black Economics, Black Political Action, and Black Leadership. Black Nationalists didn't merely talk black, they began to act black."[45] Certainly, Cleage felt he had good reason to proffer such an analysis. Yet, it obscures the ways in which post-1963 developments are organically tied to previous eras in the Black Freedom Movement.

They were hardly the first generation to take black history, art, politics, economics, and culture seriously.

Like politically engaged black ministers before him, Cleage struggled to make the black church relevant to the needs, desires, and struggles of the community it was meant to serve. He knew well that many younger activists felt alienated by the conventional teachings and practices of the church and continuously sought to provide them with a meaningful spiritual home. Like Reverend White, his old mentor, Cleage worked to maintain a truly independent institution, and like Reverend Hill, he opened the doors of his church to various organizations, coalitions, and individuals, including labor unionists, black and, yes, white, radicals, community organizers, and others.

Thus, it was in the arena of theological scholarship and activism that Cleage rendered a truly distinctive contribution. He was, as noted black theologian James Cone wrote in 1969, "one of the few black ministers who has embraced Black Power as a religious concept and has sought to reorient the church-community on the basis of it."[46] But even here we would do well to consider the similarities between Cleage's Black Christian Nationalism and the African Orthodox Church established by the Garveyite movement in the early twentieth century, as well as the Nation of Islam, both of which took the existence of a "Black God" as a point of departure.[47] Cleage not only pressed for the wide acceptance of a "Black Christ" (and Madonna and child), but he also sought to strip traditional Christianity of its "excessive mysticism." For example, the belief that Jesus was resurrected from the dead was, for Cleage, at best a mystification and at worst a lie. Tracing out the implications of this vision, he insisted that the original disciples were not primarily concerned with bodily resurrection but with the resurrection of a "Black Nation." Hence, he argued, we modern-day disciples, whether Christian, Muslim, or secular, need to get back to the original and more authentic message of Jesus' mission.[48] Not surprisingly, Cleage's political theology constantly placed him at odds with fellow clergy and not a few more conventionally religious lay people. Some, including the Reverend Charles A. Hill, even attempted to persuade other ministers to close the doors of their churches to any meetings or forums in which Cleage and his supporters organized or participated in—raising, ironically, and once again, the question, "Who Owns the Negro Church?" "I don't want anything to do with organizations which want all-black," Hill told an audience of Baptist ministers. "We should close our churches to them."[49] Undaunted, Cleage kept up the fevered pitch of radical black nationalists organizing, working with groups such as the Inner-City Organization, the Interfaith Foundation for Community Organizing, the FNP on whose ticket he ran for governor in

1964, and the League of Revolutionary Black Workers, many of whose members got their start in radical politics in UHURU and the old SWP Saturday night forums. When the 1967 urban uprising swept through sections of Detroit, Cleage saw it as a "dress rehearsal" for the revolution in politics, economics, culture, and religion yet to come. After 1967, and well into the 1970s, the embrace of Black Power and calls for programmatic implementation of black nationalism were well-established as part of the political logic in Detroit's activist communities.

Cleage did not fully revolutionize the movement or the society that gave birth to it. Although managing to erect sister temples in other locations, his Shrine of the Black Madonna eventually suffered gradual decline. It continues to exist, however, with branches in Detroit (Temple No. 1), Atlanta, Houston, and Calhoun Falls, South Carolina, despite the patriarch's recent death in February 2000. Yet, Cleage, who changed his name to Jaramogi Abebe Agyeman in the 1970s, did succeed in pushing the movement in new and interesting directions and in ways that combined an activist's faith and an unflinching political commitment. By helping to create one of the earliest black nationalist coalitions in Detroit, he played a leading role in laying the foundations for that city's ongoing struggle for black freedom. In the end, the gradual embrace of Black Power and black nationalism, including Black Christian Nationalism, constituted less of a major or radical break with the past. Rather, it represented just one more tenacious twist in a road whose tortuous path has always been structured by debates, tensions, rivalries, and new departures—a road, moreover, consistently defined by and rooted in a sense of place but never defined exclusively by region or location. In the end, it may be that Twelfth Street and Montgomery are not so far apart after all.

Notes

1. Reverend Albert B. Cleage, Jr., "An Enemy Has Done This," in *The Black Messiah* (New York: Sheed and Ward, 1969), 167.
2. According to the artist, Glanton Dowell, the painting was meant to symbolize the connections between the Madonna and "any Negro mother, an ADC [Aid to Dependent Children] mother whose child does wrong, anyone." Quoted in "Black Madonna Unveiled," *Detroit Free Press*, March 25, 1967.
3. Reverend Albert B. Cleage, Jr., *Black Christian Nationalism: New Directions for the Black Church* (New York: William and Morrow, 1972), 16.
4. Reverend Albert B. Cleage, Jr., "The Next Step," *Illustrated News*, November 1963.
5. Cleage, *Black Christian Nationalism*, 75.

6. See, for example, August Meier and Elliott Rudwick, *CORE: A Study in the Civil Rights Movement, 1942–1968* (Urbana: University of Illinois Press, 1973); Clayborne Carson, *In Struggle: SNCC and Black Wakening of the 1960s* (Cambridge: Harvard University Press, 1981); William L. Van DeBurg, *New Day in Babylon: The Black Power Movement and American Culture* (Chicago: University of Chicago Press, 1992); and William H. Chafe, *Civilities and Civil Rights: Greensboro, North Carolina and the Black Struggle for Freedom* (New York: Oxford University Press, 1980).

7. Hiley Ward, *Prophet of a Black Nation* (New York: Pilgrim Press, 1969), has a good discussion of Cleage's understanding of neoorthodox theology on pages 102–110. It remains the only book-length biography of Cleage and benefits from extensive interviews with him. On Niebuhr and his influence on the left in general, see Richard Pells, *The Liberal Mind in a Conservative Age* (New York: Harper & Row, 1985); and Niebuhr's own *Moral Man, Immoral Society* (New York: Scribner's, 1932, 1960).

8. Cleage, quoted in Ward, *Prophet of a Black Nation,* 102–103. Cleage does not, however, acknowledge Niebuhr's influence on King's theology. Nor does he credit the richness of either King's theology or, indeed, the Social Gospel tradition overall, especially in its connections to African American prophetic Christianity. See, for example, Ralph Luker, *The Social Gospel in Black and White: American Radical Reform, 1885–1912* (Chapel Hill: University of North Carolina Press, 1991); and Susan Lindley, "Neglected Voices and Praxis in the Social Gospel," *Journal of Religious Ethics* 18 (spring 1990): 75–103. For a good overview of King's theology, see Robert Michael Franklin, *Liberating Visions: Human Fulfillment and Social Justice in African-American Thought* (Minneapolis: Fortress Press, 1990), chapter 4. Jean Paul Sartre, *No Exit* (New York : Vintage, 1989).

9. Until the publication of Nick Salvatore's much-anticipated biography of Franklin, one of the best sources on Franklin remains, Jeff Todd Titon, ed., *Give Me This Mountain: Life History and Selected Sermons* (Urbana: University of Illinois Press, 1989); the Franklin quote appears on page 19.

10. Steve Babson, *Working Detroit: The Making of a Union Town* (New York: Adama, 1984); August Meier and Elliott Rudwick, *Black Detroit and the Rise of the UAW* (New York: Oxford University Press, 1979); Richard Thomas, *Life For Us Is What We Make It: Building Black Community in Detroit, 1915–1945* (Bloomington: Indiana University Press, 1992); James A. Geschwender, *Class, Race and Worker Insurgency: The League of Revolutionary Black Workers* (Cambridge, England: Cambridge University Press, 1977); Dominic J. Capeci, *Race Relations in Wartime Detroit: The Sojourner Truth Housing Controversy of 1942* (Philadelphia: Temple University Press, 1984); Elaine L. Moon, ed., *Untold Tales, Unsung Heroes: An Oral History of Detroit's African-American Community, 1918–1967* (Detroit: Wayne State University Press, 1994).

11. This relationship between select black ministers and the Ford Motor Company has been widely documented and analyzed. See, for example, Meier and Rudwick, *Black Detroit and the Rise of the UAW,* 16–18; Thomas, *Life for*

Us Is What We Make It, 272–275; Lloyd Harding Bailer, "Negro Labor in the Automobile Industry" (Ph.D. diss., University of Michigan, 1943), 113–114; and Elizabeth Anne Martin, *Detroit and the Great Migration, 1916–1929* (Ann Arbor: Bentley Historical Library Printing Services, University of Michigan, 1993), 34–40.

12. Bailer, "Negro Labor," 113; Joyce Shaw Peterson, "Black Automobile Workers in Detroit, 1910–1930," *Journal of Negro History* 64 (summer 1979): 177–190.

13. Reverend Horace A. White, "Who Owns the Negro Church?," *Christian Century* 55 (February 9, 1937): 177–178.

14. Editorial, "Mind Your Own Business," *Crisis* 44 (August 1937).

15. Homer Martin, "Address to the Convention of the National Association for the Advancement of Colored People" (June 30, 1937), Martin Papers, Archives of Labor History and Urban Affairs, Wayne State University, Detroit [Cited hereafter as ALHUA].

16. Wilkins's editorial, quoted in Meier and Rudwick, *Black Detroit,* 58; "Resolutions Adopted by the Twenty-Eighth Annual Conference of the N.A.A.C.P. in Detroit, Michigan, July 4, 1937," NAACP papers, I, B-4, Library of Congress.

17. Reverend Charles A. Hill, Oral History interview, ALHUA.

18. Coleman A. Young, *Hard Stuff: The Autobiography of Coleman A. Young* (New York: Viking, 1994), 42. A full-length published biography of Reverend Hill has yet to appear. For more details on his life and activism, see my "From the Reverend Charles A. Hill to the Reverend Albert B. Cleage, Jr.: Change and Continuity in the Patters of Civil Rights Mobilizations in Detroit, 1935–1967" (Ph.D. diss., University of Michigan, 1995).

19. Hill, Oral History interview, ALHUA.

20. *Michigan Chronicle,* October 5, 1963. Hill's contributions to the "early" phase of the movement are also chronicled in Nelson Lichtenstein and Robert Korstad, "Opportunities Found and Lost: Labor, Radicals and the Early Civil Rights Movement," *Journal of American History* 75 (1988): 790–815. The authors argue that the early phase of the civil rights movement was destroyed by the dawning of the cold war and the ravages of anticommunism. Yet, they do give enough attention to the ways in which the early phase continued to influence later developments, especially in light of interpersonal and inter-generational ties in local communities such as Detroit.

21. Cleage on White and Hill, quoted in Ward, *Prophet of a Black Nation,* 103.

22. Cleage, quoted in Ward, *Prophet of a Black Nation,* 102–103.

23. Reverend Albert Cleage, Jr., Sermon, November 1, 1967, Audio and Visual Division, ALHUA.

24. Reverend Albert Cleage, Jr., "The Negro in Detroit," *Illustrated News,* December 18, 1961; cf. E. Franklin Frazier, *Black Bourgeoisie: The Rise of a New Middle Class in the United States* (New York: Collier, 1957); and Joseph R. Washington, *Black Religion: The Negro and Christianity in the United States* (Boston: Beacon, 1964), especially chapter 2 on "Folk Religion and Negro Congregants."

25. The liberal–labor coalition was compromised of such groups as the NAACP and other race improvement organizations, factions within the UAW, labor-oriented groups such as the interracial Trade Union Leadership Council, and others who managed to survive the purges associated with anticommunism and the dawn of the cold war.

26. Reverend Albert Cleage, Jr., *Michigan Chronicle*, February 2, 1962.

27. Reverend Albert Cleage, Jr., "What's Wrong With Our Schools?," *Illustrated News*, December 18, 1961; Marilyn Gittell and T. E. Hollender, *Six Urban School Districts* (New York: Praeger, 1968); Sidney Fine, *Violence in the Model City: The Cavanagh Administration, Race Relations and the Detroit Riot of 1967* (Ann Arbor: University of Michigan Press, 1989), 41–46.

28. Richard Henry, "GOAL," *Illustrated News*, November 13, 1961.

29. Editorial, *Michigan Chronicle*, November 2, 1963.

30. "We Defeated the Millage," *Illustrated News*, April 8, 1963; *Detroit Free Press*, April 7, 1963.

31. Detroit Council on Human Relations [DCHR], "Inter-Office Correspondence, Re: UHURU," (September 15, 1963), DCHR Papers, III, Box 21, ALHUA.

32. Fine, *Violence in the Model City*, 27.

33. "UHURU Says US Has 'Racist, Savage Society,'" *Michigan Chronicle*, October 19, 1963. See also Robert H. Mast, ed., *Detroit Lives* (Philadelphia: Temple University Press, 1994); Fine, *Violence in the Model City*, 105–107; and Dan Georgakas and Marvin Surkin, *Detroit: I Do Mind Dying* (New York: St. Martin's Press, 1975).

34. Georgakas, quoted in Mast, *Detroit Lives*, 292.

35. Luke Tripp, quoted in *Michigan Chronicle*, October 19, 1963; Charleen Johnson, quoted in Mast, *Detroit Lives*, 50.

36. Reverend Albert Cleage, Jr., "The Detroit NAACP Is a Joke to People Everywhere," *Illustrated News*, March 4, 1963.

37. The march was even postponed once because of the NAACP's intransigence. *Michigan Chronicle*, May 25, June 22, 1963; *Detroit News*, June 25, 1963.

38. "Negro Ministers Vote 'Hands Off,'" *Detroit Free Press*, June 12, 1963; "Ministers Row Over March," *Michigan Chronicle*, June 1, 1963; Jose Rames, "Racial Anatomy of a City," *New University Thought* (September–October, 1963).

39. "Questions of the American Revolution: Conversations in Detroit Between James Boggs and Xavier Nicholas" (spring 1973), Labadie Collections, University of Michigan, 10; Taylor Branch, *Parting the Waters: America in the King Years, 1954–1963* (New York: Simon and Schuster, 1988), 842–843.

40. Much more deserves to be said about the FNP both nationally and in Michigan. For a good overview, see Conrad Lynn, *There Is a Fountain: The Autobiography of Conrad Lynn* (Brooklyn: Lawrence Hill, 1979. Cleage, who was chairman of the Michigan FNP, ran for governor in 1964, with others on the ticket, including Milton Henry and local activist Ernest C. Smith. "Fact Sheet on the Freedom Now Party Candidates, November 3, 1964 Elections," Ernest C. Smith Collection, Box 1, ALHUA.

41. "Plan Rights Group Patterned on King's," *Detroit News,* November 6, 1963; Franklin, quoted in *Detroit Courier,* November 16, 1963. On Lynn, Worthy, Williams, and others, see Van Gosse, *Where The Boys Are: Cuba, Cold War America and the Making of a New Left* (London: Verso, 1993), especially chapter 5; as well as Lynn, *There Is a Fountain.*

42. Del Rio, quoted in *Detroit News,* November 10, 1963.

43. Fine gives a brief overview of the development of rival conferences in *Violence in the Model City,* 28–29. "Northern Negro Leadership Conference 'A Failure,'" *Detroit Courier,* November 16, 1963; *Detroit News,* November 10, 11, 1963; "Questions of the American Revolution: Conversations in Detroit Between James Boggs and Xavier Nicholas" (spring 1973), Labadie Collections, University of Michigan, 10–11.

44. Sterling Gray, "Man of the Year: Reverend Albert B. Cleage, Jr., Architect of a Revolution," *Liberator,* December 1963, 8. Recordings of the proceedings are available in the Audio and Visual Division, ALHUA.

45. Reverend Albert Cleage, Jr., "The Next Step," *Illustrated News,* December 1963.

46. James Cone, *Black Theology and Black Power* (San Francisco: Harper, 1969, 1989), 21. Grace Lee and James Boggs discuss the importance of Cleage as "the first Christian Minister who has become a leading black nationalist spokesperson," in "Detroit: Birth of a Nation," *National Guardian,* October 7, 1967.

47. See Randall K. Burkett, *Garveyism as a Religious Movement: The Institutionalization of a Black Civil Religion* (Metuchen, N.J.: Scarecrow Press, 1978). The idea of a "Black Christ" can also be traced by to the nineteenth century in the writings of Henry McNeal Turner and others. See Kelly Brown Douglass, *The Black Christ* (Maryknoll, N.Y.: Orbis, 1994).

48. Cleage, *Black Messiah,* 92–94.

49. Hill, quoted in "Negro Ministers Here Hit Rights Group on Violence. ... " *Michigan Chronicle,* April 15, 1964; "Dexter Baptist Turns Down Freedom Now Meeting," *Michigan Chronicle,* March 21, 1964; *Detroit News,* March 16, 1964.

Chapter 7

Elijah Muhammad's Nation of Islam: Separatism, Regendering, and a Secular Approach to Black Power after Malcolm X (1965–1975)

Ula Taylor

Why would anyone become a member of the Nation of Islam after the assassination of Malcolm X (El-Hajj Malik El-Shabazz) on February 21, 1965, in New York's Audubon Ballroom? More than any other leader, Malcolm X stood at the ideological vortex in the dynamic movement for black liberation. His fiercely smart rhetoric helped to shift the dominant political struggle from a strategy of civil rights liberalism to eclectic expressions of black nationalism. As the most charismatic and visible spokesperson for the Nation of Islam, Malcolm moved beyond the Honorable Elijah Muhammad's (the Nation of Islam's undisputed leader from 1934 to 1975) call for economic self-sufficiency and his prophecy of divine intervention to a paradigm of activist nationalism. Combining an application of armed self-defense "by any means necessary" (in a political climate that hosted racist government repression in the form of the state police) along with a lethal critique of white folks as "devils," Malcolm appealed to the most socially isolated, politically dispossessed, and economically desperate members of the black proletariat. It was Malcolm's undivided commitment to create a powerful group of "believers" in the Nation of Islam that resulted in a substantial membership increase. In 1955, there were only 16 temples largely located in the urban North, but by 1960 over 50 temples were sprinkled throughout the United States with registered membership estimated between 50,000 and 250,000.[1]

Malcolm has become a militant martyr for the Nation of Islam and a "Black Power paradigm—the archetype, reference point, and spiritual adviser in absentia for a generation of Afro-American activists."[2] This chapter explores a number of issues, including the Nation of Islam's views of Africa, reparations, land, as well as poverty and progress, its focus is on the issues of separatism and the redefinition of gender roles—the creation of two allegedly complementary subjects, a masculine man and a feminine woman.[3] Clearly, Black Power advocates had multiple visions, but the Nation of Islam provides one of the most imaginative sites to explore their concerns about intimate gender relations, or what Paulette Pierce insightfully calls "boudoir politics," and the creation of a "black nation." This article is an effort to complicate our understanding of African American identity, political subjectivity, gender prescriptions, and nation building during the peak of the modern Black Power movement. Furthermore, I suggest that in the post-Malcolm X period, the religious nature of the Nation of Islam was not the major impetus for new membership. Above all, the Nation of Islam's secular programs, promising power and wealth, were the key to its expansion.

A Nation within a Nation

It is through a consideration of historical shifts in the Nation of Islam that one can locate key transformations and continuities in the meaning of Black Power. The formative years of the Nation of Islam (1930s) developed within a milieu of restrictive, second-class citizenship for African Americans. W. D. Fard Muhammad, the founder and self-proclaimed prophet of the Nation of Islam was known by his followers as a divine black messiah (Allah in the flesh), and he designated Elijah Muhammad as his last "Messenger."[4] An unorthodox version of Islam, the Nation of Islam is usually studied outside the general scope of Muslim life despite the efforts of followers to draw on orthodox Islam and Islamic cultural representations such as symbolism, extensive numerology, and codes of appropriate living. Similar to devout Muslims, Nation of Islam members conducted all daily activities with reference to religion. Although their faith was not anchored in the recitation of Arabic prayers, Islam became an organizing force that produced a community of "believers" determined to resist the bulwarks of Jim Crow (economic repression, political disenfranchisement, and social ostracism) by building an empowered independent nation within the United States.

Black people, Fard Muhammad explained, were the "original" people on the planet who ruled from "Asia." Historian Claude Clegg underscores that Fard Muhammad believed "the use of the word Africa to denote what he called East Asia" was a ploy by "whites to divide people of color who were, in his view, all Asiatics."[5] The "so-called American Negro" was in fact an "Asiatic blackman, the maker, the owner, the cream of the planet earth, God of the universe."[6] Fard Muhammad invented a history that disconnected black people in the United States from Africa and Africans, thereby detaching them from the Western imagination of blackness, which was loaded with demeaning stereotypes of African "savagery" and dehumanizing slavery.[7] At the same time, this narrative failed to critique colonialist descriptions of black Africans as "uncivilized"; rather, Fard Muhammad's rhetoric often accentuated negative myths. In effect, early Nation of Islam members wanted to build a modern black nation from a glorification of "Asiatic blackness" and a rejection of sub-Saharan Africa. This ideological structure expresses not only the internalization of black Africa as "backward," but also the very real alienation that Nation of Islam members felt as a result of colonialism, slavery, and Jim Crow. Thus, as Robert Reid-Pharr avers, the Nation of Islam's history produced an identity for black Americans that was "imagined as larger than blackness," even though "very few others are allowed to share this identity."[8]

The elevation of black Americans—most notably above black Africans—paralleled the collective grouping of Caucasians as "white, blue-eyed devils" who were "grafted out of Black people specifically to bedevil the planet."[9] Fard Muhammad advocated a separate nation from Caucasians, a place where its members were protected from a Jim Crow government and all of the "sins" from the "devil." After he mysteriously disappeared in 1934 from Detroit (the Nation of Islam's center), Elijah Muhammad continued this millennialistic mission to reject the "devil's" institutions. A complete withdrawal from American society was presumed to be the key to the resurrection of black people. So, when President Franklin D. Roosevelt instituted social security in the late 1930s, "the Messenger" told his members to refuse the identification numbers since they were the "mark of the beast." For Muhammad, social security digits not only kept individuals under surveillance but were also no different from the surnames black folks had inherited from slavery—both systems of identification represented white domination. The federal government became redefined as a "new master," who would legally chain and lock black people into an exploitative economic system.

Given that there was no area of political, economic, and social life where legal segregation did not intrude, scholar Ernest Allen concludes that converts to the Nation of Islam viewed "federal and state agencies as undistilled repositories of satanic influence."[10] The rejection of such institutions was a critique of both white supremacy and modernity. Nation of Islam leaders had responded to colonial notions that black people were outside of Western modernity, with a general repugnance toward their modern structures. Moreover, Elijah Muhammad's incessant emphasis on a particular brand of Islam—a religion that allegedly accorded black people respect and worth because men were successful patriarchal heads of their homes and women were the epitome of feminine modesty—distinguished and ultimately severed his subjects from an ostensibly corrupt nation of hypocritical white Christians.[11] Nation of Islam followers clearly defined their enemy in both racial and religious terms.

After Malcolm's 1952 prison parole, his talent was used specifically to start new temples in Boston and Philadelphia, as well as bolster membership in sagging ones. Within two years, Elijah Muhammad rewarded Malcolm's efforts by assigning him the most coveted temple outside of Chicago, Temple No. 7 in Harlem. It was in New York City that Malcolm's influence reached new heights. As the Nation of Islam's most public Minister, Malcolm proselytized not only among the hustlers, pimps, prostitutes, drug dealers, and thieves but also in churches and at political debates. He contended that the teachings of the Honorable Elijah Muhammad explained that black folks were impoverished and ethically lacking because white racists conscientiously withheld their access to "self" and neglected their most fundamental needs. After vividly detailing the failures of white America, Malcolm provided the foundation for the "so-called Negroes" to understand that they were indeed the chosen, the supreme of humankind, and that the key to their resurrection could be found in the Nation of Islam. He used his own wayward life history as a powerful example. Malcolm had sold drugs, stolen, and ended up in jail, but after he converted to the Nation of Islam while in prison (1946–52), his whole attitude and outlook on life changed. Listening to his emotionally stirring and candid testimony, Malcolm's devotees were able to recognize aspects of themselves, which pulled them closer to him and his black nationalist revelation. John Edgar Wideman argues that Malcolm delivered a message during the sixties that was "as absolute as the message runaway slaves delivered to Ole Massa." Malcolm, however, "wasn't running, and his direction was not 'away' but toward a future, a center we're still struggling to glimpse."[12]

Prior to his brutal death (Black Muslims who had been implicated in the killing were quickly dismissed by the Nation of Islam leadership as FBI infiltrators and hypocrites), Malcolm wrote in his 1964 autobiography that he knew, "[as] any official in the Nation of Islam would instantly have known, any death-talk [about him] could have been approved of—if not actually initiated—by only one man," the Honorable Elijah Muhammad. No doubt, Malcolm was a loyal convert, and prior to being ousted (in November 1963, after the assassination of President John F. Kennedy) from the Nation of Islam, his "most bone-deep personal belief, was that Elijah Muhammad in every aspect of his existence was a symbol of moral, mental, and spiritual reform among the American black people."[13] In hindsight, Malcolm told photographer Gordon Parks that as the messenger's national minister and most visible spokesperson, he had done "many things" to his regret because he was a "zombie," and "like all Muslims" he was "hypnotized, pointed in a certain direction and told to march."[14] By 1964, Malcolm and others had critiqued Elijah Muhammad as an "adulterer"who "betrayed" his followers, the Nation of Islam as an organization that was "moving too slow," and Islam as "too inactive."[15] It is difficult to fathom that during this very volatile public moment, and thereafter, a steady stream of women and men continued to be drawn into the Nation of Islam's fold.[16] Refugees from a variety of political groups who sought a structured black political organization swelled the ranks of the Nation of Islam, as the call for Black Power resonated throughout the United States.

By 1965, the Nation of Islam continued to represent a religious answer to problems of poverty and racial discrimination but also a conservative capitalist solution to these difficult circumstances. Under Elijah Muhammad's leadership, the Nation of Islam's principles and demands had crystallized. "If you want money, good homes, and friendships in all walks of life, come and follow me," said the messenger.[17] His bountiful membership call yielded a favorable response among black folks who had had a Southern experience, fled Babylon, but were still catching hell in the northern "promised land." They lived in dilapidated housing projects infested with drugs and hopelessness, representing generations of economically depressed people. More to the point, the Nation of Islam's platform offered a life chord for black people who were untouched by civil rights victories. The messenger cultivated an atmosphere of support and caring for his followers, and numerous testimonies by members suggest that he made good on his promise to improve the conditions of those who "believe." The Nation of Islam converts explain that their lives were plagued by drugs, alcohol, and lack of discipline and morals, but the messenger had extended kindness to them when others only condemned their behavior. Inside the prisons, Elijah Muhammad would make sure that jailed converts received encouraging letters, and Malcolm X recalled how he "sends money all over the country to prison inmates who write to him."[18] Brother Tomas 18X of Chicago explained that "For many years, the

Messenger has provided us with jobs" and he "has taught us how to have peace of mind, friendship, money and decent homes."[19] Under the guidance of the messenger, members remark that they had become "successful" in terms of employment and had progressed in terms of knowing "self." Sister Joan X remembered that the first time that she visited the Nation of Islam's Chicago headquarters in 1972 "it was indeed heaven on earth, all of your needs were met by sophisticated people who looked like you."[20]

Black Power

Even though activists had battled to give substance to the newly acquired social (Civil Rights Act of 1964) and political (Voting Rights Act of 1965) rights of citizenship, many of the younger freedom fighters attended college and were experiencing an increasing sense of disillusionment within the movement. Only a small percentage of middle-class black people had reaped the benefits of legal change while the predicament of the masses seemed to worsen. Occupying a precarious class position, most college students were financially strapped, but a middle-class status was within their grasp via their degrees. As a blossoming middle stratum, student activists struggled to transform institutions that produced inequalities, but at the same time they recognized that their higher degrees would position them to seize certain elite advantages. Constructing an identity within a caldron of inequalities is difficult; this is why, Sister Joan 4X spoke for many when she said, "Many of us wonder[ed] what we'll do with our education when we leave college."[21] They were not alone in terms of feeling ambiguous about their future. The urban rebellions that spread throughout the country, beginning with the Watts uprising four days after the passage of the August 1965 Voting Rights Act, evidenced the demoralization and alienation Northern black people felt in America as a result of poverty and gestapo-style policing.

The Student Nonviolent Coordinating Committee (SNCC) members certainly understood the frustrations of black urbanites. Beginning in 1960, they had courageously put their bodies on the line at sit-in demonstrations and on freedom ride treks, but by 1965 many of them were pessimistic and felt influential black leaders were willing to settle for "tokens"of racial progress. After electing Stokely Carmichael chairman in 1966, SNCC workers, especially the newly formed Atlanta Project staff, began to insist that black people think in terms of "Black Power" in order to squash "white power." An observer recalled that SNCC members in "good standing" during this period had digested Frantz Fanon's *The*

Wretched of the Earth, which detailed how the "Western man [was] deca-
dent and therefore not to be emulated by colonized peoples" and they
could "quote at length from 'Malcolm X Speaks.'"[22] In the tense aftermath
of Malcolm's death in 1965, other political organizations also began to
reshape, in the case of the Congress of Racial Equality (CORE), and new
organizations were created, notably the Black Panther Party, the Republic
of New Africa, Revolutionary Action Movement, and the League of
Revolutionary Black Workers. Black nationalist and separatist ideas, as
well as armed self-defense, were designed to give real meaning to
Malcolm's legacy and "Black Power." The postmortem period expanded
his influence in unprecedented ways. As contested debates erupted
between these groups regarding the most effective way to destroy white
hegemony, the Nation of Islam hunkered down and simply pushed to further implement its insular nationhood goals. With a long history of racial
self-determination, cultural autonomy, and black capitalism, the Nation of
Islam was able to quickly rebound from the taint of Malcolm's death to an
organization that was seen by many activists as the separatist vanguard.
Given that activists were looking for basic, but fundamentally key, elements of Black Power, it is not surprising that the post-1965 period
brought clusters of young people into the Nation of Islam who were
searching for an organization that at its core celebrated a black identity
and empowered black people on their own terms.

Anna Karriem's political activism illustrates how the problematic
dynamics within the Black Power movement could initiate a conversion to
the Nation of Islam. She had been a devoted member of SNCC between
1964 and 1967 and worked to bring "political power" to black people in
Alabama and Mississippi counties. On election day in 1967, however, she
witnessed how local registrars held loaded guns to drive SNCC members
who were supervising the process away from the polling areas and how
black sharecroppers were "driven off of their land and forbidden to take
anything with them" because they had voted for a black candidate. Karriem
found herself, "along with other SNCC workers and members of the
homeless families driving stakes into the ground and building a wooden
floor, so that we could set up tents to get them out of the cold." After 1966,
under the leadership of Carmichael, SNCC's efforts were to obtain political
and economic freedom for black people, and Karriem states that they were
"willing to arm themselves for revolution in the streets." Teaching that
"Freedom comes from the barrel of a gun," SNCC leadership, Karriem,
argued, did not teach "the outcome of armed revolution by Black people
nor did [Carmichael] teach Black people in Los Angeles in 1965 how to
restore their burned homes and businesses in Watts." Karriem was also

critical of Carmichael for not coming "around to teach the people" in Detroit and Newark in 1967 who revolted against "slum living and unemployment, how to do for self in the way of rebuilding their burned communities." "Black Power" too often led to "Black Deaths," she concluded. Karriem accepted Islam as taught by Elijah Muhammad, because she was tired of the "destruction caused by so called Black leaders who expound on ideas that [had] no foundation in reality." The messenger taught converts that "ideology is the science of ideas; we have had four hundred years to come up with ideas."[23] Karriem summarized that the Nation of Islam had moved beyond ideological rhetoric and calls for revolution; their efforts had yielded small businesses, schools, and farmland and no one had been displaced in the process. Sister Karriem also convinced other women activists to pledge loyalty to the Nation of Islam. Sister Marguerite X met Karriem while a student activist at Tuskegee. Before attending the mosque, Marguerite X was of "the radical group of college students."[24] Marguerite and Karriem's conversion helps us to understand how the Nation of Islam's conservative vision of "action" took on revolutionary meaning within a context of effete political resistance and racist violence.

Brother Preston (X) Dixon's experience also sheds additional light on an activist's conversion to the Nation of Islam. He had become involved with the Black Student Union (BSU) in Los Angeles, and "the first inkling" that "something was amiss came when the BSU central committee established a constitution and philosophy that were based on the program of the Most Honorable Elijah Muhammad—"Wants and Beliefs."[25] The Black Panther Party for Self Defense, organized in Oakland, California, October 1966, had also replicated the Nation of Islam's "Wants and Beliefs" platform in its "Ten-Point Program."[26] Huey Newton had attended mosques in both San Francisco and Oakland, spoke fairly often to a number of members, and regularly read the Nation of Islam's popular weekly newspaper, *Muhammad Speaks*. Newton would have joined them, but he "could not deal with their religion." He had been raised in a fairly strict Christian home and "had had enough of religion and could not bring [himself] to adopt another one."[27] Dixon was not turned off by the religious aspect of the Nation of Islam, but he admits that the "changeover was not immediate," for there was still considerable doubt within him. The "point of no return" came later when his local BSU organized a program and only brothers from the Nation of Islam would travel and speak to his group for free. Well-known BSU leadership, to Dixon's disgust, usually required local chapters to pay for airfare, lodging, plus honorarium. Spreading the message of Black Power soon became a fundraising tactic for some of its leadership. After 1966, Carmichael took to the speaking circuit and in "most un-Snicklike fashion, insisted on traveling first class on airplanes and receiving a thousand-dollar honorarium for a lecture." His popularity and "his appearance as a gadfly in public debates about civil rights soon earned him the nickname by friends and foes of Stokely 'Starmichael.' "[28] Brother Minister Billy X, on the other hand, was willing to travel some 200 miles, and his requirements were "just a chance to speak and teach Islam." In turn, Dixon began attending the local Nation of Islam mosque and reading Muslim literature; "almost from the start, I found myself searching for answers, and simultaneously, becoming aware of how foolish I had acted and sounded when I demanded the same person who had robbed me of the knowledge of myself, teach me back into the knowledge of myself."[29] Disgusted with displays of "selfishness and ignorance," Dixon "severed" his relations with the "BSU and stood up under the banner of Islam."[30]

Following the 1965 "summer of discontent," other new converts recall how their Nation of Islam membership was directly linked to disappointment in other political organizations, but particularly the newly formed BSUs that had spread like wildfire and therefore were the least structurally organized. Sister Linday Bryant remembered how she was initially involved in the BSU at the University of California, Santa Barbara, because she sought an organization that would give her "identity as a Black woman." Working diligently to "obtain a better education system and a better world in which to live," Bryant soon understood that the slogan "by any means necessary" to achieve the BSU goals ironically translated into "sleeping with whites and allowing them to integrate into our ranks."[31] Bryant began attending the local mosque and "became more inspired each time [she] went." Completely "disillusioned with the BSU and the phenomena of revolution," Bryant also became convinced that "the BSU did not have the solution to the Blacks' problems," so she decided to unite behind "one leader," and the only man "qualified to lead the so-called American Negro [was] the Honorable Elijah Muhammad."[32]

Sister Joan 4X also came to the Nation of Islam after membership in the BSU because she "was constantly in search of the qualities embodied in the Nation." Growing up in the South made her "aware of the evils and atrocities that white men do to my people every day of our waking lives." Joan 4X readily admits that she was "not quite ready for the caucasians on the west coast for they have placed a mental fog over the minds of our people that is much worse than any physical danger." This crisis pushed Joan 4X to become a part of "the new breed of black student trying desperately to rid themselves of the devils' influence." Putting herself on the line and shouting that she was "Black and Proud" to white administrators and officials meant that she also had to "have the courage to do something truly unique" about the conditions in the United States. As an "intelligent person," she analyzed how efficiently the white man uses the media to "choose our leaders" and then "brainwash" them and students. After becoming a member of the Nation of Islam, Joan 4X argued that the white press served as a "decoy" to keep black folks from the only true leader in America, the messenger. For Joan 4X, *The Autobiography of Malcolm X* (1964) was the most "obvious sign" to her that the "devil knows Islam is the only salvation for black people and the only vehicle that really unites us." Pointing out that when Malcolm X taught Islam, "the devils couldn't do enough to blaspheme him and the whole program of the Messenger; but when the man turned from the light of Islam, and especially now that he is dead, the white press can't put enough copies of his autobiography in the hands of our people."[33]

It is somewhat ironic that the Nation of Islam's platform was interpreted as a "Black Power" blueprint and that the waves of new members were former student activists, considering the fact that Elijah Muhammad never wavered from his conservative position that his followers eschew mainstream politics. Searching for answers to complicated, multilayered questions produced a longing to belong to something meaningful. Black Power activists were able to fill this lacuna by pushing the idea that black people at "home" and throughout the diaspora shared a collective identity and origins rooted in Africa. But Elijah Muhammad taught that Africans were a "backward" and "uncivilized" people and that the "so-called Negro" in the United States was in fact the most civilized and superior member of the human race. This diatribe against Africa at times sounded like racist, colonial gibberish, but members who may have disagreed with him were afraid to speak out against their leader. One Pan-African leader, Queen Mother Moore of Harlem, recalled how Malcolm X told her that "before he could say the word [Africa] it would have to come from Elijah."[34] This was a highly unlikely possibility since, as Malcolm X put it, Elijah Muhammad "was as anti-African as he was anti-white." In fact, Malcolm X adds, he "never had one statement that was pro-African."[35] Moore concluded that when she spent three days at the home of Elijah Muhammad, they argued because "he didn't want to hear nothing about Africa."[36] The Nation of Islam's assessment of Africa is confusing since historically and during the modern Black Power movement, Africa was always imagined as "home." The messenger justified his position with the following analysis:

> Many of my people, the so-called Negroes, say we should help the nations of Africa which are awakening. This has been said as if we owned America. We are so foolish! What part of America do you have that you can offer

toward helping Africa? Who is independent, the nations of Africa or we? The best act would be to request the independent governments of Africa and Asia to help us. We are the ones who need help. We have little or nothing to offer as help to others. We should begin to help at home first.[37]

Locating a "home" would provide the wellspring of unity, strength, and cultural meaning in the midst of the revolutionary chaos. Converts believed that the Nation of Islam, at the very least, offered a path to solving both personal and societal problems in that it linked black nationalist thought with politically transformative action. Black businesses, Muslim schools, temples, and black families were very real, tangible examples of successful nation building. At the same time, followers were encouraged to assertively critique the United States using activist language. For example, Sister Christine Delois X of Birmingham, Alabama, explained that "the white man's (devil's) civilization can offer us nothing in the way of security, education, and spirituality. In other words, this capitalist fascist-racist neocolonized society as a whole is falling (or has fallen) as our Beloved Leader and Teacher has taught for more than 40 years."[38] Writer James Baldwin was never a member of the Nation of Islam, yet he was also drawn to Elijah Muhammad's "peculiar authority." Slender and small in stature, Muhammad had a smile, Baldwin remembered, that "promised to take the burden of my life off my shoulders."[39]

Separate Territory and Institutions

Black Power advocates who shouted the slogan the loudest, Alvin F. Poussaint argues, "were those with the oldest battle scars from the terror, demoralization and castration which they experienced through continual direct confrontation" with white racism. In addition, these activists also recognized that "racial pride and self-love alone do not fill the bellies of starving black children in Mississippi."[40] Convinced that white people would never properly share resources nor concede full equality, many in attendance at the 1967 Black Power Conference in Newark, New Jersey, called for partitioning of the United States into two separate independent homelands. The Nation of Islam leadership had demanded a separate territory when activists were struggling to dismantle Jim Crow during the 1950s. Understanding that borders would move the Nation of Islam beyond an imagined state, Muhammad requested the cessation of seven or eight states. In an attempt to shame the government into a concession, Muhammad proclaimed that former slave masters were obligated to maintain and supply their needs in a separate territory for the next 20 to 25 years, given that their ancestors had earned it. Long before reparations became a popular plank among black nationalists, Muhammad and his ministers had demanded compensation for the damages done to generations of black people as "back payment" for enslaved labor. Much later, a "Black Manifesto" was issued at the April 1969 national Black Economic Development Conference in Detroit under the leadership of James Forman, which called upon the "White Christian Churches and the Jewish Synagogues in the United States and all other Racist Institutions" to give "$500 million in reparations and to surrender 60 percent of their assets to the conference to be used for the economic, social, and cultural rehabilitation of the black community."[41]

By 1965, the Nation of Islam had moved beyond cessation rhetoric, buying farmland in three states, as well as an abundance of property and small businesses near each of its temples (grocery stores, restaurants, and dry cleaning shops), valued in the millions.[42] The pursuit of economic power through the creation of separate communal institutions was a replication of Garveyism, but in terms of the modern liberation movement this strategy prefigured the late 1960s black capitalist's goals.[43] Already acting like people with power and control over their own destiny, the institutions built by the Nation of Islam were clear evidence of its material achievements. *Muhammad Speaks* published countless accounts of people who were in the "grave of ignorance and poverty" before their conversion and how they had made "real" progress with the Nation of Islam. For example, Brother Charles JX of Detroit says he became inspired to do something for himself after reading Muhammad's *Message to the Blackman* (1965). "Finally the solutions to all of my problems," Brother Charles recalled, "which had heretofore escaped me, became crystal clear." He decided to start a construction business, and he trained his son to become proficient in the field. Until he heard the teachings of Muhammad he "never thought" he could have a successful and profitable business in his lifetime.[44] Much of the followers' individual success was connected to the messenger's "Economic Freedom" plan that he introduced in 1964. Members were taught how to economize and save. Followers were told to "just save five cents a day or 25 cents a week amongst [them]selves and this would mean millions of dollars per year." At the annual Savior's Day Convention, Muhammad would spell out "the distance in dollars and cents" that had been accumulated as well as future financial expectations. The relationship between economic success and acquiring a sense of independence and power also had the objective of transforming the mind-set of members.

One of the main handicaps identified by the messenger that prevented "so-called Negroes" from achieving success was "the lack of knowledge of self." Members have given countless testimonies on how they had been formerly "brainwashed"; however, the teachings of the Honorable Elijah Muhammad explained their history. Sister Beverly Maurad, National Director of Education for the Nation of Islam in 1971, in a speech to the graduates of Muhammad Universities of Islam (secondary schools) states that even though students study some of the same subjects and read from the same books as their peers, their education is "better-more comprehensive" because "once you have been awakened it is easy to understand." The messenger taught that black people are "the original man, the maker, the owner of the planet earth. This one fact gives the true student, the true believer, a desire to regain his lost heritage" and "once again become members of a great civilization and Nation." Knowledge of self allows one to "see that you (Blackman) are the ones alluded to in your History Text books as having created wonderful civilizations with marvelous structures and using technological skills." As Black Muslim students, Maurad concludes, they have the advantage because they "know who they are," and thus they are "able to perceive and weigh and balance more clearly the curriculum presented."[45] Not surprisingly, the importance of reshaping the thoughts of followers required that the Nation of Islam create schools and curriculum "to educate self."

Black Power advocates, many of whom were enrolled or had recently attended college, also insisted on an academic curriculum that reflected the history and culture of black people. The Nation of Islam was already light-years ahead of the activists on this front. For years they had taught the members' children in separate schools that were usually located near the temples. The schools, in many ways, were the glue that held the Nation of Islam together. Sonsyrea Tate discusses how her mother stayed in the Nation of Islam so that she and her siblings would be eligible for the schools.[46] Some college students were drawn to the Nation of Islam largely because of its curriculum. Sister Joan 4X argued that black student demands for black studies departments would never be recognized and the messenger already boldly taught people "Black history."[47] The Nation of Islam's schools also became an important alternative for parents who did not want to have their children vaccinated—a requirement for public education. And, after the Tuskegee Study became public knowledge in 1972, based on medical experimentation conducted upon African American men between 1932 to 1972, authorized by the Centers for Disease Control, more African Americans feared the entire vaccination process; thus, the Nation of Islam schools were an important option.

Clearly, the religious "Islamic" nature of the Nation of Islam was not the major impetus for membership in the post-1965 period. Instead, the Nation of Islam's secular programs and exclusive black membership reinforced the new member's agenda to build a separate black nation. Essentially,

Muhammad promised to provide material symbols of power and wealth for people who had been discarded from the American populace and disinherited from the "American dream." By offering black Americans a vanguard lifestyle, Muhammad not only trumped the political struggle to extend rights of citizenship, but as T. H. Marshall would argue, his call was couched in an ideal expression of modern citizenship, "against which achievements can be measured and toward which aspirations can be directed."[48] Thus, nationhood success was predicated upon establishing a separate existence and presenting Islam as a materially empowering religion; one simply had to become a "Black Muslim" to receive the benefits.

Regendering

The making of the Black Muslim subject involved a complicated set of social relationships and obligations to the Nation of Islam. Whereas there are always rules for belonging, Roger Smith's concept of "civic myths" explains how guidelines of eligibility and exclusion are used to create political communities and thereby reflect their contested inner workings. In the case of the Nation of Islam, membership was rooted in gendered prescriptions. That is, men's and women's roles had to be reconfigured based on gendered stereotypes and hierarchies, and regulated differently in order to achieve black redemption—political emancipation, economic self-sufficiency, and social isolation from whites.

Nationalist precepts of gender promoted a conservative agenda where patriarchy took center stage. A separatist, masculine nation—the representation of a responsible, disciplined, dignified, and defiant manhood—would give black men rights and privileges denied them in white America. The centering of black men, however, pushed black women to the margin of nation building. Placing black women on the periphery served to counter/resist the master narrative of slavery that stereotypically portrays black women as jezebel's, matriarchs, and mannish women—roles that were used to both shame and usurp black manhood. Essentially, for the Nation of Islam, the emasculation of black men and their lack of masculine agency were dialectically connected to a hypersexualized, out-of-control, defiled, black woman. According to Elijah Muhammad, "There is no nation on earth that has less respect for and as little control of their women as we so-called Negroes here in America."[49]

The building of a Nation required public displays of symbols that often occurred at the site of the body. Representations of difference (men and women were essentially different by "nature") were accompanied by a prescription of particular relationships between men and women. North American slavery had created two types of victims: women who were raped and not allowed a feminine presence under the burdens of capitalism and men who were emasculated and rendered powerless. The regendering of Nation of Islam subjects returned them to a particular sense of "self" that was "natural" and denied under slavery. While a real Nation of Islam man was a masculine breadwinner and a good Nation of Islam woman was a feminine housewife, traditional roles, it was also believed, would bring a form of emotional intimacy between men and women. Boudoir politics recognizes the human need for love, and "any movement that hopes to empower" women and men "as opposed to just mobilize them" must deal with this issue.[50]

The unreal "matriarchal" legacy of slavery endured during the post-1965 Black Power movement largely because of distorted images of black female identity, for instance the fable that black women were "already liberated." Barbara Smith critiques the myth that black women were emancipated in advance of black men because the women shouldered the responsibilities of "heading families" and "working outside the home." Above all, "An ability to cope under the worst conditions is not liberation. ... Underlying this myth is the assumption that black women are towers of strength who neither feel nor need what other human beings do, either emotionally or materially." This widespread myth, codified in the 1965 Secretary of Labor Daniel Patrick Moynihan Report, insisted that black women had damned themselves and rendered black men "impotent."[51] Black male nationalists, within and outside of the Nation of Islam, presumed that women had to be controlled and assume a passive role in order for men to rise up and be "real men" in the United States. Maulana Ron Karenga led the cultural nationalists with perceptions such as "what makes a woman appealing is femininity and she can't be feminine without being submissive."[52] Moreover, as Akiba ya Elimu states, "the man" should be "the leader of the house/nation because his knowledge of the world is broader, his awareness is greater, his understanding is fuller and his application of this information is wiser," which certainly justifies why he should lead.[53] Nation of Islam male leaders added white women into this garbled misrepresentation. In fact, they accused black women of mimicking the immoral habits of white women. Utilizing racial pride rhetoric as a form of control, the messenger told black men to "stop our women from trying to look like them [white women]. By bleaching, powdering, ironing and coloring their hair, painting their lips, cheeks, and eyebrows; wearing shorts; going half-nude in public places. Stop women from using unclean language in public (and at home), from smoking and drug addiction habits."[54] In sum, slavery as well as the behavior of aggressive Western women had brought destruction to Allah's social order, generating a renegade black woman.

Restraining women, also an obsession among Middle Eastern Islamic fundamentalists, positions the Nation of Islam squarely in line with the patriarchal climate of Black Power. Muhammad, however, helped to camouflage the gender inequalities in the Nation of Islam with the affectionate rhetoric of love, protection, and respect for black womanhood. This is an important point, especially considering the scathing, sexual criticism of black women at the time. One simply has to recall Stokely Carmichael's response to a question concerning the "proper position of women in SNCC." He "jokingly" replied, "prone." Or, more to the point, the views uttered by Eldridge Cleaver, leader of the BPP, are without a doubt the most misogynistic. He wrote that he knew that "the white man made the black woman the symbol of slavery." In his mind, this view explained his lack of attraction and respect for black women. He gloated, "The only way that I can bust my nuts with a black bitch [is] to close my eyes and pretend that she is Jezebel. If I was to look down and see a black bitch underneath me or if my hand happened to feel her nappy hair, that would be the end, it would be all over."[55] Paulette Pierce insightfully analyzes that "such were the most influential musings of the fertile imagination of Black nationalists during the sixties as they labored to birth a free nation or die in the process."[56]

Within this climate, according to *Muhammad Speaks,* some women viewed the Nation of Islam as a safe, loving "home." Sister Charles Ann X said that "Islam elevates the so-called Negro woman by giving her wisdom, knowledge, culture and refinement."[57] No longer did Sandra JX consider herself "just a simple, southern girl," but in the Nation of Islam she was "the queen of the entire planet earth and the mother of all civilization."[58] Sister Vera X Lewis testified that the messenger was "not afraid to point out how the black woman has been abused for some 400 years." She was thankful that her leader "instills in black men a rebirth to their natural urge to protect black women." White men "or even misguided black men can no longer use black women for ill purposes," remarked Lewis. Historically, black women's bodies have been commodified as legal property and their sexuality exploited to justify capitalism and the perverse desires of men. Sister Mable X recalled how her "body," now that she was a member of the Nation of Islam "was overtaken with warmth and beauty." She "became very proud, rejoiceful, and thankful."[59] It seems that it did not matter (or matter enough to prevent membership) to these women that under the conditions of the Nation of Islam (as well as other black nationalist organizations) respect for their personhood and protection from seething forces hinged on their complete obedience to all paternal figures.

There are indeed complicated reasons why Nation of Islam women accepted what appears to be a second-class status. Aaronetta X Anderson remembered that when she was on the outside looking in before joining in 1966, she had many misconceptions concerning the role of women. As "quite an assertive person, and seeing how aggressive the brothers were, I assumed women had to take a back seat." After attending the Muslim's Girls Training and General Civilization Classes (MGT-GCC), it became apparent to her that it was "not so much a 'back seat' as the proper seat."[60] The fact that the "back seat" had to be addressed indicates that women had to be convinced that they were not being subjugated, and the most efficient way to rationalize limiting the participation of women was through an ideology that connected their marginalized role to the greater good of black people. It was both their racial and religious duty to sacrifice self for the liberation project. Sister Melva J. X. Walker of Oklahoma City, Oklahoma, says it best. Prior to becoming a registered Muslim on June 7, 1971, she always wanted to be "famous and beautiful." Her goal was to be a career woman, "successful, progressive and productive." Determined to finish college, she wanted to "find [her] place and really contribute something valuable to this existing system." After receiving her "X" she understood "exactly that to progress, is not just climbing to the top of the devil's society, but it means helping [her] people." The most efficient way to help was to know her "place" and "that place is not on some stage displaying [her]self, or having [her] name up in lights, and neither is that place any one of the many careers which [she] considered from Ambassador to Africa, to a Playboy bunny," but "it is a place [where she] wants to spend [her] life, Being a Woman, a Natural Black Woman in the Nation of Islam."[61]

Women like sister Melva J. X. Walker must have faced a major struggle as they transferred their allegiance from organizations that thrived on celebrating links with Africa to one that viewed Africa as backward. Most of the post-1965 Nation of Islam converts first attended the mosque, which usually had pews as opposed to prayer rugs, and wore African apparel and Afro hairstyles. Elijah Muhammad did not approve of this Afro-centric style and exercised his last resort measure to regain authority through dismissal. He concluded that if men and women are not satisfied "with the styles I give them then I am not satisfied with you being my follower."[62] Islam is a very public and visible religion, and Muhammad was clear about his dictator role as regulator of the material culture and demeanor of his followers. There was little room within the Nation of Islam to challenge prescribed practices or act as a critical citizen.

Clothing was marked as a particularly important sign of Nation of Islam identity and a means for the control over bodies and body image. Like colonial images of Africa, many Nation of Islam converts viewed Africans as a population in need of "civilization" and lacking in respectability. Elijah Muhammad "made" Nation of Islam men and women to be "respectable" and "civilized," through the adoption of a strict dress code. Men were extremely neat, and their uniform consisted of dark colored suits, usually adorned with the messenger's signature bow tie. Long hair was seen by the messenger as a "woman's" style, and he would "not tolerate" his "followers wearing such germ-catchers" as beards. Stop "imitat[ing] the non-modern man," said Muhammad. "Cut off that pillow of hair behind your head, at the nape of your neck and trim your hair-line around the back of your neck, like the modern man."[63] Women were resocialized to wear long gowns and matching head wraps. This uniform was reminiscent of the Black Cross Nurses of the Garvey movement. Although an expression of their link to black nationalism, this attire also kept women within the appropriate Muslim style, covering them from wrist to ankle. It was only a matter of time before members who initially wore colorful dashikis came to accept the messenger's stringent dress code as appropriate. Sister Marguerite X testified that she was "one of those Afro-wearers and was of the opinion that Africans or so-called Negroes imitating Africans was the only beautiful way of life. I was wrong."[64] Sister Evelyn X states: "If you see a woman dressed as a Muslim sister, you will think that she is a Muslim and treat her with the respect due a Muslim woman. By the same token, if you see a woman dressed in hot pants, halter top, afro puff wigs on her head, and mud packed on her face, you will think that she must be a loose woman and will treat her as one."[65] The tailored clothing not only combated the sexually deviant myths associated with black people but also gave the appearance of a "civilized" community with outward forms of religiosity.

Islamic law, as taught by Elijah Muhammad, rested upon the most conservative verses in the Qur'an, which dictated that wives should be obedient to their husbands. Muslim scholars debate the meaning of obedience and whether it is a requirement for good behavior rather than submission. Scholar Haleh Afshar states that "in practice, Muslim women must accept many of the dictates of patriarchy if they are to accept Islam and its teachings."[66] In 1965, Elijah Muhammad admitted that in some cities the conversion ratio was as high as five men to one woman. But he reasoned that low female support was due to the "destruction" of the black woman by the "serpent, the devil, dragon, Satan," the forces of white manipulation and not the male-centered structure of the Nation of Islam.

Conclusion

The Nation of Islam was so irresistible for men because no one articulated the aspirations of the "so-called Negro" better than Malcolm X. The need to create a new political source of black personhood and solidarity propelled activists to transform the liberation movement after his assassination. Unfortunately, a host of Black Power organizations, fraught with neophyte leadership, nepotism, and crippling masculinity, rapidly surfaced during the postmortem period. Disappointment and contention within the Black Power ranks ironically gave way to an enhanced sense of the Nation of Islam as a radical political alternative. Elijah Muhammad and his ministers weathered the tense aftermath of Malcolm's death by capitalizing on activists' disillusionment. Cultivating a constellation of theory (original "Asiatic Blackman" and "Black woman" as "queen of the universe") and practice (small businesses and schools), Elijah Muhammad was able to shift the focus away from Malcolm's demise and onto tangible evidence of nation building. The Nation of Islam became a complicated expression of Black Power, and it enables us to consider the intricate production and manifestation of political subjectivity, vis-à-vis, gender, race, class, and nation. In the end, the Nation of Islam offered young people who were constructing a political identity and searching for a stable political "home" a structured, separatist organization committed to a distinctive moral and religious sensibility. Civil agitation assumed the form of economic self-sufficiency and social isolation from whites. Certainly, Malcolm's legacy made black folks aware of the Nation of Islam, but it was his teacher's vision that brought activists into its folds during the post-1965 period.

Notes

1. E. U. Essien-Udom, *Black Nationalism: A Search for Identity in America* (Chicago: University of Chicago Press, 1962), 378.
2. Claude Clegg, *An Original Man: The Life and Times of Elijah Muhammad* (New York: St. Martin's Press, 1998), 239; William L. Van DeBurg, *New Day in Babylon: The Black Power Movement and American Culture, 1965–1975* (Chicago: The University of Chicago Press, 1992), 2.
3. For the most part, my sources on the reasons why women and men joined the Nation of Islam in the post-Malcolm X period are limited to an analysis of the Nation of Islam's weekly newspaper *Muhammad Speaks*. In terms of why they joined the organization, the members' testimonies are open to a number of interpretations—some of which I have not yet had time to explore.

4. The Nation of Islam had been founded in 1930 in Detroit under W. D. Fard. See Erdmann Doane Beynon, "The Voodoo Cult Among Negro Migrants in Detroit," *American Journal of Sociology* 63 (1938). For a discussion of the early years and Elijah Muhammad's meteoric rise, see Claude Clegg, *An Original Man.*

5. Clegg, *An Original Man,* 48.

6. Ibid., 42.

7. For example, see Winthrop Jordan, *White Over Black: American Attitudes Toward the Negro, 1550–1812* (Baltimore: Penguin Books, 1969).

8. Robert Reid-Pharr, "Speaking through Anti-Semitism: The Nation of Islam and the Poetics of Black (Counter) Modernity" *Social Text* 14:4 (winter 1996): 140.

9. Salim Mauwakkil, "The Nation of Islam and Me," in *The Farrakhan Factor: African-American Writers on Leadership, Nationhood, and Minister Louis Farrakhan,* Amy Alexander, ed. (New York: Grove Press, 1998), 296.

10. Ernest Allen, "Minister Louis Farrakhan and the Continuing Evolution of the Nation of Islam," in Alexander, *The Farrakhan Factor,* 78.

11. An important millennial idea is that a "devil stands between God's people and the heavenly kingdom." See Perry E. Giankos, "The Black Muslims: An American Millennialistic Response to Racism and Cultural Denegration," *The Centennial Review* 23: 4 (fall 1979): 439.

12. John Edgar Wideman, "Malcolm X: The Art of Autobiography," in *Malcolm X: In Our Image,* Joe Wood, ed. (New York: St. Martin's Press, 1992), 113.

13. Malcolm X, *The Autobiography of Malcolm X* (New York: Grove Press, 1964), 294.

14. Gordon Parks, "The Violent End of the Man Called Malcolm X," *Life* 58:9 (March 5, 1965): 29.

15. Malcolm X, *The Autobiography of Malcolm X,* 294–295, 316.

16. It is extremely difficult to document the numbers of people who left the Nation of Islam, as well as new members, during the post-1965 period. What is evident is that the Nation of Islam continued to be a thriving, separatist organization.

17. Elijah Muhammad, "Mr. Muhammad Calls for Unified Front of Black Men at New York City Rally," *Pittsburgh Courier,* July 19, 1958, 6.

18. Malcolm X, *The Autobiography of Malcolm X,* 169.

19. Brother Tomas 18X, "United Under Light of Islam," *Muhammad Speaks,* December 29, 1967, 25.

20. Interview by Ula Taylor of Joan X, October 21, 1999, Oakland, Calif.

21. Joan 4X, "What Islam Has Done for Me," *Muhammad Speaks,* August 29, 1969, 17.

22. Gene Roberts, "The Story of Snick: From 'Freedom High' to Black Power," *New York Times Magazine,* September 25, 1966, reprint in *Black Protest in the Sixties: Essays from the New York Times Magazine,* August Meier, John Bracey Jr., and Elliott Rudwick, eds. (New York: Markus Wierner Publication, 1991), 140–141; Frantz Fanon, *The Wretched of the Earth* (New York: Grove, 1967).

23. Anna Karriem, "The Preacher of Pan-Africanism," *Muhammad Speaks,* April 16, 1971, 15.

24. Sister Marguerite X, "Has Found Path to True Liberation, Righteousness in the Nation of Islam," *Muhammad Speaks,* August 29, 1969, 17.

25. Brother Preston X (Dixon), "Say Black Students Union Is Ersatz; Nation of Islam is the Real Thing," *Muhammad Speaks,* July 25 (1969), 17.

26. Ula Y. Taylor, J. Tarika Lewis, and Mario Van Peebles, *Panther: A Pictorial History of the Black Panther Party and the Story behind the Film* (New York: New Market Press, 1995).

27. Huey Newton, *Revolutionary Suicide* (New York: Ballantine Books, 1973), 77.

28. Charles Marsh, *God's Long Summer: Stories of Faith and Civil Rights* (Princeton, N.J.: Princeton University Press, 1997), 181.

29. Brother Preston X (Dixon), "Say Black Students Union Is Ersatz," 17.

30. Ibid.

31. Lindsay Bryant, "What Islam Has Done for Me," *Muhammad Speaks,* October 24, 1969, 13.

32. Ibid.

33. Joan 4X, "What Islam Has Done for Me," 17.

34. Audley (Queen Mother) Moore interview, June 6 and 8, 1978, in *The Black Women Oral History Project,* Ruth Edmonds Hill, ed. (Westport, Conn.: Meckler, 1991), 151.

35. Malcolm X, *February 1965: The Final Speeches,* Steve Clark, ed. (New York: Pathfinder, 1992), 205.

36. Moore interview, 151.

37. Elijah Muhammad, *Message to the Blackman in America* (Philadelphia, Penn.: Hakim Publishing, 1965), 35.

38. Sister Christine Delois X, "Dope, Alcohol and Devil's Tricks Strip Blacks of Human Dignity," *Muhammad Speaks,* January 29, 1971, 18.

39. James Baldwin, *The Price of the Ticket: Collected Nonfiction 1948–1985* (New York: St. Martin's Press, 1985), 360.

40. Alvin F. Poussaint, "A Negro Psychiatrist Explains the Negro Psyche," *New York Times Magazine,* August 20, 1967, reprint in August Meier, Elliot Rudwick, and John Bracey, Jr., eds., *Black Protest in the Sixties: Articles from the New York Times* (New York: Markus Wiener Publishers, 1991), 138.

41. John Hope Franklin and Alfred A. Moss, Jr., *From Slavery to Freedom: A History of African Americans* (Boston: McGraw Hill, 2000), 553.

42. David Jackson and William Gaines, "Nation of Islam: Power of Money," *Chicago Tribune,* March 12, 1995, 16.

43. Brother Herbert X, "Explains How Messenger Laid Out Plan for Economic Freedom in Slave Land," *Muhammad Speaks,* April 21, 1967, 25.

44. Brother Charles JX, "Found Solutions to All My Problems Laid with Islam," *Muhammad Speaks,* August 29, 1969, 17.

45. Sister Beverly Maurad, "Sister Beverley Maurad Addresses All Islam Grads," *Muhammad Speaks,* March 19, 1971, 15.

46. Sonsyrea Tate, *Little X: Growing Up in the Nation of Islam* (San Francisco: Harper Collins, 1997), 84.

47. Joan 4X, "What Islam Has Done For Me," 17.
48. T. H. Marshall, *Citizenship and Social Class* (Cambridge: Cambridge University Press, 1950), 29.
49. Muhammad, *Message to the Blackman,* 59.
50. Paulette Pierce, "Boudoir Politics and the Birthing of the Nation," in *Women Out of Place: The Gender of Agency and the Race of Nationality,* Brackette F. Williams, ed. (New York: Routledge, 1996), 235.
51. Barbara Smith, "Some Home Truths on the Contemporary Black Feminist Movement," in *Words of Fire: An Anthology of African-American Feminist Thought,* Beverly Guy-Sheftall, ed. (New York: The Free Press, 1995), 255; Daniel P. Moynihan, *The Negro Family: The Case for National Action* (Washington, D.C.: U.S. Government Printing Office, 1965).
52. Imamu Amiri Baraka, ed. *African Congress: A Documentary of the First Modern Pan-African Congress* (New York: William and Morrow, 1972), 177.
53. Baraka, ed. *African Congress,* 177, 179.
54. Muhammad, *Message to the Blackman,* 60.
55. Eldridge Cleaver, *Soul on Ice* (New York: A Delta Book, 1968), 160–161.
56. Pierce, "Boudoir Politics and the Birthing of the Nation," 223.
57. Sister Charles Ann X, "Says Islam Lifts Up the Black Woman, Giving Her Wisdom, Knowledge, Strength," *Muhammad Speaks,* June 23, 1967, 25.
58. Sandra JX, "Black Woman Finds Peace, Freedom in Folds of Islam," *Muhammad Speaks* May 26, 1967, 26.
59. Sister Mable X, "Greatest Gift She Has Ever Known," *Muhammad Speaks,* July 28, 1967, 25.
60. Aaronetta X Anderson, *Muhammad Speaks,* April 22, 1966, 25.
61. Melva J. X. (Walker), "Muslim Sister Finds Real Meaning of Black Beauty," *Muhammad Speaks,* July 16, 1971, 18.
62. Elijah Muhammad, "Warning to the MGT and GC Class," *Muhammad Speaks,* June 28, 1968, 4.
63. Elijah Muhammad, "Beards," *Muhammad Speaks,* July 4, 1969, 5.
64. Marguerite X, "What Islam Has Done for Me," *Muhammad Speaks,* August 2, 1969, 17.
65. Sister Evelyn X, "Modest Muslim Dress Dignifies Blackwoman," *Muhammad Speaks,* April 6, 1973, 18.
66. Haleh Afshar, "Why Fundamentalism? Iranian Women and Their Support of Islam," *Women: A Cultural Review* 6:4 (1995): 27.

Chapter 8

Black Buying Power: Welfare Rights, Consumerism, and Northern Protest

Felicia Kornbluh

This whole society is run on credit, especially for the rich man. So why can't we have it. The poor need it more than the rich.

—*Etta Horn, Chair, NWRO Committee on Ways and Means*

Give us Credit for Being American.

—*NWRO slogan*

The welfare rights movement and the people who joined it are paradigmatic of those who have often been left out of civil rights history.[1] Studying the South and North, scholars have begun to challenge the familiar narrative of civil rights by elaborating on the class bases of activist politics, the gender dynamics within leading movement groups, and their ideological and strategic complexity.[2] We have begun to reconceptualize the term "civil rights" to include economic redistribution and macroeconomic planning, among other issues that have often been written out of the boundaries of movement history.[3] By widening our lens to include a greater range of political activity, we have illuminated the artificial distinctions that have shaped much writing on post-1945 social movements. These include distinctions between civil rights and economic rights, between the South and North, and between a supposedly innocent early stage of movement work (in the 1950s and early 1960s) and a disruptive and ultimately tragic later stage.[4]

The social movement for welfare rights began in the urban North during the early 1960s. Although welfare rights organizing eventually reached into communities throughout the United States, its main centers were all outside the South—New York City, Cleveland, Chicago, Oakland, and Los Angeles. The overwhelming majority of movement activists were black women with children who received public assistance payments from the government. Unlike the portion of civil rights work that has received the most scholarly and popular attention—sponsored by the Southern Christian Leadership Conference (SCLC) and Student Nonviolent Coordinating Committee—the National Welfare Rights Organization (NWRO) received scant support from black churches. The welfare recipients who joined spoke in a secular language of political and constitutional rights far more than they did in a Christian language of redemption and forgiveness.[5]

Efforts to build a national coalition of welfare rights groups began in 1966 as a project of the Poverty/Rights Action Center in Washington, D.C. In 1967, a convention of locally based welfare rights groups renamed their coalition the NWRO. Like other Northern-based groups in the late 1960s and early 1970s, such as the Black Panthers and the Congress of Racial Equality (CORE), the welfare rights movement had an agenda for changing the political economy of the United States. Welfare rights activists argued that the United States should focus less on the participation of its citizens in the waged labor market and more on ensuring everyone the capacity to purchase basic goods and services. The central political demand of NWRO activists was for a guaranteed adequate income, a minimum stipend that all citizens would receive from the national government when their incomes fell below maintenance levels. NWRO members argued for guaranteeing the incomes, particularly of women who performed the socially vital work of raising children. However, they extended the benefits of the income guarantee to all U.S. citizens, including men and those without children.[6]

The NWRO and other late-1960s Northern groups differed in important ways from the mainstream civil rights organizations and classic campaigns of the Southern civil rights movement. Welfare rights organizing in the North also resembled the Southern movement in ways that bring into relief dimensions of civil rights that have often been obscured. The large portion of low-income black women among welfare rights activists, for example, recalls the Southern movement's reliance upon women's grassroots activism.

NWRO and other Northern groups also remind us that the civil rights movement was not as ideologically innocent as some chroniclers have claimed. Within the NWRO, welfare recipients mixed with liberal advocates of the federal poverty programs, community organizers trained by Saul

Alinsky, attorneys trained in the labor movement, and alumni of the 1940s–50s sectarian left. The guaranteed income idea—an idea that briefly had wide appeal across the political spectrum—was primarily a product of the libertarian left. Elsewhere in the civil rights movement, similar left-of-center affiliations and ideas were hidden in plain view. Scholarship has often underemphasized them, perhaps because charges of Communist influence were used to discredit the movement in the 1950s and 1960s. Historians have always known about the left connections of A. Philip Randolph, Bayard Rustin, and a number of those in the inner circle of Dr. Martin Luther King, Jr. Recent research has emphasized the early links between Southern black activism and the Communist Party; King's early and continued interest in socialist and social-democratic thought from his seminary days onward; and the importance of a social-democratic agenda emphasizing macroeconomic planning and full employment to a range of movement activists.[7]

Finally, the NWRO case study brings into relief the portion of civil rights protest in both the South and North that concerned the consumer dimension of the economy. It is certainly true, as Charles Hamilton and Dona Cooper Hamilton have argued, that many civil rights groups fought to remove racial barriers to jobs and employment training.[8] The movement South and North also fought for equality at the point of consumption. Consumer strategies, such as boycotts and the formation of consumer and producer cooperatives, were integral to civil rights struggles. In some instances, as in the "Don't Buy Where You Can't Work" campaigns in the 1930s and 1940s and the boycotts of major retailers in both Northern and Southern cities during the early 1960s, consumer strategies were tied to demands for increased minority employment.[9] Other strategies, such as the Montgomery Bus Boycott, the lunch-counter sit-ins, and the boycotts that accompanied the Birmingham campaign in 1963, aimed to unravel legal Jim Crow by applying economic pressure on local political and business elites. Mass consumer strategies used community solidarity to multiply the limited economic power available to individual African Americans. These struggles always contained an element of what philosopher Nancy Fraser has called "recognition justice."[10] As part of their claims for civil rights, African Americans sought the freedom to perform all of the normal public activities of post-WWII America, including buying ice-cream sodas at the five-and-dime and trying on clothes in the fitting room of a downtown department store.

In what follows, I explore the consumer dimension of struggle within the welfare rights movement. Consumerism played a special role in welfare rights because the movement was a women's movement; women have had primary responsibility throughout the twentieth century for negotiating the consumer market on behalf of their families. Consumer concerns were also central to the NWRO because consumerism suffused the daily practices of welfare departments. However, in their concern both with consumer strategies and public recognition for African American consumers, NWRO members resembled other civil rights activists more than they differed from them.

NWRO members and other activist welfare recipients criticized both private retailers and the welfare system for failing to allow welfare recipients to participate fully in the post-WWII consumer economy. Consumerist demands were constitutive of NWRO's political efforts throughout the history of the movement. Before 1968, these demands treated government agencies as almost solely responsible for meeting welfare recipients' needs. NWRO members and other welfare recipients fought authorities over the contents of the "welfare budget," the breakdown of families' needs that formed the basis of their biweekly public assistance grants. They also fought over the assessments that case workers made of what they called the "basic" and "special needs" of clients—and thus about which goods were necessities for families and which were luxuries. They used loopholes in welfare department rules, legal challenges, and confrontational tactics to gain a wide variety of goods.

By 1969, the climate in public institutions had changed. NWRO activists shifted a portion of their consumerist demands from government agencies to private retailers. Two main strategies emerged: The first was a boycott of the Sears Corporation, which involved hundreds of NWRO members and middle-class "Friends." They claimed that Sears discriminated against the poor by refusing credit applications from welfare recipients. The second strategy was a "private-sector family assistance plan," in which the NWRO offered to distribute a company's goods to its members in the hope that this would enhance the firm's reputation among low-income and African American consumers and, over the long run, help create social peace.

Consumption Politics

Aside from their immediate roots in the consumerism of the post-1945 period, welfare activists' claims for consumption rights had deep roots in traditions of social protest. Women's movements throughout U.S. history have frequently used tactics that centered on the consumer side of the economy.[11] Consumption has also been a vital part of both organized and unorganized political action within African American communities. In addition to the "Don't Buy Where You Can't Work" campaigns, the

Montgomery Bus Boycott, and other organized efforts, the claim to "lady-hood," the gendered demand for dignity and decency that welfare recipients expressed in campaigns for clothes, home furnishings, and consumer credit, recalls a rich history of individual and collective actions by African American women in the nineteenth and twentieth centuries.[12]

The 1960s and 1970s saw the emergence of a new consumer movement, which converged with the women's and civil rights movements. One major concern of this movement was access to consumer credit for women and racial minorities. Within the feminist movement, consumer consciousness provoked a campaign for women's equal credit opportunities, including credit cards in their own names for married women and improved credit access for single and divorced women. These efforts resulted in passage of the Equal Credit Opportunity Act of 1974.[13] Numerous sources raised questions about relationships between communities of color and systems of consumption, credit, and sales.

The data that fueled concern about consumer credit came primarily from a single study of practices in New York City. In the early 1960s, a coalition of settlement houses sponsored a study of the consumer behavior of black and Puerto Rican public housing tenants. The book that resulted, *The Poor Pay More*, argued that low-income consumers often paid more than those with higher incomes for goods of equal quality.[14] This occurred because low-income consumers purchased the goods on credit from local merchants or peddlers who came into their homes.[15] They bought on the installment plan at exorbitant interest rates.

Low-income African American and Puerto Rican families participated in the postwar consumer economy. Ninety-five percent of the families studied had television sets, 41 percent owned washing machines, and 23 percent had telephones "of the colored variety."[16] As with other postwar families, for poor families, "[b]ridging the gap between current income and extensive needs and aspirations is the institution of credit."[17] Even the 15 percent of families in the study who received welfare were able to buy on credit to purchase goods.[18]

Toward Black (Buying) Power

Consumer issues and other economic concerns had long been central to movement activists. In *Black Power: The Politics of Liberation*, Stokely Carmichael and Charles Hamilton made an analogy between white-black relationships and relationships between European colonial powers and their African colonies, based on the flow of consumer capital out of

African American communities.[19] They focused on the exploitative credit practices of white store owners in black neighborhoods, using the term "poverty cycle" to describe the entrapment of black urbanites in webs of installment debt. Carmichael and Hamilton added:

> The merchant has special ways of victimizing public welfare recipients. They are not supposed to buy on credit; installment payments are not provided for in the budget. Thus a merchant can threaten to tell the case-worker if a recipient who isn't meeting his payments does not "come in and put down something, if only a couple of dollars."[20]

Carmichael and Hamilton called on neighborhood groups to boycott all white-owned businesses except those that agreed to a "community rebate" of 50 percent of their profits, which could fund local employment, school scholarships, or community organization efforts.[21] In terms that resembled those in *Black Power*, social critic Harold Cruse inveighed against the "captive consumers and cheap labor reserves" in African American communities.[22]

In the late 1960s, similar calls for African American economic self-determination were heard from leaders of traditional civil rights groups. A centerpiece of the SCLC's strategy for addressing job discrimination in the North, for example, was Reverend Jesse Jackson's Operation Breadbasket in Chicago.[23] Operation Breadbasket threatened boycotts of consumer goods produced by companies that were not doing enough to provide equal employment and advancement opportunities for black workers.[24] In his last book, *Where Do We Go From Here: Chaos or Community?*, King focused on strategies that utilized the power of urban blacks as consumers. King endorsed a vigorous use of black "buying power" to further the rights struggle.[25] He singled out the "vicious circle" that low-income consumers encountered:

> You can't get a job because you are poorly educated, and you must depend on welfare to feed your children; but if you receive public aid ... you cannot own property, not even an automobile, so you are condemned to the jobs and shops which are closest to your home. Once confined to this isolated community, one no longer participates in a free economy, but is subject to price-fixing and wholesale robbery by many of the merchants of the area. [26]

The changing composition of the movement, as King and others carried it North, raised the profile of issues such as welfare and consumer purchasing in low-income neighborhoods. As James Farmer, the former head of CORE, remembered:

> [A]fter the March on Washington the young people in the inner city, who had been watching it on TV up in their slum apartments said, "Hey, let me

take a look at this." ... The young folk from the inner city were saying, "What is all this we-shall-overcome, black-and-white-together stuff? I don't know of any white folks except the guy who runs that store on 125th Street in Harlem and garnishees wages and repossesses things you buy [for missed installment payments]. I'd like to go upside his head."[27]

NWRO activists shared much with the other intellectuals and activists who worked on the problem of consumer participation for poor African Americans in the late 1960s. Arguing that in comparison to other low-income people welfare recipients were in an even weaker bargaining position vis-à-vis the exploitative local merchant, they asserted the need for consumer credit on the part of all families, whether or not they were poor. In response to these concerns, welfare rights activists sought credit at what they termed "reputable" working- and middle-class department stores like Sears, Montgomery Ward, Lerner, and Lane Bryant. They also sought to recruit corporate participation in a "Private-Sector Family Allowance Plan" that would make consumer goods available to NWRO members through vouchers.

Welfare recipients organized amidst the ubiquitous consumerism of post-WWII America. In this context, demanding a credit card at the "all-American department store" or seeking access to all-American products were ways to ask for social recognition as postwar American women. Women in the postwar United States were still responsible for negotiating the consumer marketplace in behalf of their families.[28] Welfare rights activists struggled for recognition as citizen-consumers who did the same work as all other women.

"Give Us Credit for being American": The Sears Campaign

Welfare rights activists' consumer credit campaign began in Philadelphia in the summer of 1968. Philadelphia Welfare Rights Organization (WRO) leaders such as Roxanne Jones and Margie Jefferson, and young Volunteers in Service to America (VISTAs), devised the idea of seeking department store credit exclusively for members of the WRO.[29] By August, they had agreements with Wanamaker, Lerner, Lit Brothers, and Lane Bryant stores. The group later gained limited credit access from other stores, including Sears. At the Lerner Shops, WRO members did not even have to undergo credit checks but received credit automatically. Mrs. Jefferson lauded the agreements as a way to release low-income people from exploitative local stores: "No longer are we restricted to buying inferior merchandise at high prices in the ghetto," she commented.[30] The credit benefit was a major draw to new members, and the Philadelphia WRO saw its membership double after it publicized its agreements with the stores.[31]

National welfare rights leaders were impressed with these results. As Tim Sampson, the former associate national director of the NWRO, remembered:

> Philadelphia succeeded in getting credit and welfare recipients flocked to join. So then we tried to figure out what was the best national thing that would work all over the country, and Sears was the really great connecting link ... to get the attention of local groups.[32]

NWRO staff members chose Sears, although the company was notoriously anti-union and resistant to grassroots pressure.[33] Sears's intransigence allowed NWRO to build a large-scale campaign over several months. Moreover, the NWRO sought credit from other stores and used the intransigence of the one company as a negative example to its competitors.

The aim of the credit campaign was to make local WROs intermediaries between their members and the stores. The NWRO argued that "a letter of reference from NWRO should be adequate proof that the recipient is a good credit risk, and there [should] be no other investigation."[34] With credit dependent on WRO certification, local groups would be like consumption-side hiring halls, able to choose which low-income people would have access to credit. Sears and other firms were asked to forge national agreements with the NWRO, which would be binding on all of the stores in their chains.[35]

It is difficult to establish the precise impact of the credit campaign. Scholars Frances Fox Piven and Richard Cloward have argued that the campaign had little effect. Indeed, the NWRO never persuaded Sears management to join a national agreement. However, in Philadelphia, Memphis, Pontiac, Michigan, and Portsmouth, Ohio, the WROs received credit at Sears; in Cincinnati, the local Sears store agreed to the entire NWRO plan. In Boston, certified WRO members received $50 credit lines at Filene's, Gilchrist, and Jordan Marsh in the wake of a major demonstration at Sears.[36] In Brooklyn, welfare activists protested successfully for credit at Korvette's, then received credit at Abraham and Straus without protesting. The Brooklyn agreements were followed by citywide credit arrangements for New York welfare recipients with Gimbel's and the other two chains in the wake of a major demonstration at a Manhattan Sears store.[37] At least 3,000 welfare recipients and other poor people received credit from Montgomery Ward as a result of the NWRO's negotiations with the company's national management.[38] Probably hundreds of others received credit through informal agreements. Even more received credit on what the companies claimed was an individual basis but was in fact leniency shaped by the companies' fear of demonstrations.[39]

Aside from these arrangements, WROs across the United States had active campaigns aimed at Sears. These helped to publicize welfare recipients' political agenda and their material needs, attracted members, and raised morale within the groups. WROs in 29 different areas, from Rochester, New York, to DeMoines, Iowa, and from Hinds County, Mississippi, to Pomona, California, negotiated with Sears.[40] Groups in 62 areas, from West Helena, Arkansas, to Bakersfield, California, to Waterbury, Connecticut, had conducted Sears actions of some kind by April 9, 1969. The strategies used included passing out leaflets in front of busy stores; filling out credit applications collectively (creating long lines for service) and returning frequently with a group of protesters to inquire about progress on the applications; and having middle-class "Friends" with Sears credit burn their cards (or cut them in half).[41]

The most disruptive tactic utilized by WROs in support of the Sears boycott was the "shop-in."[42] Welfare recipients would enter stores en masse and do everything in their power to complicate and slow down the sales machinery. This could include entering shoe, hat, or clothing departments and requesting help with an array of colors, sizes, and types of merchandise. NWRO staff suggested that protesters follow up by "request[ing] the manager or clerks to ask other store branches for items not available where you are."[43] When they finished choosing merchandise, WRO members took their items to cash registers. When the cashiers had finished ringing up all the merchandise, they explained that they wished to pay on credit but that Sears credit was not available for welfare recipients. Alternately, protesters would show their welfare identification cards as if they were credit cards and tell cashiers to charge the items to the Welfare Department. (New York City welfare activists "call[ed] their Welfare ID Card 'The Everything Card.'"[44]) In response to the slowdowns and long lines that resulted, welfare activists posing as ordinary customers complained loudly and created more disruption by gathering in crowds around the cash registers.[45]

WROs maximized disruption by timing their "shop-ins" to coincide with some of the heaviest shopping days in the year. In 1969, NWRO Ways and Means Committee chair Etta Horn and Wiley directed the WROs to demonstrate on the Saturday before Easter.[46] They directed members to begin with a rally outside local Sears stores and, then, to take the following steps:

— Shop for Easter and Spring clothing that you ... want to buy on credit.
— Take the merchandise to a salesperson and ask to purchase on credit NOW.

- You will be sent to the credit department—go and get all members of your WRO together there. Demand credit today and fill out applications ...
- If you have any problems, raise hell. Demand to talk to the manager, ask to have Sears headquarters in Chicago called.
- If your members get credit[,] plan to go back next week with more people to get more credit.[47]

Easter "shop-ins" combined the Sears credit demand with the desires of welfare recipients for decent things to wear, and to give their children, on the holiday. Activist welfare recipients felt similarly about buying Christmas toys. The WROs organized Sears demonstrations to coincide with the heavy shopping period between Thanksgiving and Christmas.

The Sears campaign involved middle-class allies in the work of the NWRO. "Friends" like Betty Younger—whose husband, a Cleveland minister, had helped organize welfare rights protests before his death in 1968—and leaders of the Women's Division of the Methodist Church were pleased by the Sears campaign because it offered them concrete ways to support the NWRO beyond writing checks.[48]

NWRO activists asked middle-class people to mail in postcards affirming their support of the Sears campaign and pledging financial contributions. "Dear NWRO," they read:

- I support the NWRO boycott of Sears. I do not believe that welfare recipients should be discriminated against and not receive credit.
- I have notified Sears that I will not buy from Sears until an agreement with NWRO is reached.
- I would like to do more to help welfare recipients gain equal rights. Please send more information.
- I am enclosing a contribution to help in the cause.

Of the 22 cards that survive in the archives, 20 are supportive, and 1 is ambiguous. One, received April 7, 1969, was doctored to read: "Dear NWRO":

I DO NOT support the NWRO boycott of Sears. I do believe that welfare recipients should be discriminated against and not receive credit.
THEY Get ENOUGH!
- I have notified Sears that I will buy from Sears
- I would **NOT** like to do more to help welfare recipients ...
- I am enclosing a contribution. ... **You got to Be Kidding**!
Let them go to work like we all do!

Signed
Disgusted Harder Worker
Struggling—Middle Classer![49]

Working- and middle-class consumers expressed similar sentiments to stores that acceded to the welfare recipients' demands. " 'Why make credit that easy?' a typical call went," according to a reporter for the *New York Times.* "People on public assistance shouldn't get credit at all! Are we going to have to pay higher prices to support welfare recipients on credit like we are paying higher taxes? What about people like me—people who work for a living but can't get credit because our income is too low—aren't we entitled to get credit at least as much as the welfare families?"[50]

These were not the responses that Tim Sampson and George Wiley envisioned when they imagined the Sears campaign as a link to the middle- and working-class public. However, the responses indicate that for some middle- and working-class people, access to credit (and the denial of credit to others) was part of their sense of respectability. When NWRO members demanded Sears credit cards, they asked to be included among the respectable.

Welfare rights activists used a range of arguments to pursue their claim for consumer credit. They assumed the normality of credit sales, even for poor people, and focused on the practices of local merchants and high-interest instalment contracts. In response to a letter from the president of the W. T. Grant Company denying the NWRO a credit agreement, Wiley wrote:

> The need for credit is a budgetary need. ... It should be obvious that "the poor people of this nation" need credit like anyone else. ... Admittedly, credit costs money, but credit is like a telephone or an automobile—it is to be considered a necessity, in the context of our material standard of living.[51]

He argued that credit was ubiquitous, if it was not exactly a financial or moral good. Like a telephone—the subject of intense battles between local WROs and welfare administrations—a credit card was a legitimate demand in the context of postwar America.

NWRO members and staff described the credit plan as an answer to "discrimination" against welfare recipients. By this, they meant three things at once. The first was racial discrimination. The second was status or caste discrimination, based on the position of the credit seekers as recipients of particularly despised government programs. Third was income-based discrimination comparable to what poverty lawyers were theorizing in the late 1960s and early 1970s.[52]

In the context of the Sears campaign, overcoming income discrimination required not only that NWRO members be able to apply for credit on the same terms as all other consumers. Taking into account the effects of poverty on their credit ratings and their appearance of credit unworthiness, some NWRO members claimed that they should be able to avoid credit checks altogether. Others went so far as to suggest that ability to pay was not an important consideration in granting credit, and that repayment by every client was unimportant since Sears had so many resources and welfare recipients had so few.

These three discrimination arguments mixed in NWRO pronouncements on the Sears campaign. At the start of the national Sears campaign, Etta Horn expressed her frustration at Sears President Arthur Wood in terms of income and program-status discrimination:

> WE FEEL THAT PRESIDENT WOOD IS A PART OF THE SICK SOCIETY THAT IS PREJUDICED AGAINST THE POOR. THIS WHOLE SOCIETY IS RUN ON CREDIT, ESPECIALLY FOR THE RICH MAN. SO WHY CAN'T WE HAVE IT. THE POOR NEED IT MORE THAN THE RICH.[53]

The NWRO's middle-class "Friends" used the language of discrimination to discuss the treatment of welfare recipients and other poor people by Sears. In Kansas City, for example, the "Friends" group compared the experiences of a welfare recipient and a nonrecipient in applying for credit, found that the recipient was denied credit even though she had an acceptable credit history, and concluded that antiwelfare discrimination was the cause of the discrepancy. [54]

The arguments that NWRO staff, members, and "Friends" made about discrimination were tied to arguments about credit as a right of American citizenship. Members of the Wynadotte County (Kansas City) Welfare Rights Organization wrote to managers of J. C. Penney, Sears, Montgomery Ward, and W. T. Grant, requesting credit agreements (and threatening protest the day after Thanksgiving), in which they argued:

> One of the main problems we have had in helping ourselves is that reputable stores such as yours refuse to allow credit to welfare recipients, no matter how good we may be at paying our bills. This forces us to have to deal with less reputable stores who often charge excessive interest rates.
>
> Sir, we want you to grant members of our group the same right that all other citizens have. That is, we should not be discriminated against by you just because we are on welfare.[55]

A leaflet from the Chicago WRO made the idea of discrimination against the poor even more stark:

> According to Sears, 3 out of every 5 families in America, have charge accounts at Sears. ... Sears deals with 80% of the population ... the lower 10% are poor people and WELFARE RECIPIENTS. ... WE WANT TO BE INCLUDED LIKE EVERYONE ELSE. ... SEARS DISCRIMINATES AGAINST WELFARE RECIPIENTS BY REFUSING TO ALLOW THEM THE BENEFITS OF CREDIT PURCHASES.[56]

NWRO leaders revealed their perspective on credit rights. A list of proposed slogans for the Sears campaign included: "The Rich get cash & credit at least give the poor credit"; "How Many credit Cards do you have? We only want ONE[,] a SEARS credit card for all poor people"; and "Give us Credit for Being American."[57]

Welfare rights activists saw themselves as entitled to credit because they were entitled to social recognition in a consumer society. The right to buy essential items for oneself and for one's children was bound up with postwar ideas of womanhood and motherhood. Members of the Chicago WRO expressed the link between consumer credit and their roles as mothers and decently presented women during a protest at a Sears fashion show:

> Welfare mothers, all members of the National Welfare Rights Organization, are at this Sears fashion show today because we are trying to gain the attention of all people, to let them know that Sears, Roebuck and Co. discriminates in their credit policies, against welfare recipients and poor people.
> ... These accounts will give us the opportunity to 'buy better' clothing for our loved ones and children. ... The fashions we are modeling today, were all current fashions 5 to 8 years ago. If Sears granted us our accounts, we could also wear the current fashions that Sears, Roebuck and Co. [are] modeling today.[58]

The women claimed that even "welfare mothers" deserved the opportunity to consume decent, up-to-date goods themselves, and to buy nice things for their children. The role of aspirations for dignity and material adequacy in the Sears campaign also emerges in a composition written by Dorothy Perry, the 12-year-old daughter of the "Action Chairman" of the Newark WRO. While sitting in at Sears, she wrote:

> One thing I can truely [sic] say is that while I am on welfare my mother is learning her rights and believe me she is getting them. We have had many

Demostrations [*sic*] and they have made a Lot of change to Blacks and whites and have given them more courage to Fight For there [*sic*]rights. Today we went to Sears to ask them could we have credit in there [*sic*] store[;] they don't want any part of us welfare people. They don't know what it is to be poor and to try to have the better things in Life.[59]

The testimony of Dorothy Perry, and others cited above, indicates that the desire to "have the better things in Life" informed social action within the movement culture of the late 1960s.

A Private-Sector Family Allowance

As in the boycott of the Sears Corporation, and in their private-sector voucher plan, welfare rights activists revealed their sense that private firms owed something to them. The "private-sector family allowance" idea transposed the Western European idea of a family allowance—a grant to each procreative family from the national government to help in raising the next generation of citizens—to the private consumer market. The language NWRO leaders used to describe the plan was similar to that they used with Sears, in which they claimed that this highly profitable company should issue credit cards even to people who might not pay their bills. They pointed to the excess profits of consumer products firms, which they argued the firms should convert into low- or no-cost goods for members of NWRO. Utilizing the rhetoric of the incoming Nixon Administration, George Wiley, Tim Sampson, NWRO Chair Johnnie Tillmon, and Ways and Means Committee Chair Etta Horn sought the help of profit-making firms to secure welfare rights. The firms declined the opportunity.

The NWRO "plan" consisted of an offer to large national firms that they make it possible for poor people to buy their products by donating vouchers, or coupons, for the products to the NWRO. The NWRO would distribute the vouchers to its members. As with the Sears plan, the NWRO would gain in the process a concrete material benefit to offer members or potential members in exchange for participation.[60] "The National Welfare Rights Organization has a nationwide network of welfare rights organizations," boasted a *precis* of the voucher idea. "These affiliates are located in more than 100 cities and 45 states. We are offering our network as a distribution system for these coupons."[61] The NWRO suggested that the companies provide packages of $5 or more of coupons for the family of each member, distributed in small denominations and redeemable, like sales coupons, in local grocery and drugstores. "If a number of companies participated," NWRO leaders argued, "this could amount to a significant direct subsidy of poor people without any intervention or involvement of government agencies."[62]

The exchanges between welfare rights leaders and officials of various firms on the subject of vouchers illuminate both the wide berth that social movement activists of the late 1960s believed they had to interpret standard arrangements *and* the distance between these activists and the people who managed the consumer economy. In an exchange between Tillmon and Wiley and officials of General Mills, the welfare rights goal of ameliorating the material disfranchisement of welfare recipients met only confusion. Wiley and Tillmon presented their request for free goods as a corporate opportunity. "President-elect Richard M. Nixon has called for voluntary efforts from the private sector to assault the problem of poverty," they began. "The National Welfare Rights Organization is offering your company an opportunity to play a direct and vital role in this effort."[63] They proposed the welfare rights movement as a particularly apt partner for the behemoth firm: "NWRO," they claimed, "is the only nationwide organization of, by and for poor people vigorously striving for a fuller share of the abundance of our affluent society." Even as they expressed a kind of fealty to President Nixon's ideal of private-sector rather than governmental solutions to social problems, NWRO leaders called into question the morality of limitless profits:

> Since poor people do not have enough *money,* we ask that your company distribute a share of your great wealth to those poorest of the poor. This could be in the form of coupons distributed through NWRO, which are redeemable for your products. The value of the coupons distributed would be commensurate to your commitment to the eradication of poverty. Furthermore, distributing your contribution in this way would especially reward those people who had the initiative to develop their own independent organization in the democratic spirit of our country. [64]

The welfare rights leaders assured General Mills executives that donating products to the NWRO would help in accessing the low-income market. They proposed an NWRO "honor roll of participating companies and their products, so that our members, as well as friends of poor people everywhere, may direct their dollars toward the products of companies seriously commit[t]ed to accepting Mr. Nixon's challenge."[65] In their outline of the voucher plan, NWRO leaders added two additional points on the side of corporate self-interest in the project: An estimate of the "buying power of the [nine] million welfare recipients alone to be in the neighborhood of $10 billion annually" and the idea that, because of charitable giving laws, "[t]he cost of this program would be largely born[e] by the federal government through tax write offs."[66]

The response to the NWRO offer, from a General Mills community relations officer, revealed his befuddlement and resistance to giving things away: "Dear Mrs. Tillmon," he wrote, "Although your letter outlines in general terms a cooperative approach toward solving the problems of poverty, I must confess that I remain confused as to the exact means."[67] Although he invited Tillmon to send additional information about the plan, General Mills and NWRO never made any progress toward a voucher program. Welfare rights leaders had no more success with the other corporations to which they offered the private-sector family allowance "opportunity."[68]

In the Sears campaign and their efforts to gain a "private-sector Family Allowance Plan" NWRO activists ventured into battle as American consumers who deserved equal treatment, although they might be poor, black, female, and recipients of government benefits. In politicizing their identities as consumers, they illuminated their understandings of the public responsibilities of private firms such as Sears and General Mills. Activists whose claims for welfare rights encompassed Sears credit cards and vouchers with which to buy brand-name household goods expressed a deep yearning for social inclusion in postwar society.

Women of color who received public assistance experienced and contested deprivation in postwar society. As much as at the ballot box, the jury box, or the bus station, Northern women of color who fought for welfare rights experienced inequality in the welfare office, on the job-training site, and on the sales floor of the department store. Women who mobilized for welfare rights developed key parts of their social and political identities negotiating the consumer economy on behalf of their families. Although they were on the far margins of the "affluent society," in their campaigns for consumer credit and brand-name goods, they claimed the rhetorical space of that society as their own. When these women spoke as postwar American consumers, and as rights-conscious citizens, they spoke in a powerful 1960s argot.

By politicizing the relationships of power, privilege, and deprivation that women of color and other poor people experienced in the grocery store and social service office, welfare rights organizers built a unique social movement in the late 1960s. Still, welfare recipients made only small gains against the powerful institutions they faced. The victories they achieved against postwar capitalism, a consumer society sustained by personal credit, ethnic, racial, and linguistic hierarchies that were as prevalent in the urban North as the rural South, and gender-based structures of power, were mostly temporary.

Today, the very idea of "welfare rights" seems outlandish to most Americans—much less the idea of consumer rights for people who cannot afford to shop without government aid. In part, because such ideas seem politically irrecoverable, the NWRO and other challenging Northern groups have sometimes been left outside the history of the civil rights movement. At the same time, scholars have depicted the Southern movement in ways that narrowed its reach and flattened its ideological range. With the cold war a memory and the flames of 1960s ideological debates settling into embers, the time has arrived for a new, more expansive, and more generous view of the history of civil rights in the United States.

Notes

1. Welfare rights has *not* been left out of the literature on modern black women's history or the history of poverty policy. For the former, see Deborah Gray White, *Too Heavy A Load: Black Women in Defense of Themselves, 1894–1994* (New York: W. W. Norton, 1999), esp. 223–242; Jacqueline Jones, *Labor of Love, Labor of Sorrow: Black Women, Work, and the Family from Slavery to the Present* (New York: Basic Books, 1985); Paula Giddings, *When and Where I Enter: The Impact of Black Women on Race and Sex in America* (New York: Bantam Press, 1984), 312–13, 326. For the latter, see Michael B. Katz, *The Undeserving Poor: From the War on Poverty to the War on Welfare* (New York: Pantheon, 1989), 106–108, and James Patterson, *America's Struggle Against Poverty, 1900–1980* (Cambridge, Mass.: Harvard University Press, 1981), 153, 180, 195.

2. More recent scholarship that both expands the range of political activity covered and sheds new light on the black civil rights movement in the South includes: Jennifer Frost, *An Interracial Movement of the Poor: Community Organizing and the New Left in the 1960s* (New York: New York University Press, 2001); Gail Williams O'Brien, *The Color of the Law: Race, Violence, and Justice in the Post–World War Two South* (Chapel Hill: University of North Carolina Press (UNC), 2000); Pete Daniels, *Lost Revolutions: The South in the 1950s* (Chapel Hill: UNC Press, 2000); Timothy Tyson, *Radio Free Dixie: Robert F. Williams and the Roots of Black Power* (Chapel Hill: UNC Press, 1999); Nancy Naples, *Grassroots Warriors: Activist Mothering, Community Work, and the War on Poverty* (New York: Routledge, 1998); Nell Irvin Painter, *The Narrative of Hosea Hudson: The Life and Times of a Black Radical* (New York: W. W. Norton, 1994); James Goodman, *Stories of Scottsboro* (New York: Vintage Press, 1994); Robin Kelley, "Congested Terrain: Resistance on Public Transportation," and "Birmingham's Untouchables" in his *Race Rebels: Culture, Politics, and the Black Working Class* (New York: Free Press, 1994), 55–100; John Egerton, *Speak Now Against the Day: The Generation Before the Civil Rights Movement in the South* (Chapel Hill: UNC Press, 1994); Charles Payne, *I've Got the Light of Freedom* (Berkeley: University of California Press, 1993); James R. Ralph, Jr., *Martin Luther King, Jr., Chicago, and the Civil Rights Movement* (Cambridge, Mass.: Harvard University Press, 1993); Robin Kelley, *Hammer and Hoe: Alabama Communists*

During the Great Depression (Chapel Hill: UNC Press, 1990); and Jo Ann Gibson Robinson, with David Garrow, *The Montgomery Bus Boycott and the Women Who Started It* (Knoxville, Tenn.: University of Tennessee Press, 1987).

3. For correctives, see Charles Hamilton and Dona Cooper Hamilton, *The Dual Agenda: Race and Social Welfare Policies of Civil Rights Organizations* (New York: Columbia University Press, 1987), and Thomas F. Jackson, "Beyond Civil Rights: African-American Political Thought and Urban Poverty, 1960–1973" (Ph.D. diss., Stanford University, 1995).

4. Such contrasts have appeared in a range of journalistic, first-person, and scholarly accounts. See, for examples, Vincent Cannato, *The Ungovernable City: John Lindsay and His Struggle to Save New York* (New York: Basic Books, 2001), esp. 189–227; Thomas Edsall, with Mary Edsall, *Chain Reaction: The Impact of Race, Rights, and Taxes on American Politics* (New York: W. W. Norton, 1992); Nicholas Lemann, *The Promised Land: The Great Black Migration and How it Changed America* (New York: Knopf, 1991); Jim Sleeper, *The Closest of Strangers: Liberalism and the Politics of Race in New York* (New York: W. W. Norton, 1990); Todd Gitlin, *The Sixties: Years of Hope, Days of Rage* (New York: Bantam Books, 1987); Allen Matusow, *The Unraveling of America: A History of Liberalism in the 1960s* (New York: Harper Torchbooks, 1984). Such a contrast is suggested by the chronological and thematic boundaries of Taylor Branch, *Parting the Waters: America in the King Years, 1954–1963* (New York: Simon and Schuster, 1988) and is implicit in the sense of tragedy that informs August Meier and Elliott Rudwick, *CORE: A Study in the Civil Rights Movement* (Urbana: University of Illinois Press, 1975).

5. Felicia Kornbluh, "A Right to Welfare? Poor Women, Professionals, and Poverty Programs, 1935–1975" (Ph.D. diss., Princeton University, 2000), 1–34.

6. Ibid., 78–189.

7. On left influences and content, see Tyson, *Radio Free Dixie;* Painter, *Narrative of Hosea Hudson;* Kelley, *Hammer and Hoe;* and Jackson, "Beyond Civil Rights."

8. Hamilton and Hamilton, *Dual Agenda.*

9. On these boycotts, see St. Clair Drake and Horace Cayton, *Black Metropolis: A Study of Negro Life* (Chicago: University of Chicago Press, 1945), 293–296; Sleeper, *Closest of Strangers,* 48–50.

10. Nancy Fraser, "From Redistribution to Recognition? Dilemmas of Justice in a 'Postsocialist' Age," from her *Justice Interruptus: Critical Reflections on the 'Postsocialist' Condition* (New York: Routledge, 1997), 11–39. For a similar discussion that focuses particularly on African American consumption as access to public space, see Regina Austin, "'A Nation of Thieves': Consumption, Commerce, and the Black Public Sphere," *Public Culture* 7:1 (fall 1994): 225–248.

11. For a historical overview of gender and consumption, see Victoria de Grazia, with Ellen Furlough, eds., *The Sex of Things: Gender and Consumption in Historical Perspective* (Berkeley: University of California Press, 1996). For theoretical treatments of consumption as work that women perform, see Laura

Balbo, "Crazy Quilts: Rethinking the Welfare State Debate from a Woman's Point of View, " in *Women and the State,* Anne Showstock Sassoon, ed. (London: Unwin Hyman, 1987), 45–71, and Batya Weinbaum and Amy Bridges, "The Other Side of the Paycheck: Monopoly Capital and the Structure of Consumption," in *Capitalist Patriarchy and the Case for Socialist Feminism,* Zillah Eisenstein, ed. (New York: Monthly Review Press, 1979), 190–205.

12. See, for examples, Jones, *Labor of Love, Labor of Sorrow,* 68–70; Evelyn Brooks Higginbotham, *Righteous Discontent: The Women's Movement in the Black Baptist Church, 1880–1920* (Cambridge, Mass.: Harvard University Press, 1993); Giddings, *When and Where I Enter,* 22–23. On the problematic and political claim of African American women to "ladyhood" at the turn of the twentieth century, see Kevin Gaines, "Rethinking Race and Class in African-American Struggles for Equality, 1885–1941," *American Historical Review* 201:2 (April 1997): 378–387; Kevin Gaines, *Uplifting the Race: Black Leadership, Politics, and Culture in the Twentieth Century* (Chapel Hill: UNC Press, 1996); Stephanie Shaw, *What a Woman Ought to Be and to Do: Black Professional Women Workers During the Jim Crow Era* (Chicago: University of Chicago Press, 1996); Giddings, *When and Where I Enter,* 49, 178;

13. Flora Davis, *Moving the Mountain: The Women's Movement in America Since 1960* (New York: Simon and Schuster, 1991), 147–148.

14. David Caplovitz, *The Poor Pay More: Consumer Practices of Low-Income Families* (New York: The Free Press, 1967). Other important studies include Federal Trade Commission, Economic Report on Instalment Credit and Retail Sales Practices of District of Columbia Retailers," excerpted in *Consumerism: Search for the Consumer Interest,* David Aaker and George Day, eds. (New York: The Free Press, 1971), 374–381, and Eric Schnapper, "Consumer Legislation and the Poor," *Yale Law Journal* 76 (1967): 745–792.

15. Caplovitz, *The Poor Pay More,* 81.

16. Ibid., 37, 41. Of course, high levels of consumption were not unique to Puerto Rican and African American migrants to U.S. cities. For one telling comparison, see Jenna Weissman Joselit, *The Wonders of America: Reinventing Jewish Culture, 1880–1950* (New York: Hill and Wang, 1994), 142–148.

17. Caplovitz, *The Poor Pay More,* 47.

18. Ibid., 9, 30, 50.

19. Stokely Carmichael and Charles V. Hamilton, *Black Power: The Politics of Liberation* (New York: Vintage Press, 1992—originally published in 1967), 18. For further discussion of Black Power and the colonial analogy, see Katz, *The Undeserving Poor,* 55–57. For theories of colonialism from the political left of the late 1960s, see Andre Gunder Frank, *Capitalism and Underdevelopment in Latin America* (New York: Monthly Review Press, 1967).

20. Carmichael and Hamilton, *Black Power,* 20–21.

21. Ibid., 173.

22. Harold Cruse, *The Crisis of the Negro Intellectual: A Historical Analysis of the Failure of Black Leadership* (New York: Quill/Morrow, 1984—originally published in 1967), 94–95.

23. Southern Christian Leadership Conference, *Operation Breadbasket* (newspaper), n.d., and n.a., "Operation Breadbasket Seminar—Negro Businesses," *The Woodlawn Observer* March 8, 1967, 11, from "Operation Breadbasket" file, Social Action Vertical File, State Historical Society of Wisconsin.

24. Ralph, *Northern Protest: Martin Luther King, Jr., Chicago, and the Civil Rights Movement* (Cambridge, Mass.: Harvard University Press, 1993), 67–69. For other private-sector aspects of SCLC's Chicago campaign, including its emphasis on nondiscriminatory access to credit for homes and businesses, see " 'A Proposal by the Southern Christian Leadership Conference for the Development of a Nonviolent Action Movement for the Greater Chicago Area,' January 5, 1966," and "Demands Placed on the Door of Chicago City Hall by Martin Luther King, Jr., July 10, 1966," in *The Eyes on the Prize Civil Rights Reader,* Clayborne Carson, David Garrow, Gerald Gill, Vincent Harding, and Darlene Clark Hine, eds. (New York: Penguin Books, 1991), 291–303.

25. Martin Luther King, Jr., *Where Do We Go From Here? Chaos or Community* (New York: Harper and Row, 1967), 38.

26. Ibid., 116. His increasing emphasis on consumer practices was part of a larger economic turn in King's thinking. Like NWRO members, King in 1967 argued that it was imperative either to create full employment or to ensure all citizens adequate income. "We have left the realm of constitutional rights," he wrote, "and we are entering the area of human rights" (ibid., 130). For evidence from other civil rights leaders, see Clayborne Carson, *In Struggle: SNCC and the Black Awakening of the 1960s* (Cambridge, Mass.: Harvard University Press, 1981), 103, 172, 255, 269; Meier and Rudwick, *CORE,* 187, 234, 262.

27. James Farmer, remembrance, in "After the Revolution," by Henry Louis Gates, Jr., *The New Yorker* 72:10 (April 29 and May 6, 1996): 60.

28. On postwar gender relations and consumption, see Elaine Tyler May, *Homeward Bound: American Families in the Cold War Era* (New York: Basic Books, 1988), 162–182.

29. Nick Kotz and Mary Lynn Kotz, biographers of NWRO Executive Director George Wiley, grant Jones, an African American welfare recipient, exclusive credit for the credit card campaign. Jones had organized previous campaigns to meet the needs of low-income consumers of color. These included successful challenges of the Philadelphia health department's practice of ignoring the quality of food sold in grocery stores in all-black neighborhoods, and of the telephone company's routine practice of charging higher deposit fees for telephone service to low-income people than they charged to the wealthy. Kotz and Kotz, *A Passion for Equality: George A. Wiley and the Movement* (New York: W. W. Norton, 1977), 235–236. Tim Sampson remembered the VISTA volunteers being involved in the origins of the campaign (Sampson telephone interview, February 12, 1996). Also see discussion of the Philadelphia credit campaign in Larry R. Jackson and William A. Johnson, *Protest by the Poor: The Welfare Rights Movement in New York City* (Lexington, Mass.: D.C. Heath and the Rand Corporation, 1974), 41. Roxanne Jones was later elected to the Pennsylvania State House, where she served until her death in 1996.

30. Unsigned article, "Wanamaker and Lerner Agree To Give Relief Clients Credit," *The Philadelphia Tribune*, August 20, 1968 (no page) from "NWRO ACTION Leadership Packet No. 3," Library of the Welfare Law Center, New York City, file titled "NWRO."

31. [Tim Sampson?], "Nationwide Sears Credit Campaign," notice from the NWRO to all WROs, n.d. [March 1969?] from Box 2038, File titled "NWRO Sears Materials," NWRO papers.

32. Sampson interview, February 12, 1996.

33. The Retail Clerks International Association, AFL-CIO, began a boycott of Sears for its anti-union activities in July 1960 that continued until May 1967 without any success. The immediate precipitant of the union action was Sears' firing of clerks who refused to cross a picket line, but this was, according to the union, "only the climax of a long series of anti-labor acts by the world's largest general merchandising corporation." See Memorandum, From: Retail Clerks International Association, To: George Meany, President, AFL-CIO, Re: Boycott against Sears, Roebuck & Company, May 9, 1967, from Box 2038, File titled "Sears Research," NWRO papers.

34. NWRO, "Nationwide Sears Credit Campaign," from NWRO ACTION Leadership Packet No. 3, Library of the Welfare Law Center, File titled "NWRO."

35. Ibid. For the plan offered to stores other than Sears, which was substantially the same as the Sears plan, see "NWRO Credit Plan," *NOW! News*, April 1, 1969, p. 2, Box 15, Folder 2, George Wiley papers.

36. [Tim Sampson?], "Summary of NWRO Credit Agreements," n.d., from Box 2038, File titled "Sears Correspondence," NWRO papers.

37. On Brooklyn, see Jacqueline Pope, *Biting the Hand That Feeds Them: Organizing Women on Welfare at the Grass Roots Level* (New York: Praeger Press, 1989), 105–110. On New York City as a whole, see Isidore Barmash, "3 Big Stores Agree on Extending Credit to Relief Recipients," *New York Times*, July 23, 1969, 1; Jackson and Johnson, *Protest by the Poor*, 41.

38. Press Release, Montgomery Ward Company, on its Agreement with the National Welfare Rights Organization, December 8, 1969, Box 2038, File titled "Montgomery Ward," NWRO papers, and "Memorandum of Agreement between the National Welfare Rights Organization and the Montgomery Ward Company for a Pilot Program Extending Credit to Welfare Recipients," September 10, 1969, Box 21, Folder 5, Wiley papers. See discussion in Kotz and Kotz, *A Passion for Equality*, 237 and Jackson and Johnson, *Protest by the Poor*, 41. Tim Sampson also emphasized the Montgomery Ward agreement as a positive outcome of the Sears boycott (interview, February 12, 1996).

39. In Pontiac, for example, the local welfare recipient/leader reported to NWRO headquarters that "she knows several women who are presently being hounded by collection agencies who did get the credit" from Sears, although the firm said it was evaluating customers individually. See "Pontiac's Agreement With Sears," n.d., Box 2038, File titled "Local WRO Sears Material," NWRO papers.

40. "NWRO Sears Action," tally, n.a., n.d. [March 1969?], Box 2038, File titled "Consumer Credit," NWRO papers.

41. National Welfare Rights Organization, "Sears Boycott Action List," April 9, 1969, Box 15, Folder 2, Wiley papers.

42. This is a tactic that NWRO activists appear to have inherited from CORE. However, CORE "shop-ins" aimed to increase the employment of African Americans while the NWRO "shop-ins" sought to improve conditions for consumers. Meier and Rudwick, *CORE,* 236. For CORE boycotts and protests of major stores or consumer product companies, see 30, 47, 57, 59, 234.

43. NWRO, "Call To Action" on Sears campaign, n.d. [March 1969?], Box 2038, File titled "NWRO Sears Materials," NWRO papers.

44. Ibid.

45. See description of tactics in Pope, *Biting the Hand,* 106–108.

46. The Ways and Means Committee was the NWRO committee assigned to negotiate with Sears and other private-sector firms. The name echoed that of the extremely powerful committee of the House of Representatives that had jurisdiction over public assistance legislation.

47. Memo To: All WROs, From: Etta B. Horn, Chairman, NWRO Ways and Means Committee, and George A. Wiley, Executive Director, Subject: Sears Action, n.d. [March–April 1969], Box 2038, Folder titled "Sears Correspondence," NWRO papers.

48. Letter from Better Younger, Pittsburgh, Pennsylvania, to Johnnie Tillmon and Letter from Mrs. Wayne W. Harrington, President, Women's Division of the Methodist Church, to Arthur M. Woods [*sic*], President, Sears, Roebuck Company, Chicago, March 18, 1969, Box 2038, Folder titled "Sears Correspondence," NWRO papers.

49. Mail-in Cards on the Sears Campaign, Box 2038, File titled "Correspondence With People About Sears," NWRO papers.

50. Isidore Barmash, "As Those on Relief Get an Offer of Credit," *The New York Times,* July 20, 1969.

51. Letter from R. W. Mayer, President, W. T. Grant Company, New York, to Mrs. Etta Horn and Mr. George Wiley, National Welfare Rights Organization, Washington, D.C., September 16, 1969, and [George Wiley], Draft response, n.d., Box 2038, File titled "NWRO Credit Plan," NWRO papers.

52. For a record of lawyers' efforts to encode income discrimination in constitutional doctrine, see Laurence H. Tribe, *American Constitutional Law* (Mineola, N.Y.: The Foundation Press, 1978), 1098–1136; Aryeh Neier, *Only Judgment: The Limits of Litigation in Social Change* (Middletown, Conn.: Wesleyan University Press, 1982), 127–140; and Martha Davis, *Brutal Need: Lawyers and the Welfare Rights Movement, 1960–1973* (New Haven: Yale University Press, 1993). For efforts to theorize income discrimination, and the concomitant public obligation to provide subsistence, see Frank Michelman, "The Supreme Court 1968 Term—Forward: On Protecting the Poor Through the Fourteenth Amendment," *Harvard Law Review* 83:7 (1969): 7–59; A. Delafield Smith, *The Right to Life* (Chapel Hill: UNC Press, 1955).

53. "Mrs. Etta Horn," WRO's in ACTION vol. 1, no. 1 (April, 1969), p. 2, from Box 2038, File titled "Sears," NWRO papers.

54. See Friends of Welfare Rights, Kansas City, Kansas, "Do Welfare People Have a Case?" Box 2038, File titled "Local WRO Sears Material," NWRO papers. For use of discrimination language by "Friends," see Letter from Edward E. Goode, Assistant Director, Social Service Department, [Hartford, Conn.] to Mr. Arthur Wood, President Sears, Roebuck & Co., Chicago, June 26, 1969, Box 2038, File titled "Sears Correspondence," NWRO papers. Goode included half of his Sear's credit card with the copy of his letter he sent to NWRO.

55. Letter from (Mrs.) Ruther Lee Williams Chairman, Wynadotte County Welfare Rights Organization and (Mrs.) Vera Walker, Kansas Representative National Welfare Rights Organization to Store Managers, November 22, 1968 (Attached to Report to NWRO from Bob Agard, Executive Director, Kansas City Welfare Rights Training Project, n.d.), Box 2038, File titled "Local WRO Sears Material," NWRO papers.

56. Chicago Welfare Rights Organization, "Don't Buy At Sears," April 7, 1969, Box 2038, File titled "Local WRO Sears Material," NWRO papers. The math here is a bit off; if three out of five families had Sears charge cards, then 60 percent, not 80 percent, of Americans would have had access to Sears credit.

57. "List of possible slogans for the Sears campaign," n.a., n.d., Box 2038, File titled "NWRO Sears Materials," NWRO papers.

58. Chicago Welfare Rights Organization/NWRO, "Press Release," April 7, 1969, Box 2038, File titled "Local WRO Sears Material," NWRO papers.

59. Dorothy Perry, "Composition—'Welfare Rights,'" April 8, 1969, from Box 2038, File titled "Local WRO Sears Material," NWRO papers.

60. Coupons for consumer goods would have facilitated the kind of benefit-based organizing that Tim Sampson learned from Fred Ross of the United Farm Workers. For a critique of this kind of organizing, see Lawrence Neil Bailis, *Bread or Justice: Grassroots Organizing in the Welfare Rights Movement* (Boston, Mass.: Lexington Books, 1974).

61. National Welfare Rights Organization, "NWRO Private Sector/Family Allowance Plan," n.d., from Box 2038, Folder titled "NWRO Sears Stuff," NWRO papers.

62. Ibid.

63. Letter from Mrs. Johnnie Tillmon, National Chairman, and George Wiley, Executive Director, National Welfare Rights Organization, Washington, D.C., to Mr. J. F. McFarland, President, General Mills, Inc., Minneapolis, Minnesota, December 16, 1968, from Box 2038, folder titled "Consumer Credit," NWRO papers.

64. Ibid.

65. Such promotion of a company among members of a particular community was the reverse of a boycott—and the suggestion of such an "honor roll" probably bore with it the implicit threat of a boycott of firms that failed to participate. NWRO officials made the threat of a boycott more explicit in correspondence with the leadership of Proctor & Gamble: "[W]e wrote you to solicit your cooperation in a private sector assault on poverty. We requested

a meeting with your or representatives of your company to discuss a positive program. To date, we have not even had the courtesy of a reply. . . . As you undoubtedly know, we are presently boycotting Sears, Roebuck & Company because of Sears' insensitivity to the credit problems of poor people. At our May 23rd meeting, we will consider if any action should be taken against Proctor & Gamble." Letter from (Mrs.) Etta Horn, Chairman, Committee on Ways and Means, and George Wiley, Executive Director, National Welfare Rights Organization, Washington, D.C., to Mr. H. J. Morgens, President, The Proctor & Gamble Company, Cincinnati, Ohio, May 16, 1969, in Box 2038, folder titled "Proctor & Gamble," NWRO papers.

66. "NWRO Private Sector/Family Allowance Plan."

67. Letter from Thomas L. Olson, Manager of Community Relations, General Mills, to Mrs. Johnnie Tillmon, December 31, 1968, from Box 2038, folder titled "Consumer Credit" NWRO papers.

68. See, for example, Letter from Johnnie Tillmon and George Wiley to Mr. D. J. Fitzgibbons, President, The Sterling Drug Company, New York, New York, December 16, 1968 (same text as General Mills letter), in Box 2038, folder titled "Consumer Credit," NWRO papers. On the high-priority targets for the NWRO, see also Note from [Tim Sampson] to Joyce [Burson], n.d., in Box 2038, folder titled "Consumer Credit" NWRO papers: "Proctor & Gamble, General [Foods], Bayer Aspirin, General Mills. Joyce, George wants these to roll!"

Chapter 9

The Politics of Culture: The US Organization and the Quest for Black "Unity"

Scot Brown

The US Organization is one of the most controversial and misunderstood Black Power groups of the late 1960s. Despite the fact that many are aware of, and millions practice, the Kwanzaa holiday ritual and celebration created by Maulana Karenga and the US Organization, the political thrust of the US Organization remains largely an untold story. While the past decade has seen an impressive amount of autobiographical reflections on "The Movement," many of the feuds and rivalries of the past continue to paint a skewed picture of this organization's activism. Even the meaning of the group's name, "US," has been misinterpreted. Critics and rivals of the organization, in the late 1960s, derogatorily referred to it as "United Slaves," and that slur is persistently used, erroneously, in historical accounts of the period. This essay seeks to open a new dialogue on US by examining its political orientation and the intellectual bases for its approach to united front politics.

The US Organization had a very distinctive style. US members called themselves "advocates," and oftentimes their identification with the organization visually demonstrated a new black consciousness with "afro" hairstyles, shaved heads, and colorful African-inspired clothing. Demonstrating their commitment to developing an alternative culture and aesthetics, US advocates took African names and practiced African-inspired rituals and customs on a daily basis. The cultural nationalism of US was also influenced by contemporary radical trends coming out of Africa.

Black Power era critics of the US Organization held that its cultural nationalism lacked any serious political dimension. Some purported that US urged African Americans to turn inward rather than confront the established order of the day.[1] In the 1998 study, *Just My Soul Responding: Rhythm and Blues, Black Consciousness and Race Relations,* Brian Ward states, "As many of his critics, led by the Black Panther Party, noted, Karenga and his acolytes appeared to be making ego-gratifying fetish and healthy profit out of these pseudo-African trappings while doing little to convert the racial consciousness and solidarity they promoted into meaningful challenges to white power." Thus, recent scholarship on the Black Power era largely reiterated the allegations made by US's 1960s rivals.[2] In fact, scholars of the civil rights and Black Power movements have almost completely overlooked the US political program. However, an analysis of the organization's Black Power activism in Los Angeles reveals that in terms of politics, the US advocates regarded themselves as organizers of organizations. Specifically, they attempted to "programmatically influence" the political and cultural projects within the black community in a nationalist direction, by leading interorganizational caucuses (e.g., the Temporary Alliance of Local Organizations [TALO] and the Black Congress); working for self-determination, regional autonomy, and Black representation in electoral politics; agitating against U.S. military aggression in Vietnam; and organizing a series of local and national Black Power conferences to spread black nationalism and build united fronts. In their view, US had no need for mass membership recruitment. The goal was to ideologically influence other organizations with its united front approach and thus direct the course of the coming "cultural revolution." Of course, that united front strategy did not stop the US Organization from its own involvement in urban uprisings, school walkouts, and student strikes. Furthermore, US's establishment of African American holidays in the late 1960s was inextricably tied to the struggle for local Black community control and the wider black nationalist and Latino alliances, spanning the country.

African Languages, Anthropology, and the American Academy

The origins of the US united front approach to political activism preceded the organization's 1965 birth. After graduating from high school in 1958, Karenga, born Ron Everett, moved to Los Angeles from his rural hometown Parsonburg, Maryland, and lived in Los Angeles with his older brother, Chestyn Everett, an artist and schoolteacher.[3] There, Karenga acquired California state residency and attended Los Angeles City College (LACC) and later University of California at Los Angeles (UCLA).[4] Persistent activism and leadership paved the way for his 1961 election as student body president at LACC.[5]

Karenga attributed his victory to having built a large constituency among international students. This support was reflected in his election platform, calling for "a more extensive international students program."[6] In part, these connections to international students inspired Karenga's interest in Africa. The climate at LACC also facilitated his encounter with various aspects of African culture. LACC introduced an African history course to the curriculum in the spring of 1961.

"I started [studying Kiswahili] at City College," Karenga remembers, "I said to myself 'I'm African, why don't I know an African language?' "[7] Kiswahili, also called Swahili, had a special appeal to him and eventually other African American cultural nationalists, as it is spoken by a broad range of ethnicities and regions throughout Eastern, Central, and parts of Southern Africa.

By 1965, Karenga had completed a bachelor of arts at UCLA in political science, and a masters in the same field, with a specialization in African affairs. Throughout his time at UCLA, Karenga continued to study Kiswahili and Arabic.[8] Many of the texts on Africa that Karenga read during this period were anthropological and ethnographic studies that influenced his view of culture as a holistic composite of a given group's thought and practices, rather than simply a people's arts and folkways. Most influential on Karenga's thought were studies of African cultural groups and ethnicities that attempted to present an overview of the entire way of life of a given people. These studies viewed politics and economics as sub-divisions or categories within a larger cultural whole, a conception of culture that informed the US Organization's own "seven criteria for culture" analysis: mythology, history, social organization, political organization, economic organization, creative motif, and ethos.[9] Critics of the organization who misunderstand this anthropological view of culture have incorrectly described US philosophy as nonpolitical and solely dedicated to the arts and aesthetic expression. However, as far as US was concerned, its perspective was summarized best in *The Quotable Karenga:* "Everything that we do, think, or learn is somehow interpreted as a cultural expression. So when we discuss politics, to US that is a sign of culture. When we discuss economics, to US that is a sign of culture. ... In other words, we define culture as a complete value system and also means and ways of maintaining that value system."[10]

The Afro-American Association, the Assassination of Malcolm X, and the Watts Uprising

In 1963 Karenga met with Donald Warden, a Bay Area nationalist and activist who headed the Afro-American Association. Bay Area activists

Ernie Allen, Jr. (Ernie Mkalimoto), Huey Newton, Bobby Seale, and Ken Freeman were also members of that group. Karenga accepted Warden's invitation to head the Los Angeles chapter of the group.[11] Ayuko Babu, Tut Hayes, Akida Kimani, and Lloyd Hawkins figured prominently in the association's Los Angeles chapter.[12] The association functioned primarily as a study group and lecture forum, although group members also frequently spoke outdoors to black community audiences ("street speaking").

Karenga apparently remained with the Afro-American Association until 1964—one former member stated that the group disbanded as a result of "strong personalities vying against each other and a lack of discipline."[13] Even after Karenga left the association and started what would become US, several of the association's tenets, particularly its call for black community control and economic self-reliance, remained key facets of his cultural nationalist project.[14]

The year 1965, the turbulent period during which US emerged, was marked by the assassination of Malcolm X in February, and by the uprising in the Watts section of Los Angeles in August. Those two developments paved the way for the formation of the US Organization and made a deep imprint on its formative period. Militancy was widespread; a yellow sweatshirt with an imprint of Malcolm X's face and the phrase, "St. Malcolm"—worn by various Black activists in Los Angeles during the revolt's aftermath—came to symbolically represent the intimate connections between the two events.[15]

US Organization

In the fall of 1965, Maulana Karenga, Hakim Jamal, Dorothy Jamal, Tommy Jacquette-Mfikiri (Halifu), Karl Key-Hekima, Ken Seaton-Msemaji, Samuel Carr-Damu (Ngao Damu), Sanamu Nyeusi, and Brenda Haiba Karenga were among the early members of a newly formed organization called "US." The term "US" was chosen as a dual reference to the organization and the community its members pledged to serve: "*us Blacks as opposed to 'them' Whites.*"[16] According to Hakim Jamal (who claimed ownership of the term US), the organization was not formed in one singular meeting but instead it grew out of a study group called the Circle of Seven, led by Karenga, which had met regularly at the black-owned Aquarian Bookstore in Los Angeles.

Jamal was a close associate of Malcolm X, going back to Malcolm's days as a Boston hustler and moving with him throughout his political career with the Nation of Islam (NOI) to the Organization for Afro-American Unity (OAAU). Upon joining forces with the study group, Jamal led a push to anchor Malcolm as US's main ideological and inspirational reference. The US Organization's first newspaper, *Message to the Grassroots,* which appeared in May 1966, designates Karenga as the "chairman" of US, and Jamal as its "founder." The first issue acknowledged its dedication to "Mrs. Betty Shabazz the widow of our slain nationalist leader."[17] By the summer of 1966, Jamal had parted company with US, and Karenga stood as the organization's acknowledged leader and ideologue. The split was likely to have resulted from differences over US's philosophy and leadership directions. Jamal's preference for a political program based on the teachings of Malcolm X seems to have ultimately clashed with Karenga's rapidly expanding dominance over US. By the late summer of 1966, Karenga had become the organization's central ideologue and maximum leader.[18]

The centrality of Karenga's leadership notwithstanding, the US members, from the outset, had specialized and essential roles to play in the functioning of the organization. Samuel Carr-Damu led the paramilitary wing. James Doss-Tayari and Karl Hekima were Vice Chairmen. Haiba Karenga and Dorothy Jamal led the "School of Afroamerican culture." Sanamu Nyeusi was both a teacher in the school and secretary-treasurer of the organization. Samuel Carr-Damu, later known as Ngao Damu was a key original member of US who had a great deal of influence on the US's paramilitary wing (which he led) called the Simba Wachanga (Young Lions).[19] Apparently an "ex-Army Sergeant," Korean War veteran, and US's first real "soldier," Damu's military experience and training proved vital to the new organization's ability to survive amidst the competitive and sometimes hostile world of Los Angeles radical politics.[20] When US was featured on the cover of *Life* Magazine in July of 1966, a picture of Damu drilling and roaring orders to members of black youth added further evidence that one of the legacies of the 1965 Watts revolt was a radical black nationalist trend, defiantly opposed to nonviolence.[21] James Doss-Tayari who became vice-chairman sometime in late 1966, recalls that Damu was known as the "Old Lion" because of his military expertise. Similarly, Tayari was also known for his a serious, tough, and robust presence.[22] By contrast with Damu, Tayari had previous experience as an activist in interracial and socialist movements in the Los Angeles area, from 1963 until 1965, such as the W.E.B. Du Bois Club, a group affiliated with the Communist Party.[23]

Women were also key players in the early days of US. The wives of Maulana Karenga and Hakim Jamal, Haiba Karenga and Dorothy Jamal, organized the US School of Afroamerican culture—one of its most important institutions serving children of members as well as those from nationalist-minded families in the Los Angeles area. Sanamu Nyeusi was secretary-treasurer of US and a teacher at the School of Afroamerican culture.[24] Her personal charisma helped her recruit a number of the groups rising leaders, including two brothers, Oliver Massengale-Heshimu and Charles Massengale-Sigidi.

Another major force in the organization's early years was an influx of people who joined US from Pasadena. Many of them were first-generation students at Pasadena City College (PCC). Clyde Daniels-Halisi, one of the founders of the Black Student Union there and later a college professor, played a large part in drawing his friends and associates to US. Halisi remembers having first seen Karenga and Hakim Jamal on a local television program sometime in late 1965 and 1966.[25] He remembers after watching, "at that point I was convinced that I wanted to join such an organization."[26] Similarly, James Mtume, George Subira, Joanne Richards-Kicheko, Buddy Rose-Aminifu, Amina Thomas, and a host of other students from PCC encouraged some of their relatives, friends, and other African American students to come to US's weekly forums and eventually join the organization.[27]

High School Recruitment and the Politics of the Malcolm X Holiday

On February 22, 1966, US convened its first public event, a memorial observance for Malcolm X, who had been assassinated the previous February. US called the event a Dhabihu (sacrifice) service, and declared the day a special holiday to pay homage to Malcolm X's sacrifice of his life for the cause of black liberation.[28] Karenga was featured as the keynote speaker at the service, which was attended by about 200 people.[29] The Dhabihu gave Karenga a plat-•form to introduce the organization's political views to a larger community, especially the political basis for what would become his organization's opposition to the Vietnam War. The anti-imperialist service also included a candle lighting ritual, an activity also associated with the first Kwanzaa celebration to occur some 10 months later. [30]

Karenga and other younger nationalists activists strongly identified with Malcolm X's advocacy of self-defense and black community economic and political control. US and other local nationalists were openly defying the NOI by organizing this public event—especially when considering that the Dhabihu took place at a time when the NOI vehemently argued that Malcolm X was a befallen traitor.

By spring 1967, US had already initiated the first Kwanzaa celebration (in December of 1966), a week-long commemoration of the organization's seven principles (Nguzo Saba) celebrated throughout the African diaspora. Even though those who attended the first Kwanzaa celebration remember it as a small intimate gathering, the organization's members, in all likelihood, felt a collective confirmation that diligent activism would bring forth a wider acceptance of their new black culture. This is evident in the US call, the following spring, for African Americans to boycott work or school on May 19 or the closest weekday to it, in observance of a new black national holiday Kuzaliwa, Malcolm X's birthday. The response in Los Angeles was overwhelming and partly responsible for US's growing appeal to African American youth in Los Angeles.

The *Los Angeles Sentinel* reported "a wave of absenteeism hit Los Angeles in response to a call from Ron Karenga, of US, to make the birthday of the late Malcolm X a national Negro holiday."[31] At one high school, an estimated 1,500 students walked out.[32] After walking out, students from all over Los Angeles assembled at a park, for what the *Sentinel* described as "a peaceful day of picnicking."[33]

In the spring of 1967, Charles Johnson-Sitawisha was in the eighth grade at Horace Mann Junior High School. Following the example of his older brother, who had been attending the US community forums and lectures, Sitawisha decided not to attend school on May 19. Reflecting on what transpired when he returned on the following school day, he stated that, "the teacher asked me for an absence slip. I told her I didn't have one and she asked why." "I said," he continued " 'because it was a holiday yesterday,' and the whole class laughed at me." He remembers remarking to his classmates, "'If it's funny to you, that's fine, but I choose to do that as a Black man,' and I told the teacher if she wanted to mark me truant, that's fine, but I stand by that."[34] The following year Sitawisha joined the Simba Wachanga, the wing of the US Organization comprised mainly of teenage and young adult males.[35]

The challenge that the mass walkouts presented to public school administrations in the Los Angeles area did not stop with the Malcolm X holiday. Other community demands for increased responsiveness from the public schools, to local African American concerns, persisted throughout 1967. In August of that year, Kenneth Hahn, the Los Angeles county supervisor, warned in an internal memo that "[m]ilitant forces seem intent on trying to disrupt every university, college and high school campus."[36] Urging a countywide crackdown, he declared, "[w]e cannot have anarchy existing in California."[37] That fall, a coalition of concerned parents and community groups organized protests demanding the ouster of Robert Dehamy, the principal of Manual Arts High School. Among their various grievances was the charge that he routinely expelled or suspended students without consulting or adequately advising parents.[38] An article on a particular demonstration at Manual Arts is accompanied by a photo of Karenga, who was present at the rally, alongside a woman toting a placard that stated, "We Are Sick of Our Children Being Mistreated!!"[39] The demonstrations apparently went on for months. The cover of the November 17, 1967, issue of the US Organization's newspaper, *Harambee*, displays a photograph of a police officer that has a black female in a choke-hold. The police were apparently in the process of breaking up a protest at the school. The front-page headline of the newspaper read, "Another View of Manual."[40]

The heyday of US's effectiveness from mid-1966 until early-1969, reflects the strength of the broader resurgent black nationalist movement in those years. The excitement generated by the movement's growth gave rise to a sense of cooperation and shared purpose among Black Power organizations. Uhuru Day, another holiday created and celebrated by US, became a building block for the organization's alliances and relationships with other activists during the group's early years. The holiday, first cele-brated on August 11, 1966, commemorated the one-year anniversary of the Watts uprising.[41] Since US came into existence in part as a result of the rise in the popularity of black nationalism in Los Angeles following the Watts revolt, Uhuru Day had a special significance for US advocates and a broad range of community activists, who were fashioned into a militant political community by the uprising.

The 1967 Uhuru Day rally revealed the growing political consensus and commitment to alliance building among black nationalist organizations. Demonstrating their militant unity, H. Rap Brown, national chairman of the Student Nonviolent Coordinating Committee (SNCC), and Huey Newton, minister of defense of the Black Panther Party for Self-Defense, joined Karenga as keynote speakers for the event. Newspapers reports indicate that between 3,000 and 5,000 people attended the event, which was held outside of the US headquarters.[42]

US, SNCC, and the Black Panther Party were united in support of the Uhuru Day theme, in advocacy of the right to self-defense, and in adher-ence to Malcolm X's vision of a black united front based on the principle of group solidarity despite ideological differences. From a historical per-spective, Newton's presence at the rally is particularly significant given that the US Organization and the Black Panther Party would embark on a vio-lent feud within two years. In 1967, however, the rally exemplified the early tendency for both organizations to work together on projects that reflected a mutual commitment to fulfilling Malcolm X's vision.

H. Rap Brown's appearance at Uhuru Day is even more of a testimony to a sense of unity among black nationalists at that time. A couple of weeks before the rally, both federal and Maryland state authorities had issued warrants for his arrest in connection with a speech that he delivered in

Cambridge, Maryland, which was followed by an outbreak of violence.[43] Just days following his speech in Los Angeles, Brown was arrested by federal authorities in Washington D.C.[44]

US Program and Philosophy

As young militants joined the US Organization and as radical Black Power groups aligned themselves around the revolutionary legacy of Malcolm X, Karenga and his associates paid more attention to program, philosophy, and organization. US's political program and philosophy mirrored its leader's own intellectual journey. Based on his readings in black nationalist literature and contemporary academic scholarship on African and African American cultures and histories, Karenga concluded that enslavement and other forms of oppression in the United States robbed African Americans of the basic elements that constitute a people's or a group's culture. In his view, African Americans did not possess a culture of their own but rather had imitatively embraced the culture of their oppressors.[45]

US set out to construct and propagate a new black culture based on selected African traditions, for the purpose of launching a cultural revolution among African Americans. The organization regarded itself both as the vanguard of this "black cultural revolution" and the archetype of a new black nation within the United States. US members used the African language Kiswahili and sometimes other African languages, such as Zulu, to express their cultural concepts and rituals. Central to that cultural revolution were the Nguzo Saba (seven principles)—*umoja* (unity), *kujichagulia* (self-determination), *ujima* (collective work and responsibility), *ujamaa* (cooperative economics), *nia* (purpose), *kuumba* (creativity), and *imani* (faith)—as well as the seven-day holiday commemorating them, called Kwanzaa; those are two enduring legacies of US's cultural nationalism.[46]

The structure and hierarchy of US in the late 1960s reveals an extensive use of African culture and languages, not only for its alternative rituals but also for stratification of member responsibilities. The organization had developed several subunits; e.g., the Simba Wachanga the young male paramilitary wing; the Saidi (Lords) "older" men, usually over 20; the School of Afroamerican culture; the Mwalimu (teacher) unit of those studying the US religious outlook called Kawaida; and the Muminina, the women of the organization. Alongside those social units were committees focused on issues and tasks.

The two main governing bodies of US, during this period, were the Circle of Administrators and the Circle of Isihlangu. A Zulu word,

Isihlangu means "shield." That particular circle served as an executive governing committee.[47] At the end of 1967, Isishlangu's membership and ranking were: (1) Maulana Ron Karenga, founder-chairman; (2) Mwalimu Jim Tayari, vice-chairman; (3) Shahidi Karl Hekima, second vice-chairman; and (4) Ngao Sam Damu, security chairman.[48] Karenga described the Circle of Administrators as "chairs over chairs," guiding the various specific task-oriented committees.[49] Some of those listed as part of the circle in December 1967 were Reginald Endesha, finance; Clyde Halisi, advocacy-propaganda; Mwalimu Oliver Heshimu, Simba Wachanga; Shahidi Karl Hekima, labor; Mwalimu Ramon Imara, Kawaida; Ujima Imara, Muminina; Haiba Karenga, education; Ahera Msemaji, Third World Alliances; and Mwalimu Charles Sigidi, Saidi.[50]

While the US Organization was distinctive in its organizational structure and its rituals, much of its united front approach to politics as well as its views on "cultural revolution" were borrowed from Malcolm X and his OAAU. His sojourn into political and secular nationalism after leaving the NOI encouraged Karenga's views about cultural revolution. The OAAU's view of culture—as expressed in its "Statement of Basic Aims and Objectives"—was a precursor to US's cultural nationalist assertions, declaring, "We must recapture our heritage and our identity if we are ever to liberate ourselves from the bonds of White supremacy. We must launch a cultural revolution to unbrainwash an entire people."[51] The OAAU's "Basic Unity Program," also influenced Karenga and US. The program called on "Afro-American people" to "launch a cultural revolution which will provide the means for restoring our identity that we might rejoin our brothers and sisters on the African continent, culturally, psychologically, economically, and share with them the sweet fruits of freedom from oppression and independence of racist governments."[52]

Malcolm X modeled the OAAU after the Pan-African structure for governments, the Organization of African Unity.[53] The OAAU's quest for a coalition of diverse black nationalist participant members inspired the US theory of black unity and organizing strategies. Malcolm X's "The Ballot or the Bullet" outlined the OAAU's position, not demanding that organizations become subordinate to or merge with one particular group, but rather to accept the broad principles of black nationalism and simultaneously remain independent and autonomous. US later called this same approach "operational unity"—describing it as "unity without uniformity"—and employed it as the theoretical basis for several umbrella organizations and coalitions.[54]

US's early activism underscores the organization's quest to actualize this united front ideal, urging the advocates to engage existing public venues affecting black consciousness. It also functioned as a mandate to continue providing new spaces for African Americans to discover their "Blackness." The task of changing African American minds and culture carried with it a political struggle for control of the instruments and institutions that impact black consciousness.

Electoral Politics, Freedom City, and TALO

US members had long expressed great respect for SNCC and its leaders for their efforts to build independent African American political organizations in the South. Black nationalists in the North and West were struck by the bold efforts of the Lowndes County Freedom Organization, a SNCC-organized political force that had been challenging, since 1965, white political control in the heart of the Alabama Black Belt. In 1966, Clifford Vaughs, director of the Los Angeles chapter of SNCC, attempted to build a similar kind of black political organization in Watts to lead a campaign to secede the area from Los Angeles and establish an independent municipality called "Freedom City."[55] Karenga served as the movement's "public relations director."[56] Watts had, in fact, been an independent municipality prior to 1926, when, as Raphael Sonenshein has noted, discriminatory housing practices elsewhere in the area inspired thousands of African Americans to move to Watts. As a result, the municipality "was quickly incorporated into Los Angeles ... thereby preventing a Black-dominated local government."[57]

The Freedom City movement received a significant amount of national attention as the media attention focused on Watts on the first anniversary of the 1965 rebellion. Several feature articles on Watts in national news magazines portrayed black nationalism as an ominous specter of further violence.[58] Among the Los Angeles black nationalist activists and groups discussed in these articles, Karenga's US was seen as especially dangerous.

Journalists, inspired by an alarmist white backlash against Black Power, interpreted US's role in the Freedom City movement as further evidence of the rising black nationalist peril.[59] While Karenga wrote press releases for the initiative, US members canvassed door to door in the election precincts. Ultimately, the advocates of Freedom City failed to acquire the 217,543 signatures on a petition necessary for initiation of the secession process. Historian Clayborne Carson regards this result as indicative of the broader failure of SNCC Northern activists to transform their Black Power rhetoric into "actual political power."[60] For US, however, the Freedom City movement established what would be the hallmark of the organization's

Black Power legacy—its constant effort to participate in, form, or lead African American umbrella organizations modeled on Malcolm X's united front ideal.

Beyond the effort to form an independent black-governed municipality in Watts, US members worked to elect Yvonne Braithwaite Burke to the California State Assembly in 1966. Ken Msemaji, the head of community relations for US, coordinated the group's participation in neighborhood canvassing, literature distribution, and other precinct work. Likewise, US members helped elect state Assemblyman Mervyn Dymally to the California State Senate in1967. US regarded electoral politics as critical terrain in the struggle for black self-determination and community control. Msemaji recalls that when talking to potential voters, at the time, he was "trying to emphasize why it's important to get Black people elected to office and not be represented by Whites."[61]

During the summer of 1966, US joined another coalition called TALO. TALO included individuals from several Los Angeles black organizations: CORE [Congress of Racial Equality], Central L.A. NAACP, SLANT [Self Leadership for All Nationalities Today], US, and the "United Civil Rights Committee."[62] Among TALO's major achievements was the partial funding of the Community Alert Patrol, a group formed to monitor police activities in South Central Los Angeles. US pulled out of TALO during that fall, however, because Karenga felt "TALO didn't have a program beyond the Community Alert Patrol." He also criticized the alliance for its ineffective decision-making procedures.[63]

As the organization became increasingly steeped in Karenga's own unique ideology, US sought coalition arrangements where his ideas could dominate the agenda. This underscored the explosive tension between the organization's political aspirations and its own self-image. As a self-declared representative of the progressive black future, the US Organization frequently clashed with other constituent member groups in several umbrella formations.

The Black Congress, Vietnam, and UCLA

In the fall of 1967, US joined forces with the Black Congress, a newly formed alliance of African American organizations, businesses, and associations. Black Congress Chairman Walt Bremond, an experienced activist and student of Saul Alinsky's protest strategies, had previously led a Los Angeles organization called the Social Action Training Center, which "taught two alternatives to violence—community organization and community development."[64] The Black Congress consisted of over

20 participating groups identified with social issues, civil rights, public policies, and the community, including the Black Anti-Draft, Black Resistance Against Wars for Oppression and the Freedom Draft Movement, Black Panther Party of California, Black Youth Conference as well as Black Student Unions of California State University at Los Angeles, Compton City College, Los Angeles City College, Black Unitarians for Radical Reform and Immanuel Church, Citizens for Creative Welfare and County Welfare Rights, L.A. CORE and NAACP, SLANT, Underground Musicians Association, US, and many other organizations.[65]

The Black Congress embraced US's concept of "operational unity" to guide its effort to promote cooperative activism. Specifically, the congress brought together black organizations of diverse ideological perspectives under one umbrella. In fact, most of the participating organizations moved their headquarters to the Black Congress building or had auxiliary offices there. The programs or services offered by an individual organization functioned within the framework of the congress's larger united front agenda.[66] Using a model similar to that of the United Nations, representatives from member groups took part in specific subdivisions in the congress called councils, for example, finance council, education council, security council. Those involved with the housing council, for instance, were charged with the task of "aggressively and ruthlessly mov[ing] against all 'slumlords' with legal, political boycotts, 'rent strikes' and any other means necessary."[67]

That structure inspired supplementary and interorganizational support for initiatives previously seen as the domain of a particular group or individual and made the congress an extraordinary force in the balance of political power in Los Angeles. For example, Margaret Wright, a persistent advocate for black community control in the school system, who was head of the United Parents Council and the Black Educators, received additional support for her efforts from the attorneys and legal rights advocates of the legal council. Mwalimu Oliver Heshimu, who represented US on legal council, reported that during one meeting, he and others discussed launching retaliatory legal measures, should the Board of Education "fail to approve teaching of Black History as [United Parents Council and] Black educators have demanded."[68]

US identified completely with this alliance, moving its *Hekalu* (temple) to the Black Congress building, and transforming its newspaper, *Harambee*, to become the organ of the congress. Whereas Karenga had been the paper's editor in 1966, by the fall of 1967, *Harambee*'s leadership and content had changed. John Floyd of the Los Angeles-based Black Panther Political Party (entirely different and unaffiliated with the

Panthers in Northern California) became the editor, and Elaine Brown—later a prominent leader in the Oakland Black Panther Party—served as one of the paper's reporters. Under Floyd's editorship, *Harambee* described the paper's mission in the same terms as the US Organization's definition: "HARAMBEE, a Swahili word that means, 'let's pull together,' is a black community newspaper published by the Los Angeles Black Congress."[69]

In addition to collective local projects in community development, the congress fostered a policy consensus on key national and international issues—for example, alliances with people of color, and opposition to the Vietnam War. On October 22, 1967, US was among a group of organizations in the Black Congress that signed the "Treaty of Peace and Harmony, and Mutual Assistance," with the Spanish-American Federal Alliance of Free City States—a consortium of Chicano activists and organizations seeking political autonomy in the Southwest.[70]

The US Organization's involvement in the "Treaty of Peace and Harmony, and Mutual Assistance" also underscored its belief that nations of color should form an international political bloc, or third force (neither capitalist nor communist). This perspective figured prominently in the organization's positions on domestic and international issues. The view that African Americans and other people of color, in the United States and abroad, should be natural political allies extended to the congress's anti-Vietnam War position. The antiwar position brought numerous organizations into its ranks. A 1967 article in *Harambee* described an antiwar rally at which Karenga shared the rostrum with representatives of Black Panthers, CORE, and the Black Student Union Alliance.[71]

Using the seven principles as an explanatory framework, a 1967 "US Statement on the Viet Nam War" relates its opposition to the war with the assertion that African Americans and Asians share a common quest for self-determination. Indeed, some members of the US Organization's *Kawaida* faith were conscientious objectors to the war in Vietnam:

> As members of the Kawaida faith we oppose the war because it violates two basic principles upon which our faith is based. (1) It violates the sixth principle KUUMBA which is creativity. As members of the Kawaida faith we are pledged to be creative rather than destructive. We consider creative that which promotes human life and development; and we consider destructive that which is negative to human life and development. (2) The Viet Nam war also violates our second principle, KUJICHAGULIA which is self-determination for it is a war that denies people of color of Asia their right to choose their own form of government and to promote human life and development in the way they see is beneficial to them and to their own

needs and desires. We, ourselves, are struggling for the right of self-determination on every level. We would be against ourselves if we fought to deny others of the same right. [72]

The antiwar position of the US Organization and the Black Congress inspired a group of black marines to form an affiliate chapter of US in Vietnam. In the late spring of 1967, a group of black marines temporarily stationed at the aviation squadron at El Toro, California, attended the US and Black Congress meetings while on leave.[73] Prior to leaving California for Da Nang, Vietnam, they adopted Kiswahili names.[74] In Vietnam, they set up their own *Hekalu* modeled on the US headquarters in the Black Congress building. Thomas Nrefu-Belton, a marine who assisted in establishing the US affiliate chapter in Vietnam, recalls that this activism led him to question the morality of the war and white military authority.[75] US was among a series of radical organizations, along with the Mau Mau and the Black Panther Party, that had sympathizers or corollary chapters among black soldiers and marines stationed in Vietnam.[76]

While in Vietnam, black marines' use of African names, special handshake greetings, hairstyles, and other outward expressions of solidarity with elements in the Black Power movement became a source of major concern to military authorities, who viewed the actions as threats to authority and challenges to leadership.[77] Black marines, affiliated with US, set up their own *Hekalu* in Chu Lai, Vietnam, which became an exclusive black domain, where critical and explicit political dialogue occurred. Marines' association with the US Organization played an important role in their resistance to racism in the American military. US's cultural nationalism, along with other radical ideologies of the late 1960s, may have encouraged some African American marines to rebel. During the late 1960s and early 1970s—the height of the Black Power movement and its subsequent impact on black servicemen—the marines and other armed forces experienced an abnormal amount of fraggings (attacks against officers by lower ranking servicemen). A significant number of these incidents were a product of racial tensions in the military.[78]

While US and the Black Congress contributed to the consolidation of widespread African American opposition to the Vietnam War, challenges to the discipline of interorganizational unity emerged as the alliance's effectiveness peaked. The early months of 1968 marked a high point, both in the Black Congress's public profile and in the US ability to position itself as the leading organization within that united front. On February 18, 1968, an estimated 5,000 people attended a Black Congress-sponsored rally at the Los Angeles Sports Arena to support the incarcerated Minister of Defense of the Black Panther Party, Huey Newton, who had been arrested and charged with murdering a police officer. The range of speakers at the rally—Maulana Karenga, Kwame Toure (Stokely Carmichael), Reverend Thomas Kilgore, H. Rap Brown, Bobby Seale, and Reis Tijerina—revealed a continued sense of unity, albeit fragile, that Newton's case had generated among nationalists and other radicals around the issue of self-defense.[79] On one hand, the rally was a practical expression of Karenga's vision of operational unity, yet it also revealed US/Black Panther party infighting as differences over security matters led each group to view the other with distrust and suspicion.[80] Throughout the latter half of 1968, rivalries and internal dissension consumed the Black Congress, US, and the Panthers. The rift between the congress's two most powerful member organizations disrupted any sense of "operational unity." From early 1968 through 1970, US and the Black Panther Party competed for dominance in the public sphere—from community meetings and street corners to college campuses.

In April 1968, the Black Congress organized several events immediately after the assassination of Martin Luther King. Violent revolts occurred in several American cities in response to King's death, but the Black Congress succeeded in directing the collective rage felt in the Los Angeles African American community away from retaliatory violence, and toward a plan for organized, antiracist community action—a plan based on US's concept of operational unity. Although the Black Congress as a whole had taken the position against violent retaliation, some media had incorrectly attributed this solely to the US Organization. An extensive profile on Karenga that appeared on the front page of the *Wall Street Journal,* in July of 1968, "Black Enigma: A West Coast Militant Talks Tough but Helps Avert Trouble,"[81] noted that "Karenga's prestige also rose after his open participation in an 'operational unity steering committee,' formed by the Black Congress only hours after King's death." "The committee's main purpose," it continued, "was to prevent Negro rioting here."[82]

The article raised two other specific issues that would subsequently fuel charges that US was either committed to diverting mass radical sentiment or was a direct operative of the U.S. government. The first allegation cited was that Karenga had "met clandestinely with Los Angeles Police Chief Thomas Reddin after Mr. King was killed."[83] This claim emerged in the context of the article's thesis that Karenga was a master manipulator who used the language and imagery of militancy to mask his own personal accommodation with traditional white-dominated centers of political power. Without revealing its sources, it contends that, "[c]ivil rights observers agree that Karenga is typical of many militants who talk of looting and burning but actually are eager to gather influence for quiet bargaining with the predominately White power structure."[84]

Karenga never denied meeting with the police chief. He noted, moreover, that the meeting was *not* clandestine and that it occurred with the presence of other members of the Black Congress.[85] When asked about this matter in an interview, Karenga said, "When we met with Reddin we were meeting as the Black Congress, as a collective group with Walt Bremond, with Reverend Edwards and other people who were on that committee."[86] He also rejected the notion that meeting with elements of the "white power structure" is taboo and added that the objective of the meeting was an attempt to thwart police misconduct. "That is necessary at times," he argued, "for us to meet with different factions in society and try to ease the oppression and repression that's going to constantly occur."[87] As far as the result of the meeting was concerned, he concluded "we were able to change the amount of police in the community for a while."[88]

More difficult for Karenga and US to defend, however, was another issue raised in the *Wall Street Journal* profile—Karenga's having gone to Sacramento "a few weeks after the assassination of Martin Luther King," for "a private chat with Governor Ronald Reagan, at the governor's request."[89] By the time of King's assassination, Governor Reagan, elected in 1966, had already earned a reputation for law and order politics. Radicals and black nationalists throughout California found him an easy negative symbol, representing the very worst of the state's right wing constituency.[90] In any case, Karenga conceded that he attended the meeting and expressed regret at having done so. Discussing his reasons for attending the meeting, he stated that "Reagan called my house and I had a lot of people [from the US Organization] in jail and in prison and I thought that was an outlet where we could get some of our people out of prison."[91] In another instance, responding to the allegation that the meeting with Reagan was clandestine, Karenga mentioned that it was not possible for him to "slip into Sacramento" due to his conspicuous shaved head, African clothing, and eight other US members who traveled with him.[92]

However, looking back at that the meeting with Reagan, Karenga said that it was "the wrong move."[93] For him, the mistake was tactical and, in a vague sense, ideological—although he maintained the position that the very notion of conferring with the governor did not pose any inherent ethical problems. He also concluded that the manner by which the meeting transpired added to accusations that he and US were collaborating with reactionary government agencies.[94] The decision to meet unilaterally with the governor, without representatives from other congress organizations, is a likely indicator of the careless arrogance that accompanied US's sense that it could operate as the leading group within a supposedly cooperative alliance. In any case, reports of the meeting increased the already mounting tensions in the Black Congress.

Apart from its clash with the Black Panther Party for Self-Defense, US was notorious for using violent strong-arm tactics against dissenting individuals and organizations who disagreed with the US position within the congress's internal deliberations.[95] The Black Panther Party also used force and intimidation to get its way with the congress—especially with respect to the Los Angeles-based Black Panther Political Party that included Angela Davis, John Floyd, and Ayuko Babu.[96] In fact, SNCC's James Forman went to Los Angeles several times to mediate both the US/Panther conflict and the strife between the two Panther organizations.[97] The Federal Bureau of Investigation (FBI) took note of these independent efforts to quell the feud and intensified its campaign to destabilize both organizations. The atmosphere in the Black Congress grew particularly tense when a series of FBI-created anonymous letters were sent to leaders and rank-and-file members of both groups, some of which urged the Black Panther Party to "takeover" US while other letters warned US about a planned takeover.[98]

In late September 1968, the Los Angeles FBI stated that it had been informed of "considerable friction between the Black Panther Party and the 'US' organization headed by RON KARENGA," and that, as a result, the Black Panther Party had recently withdrawn from the Black Congress.[99] The memo also mentioned that "information has been received that the BPP has issued instructions that RON KARENGA, Chairman of 'US' is to be killed."[100] Two months later, on November 29, the Los Angeles office reported that it was "currently preparing an anonymous letter for Bureau approval which will be sent to the Los Angeles Black Panther Party (BPP) supposedly from a member of the 'US' organization in which it will be stated that the youth group of the 'US' organization is aware of the BPP 'contract' to kill RON KARENGA, leader of 'US,' and they, 'US' members in retaliation have made plans to ambush leaders of the BPP in Los Angeles."[101] The special agent in charge made the objective of this operation ominously clear: "It is hoped this counterintelligence measure will result in an 'US' and BPP vendetta."[102] There may have been no truth to the bureau's information about an actual assassination plot. It is quite probable that as a war of words escalated between these groups, the climate of heightened rhetoric yielded that kind of "talk" among rival partisans. Even more disturbing, however, is the FBI's apparently gleeful enthusiasm and coldly deliberate inaction with respect to a prospective murder conspiracy.

By early 1969 the conflict had moved onto the UCLA campus. In a fracas that ensued after a Black Student Union meeting, Panther leaders Alprentice "Bunchy" Carter and John Huggins were shot to death, and US member Larry Stiner-Watani sustained a gunshot wound to the shoulder. How the clash transpired is not altogether clear. Eyewitnesses testified that US member Claude Hubert-Gaidi (also known as Chochezi) shot Carter and Huggins while they were involved in a violent struggle with US member Harold Jones-Tawala who, just moments before, was engaged in a heated argument with Black Panther Elaine Brown.[103] Former Black Panther deputy minister of defense, Geronimo Pratt, was Carter's head of security at the time.[104] Recalling the incidents, he insists that it was not a conspiracy, but rather a spontaneous shootout. Pratt stated that the altercation with Huggins, Carter, and Tawala, "caused one of the Panthers to pull out a gun ... which subsequently caused US members to pull out their guns to defend themselves."[105] "In the ensuing gun battle," Pratt continued, "Bunchy Carter and John Huggins lay dead."[106] Karenga and US members have described the UCLA tragedy with an emphasis on some of the same points mentioned in the version articulated by Pratt.[107] In any case, shortly after the deaths of Carter and Huggins, the Black Panther Party maintained an official position that what had transpired was, indeed, a planned assassination, orchestrated by Karenga in fulfillment of a government directive.[108] Many historical accounts of the UCLA incident accept this partisan view without question or scrutiny.[109] The view that the deaths were the result of a planned conspiracy was also employed by Los Angeles District Attorney's prosecutor Stephen Trott in his case against three US members of the Simba on trial for the shootings.[110] Shortly after the UCLA incident, George Stiner-Ali, his brother Larry Stiner-Watani, and Donald Hawkins-Stodi surrendered to the police, who had issued warrants for their arrests. The three of them were subsequently tried and convicted for conspiracy to commit murder and two counts of second-degree murder.[111] The person who allegedly did the shooting, Claude Hubert-Gaidi, was never found, and neither was Harold Jones-Tawala. The Stiner brothers both received life sentences, whereas Stodi, because he was only 20-years old, served time in California's Youth Authority Detention.

The shootout had an immediate crippling effect on the Black Congress. Shortly afterward, the congress chairman, Walt Bremond, resigned.[112] Even more damaging, another group of organizations, some previously belonging to the Black Congress, formed a counter-united front coalition called the Black Alternative.[113] By the spring of 1969, the Black Congress was virtually defunct, and the US quest for a united front in Los Angeles had come to an end.[114] While US experienced harsh opposition to its version of united front politics in Los Angeles, paradoxically the organization played an integral and positive role during this same period in the Northeast.

The NewArk Laboratory: The Black Power Conferences and Electoral Politics in Newark

Long before the shootout with the Panthers, Karenga and Amiri Baraka (then LeRoi Jones), the literary genius and activist, met for the first time in late 1966 or sometime in early 1967. Karenga was in New Jersey for meetings with Nathan Wright that resulted in the Newark Black Power Conference of July 1967. And soon thereafter, Baraka took a look at the US Organization on a visit to Los Angeles. The alliance between these two leaders and their respective organizations led to a series of concrete political achievements in Newark—the most noteworthy of which was the election of the city's first black mayor in 1970.

Komozi Woodard's *A Nation Within A Nation: Amiri Baraka (LeRoi Jones) & Black Power Politics* maintains that the goals of independent politics and black nationality formation were key developments in Black Power era cultural nationalism. A centerpiece in this process was the launching of, what Woodard has termed, the Modern Black Convention Movement—the 1966, 1967, and 1968 Black Power Conferences, 1970 and 1972 Congress of African People Conventions, the 1972 National Black Political Convention in Gary, and a series of other major political gatherings. Through networks established with East Coast nationalist organizations, far away from the contentious regional struggles for power in Southern California, US was able to assume a dominant role in this budding convention movement. The US political relationship with Newark began with planning the first National Conference on Black Power. A participant in the Black Power Planning Conference on September 3, 1966, organized by Representative Adam Clayton Powell, in Washington D.C., Karenga emerged as one of the five members of the continuations committee that would play a leading role in planning the 1967 conference.[115] The 1966 Black Power Planning Conference brought together 169 delegates from 37 cities, 18 states, and 64 organizations.[116]

The Continuations Committee decided that the National Conference on Black Power was to be held the following year in Newark, New Jersey. This decision would have an unanticipated level of political importance given that the four-day conference was scheduled to begin July 20, 1967.

On July 11 of that year, a violent rebellion erupted in Newark—as had been the case in Watts in 1965—that raged on for almost a week. As a result of this turn of events, 26 people were killed and over 1,000 were injured.[117] The committee was pressured by numerous city officials to postpone the conference. However, they decided to continue with the conference as it had been originally scheduled.[118] It became, as a result, not merely an avenue for creating a strategy for Black Power on a national level but also a forum to address the local political and economic bases for the rebellion.[119]

The conference consisted of a series of workshops and general sessions where participants voted on specific resolutions. Nathan Hare, Hoyt Fuller, Ossie Davis, Faye Bellamy, James Farmer, Vivian Braxton, William Strickland, and Cleveland Sellers were among the group of those who facilitated workshops.[120] Significantly, Karenga was the coordinator for one called, "Black Power in World Perspective: Nationalism and Internationalism."[121] As had been the case with the Black Congress, Karenga emerged as a central theorist who provided a model for the conference's participating organizations of diverse ideological positions to function cooperatively.

The conference resolution calling for a political task force to assist in unseating Newark Mayor Hugh Addonizio became a focal point of an emerging alliance between US and various political forces in Newark.[122] Baraka, who had been injured in a police beating, became even more active in Newark politics after the rebellion. He was in close contact with, and in certain instances a leading member in, a few key organizations that would collectively ignite a campaign to increase African American political representation in Newark; the United Brothers, Black Community Defense and Development (BCD), and a collective of local artists called the Spirit House. Eventually, these forces merged and became a sort of East Coast affiliate chapter of the US Organization. Baraka recalled, "It was Karenga, who on one of his visits, suggested that we formally bring together the United Brothers, BCD, and the Spirit House forces. ... Karenga suggested the name Committee for a Unified Newark (CFUN)."[123]

This new alliance's first major public effort toward organizing in electoral politics was the Black Political Convention in Newark June 21–23, 1968.[124] Karenga spoke at a plenary session. His effectiveness was bolstered by an ability to expose convention participants to a theoretical model that assisted them in conceptualizing a strategy for gaining political power.[125] His own doctrine's catechisms specified various objectives and steps for achieving political power. Most noteworthy are the four areas of political power: (1) political office, (2) community organization, (3) coalitions and alliances, and (4) disruption.[126] The convention was a major step in launching CFUN's electoral campaign that ran Ted Pinkney and Donald Tucker for city council seats for the November 1968 election. This effort was called the "Peace and Power" campaign. Baraka recalled, "Karenga came to town especially to help with the campaign." He went on mention that "It was ... [Karenga] who named the campaign 'Peace & Power,' hoping to capitalize on the peace movement that was one aspect of the anti-Vietnam protests as well as the Black Power movement."[127]

The National Conference on Black Power in August 1968 presented CFUN with an opportunity to gain national support for the Peace and Power Campaign. By that time, Karenga was the head of the Black Power Continuations Committee. The conference further solidified the alliance between US and CFUN. A large contingent of US members attended the conference.[128] Wesely Kabaila, a former US member who attended the Philadelphia conference, recalls that just afterward, a group of them "left Philadelphia and went directly to Newark to help organize."[129] Kabaila also remembers this contingent of US members staying in Newark for nearly one month assisting with the campaign and teaching the US doctrine and practice to the BCD and CFUN members.[130]

In addition to direct input from this cadre, Karenga personally assisted CFUN in the development of its day-to-day organizing efforts—especially voter registration and fund-raising. Evidently, Karenga and US's experience with voter registration drives in the Freedom City movement and other organizing efforts in Los Angeles informed their ability to play an advisory role in the beginnings of their relationship with CFUN. The Peace and Power campaign fell short of achieving the election of its candidates to the city council. However, this entree into electoral politics laid the basis for CFUN's electoral triumph in its 1970 mayoral campaign that produced the election of Newark's first black mayor, Kenneth Gibson.

US's participation in united front politics declined in the early 1970s, when sectarian conflict and government repression undermined the organization's overall effectiveness. Stress from the US/Panther conflict eventually undermined the alliance it had formed with Amiri Baraka and others and damaged the day-to-day functioning of the organization as a local force in Los Angles. The resulting US leadership breakdown is dramatically evidenced in the 1971 conviction of Karenga and three others for assault and false imprisonment in association with the torture of two US members.[131] The internationalization of the Modern Black Convention Movement continued without the US Organization's participation during the mid-1970s—giving way to the African Liberation Support Committee and an extensive African American presence at the 1974 Sixth Pan-African Congress in Tanzania.

Conclusion

Culture and politics are more inseparable than dichotomous—especially within the framework of the African American struggle against oppression in the United States. Unfortunately, legacies rooted in the war of words and guns, between US and the Black Panther Party, persistently distort historical knowledge of the US role in the politics of the black nationalist resurgence of the 1960s and early 1970s. Rivalries between these two groups generated a misleading debate, incorrectly juxtaposing the *cultural* nationalism of US against the *revolutionary* nationalism of the Black Panther Party. Those opposed to US in the late 1960s characterized its activism as nonthreatening to "the system," preoccupied with cultural symbols and rituals, and void of substantive political content. Some recent studies on the period duplicate a similarly binary view and are as woefully negligent in assessing the US political legacy as those activists embroiled in the feud over thirty years ago.[132]

The story of US reminds us that resistance is almost always multidimensional and complex. Not only did US challenge white power, but it was a central force in the Black Power movement, as well as at the core of the Modern Black Convention Movement. African American leadership has a long tradition of establishing black interorganizational umbrella formations, and US embodied this as it attempted to fulfill united front ideals articulated in Malcolm X's blueprint for the OAAU. While US's strategy of "programmatic influence" contributed to the budding Modern Black Convention Movement and the electoral political action of Amiri Baraka's Committee for a Unified Newark, it did not create a lasting black alliance capable of enduring ideological and political conflict—an objective to this day beyond the grasp of African American activism. During the Black Power period, many other organizations and factions similarly regarded themselves as vanguard leaders and ultimately challenged the US authority in the movement. Nonetheless, these potentially explosive united front efforts helped forge and solidify a consensus on critical issues of the time, including community control in schools, the right of black self-defense, adequate black representation in urban politics, and opposition to the Vietnam War. Indeed, the zeal with which US members embraced a new world for themselves, replete with alternative rituals and institutions, mirrored their larger effort to transform American society. The multiple spaces in which power, conflict, disheartenment, vision, and collective sacrifice flourished are best captured in the US Organization's own motto: "Anywhere we are, US is."[133]

Notes

1. Linda Harrison, "On Cultural Nationalism," *Black Panther,* February 2, 1969, 6; Huey Newton, "Huey Newton Talks to the Movement about the Black Panther Party, Cultural Nationalism, SNCC, Liberals and White Revolutionaries," in *Black Panthers Speak,* Philip Foner, ed. (New York: J. B. Lippincott, 1970), 50–51.

2. Gerald Horne, *Fire This Time: The Watts Uprising and the 1960s* (Charlottesville: University Press of Virginia, 1995), 187, 202–203; Bruce Tyler, "The Rise and Decline of the Watts Summer Festival, 1965–1986," *American Studies* 31:2 (1990): 63; Herbert Haines, *Black Radicals and the Civil Rights Mainstream, 1954–1970* (Knoxville: University of Tennessee Press, 1988), 64; Jennifer Jordan, "Cultural Nationalism in the 1960s: Politics and Poetry," in *Race, Politics and Culture: Critical Essays on the Radicalism of the 1960s,* Adolph Reed, ed. (Westport: Greenwood Press, 1986), 35–38. Jordan's essay makes the rather curious assertion that US and other cultural nationalists were only rhetorically critical of the Vietnam War and did not actively participate in the antiwar movement.

3. Scot Brown, "Interview with Maulana Karenga" (audio recording, July 11, 1998), side 1.

4. Scot Brown, "Interview with Maulana Karenga" (transcript, October 11, 1994), 1–5.

5. "25 'Orators' Reach Speech Semi-Finals," *Los Angeles Collegian,* May 13, 1960, 1; "Bein, Everett Unopposed for Top Posts," *Los Angeles Collegian,* May 24, 1966, 1; "Everett Wins: VP Defeats AS Treasurer," *Los Angeles Collegian,* January 13, 1961, 1; Brown, "Interview with Maulana Karenga," 3.

6. Brown, "Interview with Maulana Karenga," 3; "AS Prexy Candidate Explains Platform," *Los Angeles Collegian,* January 10, 1961, 2.

7. Brown, "Interview with Maulana Karenga," 12.

8. At some point, Karenga also learned French. He read both African literature and politics in French from the then yet to be translated writings on negritude to the political tracts of Sekou Toure on African socialism.

9. Maulana Ron Karenga, in *The Quotable Karenga,* Clyde Halisi and James Mtume, eds. (Los Angeles: US Organization, 1967), 7.

10. Ibid., 15.

11. Brown, "Interview with Maulana Karenga," 25.

12. John Floyd, "Marcus, Marx, Malcolm, and Militants," *Los Angeles Sentinel,* May 20, 1971, 5.

13. Ibid.

14. Ron Karenga et al., "What is Black Power," audio recording of panel discussion (Los Angeles: Pacifica Radio Archive, July 23, 1966), tape 1, side 1.

15. Bill Ray (photographer), "Watts Today," *Life Magazine,* July 15, 1966, 53; Budd Schulberg, ed., *From the Ashes: Voices of Watts* (New York: The New American Library, 1967), 18.

16. C. Batuta, "US—Black Nationalism on the Move," *Black Dialogue* 2:7 (Autumn 1966), 7; Brown, "Interview with Maulana Karenga," 44; Scot Brown, "Interview with Karl Key-Hekima, (transcript, November 11, 1996), 4–5.

17. *Message to the Grassroots,* May 21, 1966, 1, 5. This newspaper was short-lived and may have folded just after the first issue went into print. It had certainly been discontinued by the time that Jamal left US in the late spring or summer of 1966. In August 1966, US introduced a new official newspaper called *Harambee*—its first edition commemorated the anniversary of the Watts revolt. This author was able to locate one edition of the paper in the personal papers of Terry Carr-Damu.

18. By 1968, Jamal had founded the Malcolm X Foundation, based in Compton, which he argued was the true heir to Malcolm X's revolutionary legacy. Jamal also grew to become a critic of US's cultural nationalism, contending that its emphasis on African culture diverted its members from participating in revolutionary action. See "'Operational Unity' Leaves Jamal Cold," *Los Angeles Sentinel,* April 18, 1968, A11; "An Interview with Hakim Jamal," *Long Beach Free Press,* September 17–October 1, 1969, 6, 12, 14.

19. Scot Brown, "Interview with Oliver Massengale-Heshimu and Charles Massengale-Sigidi" (transcript, November 11, 1997), 7.

20. Scot Brown, "Interview with James Doss-Tayari," (November 12, 1996), 18.

21. Ibid., 18–19.

22. Scot Brown, "Interview with Ngoma Ali" (transcript, November 10, 1996), 5; Brown, "Interview with Karl Key-Hekima," 42; Amiri Baraka, *The Autobiography of LeRoi Jones* (Chicago: Lawrence Hill Books, 1997), 356.

23. Brown, "Interview with James Doss-Tayari," 1–2.

24. "Natural Beauty of the Week," *Harambee,* August 11, 1966, 6.

25. Scot Brown, "Interview with C. R. D. Halisi" (transcript, November 11, 1996), 3; "Masters of Trickology," *Herald Dispatch,* July 30, 1966, 1; Brown, "Interview Oliver with Massengale-Heshimu and Charles Massengale-Sigidi," 2.

26. Brown, "Interview with C. R. D. Halisi," 4.

27. Scot Brown, "Interview with Joann Richardson-Kicheko" (transcript, April 22, 1997), 1.

28. Clay Carson, "A Talk with Ron Karenga," *Los Angeles Free Press,* September 2, 1966, 12.

29. "First Annual Memorial Staged for Malcolm X," *Los Angeles Sentinel,* March 3, 1966, A11.

30. Ibid.

31. "Riots Disrupt Malcolm X Meeting," *Los Angeles Sentinel,* May 25, 1967, A3.

32. Ibid.

33. Ibid.

34. Scot Brown, "Interview with Charles Johnson-Sitawisha" (transcript, September 9, 1995), 4.

35. Ibid., 5–6. The US flyer for Malcolm X's birthday in 1968 urges the Los Angeles community. "'PEOPLE GET READY' for a BLACK HOLIDAY, No

School, No Work to celebrate KUZALIWA (The Birth Of Malcolm X)" in "[Flyer for Kuzaliwa, May 17, 1968]," Personal Papers of Charles Johnson-Sitawisha.

36. "From the Office of Kenneth Hahn [re: demonstrations in Los Angeles Area High Schools and Colleges]," Kenneth Hahn Papers, Huntington Library, Box 273, Folder 2a.

37. Ibid.

38. "Parents Demand Changes," *Los Angeles Sentinel*, September 14, 1967, A1, A8.

39. Ibid., A8.

40. "Another View of Manual," *Harambee*, November 17, 1967, 1.

41. John Dunne, "The Ugly Mood of Watts," *Saturday Evening Post*, July 16, 1966, 86.

42. "Festival Welcomes Uhuru Militants," *Los Angeles Free Press*, August 18–24, 1967, 3.

43. Clayborne Carson, *In Struggle: SNCC and the Black Awakening of the 1960s* (Cambridge: Harvard University Press, 1981), 255–257.

44. "Exclusive: Rap Brown Raps With Free Press," *Los Angeles Free Press*, August 18–24, 1967, 1.

45. Maulana Ron Karenga, in Karenga, *The Quotable Karenga*, 7.

46. Imamu [Clyde] Halisi, ed., *Kitabu: Beginning Concepts in Kawaida* (Los Angeles: Us Organization, 1971), 7–8; For an earlier reference to the Nguzo Saba, see Carson, "A Talk With Ron Karenga: Watts Black Nationalist," 12.

47. Scot Brown, "Interview with Maulana Karenga" (transcript, October 11, 1994), 53.

48. "Maulana Ron Karenga to LeRoi Jones," December 19, 1967, Personal Papers of Komozi Woodard. The names and titles of members of both circles are listed on the letterhead.

49. Brown, "Interview with Maulana Karenga," 53.

50. "Karenga to Jones," papers of Komozi Woodard.

51. Malcolm X, "Statement of Basic Aims and Objectives of the Organization of Afro-American Unity," in *New Black Voices: An Anthology of Contemporary New Black Literature*, Abraham Chapman, ed. (New York: New American Library, 1972), 563.

52. Organization of Afro-American Unity, "Basic Unity Program," in *February 1965: The Final Speeches, Malcolm X*, Steve Clark, ed. (New York: Pathfinder Press, 1992), 258.

53. William Van DeBurg, *New Day in Babylon: The Black Power Movement and American Culture, 1965–1975* (Chicago: University of Chicago Press, 1992), 3.

54. "Ron Karenga Speaks on 'Unity Without Uniformity,'" *Los Angeles Sentinel*, April 11, 1968, B5; Karenga, in his *The Quotable Karenga*, 17; Booker Griffin, "Operational Unity: A Positive Concept," *Los Angeles Sentinel*, February 22, 1968, 10B; Alphonso Pinkney, *Red, Black and Green: Black Nationalism in the United States* (New York: Cambridge University Press, 1976), 141.

55. "Will Watts Secede?" in *The Movement 1964–1970*, Clayborne Carson, ed. (Westport: Greenwood Press, 1993), 132.

56   "Opposition Shown to Freedom City," *Los Angeles Sentinel,* July 28, 1966, 1A.

57.   Raphael Sonenshein, *Politics in Black and White: Race and Power in Los Angeles* (Princeton: Princeton University Press, 1993), 27.

58.   Dunne, "The Ugly Mood of Watts," 83–87; "Watts Waiting for D-Day," *The New Republic,* June 11, 1966, 15–17; "Watts Today," *Life,* July 15, 1966, 62.

59.   "Watts Today," *Life,* 62; Dunne, "The Ugly Mood of Watts," 86.

60.   Carson, *In Struggle,* 233; Also Carson notes that the SNCC national leadership regarded the demise of the Freedom City campaign as an indication of Clifford Vaughs's lack of effectiveness and asked for his resignation and closed the Los Angeles office (233). Another Los Angeles chapter of SNCC would be revived later in 1968.

61.   Scot Brown, "Interview with Ken Msemaji," May 20, 2001, 7.

62.   "There is a Movement Starting in Watts," in Carson, *The Movement 1964– 1970.*

63.   Clayborne Carson, "A Talk With Ron Karenga," *Los Angeles Free Press,* September 2, 1966, 12.

64.   "Dr. King's Death Unifies LA Black Community," *Los Angeles Free Press,* April 12, 1968, 3.

65.   "Partial List of Black Congress," *Harambee,* November 17, 1967, 8.

66.   Black Congress Aircheck" [audio recording] (Los Angeles: Pacifica Radio Archive, 1968), tape 2, side 2; "Soul Brothers Air Grievances," *Los Angeles Sentinel,* January 1, 1969, A1, B10.

67.   "Black Congress Programs," [no date], 3. Personal Papers of Alfred Moore.

68.   Mwalimu Ken Msemaji to Mwalimu Oliver Heshimu, September 3, 1968, Papers of Maulana Karenga and the Organization US, African American Cultural Center, Los Angeles.

69.   *Harambee,* August 11, 1966, 3; *Harambee,* September 15, 1966, 3; *Harambee,* October 13, 1966, 3; *Harambee,* November 17, 1967, 2; *Harambee,* December 28, 1967, 2.

70.   "Introduction to Treaty," *Harambee,* November 17, 1967, 6.

71.   "San Diego Rally Seeks To End Vietnam War," *Harambee,* December 28, 1967, 8. It should be noted that SNCC's early antiwar stance had a strong influence on what would become that of US and other organizations during the late 1960s.

72.   "US Statement on the Viet Nam War, 1967," Personal Papers of Wesely Kabaila.

73.   Scot Brown, "Interview With Thomas Belton," (audio recording, November, 27, 1998), side 1.

74.   Gary Solis, *Marines and Military Law in Vietnam: Trial by Fire* (Washington, D.C.: History and Museums Division Headquarters, U.S. Marine Corps, 1989),129.

75.   Brown, "Interview with Thomas Belton," side 1.

76.   Wallace Terry, "Bringing the War Home," *Black Scholar* (November 1970): 8.

77.   Solis, *Marines and Military Law in Vietnam,*129.

78.   Robert Mullen, *Blacks in America's Wars: The Shift in Attitudes from the Revolutionary War to Vietnam* (New York: Pathfinder Press, 1973), pp. 80–81.

79. "Black Power, 'Every Negro is a Potential Blackman,'" *Herald Dispatch,* February 22, 1968, 3, 8; Angela Davis, *Angela Davis: An Autobiography* (New York: Bantam Books, 1974), 165–166.

80. Carson, *In Struggle,* 282–283.

81. "Black Enigma: A West Coast Militant Talks Tough but Helps Avert Trouble," Wall Street Journal, July 26, 1968, 1, 15.

82. Ibid., 15.

83. Ibid., 1.

84. Ibid.

85. "Karenga Speaks About Conflict With Panthers," *Los Angeles Free Press,* February 7, 1969, 1.

86. Earl Ofari and Ruth Hirshman, "Victim of Watergating, Ron Karenga: Interviewed by Ofari and Hirshman," [audio recording] (Los Angeles: Pacifica Radio Archive, 1974), side 1.

87. Ibid.

88. Ibid.

89. "Black Enigma," 1.

90. Van DeBurg, *New Day in Babylon,* 85–86; Sonenshein, *Politics in Black and White,* 85; Gilbert Moore, *Rage* (New York: Carrol & Graf Publishers, 1993), 91; Kenneth O'Reilly, *"Racial Matters" The FBI's Secret File on Black America, 1960–1972* (New York, The Free Press, 1989), 295, 336.

91. Ofari and Hirshman, " Interview with Ron Karenga," side 1.

92. "Karenga Speaks About Conflict With Panthers," 1.

93. Ofari and Hirshman, " Interview with Ron Karenga," side 1.

94. Ibid.; While Karenga, in the interview with Ofari and Hirshman, conceded his tactical error in meeting with Reagan, he also pondered, "Why is it that Black people and White people in this country believe that if a Black man meets with a White man, that [the] White man automatically is more intelligent than he is, automatically more shrewd politically than he is and automatically is going to make a fool of him and make him a patsy and a sell-out for the people?"

95. "Militants Fight Blacks, White Men Settle Dispute," *Herald Dispatch,* July 20, 1968, 1, 3. It should be noted that Pat Alexander, the editor of the *Herald Dispatch,* had a general mistrust of militant organizations of the Black Power movement. In different instances, she characterized both US and the Black Panther Party as fascistic. As a result, the paper's articles pertaining to local black nationalist politics were oftentimes unapologetically polemical; "Members of US Blamed," *Los Angeles Sentinel,* July 11, 1968, A1, A8; Elaine Brown, *A Taste of Power: A Black Woman's Story,* 115–116.

96. Davis, *Angela Davis,* 162; Brown, *A Taste of Power,* 124.

97. James Forman, *The Making of Black Revolutionaries* (New York: Macmillan, 1972), 524, 528; Scot Brown, "Interview with Ayuko Babu" (audio recording, November 9, 1996), tape 1, side 2; Davis, *Angela Davis,* 163; Carson, *In Struggle,* 281; "Black Congress Chairman Quits," *Los Angeles Sentinel,* January 30, 1969, A1, A10.

98. Federal Bureau of Investigation, "SAC San Diego to Director," November 22, 1968, Black Nationalist Hate Groups File (100-448006, section 5), 1, in *COINTELPRO: The Counter Intelligence Program of the FBI.*

99. Federal Bureau of Investigation, "SAC Los Angeles to Director," September 25, 1968, Black Nationalist Hate Groups File (100-448006, section 3), 1, 3, in *COINTELPRO.*

100. Ibid., 3.

101. Federal Bureau of Investigation, "SAC Los Angeles to Director," November 29, 1968, Black Nationalist Hate Groups File (100-448006, section 5), 1, in *COINTELPRO.*

102. Ibid.

103. "'US' Member Shot Panther in Back," *Herald Dispatch,* August 21, 1969; "Panther's 'Sex Problems' Told in Murder Hearing," *Los Angeles Sentinel* [author's files, no date] A1, A11.

104. James Mtume, "Interview with George Stiner-Ali and Claude Hubert-Gaidi," October 1998 [notes from audio recording].

105. Bakari Kitwana, "A Soldier's Story," *The Source,* February 1998, 132.

106. Ibid.

107. "Karenga Denies Shooting of UCLA Black Panthers," *Los Angeles Free Press,* January 31–February 7, 1969, 1; M. Ron Karenga, "A Response to Muhammad Ahmad," *Black Scholar* 9:10 (July/August 1978): 55–57; Scot Brown, "Interview with James Mtume" (transcript, January 16, 1997), 31–32; Mtume, "Interview with George Stiner-Ali and Claude Hubert-Gaidi."

108. "Cowardly Snakes Kill Panthers," *The Black Panther,* February 2, 1969, 6; "Panthers Promise to Avenge Deaths," *Berkeley Barb,* January 24–30, 9; "Bobby Seale Talks to The Movement about L.A. Assassinations, Cultural Nationalism, Exhausting All Political Means, Community Programs, Black Capitalism," in Carson, *The Movement 1964–1970,* 562–64; "Los Angeles Panthers Await Justice For US Organization Pigs," *The Black Panther,* February 2, 1969, 4.

109. Ward Churchill and Jim Vander Wall, *Agents of Repression: The Secret Wars Against the Black Panther Party and the American Indian Movement* (Boston: South End Press, 1988), 42–43; Ekwueme Michael Thelwell, "Just To See What the End Will Be," [Afterword] in Moore, *Rage,* 300–301; Bruce Tyler, "Black Radicalism in Southern California, 1950–1982" (Ph.D. diss., UCLA, 1983), 376. In separate published statements, two persons, Louis Tackwood and a shadowy unidentifiable man calling himself "Othello," claimed that they had worked for the FBI or local police and funneled weapons to and worked with infiltrators in US for the purpose of destabilizing the Black Panther Party. Othello's account, mysteriously told in an interview with *Penthouse* magazine, is cited in Huey Newton's dissertation, *War Against the Panthers: A Study of Repression in America* (New York: Writers & Readers Publishing, 1998), 104–10. Tackwood's story can be found in a book entitled *The Glass House Tapes* (New York: Avon, 1973). His account added fuel to scholarly attempts at advancing similar allegations against US and Karenga.

Somewhat troubling is the ease with which some historians have accepted the snitch-to-truth-teller conversion narratives offered by Tackwood or "Othello"—see Rod Bush, *We Are Not What We Seem: Black Nationalism and Class Struggle in the American Century* (New York: New York University Press, 1999), 217, for problematic use of Othello's story. Prior to the publication of *The Glass House Tapes,* Tackwood's credibility was shattered by constant changes in his story, and evasive and poor performance on a lie detector test for the *Los Angeles Times* and *Newsweek,* conducted by Chris Gugas, who at the time was the former president and current board chairman of the American Polygraph Association; see *Los Angeles Times,* October 17, 1971, 1, B1, B4, for details. While taking the test, he specifically refused to answer questions relating to his claim that he supplied Karenga with guns and money to disrupt the Black Panther Party.

110. "US Members Lose Battle," *Los Angeles Sentinel,* September 11, 1969, A1, A12; "Tight Security at Panther's Trial," *Herald Dispatch,* July 12, 1969, 2.

111. "Arguments Rage in Murder Trial," *Los Angeles Sentinel,* July 24, 1969, A1; "Stiner Brothers Get Life Sentence," *Los Angeles Sentinel,* November 30, 1969, A1, A9.

112. "Black Congress Chairman Quits," *Los Angeles Sentinel,* January 30, 1969, A1, A10.

113. "Black Power Thugs Warn Margaret Wright," *Herald Dispatch,* January 18, 1969; "Soul Brothers Air Grievances," *Los Angeles Sentinel,* January 1, 1969, A1, 10B.

114. "Maulana Karenga Urges Conference on Community Unity," *Harambee,* April 25, 1969, 8. At the time of the publication of this edition of *Harambee,* the newspaper had returned to being an exclusive organ of the US Organization. Its entire editorial staff was composed of US members.

115. Chuck Stone, "National Conference on Black Power," in *The Black Power Revolt,* Floyd Barbour, ed. (Boston: Extending Horizons Books, 1968), 190.

116. Ibid.

117. Ibid.

118. Komozi Woodard, *A Nation Within A Nation: Amiri Baraka (LeRoi Jones) & Black Power Politics* (Chapel Hill: University of North Carolina Press, 1999), 84–85; Komozi Woodard, "The Making of the New Ark: Imamu Amiri Baraka (LeRoi Jones), and the Newark Congress of African People, and the Modern Black Convention Movement. A History of the Black Revolt and the New Nationalism, 1966–1976" (Ph.D. diss., University of Pennsylvania, 1991), 104–105; Stone, "National Conference on Black Power," 190.

119. Stone, "National Conference on Black Power."

120. Nathan Wright, Jr., *Let's Work Together* (New York: Hawthorne Books, 1968), 146.

121. Ibid.

122. Stone, "National Conference on Black Power," 196.

123. Baraka, *The Autobiography of LeRoi Jones* (Chicago: Lawrence Hill Books, 1997), 385.

124 "Black Convention: Prelude to Self-Government," *Black Newark* 1:2 (July 1968): 12.

125. Woodard, "The Making of the New Ark," 161.

126. "Black Power Rally" [audio recording] (Los Angeles: Pacifica Radio Archive, 1968) side 2; Baraka, *The Autobiography of LeRoi Jones,* 393.

127. Baraka, *The Autobiography of LeRoi Jones,* 385.

128. Scot Brown, "Interview with Amina Thomas" (transcript: November 10, 1996), 7; Brown, "Interview with Oliver Massengale-Heshimu and Charles Massengale-Sigidi," 29; there was an apparent clash involving US Simba and the Revolutionary Action Movement's Black Guards. This is briefly mentioned in an article by Nikki Giovanni, "Black Poems, Poseurs and Power," *Negro Digest* 18 (June 1969).

129. Scot Brown, "Interview With Wesely Kabaila" (transcript: October 11, 1994), 28.

130. Ibid., 29.

131. "Karenga, 2 Others Found Guilty of Torturing Woman," *Los Angeles Times,* May 30, 1971, B26. "Ron Karenga Convicted, Gets Ten Year Sentence," *Herald Dispatch,* June 3, 1971, 1, 10; "US Leader Held in Asian-Type Torturing," *Los Angeles Sentinel,* A1, A8; Superior Court of the State of California for the County of Los Angeles, "A 264 545 Everett-Karenga, Ron N. et al.," Dept. 102, Arthur Alarcon, Judge.

132. Brian Ward, *Just My Soul Responding: Black Consciousness, and Race Relations* (Los Angeles: University of California Press, 1998), 348.

133. "Karenga to Jones," Personal Papers of Komozi Woodard. The slogan "Anywhere we are US is" is used as a logo at the top of the US Organization's letterhead.

Chapter 10

Between Social Service Reform and Revolutionary Politics: The Young Lords, Late Sixties Radicalism, and Community Organizing in New York City[1]

Johanna Fernandez

Among the many developments of the late 1960s and early 1970s, a generation of largely inexperienced young radical activists from diverse racial backgrounds established influential organizations in the volatile environment of Northern ghettos. These groups formed, in the aggregate, part of a growing grassroots movement of poor and working-class urban dwellers, mostly minority, that gave political and social direction to the insurgent mood prevalent in Northern cities in the second half of the 1960s and the early 1970s. The example was set by the Black Panther Party (BPP) when, in 1966, following the first wave of urban upheavals, its founding members resolved to organize the radicalized sections of poor and working-class black Northerners. The appeal of the BPP among black urban dwellers was rooted in the group's program, which expressed in urgent and uncompromising language the totality of basic political and economic grievances that had motivated civil rights protests in the North since the movement's emergence in the 1940s.[2] The Panthers' tenets called for "the power to determine the destiny of our Black Community, ... full employment for our people, ... an end to the robbery by the white man of our black community, ... decent housing, fit for shelter of human beings, ...

education, ... an immediate end to police brutality, ... [and] clothing, justice, and peace."[3] Moreover, in formulating an overarching critique of capitalism and proposing an alternative view of how society might be organized upon more humane priorities, the BPP gave Northern protests a deeper purpose and meaning at precisely the time when radicalization was becoming widespread.

As the decade came to a close, the BPP's compelling precedent and model of political organizing awakened radical movements, especially among groups with a history of racial oppression in the United States, about which we know little. These include the Revolutionary Union Movements (RUM), the Health Revolutionary Unity Movement (HRUM), the Young Lord's Organization (YLO), the Brown Berets, I Wor Kuen, the American Indian Movement (AIM), the Young Patriots, and many others.[4] Anchored for the most part in urban centers where an ever-growing number of people of color settled beginning in the 1940s, these organizations waged formidable struggles against the growing concentration of poverty that enveloped Northern, inner-city neighborhoods in the post-WWII period. Their movements were among the first to highlight the social consequences of the new poverty in the cities, what is commonly known today as the contemporary urban crisis. Examined together, the composition of these organizations stretched across the racial spectrum of American society, and in their politics and activism each expressed the class character of the Northern movements for racial equality, especially in the latter half of the 1960s.

This essay outlines the rise of the YLO, a Puerto Rican revolutionary nationalist formation analogous to the BPP, focusing primarily on the New York chapter and its impact on that city. I explore the emergence of the YLO as a product of deep social and economic changes in the postwar period, a context that created social inequality distinct from what had previously been observed in Northern cities. The chapter also examines the YLO's response to these conditions as it helped orchestrate militant protests of poor urban dwellers that addressed specific local grievances and simultaneously advanced a broader political movement whose aim was to rebuild society anew.

Through most of its active life, the YLO in New York (later renamed the Young Lords Party) led militant community-based campaigns to alleviate the most visible manifestations of urban poverty: inadequate health care, dilapidated housing, hunger, and irregular sanitation services. The group also endeavored to expose and challenge the ubiquity of police-inflicted violence against people of color in urban neighborhoods and the pervasiveness of racial discrimination in the courts. In linking local economic grievances with issues pertaining to structural racism and Puerto Rico's neocolonial relationship with the United States, the YLO acquired a large following both within New York's Puerto Rican enclave and among city activists.

Studying the Puerto Rican-led YLO alongside the struggles of native-born African Americans examined in this volume is particularly instructive. As an ethnic group of racially mixed stock, Puerto Ricans, who lived alongside African Americans, provide a tangible comparison for understanding the context-driven logic of racial ideology. By virtue of its dark and mulatto complexion, a significant section of the Puerto Rican population forms part of the black diaspora and therefore encountered many of the same racial barriers as did black Southerners migrating to Northern cities in the postwar years. For this reason, numerous members of the Young Lords considered joining or were members of black protest groups until the Young Lords emerged. Pablo Guzmán, a leading member of the New York YLO of recognizable African ancestry, considered joining the BPP in 1969.[5] Similarly, Felipe Luciano, chairman of the New York branch of the group, was involved with Amiri Baraka's Black Arts movement. Even Rafael Viera, a fair-skinned Puerto Rican, was a member of a black cultural nationalist organization in Detroit before joining the YLO in New York.

Yet, having been reared in a social context governed by different conceptions of race forged under Spanish rather than British colonialism in Puerto Rico, for Puerto Ricans it is counterintuitive to adhere to the dominant U.S. practice of subordinating cultural to racial identification.[6] Rather, Puerto Ricans are more likely than Americans to identify cultural heritage as the primary formative element in their social identity.[7] Additionally, because of the island's neocolonial relationship with the United States, which began at the turn of the nineteenth century, its identity is more nation-based than it is defined by race.[8] These factors complicate dominant conceptions of race in the United States as an impermeable black/white dichotomy, where racial differences are often essentialized and the possibility of solidarity on a basis other than race is rarely envisioned.

But perhaps the most compelling reason for comparing the Puerto Rican and African American movements is that, despite their distinct histories of oppression and the contrasting racial orders within which each was reared, both shared a similar relationship to the established political and economic structure of American society in the postwar urban North, where they often lived alongside each other. Notwithstanding the nationalist undercurrent of most radical organizations of the period, a comparison of the radical Puerto Rican and African American movements of the late sixties suggests that their activities, political ideas, and alliances were driven by a strong class impulse.

From the movement's inception, its leaders—challenged with the task of increasing their ranks and recognizing that black oppression was not attributable to race alone—broadened their protest demands. Issues commonly raised by the movement, such as greater job opportunities in private and public industry and improved housing, were meant to reflect the interests of the largest sections of African Americans and Latinos possible and to motivate them to take the risks involved in political activism.[9]

While the history of the civil rights movement has been primarily understood within the framework of African American citizenship rights, the issues raised by the Young Lords movement paint a portrait of struggle that is more composite. In many ways, the activism of the Lords reflects, with greater accuracy, the range of social and economic problems with which the civil rights movement was concerned.[10]

This essay challenges mainstream depictions of the civil rights movement through its examination of the YLO and the group's community actions. I suggest that although racial inequality in America impelled the movement's emergence, the objectives and character of protest were integrally woven with grievances of social and economic import. In New York, finding solutions to the seemingly pedestrian problems of garbage collection and lead poisoning in dilapidated urban dwellings increasingly informed the logic and aims of the movement. The Young Lords' skillfulness in probing different issues and methods of protests and pinpointing those, which resonated most with a specific community, ensured the group's success.

The Rise of the Young Lords and the Social Roots of Urban Radicalism in the North

The YLO first emerged in Chicago in the 1960s as a politicized gang.[11] It was one of numerous inner-city gangs to relinquish its defensive competition over "turf" control and to move toward progressive and overtly political community organizing, partially as a result of organic grassroots leadership in inner-city neighborhoods and the conscious interventions of political groups such as the BPP. The primary architect of the Young Lords' conversion was its chairman, Jose "Cha Cha" Jimenez. Like many black and Latino urban youth of his time, the Puerto Rican gang leader turned activist was radicalized through his countless encounters with the penal system and the excessive use of police force in the racially shifting neighborhoods of Chicago's North Side. While serving time in prison, Jimenez met fellow inmate and Chicago Black Panther leader Fred

Hampton, with whom he developed a close political relationship. Clearly persuaded by Hampton, upon release from prison, Jimenez resolved to use his influence as leader of the Young Lords, still in its gang incarnation, to negotiate a general truce between Chicago's white and Latino gangs. He eventually transformed the Young Lords into the BPP's Puerto Rican counterpart.

Transformed into a political group in 1967, the YLO is an example of a radical formation that evolved out of a confluence of social forces in the post-WWII urban experience and the escalation of protest movements in the sixties. The rise of urban militant formations in the 1960s was rooted in the social and economic structure of the postwar urban landscape, which had thrust major Northern cities in a labyrinthine course of ever increasing racial segregation and chronic unemployment. By 1960, the wave of predominantly black, Puerto Rican, Mexican, Native American, and, to a lesser extent, white Appalachian migrants who were beckoned from their rural dwellings into Northern cities by the promise of wartime jobs found themselves struggling amidst a transformed postwar urban economy no longer dependent on unskilled labor.[12]

Northern manufacturing industries that had previously provided employment to new migrants were relocating to the suburbs and the South by stages in search of lower production costs and cheaper, nonunion wages. During the same period, the infusion of technological advancements in industry eliminated demands for yet more unskilled, blue-collar jobs.[13] These developments provide a context for understanding how and why the BPP, the YLO, and the Young Patriots, a group of progressive poor whites from Appalachia, embraced interracial political collaboration on the basis of shared class interests. In Chicago, these three groups formed an activist alliance in the late 1960s, which they called the Rainbow Coalition.[14]

Yet, as the internal population shifts occasioned by wartime labor demands triggered a long-term flow of predominantly black and Latino migrants into the cities, the burden of poverty was disproportionately borne by people of color. In New York, the postwar transition from manufacturing to a predominantly service-based economy also created pockets of joblessness. Bureau of Labor Statistics studies published throughout the 1960s demonstrated an emerging concern over groups of predominantly black and Puerto Rican men in their prime working years living in New York's poorest slums. Relative to the labor participation of black and white men, lack of job activity was lowest among Puerto Ricans. In 1966, 47 percent of Puerto Ricans in New York were either unemployed, underemployed, or permanently out of the labor force for lack of success in finding employment.[15]

Radical grassroots movements cohering in the second half of the decade reflected the distinctive social features of the urban environment in which they emerged. At the same time that cities entered a sustained process of industrial decline, the mass exodus of upwardly mobile whites to the suburbs depleted the cities' residential tax base. As the new migrants moved into neighborhoods in transition being vacated by suburbia-bound white residents, racial tensions soared. The increased segregation in the cities contributed to the race-based character of urban politics, a politics that young radicals like the Young Lords and the Black Panthers adopted. Moreover, the inclement conditions of postwar city life that led to the riots of the 1960s also provided the breeding ground for militant insurgent groups and determined their fearless temperament. The intrepid style and politics of the YLO and other similar formations achieved widespread appeal among racially diverse sectors in the inner city because they captured and expressed the experience of these decaying urban communities.

The impulse of emerging radicals was to channel the raw discontent that existed among the unemployed by initiating campaigns on public policy issues directly affecting poor and working people where they lived. Between 1968 and 1969, the Chicago YLO led a series of militant campaigns with a social service temper akin to the BPP's "Survival Programs." Working in Chicago, a stronghold of the War on Poverty initiative, the YLO established tactical alliances with social service professionals and government antipoverty programs. The protest actions of the YLO include the occupation of the Armitage Street Church in Chicago, following numerous failed attempts at convincing its leadership to allow the group use of the space for the purposes of administering a day care program and a health clinic. In collaboration with other radical organizations and various social service groups, the Chicago YLO successfully halted an urban renewal plan for construction of middle-income homes in the city's West Lincoln Park neighborhood, which would have displaced Puerto Ricans and other Latinos.[16] The Puerto Rican radicals inspired the formation of sister organizations in other cities, the most influential of which was based in New York City. The New York Young Lords eventually duplicated the protest campaigns of the Chicago branch in Puerto Rican neighborhoods, including East Harlem and the South Bronx.

In New York, the community health issues addressed by the Young Lords in their campaigns and the coalitions they built with the HRUM corresponded to the concentration of Puerto Ricans and black workers as orderlies in public and voluntary hospitals. The hospital industry was one of the few service sector areas where minorities were hired in large numbers. Influenced by the community action ethos of the period, the hospital-based

HRUM endeavored to broaden the parameters of its struggle beyond traditional bread-and-butter workplace issues. In collaboration with the HRUM, the YLO campaigned against the grievances expressed by hospital patients, mainly hospital privatization, the ill treatment of patients on the basis of race, and the proliferation of epidemics brought on by poor sanitation and conditions of poverty such as tuberculosis, anemia, and lead poisoning.

The Emergence of the Young Lords in New York

In the summer of 1969, Puerto Rican radicals in New York established what would become a much more organizationally cohesive group than its Chicago counterpart. Its members determined to build what they deemed a more disciplined revolutionary group committed to the struggle for Puerto Rican liberation on the island and on the mainland.

The New York group was led by college-educated youth, the children of poor and working-class Puerto Rican migrants to the city. Its membership included ex-students, working-class youth, former gang members, former drug addicts, and people who had at one time or another been institutionalized for petty crime. Although the organization was composed primarily of Puerto Ricans born in or raised on the mainland United States, close to 30 percent of its members were African Americans and non-Puerto Rican Latinos.

By 1971, the New York Lords claimed approximately 1,000 members and had spread rapidly along the northeastern corridor and in Puerto Rico, building branches in Bridgeport, Newark, and Philadelphia and in Ponce and Aguadilla, two cities in Puerto Rico. Eventually, the New York YLO established a more politically directed chapter of the organization, prioritizing education, organizational discipline, and ideological cohesion as an integral part of their activist work. On this basis, the group severed its ties to the Chicago YLO in May 1970 and renamed itself the Young Lords Party.[17]

One of the predecessors of the YLO in New York was the Sociedad de Albizu Campos (SAC).[18] The SAC was one of many reading circles that cropped up across the nation in the aftermath of the watershed events of 1968 where activists engaged in intense ideological discussions on theories of imperialism, national liberation struggles, the origins of class divisions in society, and the roots of race and gender oppression. Named after the father of the Puerto Rican national independence movement, Don Pedro Albizu Campos, the organization started as a reading group composed of students from the newly chartered State University of New York at

Old Westbury who were concerned with Puerto Rican history in general and with the history and politics of Puerto Rico's national liberation movements, in particular.[19]

The watershed campus protests of 1968 provided fertile ground for the radicalization of large numbers of students, especially minority youth who had matriculated at universities across the nation in record numbers following the institutionalization, between 1964 and 1966, of special university admissions opportunities for black and Latino students administered by SEEK (Search for Education, Elevation, and Knowledge) and the College Discovery programs.[20] Once in college, young radicals began to meet to discuss issues of campus discrimination, financial aid, and the narrow scope of their colleges' core curriculums. Some formed their own race-based coalitions to address these grievances, while others joined existing activist organizations. The Puerto Rican Student Union (PRSU) coordinated the efforts of various Puerto Rican student groups emerging in colleges across New York. The PRSU chapters at Queens and Herbert Lehman colleges in particular provided resolute leadership to the nascent Puerto Rican student movement in New York by broadening the political range of the issues it discussed.[21] The most politically conscious elements of this group linked their grievances to the movement for Puerto Rican independence and the mounting struggles in the University of Puerto Rico against on-campus military recruitment for the Vietnam War.[22]

As tens of thousands of once "nonideological" students began to question the logic and structure of American society, many ex-student activists, such as those who eventually founded the YLO in New York, also began to look outside the university to poor communities for more permanent and impacting sites of struggle. Denise Oliver, an African American member and one of the first women to hold a position in the formal leadership of the organization, left her university studies to join SNCC (Student Nonviolent Coordinating Committee) and later worked in a federally funded program in East Harlem before joining the Young Lords in 1969. Similarly, upon leaving Columbia University, Juan Gonzalez, a founding member of the YLO in New York, took a job as a Neighborhood Youth Corp trainer in Washington, D.C. It was during this time that Gonzalez began to read Marxist texts in earnest: "I needed to read some Marxism because I really felt totally ill-equipped even to engage in discussions with a lot of the SDS [Students for a Democratic Society] folks because I didn't have any kind of grounding."[23] Like other radicals of the time, Gonzalez was in search of a theoretical understanding of power and politics in society and looked toward community organizing as the next phase in the movement.

Gonzalez's previous experience, as a leading member of the coordinating committee of the Columbia Strike of 1968 and member of the SDS, helped shape his political outlook. The activist was one of two Columbia student protesters who forfeited rights to his diploma when he refused to sign a compromise document with university officials expressing regret for participation in the student-led building occupations and strike at Columbia. Gonzalez was among the thousands of young activists who emerged from their student tenure feeling that "something" had to be done. The manifold campaigns raging in college campuses, combined with the shock occasioned by events of the year such as Martin Luther King's assassination, fueled this feeling of urgency. Shortly after leaving Columbia, Gonzalez, who was well known in activist circles, was approached by members of the SAC.

Although the SAC had a revolving membership, it had a core group of attendees who met regularly. The growing sentiment in favor of the concept of "community control" in New York, after the Ocean Hill—Brownsville controversy, the battle for community governance over curricular offerings and administrative control of New York's public schools, as well as the black movement's ardent call for black independent political power aroused members of the fledgling group to connect ideological discussions with actions in the Puerto Rican neighborhood of East Harlem. When their visits home to New York coincided, members of the SAC would arrange to meet in a space provided by the Real Great Society, a government antipoverty program in East Harlem.[24]

At one of their Saturday study sessions in East Harlem in June 1969, the Puerto Rican radicals learned about the Chicago-based YLO, which would eventually provide the SAC an organizational model to pioneer a Puerto Rican revolutionary formation in New York. At this session, members discussed a Panther interview with "Cha Cha" Jimenez in which he explained the evolution of the Chicago YLO.[25] Jimenez also discussed the colonial relationship between Puerto Rico and the United States and cited Cuba and China as allies in the struggle for Puerto Rican independence. Jimenez identified his group with the growing number of radicals in the United States whose politics were becoming internationalist in scope as they studied and supported movements in "third world" nations against colonization, particularly U.S. military intervention in Vietnam. At that Saturday meeting, the SAC resolved to drive to Chicago to learn more about the YLO.

After meeting with Jimenez in Chicago, members of the SAC called on two other New York organizations to discuss a merger that would launch a New York chapter of the YLO. The New York radicals formally announced their new organization at a Tompkins Square Park demonstration on the

Lower East Side on Saturday, July 26, 1969. The newly formed group appeared clad in fatigues resembling the BPP and holding aloft a banner of a rifle over the Puerto Rican flag as their insignia. Although the members of the YLO in New York had not yet carved out a definite political strategy, the date of their coming out revealed the organization's ideological inclinations.[26] On July 26, 1953, student militants, led by Fidel Castro, launched the first offensive of the Cuban revolutionary struggle at the Moncada Fort in Santiago de Oriente. By 1969, Cuba had realized its struggle for national liberation and was one of the main challengers of U.S. imperialism.[27]

Preoccupied with organizing the poorest sections of society, the New York Lords embraced what Karl Marx identified as the lumpen proletariat, the group of permanently unemployed and discouraged workers living on the margins of society, which through the group's Maoist interpretation was regarded as the social class with the greatest revolutionary potential. As it set out to challenge the degraded status of poor Puerto Ricans in New York, the YLO employed a militant and confrontational style of protest in their campaigns. Their aggressive protests, which sought to shock and disable normal city life, were an adaptation of guerrilla warfare to the urban environment. As anticapitalist community activists, they initiated local struggles on issues directly affecting poor and working people, which they often attempted to connect to a global politics.

An Urban Movement of the Poor—Part I: The Garbage

In July of 1969, the newly formed New York YLO launched an ambitious and fast-paced course of community-oriented protests that involved thousands of people and addressed the most pressing social problems in East Harlem: sanitation, lead poisoning, tuberculosis, police brutality, housing, and hunger.

The Young Lords termed their first grassroots initiative the Garbage Offensive, a campaign for improved sanitation services in East Harlem. While the reference to the Tet Offensive implied their solidarity with the Vietnamese struggle, the juxtaposition of an issue as unremarkable as sanitation with the era's most dramatic military operation was a telltale sign of the group's ability to link international crises with local concerns.

For several weeks in the summer of 1969, the Young Lords attempted to call attention to the large quantities of accumulated garbage in East Harlem, the consequence of irregular pickups by the sanitation department and a dearth of trash receptacles on New York's street corners, especially in poor New York neighborhoods.[28] Over the course of approximately three consecutive Sundays, the Young Lords swept sections of the neighborhood and deposited the refuse in large bags, only to find that the garbage was not collected regularly throughout the week—and when it was, the sanitation crew left half of it strewn in the streets.[29] David Perez, a founding member of the YLO who relocated to New York from Chicago, observed years later:

> Until I came to New York, I had never seen so much garbage and dirt in the streets. Not that Chicago was a clean place, but it was not as filthy as Manhattan. The garbage was not stacked up on the streets. [In Chicago] there were alleys in which to stack garbage, so that ... you didn't have it piled up on the front stoop, where people sat during the hot weather.[30]

After an informal neighborhood inquiry conducted by the group on East Harlem's most pressing problems, the Young Lords identified an issue they believed could resonate with a broad section of neighborhood residents and might rouse some to join them in their efforts.[31] The garbage crisis epitomized all that was wrong with the way Puerto Ricans, the second largest racial minority group in New York, were treated in the city. In their estimation, the failure to resolve issues as basic as sanitation was an indication that local government did not view poor people of color as deserving of municipal services.

On Sunday, July 27, 1969, approximately a dozen members of the newly formed YLO erected a peculiar traffic barrier in East Harlem. They raised barricades of garbage to protest the lack of sanitation services to New York's major Spanish-speaking neighborhood. After clearing the neighborhood's empty lots and sweeping its dirty streets, the Young Lords proceeded to dump the trash they collected on Third Avenue at 100th Street. While a group of Young Lords coordinated the unloading of abandoned furniture and garbage onto the middle of the street, other members of the group explained the meaning of their protest to the crowd that had gathered to watch what was, in effect, an outdoor town meeting.

The audacious style of the Young Lords' protest action, that Sunday afternoon, exemplified the second phase in their street cleaning campaign. Weeks earlier, the YLO had swept the streets. Placing a greater emphasis on civil disobedience, the Lords now endeavored to involve larger numbers of neighborhood residents in their campaign. The group's new direction was markedly different from its initial efforts at organizing on behalf of "the people," a latent theme throughout the life of the organization.[32]

The service temper of the Young Lords' campaigns reflected, in part, their belief in community. Part of the first generation of mainland-born Puerto Ricans following the ethnic group's mass migration to New York in the 1940s and 1950s, many members of the Young Lords retained some of the small-town Puerto Rican values of their parents. They were deferential to elders and possessed a deep sense of moral and cultural obligation to family and community. These first-generation, college-educated Puerto Rican radicals, who seemed for the first time able to leave behind the poverty and inequality in which they grew up, felt compelled to return home and organize against social injustice.[33]

Moreover, the service-oriented spirit of the group's initial street cleaning protest was influenced by the dominant practice and ideas of the New Left around the world. The widespread conception of the revolutionary as a self-sacrificing "servant of the people" among radicals in the late 1960s was derived from theories espoused by Mao Tse Tung and Che Guevara. Popularized in great measure by the BPP in the United States, revolutionary practice became synonymous with "serving the people." At the same time, the do-it-yourself model of community intervention fostered by local antipoverty programs influenced urban radicals. While the Young Lords were critical of the limitations of poverty programs, they often adopted some of their methods.

But it was not until the Young Lords combined their service-oriented work with political agitation that they succeeded in attracting greater numbers of people to their campaign. By stopping traffic and creating a quasi, outdoor town meeting, the Young Lords' new protest strategy captured the attention of various local government leaders and aroused the interest of thousands of neighborhood residents. The YLO's politicization of the issue of uncollected garbage in East Harlem was manifested a few weeks before the first garbage demonstration, when they organized approximately 35 people on a visit to the local sanitation depot to register complaints and ask for brooms. The Lord's insistence on obtaining brooms from the sanitation department was a reflection both of their political inexperience and the widespread sentiments generated by antipoverty programs, which often gave residents in the country's poorest districts a false sense of their leverage and power over local governance. The group claimed they were met with intransigence and racial slurs by the staff of the district's sanitation headquarters, which denied them brooms.[34] Spurred on by the altercation with the sanitation department, the YLO was determined to intensify its efforts by pursuing more aggressive tactics.

As they assembled the garbage on the intersection of 110th Street and Third Avenue, some of the onlookers joined the action, pouring gasoline on the refuse heaps and setting them aflame. But the protest quickly escalated into a riot, and when the local fire department intervened, the firemen were pelted with trash. Concerned by the confrontation they had inadvertently set off, the Young Lords attempted to direct social resentment away from the firemen and to diffuse the potential for violence.[35]

Confrontations like these, between firefighters and black and Latino residents, had become habitual features of urban life during the decade's numerous riots. The fire department was among the most stridently discriminatory institutions nationwide in terms of employment and could be aptly described as an exclusive civil service fraternity. In 1963, out of close to 2,500 fire fighters in New York City, 38 were black and only 1 was Puerto Rican. As late as 1979, African Americans accounted for only 5 percent of the department and Puerto Ricans a scandalous 1 percent.[36] Accordingly, eruptions of rage during urban riots were often directed at fire departments (and their members) as these came to symbolize a link in the chain of social institutions responsible for the conscious exclusion and oppression of racial minorities.[37]

The Young Lords led their garbage dumping protests until September of 1969. In one instance, the *New York Times* reported that "residents of the area around Park Avenue and 110th Street joined in heaping and burning garbage at several intersections. Several abandoned cars were burned and overturned, traffic was blocked and heavy police reinforcements were called to the area to protect sanitation men called to remove the refuse."[38] The continued incineration of garbage heaps, in one of Manhattan's major connecting points for commuters to the outer boroughs, created undue pressures on the city.

Throughout the month of August of 1969, local mainstream television and print media covered what the newspapers called "garbage-dumping demonstrations," marking the Young Lords' public reputation as New York's emergent and dynamic militants. Animated by Saul Alinsky's exhortations that community organizing be inventive, irreverent, humorous, and directly focused on day-to-day issues of life, the group was extraordinarily effective in obstructing sections of the city's central transportation artery and generating a kind of media fascination with these new radicals. An article featured in the foremost left-liberal newspaper of the time, the *Guardian,* gives a sense of the small group's influence on the neighborhood and on the city. According to the newspaper, hundreds of local residents joined the six demonstrations organized by the Young Lords that summer, the most successful of which obstructed traffic for 30 city blocks.[39]

The Garbage Offensive tapped into a subject of increasing local and national concern. In 1969, the *New York Times* ran a series of lead articles addressing the problem of garbage disposal across the country.[40] On a national scale, the rising affluence of American society and the sharp changes in the consumption patterns of broad sectors of U.S. workers during the

1950s and 1960s led to an exponential increase in the production of house-hold, commercial, and industrial wastes.[41] As the amount of refuse material produced by society grew beyond the country's limited disposal capacity, local governments were forced to seek solutions to the implacable problem. The crisis of garbage disposal in New York was exacerbated by the sanitation department's outdated and corroding equipment; it was the only major city in the United States without high-capacity trucks for compressing garbage.[42]

Although New York had long been notorious for its dirty streets, the battle waged by public employees during the 1960s for private industry salaries created a crisis in the dispensation of sanitation services in the city. Approximately a year before the Young Lords began organizing around sanitation in East Harlem, a sanitation strike had highlighted the problem of garbage disposal with 10,000 tons of garbage accumulating each day sanitation workers were not at work.[43] For the duration of the strike, New York was hostage to a garbage blight that led the health commissioner to issue a state of emergency alerting citizens to possible outbreaks of typhoid, hepatitis, and other infectious diseases.[44]

Following the strike, the local media printed a series of feature stories on New York's sanitation problems and reported on a special initiative by the Department of Health to combat the city's rodent epidemic. In most instances, Department of Health representatives cited the improper dis-posal of garbage in the ghettos as an aggravating factor in the spread of disease and the growth of the rat population in the city. The special initia-tive proposed to focus on the poorest housing districts in the city in West and East Harlem, the Mott Haven section of the Bronx, and Brownsville in Brooklyn, where the rat population was heavily concentrated.[45]

To be sure, the Young Lords chose to agitate around an issue of concern to different sectors of the city that had been previously addressed in countless one-time garbage dumping demonstrations by community activists.[46] But the success of the Garbage Offensive was also due to its tim-ing. The Young Lords' garbage protests came at a time when the issue of sanitation had been prominent in the city's political debate.

The YLO's offensive in East Harlem in the summer of 1969 coincided with a heated mayoral election race. Although, at the time, the organiza-tion did not consciously follow the formal politics of the city as a means of propelling its ideas and demands into the larger political terrain, their actions advanced the issue within the political debate and forced the can-didates to respond to the problem of sanitation with concrete solutions in order to gain votes. Organizing with determination and creative flare dur-ing the heightened political milieu of the elections, the Young Lords were well positioned to score a victory and raise their profile in the city.[47]

By the end of the summer, as organized pressure mounted, the city's sanitation became a major issue in the weeks leading up to the mayoral elections of November 1969. When Democratic mayoral candidate Mario Procaccino wrote a position paper on what it would take to keep the city streets clean, recommending a 1,000-person increase in sanitation personnel, the defensive incumbent Republican Mayor, John Lindsay, launched a special effort calling first for 1,100, and later 1,300, sanitation men to work overtime for four Sundays in the month of September to clear lots, remove "household bulk," and sweep and wash New York's streets.[48]

As the garbage actions of the YLO received increasing local coverage by mainstream media networks, and as the group involved greater numbers of people in their protests, the Young Lords grew in size. In a relatively short period, during the summer months of 1969, they established organizing credibility and a reputation as the group that could confront the problems of Puerto Ricans and East Harlem head-on. The Garbage Offensive also vested the organization with valuable experience. The group learned how to involve larger numbers of people in their urban guerrilla actions while avoiding the police and mass arrests. Despite their insistence that sanitation services remained inadequate in East Harlem, the group viewed their campaign as a success. To the credit of the organization and the pressure they mounted on the city, the sanitation department conceded to a series of meetings with the Puerto Rican community to discuss their concerns.[49]

Having grown in membership and influence following this victory, the group moved to formalize their presence in East Harlem by establishing a storefront office on 110th Street and Madison Avenue. During this period, they established a division of work whereby different members specialized in distinct areas of concern to the community such as community health and political education. These changes allowed the group to launch several campaigns simultaneously and involve larger numbers of people in the process. The organization's new division of labor also permitted its subgroups to devise campaigns on their own, which facilitated the development of leadership among its membership and let newcomers feel a part of a working organization they could actively help shape.

An Urban Movement of the Poor—Part II: Lead-Based Paint

In the fall of 1969, YLO members working on community health issues focused on lead poisoning, one of the most long-standing and critical public health problems in the history of medicine.[50] The Young Lords seized on lead poisoning as a campaign issue following a nearly fatal case treated in East Harlem's Metropolitan Hospital in September of 1969. After falling into a coma due to advanced levels of lead poisoning in his bloodstream, two-year-old Gregory Franklin emerged from the hospital with permanent, severe brain damage.[51] The tragedy of the young boy had been the latest in a string of cases of plumbism, or chronic lead poisoning, among children in the city.

In November 1968, the city's health department announced that 600 cases of lead poisoning had been recorded in a period of ten months, 3 of which had resulted in fatalities.[52] By September of 1969, several children had died from the same cause in New York City and its environs.[53] Yet, while only 600 cases had been recorded in New York in each year between 1966 and 1969, public health reports estimated that between 25,000 and 35,000 children were afflicted with the disease each year.[54]

The issue of lead poisoning among children pointedly illustrated the Young Lord's critique of the society in which they lived. Identified as a distinct condition in the late 1900s, childhood lead poisoning—a more serious and potentially fatal disease than its counterpart among adults—is acquired, in large part, through contact with objects that contain lead. Although the toxic nature of lead has been recognized since antiquity, the continued use of lead paint for toys, furniture, and interiors of dwellings has generally persisted unchecked in the United States and through much of the industrialized world because of the leniency of government regulations.[55] But with increased scientific knowledge of lead's toxicity, contamination among humans has depended largely on social and economic factors.

Poor undernourished children, likely to develop an abnormal craving for dirt and other nonnutritive substances, a condition known as pica, are at risk of becoming victims of lead poisoning from eating chips of paint that fall from old walls in decaying housing structures. Although lead-based paint was discontinued in the 1940s, the failure of municipal governments to enforce housing codes requiring landlords to remove old coats of lead paint from apartment walls has contributed to the crisis. In the New York of the 1960s, 43,000 "old law" housing tenements, which were deemed "unfit for human habitation" in 1901, continued to house predominantly black, Puerto Rican, and Chinese tenants. The deadly threat of lead contamination among children in these tenements was ubiquitous.[56]

The case of Gregory Franklin illustrated the depth of the health and housing crisis. According to media interviews with the family, prior to Franklin's hospitalization, his parents had waged a fruitless 18-month battle with their landlord to get the flaking and falling walls of their apartment repaired. After Franklin's sister also tested positive for lead in her bloodstream, it was suspected that a great number of children in the tenement where the Franklin family lived were in danger, especially since the Harlem building had close to 100 outstanding violations.[57] After the health department reported that the Franklin children contracted lead poisoning from "rusty pipes, which polluted the drinking water," the Citizen's Committee to End Lead Poisoning, a group of independent activists, concerned citizens, and lawyers working in the field, conducted tests on the building's flaking walls in an attempt to show the landlord's culpability.

In response to the incident, the Lords held a series of meetings in East Harlem and at Metropolitan Hospital framing the problem in terms of racial justice. Before they launched their Lead Offensive, the Young Lords had rallied with auxiliary workers and health professionals at Metropolitan in support of a hospital governing board composed of workers and members of the community. Having established a political relationship with auxiliary workers and health professionals in September, the Young Lords were well positioned to learn about and agitate around the politics of lead poisoning.

The group initiated a lead-testing program in collaboration with the hospital's medical residents. For several weeks they distributed leaflets and informed residents of their impending door-to-door campaign. One of their flyers read:

> We are operating our own lead poisoning detection program with students from New York Medical College, beginning Tuesday November 25, on 112th Street. The Young Lords and medical personnel will knock on your door Tuesday and ask to test your children for lead poison. Do not turn them away. Help save your children.[58]

When Metropolitan refused to provide the Young Lords and their allies the free tests they were promised, the activists decided to take their grievance to the Department of Health.[59] On November 24, the lords led a sit-in at the department. This action, combined with the burgeoning media attention their campaign was receiving, forced the city administration to take decisive action to address the crisis.[60]

In the aftermath of Gregory Franklin's tragedy, city councilman Carter Burden and housing organizer Paul Du Brul had held a press conference at the Franklin family's home at which Burden proposed "an apartment by apartment testing program to be conducted by the Neighborhood Youth Corps."[61] And in response to an incident of lead poisoning in the Bronx earlier that year, Representative Edward Koch wrote a series of letters to Mayor Lindsay informing him that even the conservative mayor of

Chicago, Richard Daley, had a more advanced lead poisoning prevention program than New York. These efforts helped build a growing awareness of the issue, without which the Lords' campaign would not have resonated as broadly as it did.[62]

The YLO reached a decisive point in their lead poisoning campaign when they forced a confrontation with the city agency responsible for overseeing the problem. The Young Lords' Health Ministry, chaired by Rafael Viera, led a sit-in at the office of Dr. David Harris, the deputy commissioner of the Department of Health. Approximately 30 Young Lords participated in the action, alongside a number of nurses, health industry workers, and medical students, including Gene Straus, the chief medical resident at Metropolitan Hospital.[63] The Young Lords and their supporters demanded the release of 200 lead-testing kits for use in their testing drive. According to the protesters, the kits were allowed to languish unused at Metropolitan Hospital, despite the growing proportions of lead-poisoned victims in the city.

Fueling the actions of the Young Lords was a rumor that the health department had refused to accept 40,000 prepackaged urinary aminolevulinic acid (ALA) lead screening kits, donated to the city by Bio Rad Laboratories.[64] The unsubstantiated news had invited derision from community activists, who viewed the alleged refusal of the department as proof of the callousness and opportunism of its officers, especially since in October, at the height of the mayoral elections, the department had issued a press release announcing a crash lead-testing drive, partly in response to the Gregory Franklin tragedy.[65]

Public pressure mounted on the department as the Young Lords and their medical allies at Metropolitan Hospital generated public attention while conducting door-to-door tests in the days following the sit-in. In the course of one day, members of the YLO and their allies tested up to 60 children.[66] The Young Lords' consistent use of press conferences and releases to publicize their efforts and findings and to expose bureaucratic inaction was critical in mounting pressure on local government. Starting in the early fall, immediately following their garbage protests, founding member Pablo Guzmán led the group in an aggressive pursuit of positive media coverage. As "Minister of Information," Guzmán primed members on the image Young Lords should project to the media. The Young Lords determined that "the camera should be used as an organizing tool ... an avenue to the audience [they] wanted to reach."[67]

As the activists announced that 30 percent of the tests they conducted yielded lead-positive results, *Village Voice* columnist Jack Newfield noted that the "Young Lords [were doing the] City's work in the Barrio," an indication of the group's growing support among a section of journalists in the city.[68] With the news blazing through parts of the city that one-third of children living in slums were infected with lead, the department was forced to either disprove the Young Lords' findings or propose a comprehensive program for treatment and prevention.

The Department of Health issued a statement explaining that plans to use the 40,000 tests had been suspended because of the inaccuracy of the ALA test. However legitimate the reasons, the department's credibility was seriously damaged. With health professionals and Young Lords at Metropolitan Hospital exposing a health crisis in numbers and with the names and faces of victims, news of the department's refusal to accept the 40,000 testing kits created an instant public scandal. At different times during their campaign, *New York Times* headlines read "Criticism Rising Over Lead Poisoning" and "City Held Callous on Lead Poisoning." Even the president of the American Public Health Association, Dr. Paul B. Cornely, criticized the department for refusing the tests and for neglecting the victims of lead poisoning, suggesting that the race of the predominantly black and Puerto Rican victims played a role in the way the city handled the crisis.[69]

A letter to the editor written by a Bio Rad Corporation salesmen in response to one of Jack Newfield's columns cast further doubt on the department's explanations. Acknowledging Jack Newfield's description of the health department as an office of bureaucratic indifference, he wrote,

> I think Newfield and the Young Lords are operating on false hopes. It is my personal opinion that the city does not want a large-scale screening of children for lead poisoning. Dr. McLaughlin [New York's health commissioner] does not want to know for sure how many children are lead-poisoned, because then the city will be obligated to do something about the situation. And there is only one solution to the lead poisoning problem—the walls and ceilings of the apartments must be removed and replaced.[70]

Although the department declined to use the ALA tests en masse for reasons that were scientifically demonstrable, there was truth in the salesman's assertions. Dr. Mary McLaughlin, New York City's commissioner of health in 1969, was a specialist in the area of lead poisoning. She recognized the magnitude of the problem and the need for a comprehensive program. But, according to McLaughlin, without appropriate funds the department could not hire someone to design such a program. Moreover, due to its lack of prosecutorial authority, the department was incapable of addressing the source of the problem: an epidemic of housing violations by landlords that was feeding the crisis of lead poisoning in the city.[71]

The notoriously lenient prosecution of housing code violations in New York City did not help the matter either: It failed to enforce laws prohibiting the presence of lead paint in the interior walls of dwellings. A study in 1965 found that, on average, in cases involving exposure to lead, landlords were fined a total of $14 and an average of $50 per violation.[72]

While Dr. Mary McLaughlin published a candid analysis of the political dimensions of the problem in a medical journal, she never provided the same explanation in the mainstream public media or in the press releases of the department. Instead of providing a clear explanation of the problem that outlined the department's limited powers in solving a crisis of political proportions, the department opted to propose symbolic program measures year after year. The department's toothless proposals served more to appease the public than to address the problem in earnest. After awhile, the proposal to continue the study of a problem that was well defined was offensive to the good judgment of community residents, activists, and health providers. To the Young Lords, lead poisoning among children exposed the ways in which factors of class, politics, and power functioned as barriers to Puerto Rican progress, as well as barriers to the solution of problems within society's reach.

Of the political activities the Young Lords initiated in the fall and winter of 1969, their campaign to bring attention to the high incidences of lead poisoning among poor black and Puerto Rican children in New York City proved to have the most lasting impact on the city. Just weeks after the YLO underscored the negligent disposition of the Department of Health regarding potentially lead poisoned children living in city slums, New York's local government established a more exacting lead clause within the housing code and the Emergency Repair Program, a subsidiary of the Housing Development Administration, to remove lead paint from tenement walls. The new rule dictated that if landlords who had been given court orders to remove lead hazards from their buildings did not do so within five days, the emergency team would make the repairs and bill the landlord for the job.[73] Moreover, the health department created an office, the Bureau of Lead Poisoning Control, whose sole responsibility was to launch programs in the city to combat the problem. As a result, the number of children tested in the first half of 1970 was five times that tested by the Department of Health in all of 1969.[74]

Although the Young Lords were not the only group that attempted to bring attention to the issue of lead poisoning in the city, their brash actions were most successful in eliciting more than a token gesture response from government. In 1974, an appraisal of New York's lead screening program, published in the *American Journal of Public Health,* linked the Young Lords' activism to the upsurge of criticism leveled at the Department of Health by the press and other community groups for its handling of the problem. The young radicals' success was due to the skillful campaign they launched, which integrated direct action with community outreach, in this case, door-to-door testing. While relatively few people participated in their sit-ins, their confrontational actions provoked a crisis in the offices of a lethargic city bureaucracy that invited publicity and forced a government response.

Alternatively, their home visits represented a form of itinerant, grassroots organizing that carried the Young Lords campaign to a much larger number of people beyond their periphery. The painstaking door-to-door testing, which the Young Lords performed alongside health professionals, endowed the group with a measure of moral authority and helped to establish their reputation as dedicated young radicals. The Lords' use of the media to publicize their findings, in combination with their confrontational actions, simultaneously exposed and shamed local government into action. The bold approach with which the YLO addressed the issue of lead poisoning finally brought a crisis that had been simmering beneath the surface to its boiling point.

The experience of organizing door to door and witnessing, in the process, some of the worst conditions of poverty in the country radicalized the membership of the organization. In a live radio broadcast show at the Pacifica Radio Headquarters on the West Coast, Rafael Viera explained that, even though he had grown up in a poor neighborhood like East Harlem, he was shocked when he encountered such severe cases of ringworm and tuberculosis while conducting lead tests in East Harlem. This early organizing experience instilled, in many of those who participated in it, a strong sense of moral indignation against their society that solidified their enthusiasm and commitment to the organization.

In his widely read and controversial 1964 assessment and prospective of the Southern civil rights movement, Bayard Rustin attempted, among other things, to define the character of its Northern counterpart, suggesting that in Northern ghettos the civil rights movement was "perhaps misnamed." Rustin, the skillful strategist of the civil rights movement and foremost political commentator of his time, proclaimed that, in the North, "at issue, after all, is not civil rights, strictly speaking, but social and economic conditions. Last Summer's riots were not race riots; they were outbursts of class aggression in a society where class and color definitions are converging disastrously."[75]

By the 1960s, postwar deindustrialization, white flight, and residential tax-base erosion in the cities had produced unprecedented levels of racial segregation, permanent unemployment, and all the attendant problems of urban decay: poor education, health, and housing, a disfigured physical landscape, and explosive tensions between the community and the police. It was against this backdrop that the Northern movement emerged. The temperament of Young Lord militant activism and the group's insurgent politics were rooted in deep social disenchantment at worsening objective conditions conjoined with the hopes for social change nurtured by years of struggle and direct action in the civil rights movement.

At the heart of the burgeoning community action movement in which the YLO played so pivotal a role was the determination to introduce the grievances of the poorest classes into the public discourse. The movement reflected a growing preoccupation among activists to concretize the struggle for racial equality by raising questions concerning structural class inequality and lack of access to local political power. Increasingly, the Young Lords, as well as activists of other political persuasions, sought greater influence and power over major local institutions. For a brief moment in the late sixties and early seventies, they pursued the goals of "community control," motivated by the idea that by taking possession of major local institutions—schools, hospitals, churches, and police precincts—local communities could begin to exercise genuine direct democracy.

Unhampered by the same levels of government repression to which the Panthers were subjected, the New York Lords injected the BPP's model of organizing with their own savvy protest style. In many instances, the YLO was able to accomplish more than traditional social service institutions because they were prepared to break the law and mount social pressure on local government to obtain the resources and authority they needed to address, however modestly, a given problem. Nevertheless, in "doing the city's work" the group straddled a strange middle ground between traditional social service organization and political organization, with an eye on fundamentally transforming society. While the group attempted to provide a critique of capitalism, their service-oriented strategy alone, however militant, lacked the muscle necessary to qualitatively affect the deep structural changes taking place in the cities, much less transform society.

Although the YLO had brilliant tactics, the group's long-term political aims were hampered by the poverty of the leftist tradition in the United States, especially following the expulsion of communists, radicals, and progressives from American institutions during the Red Scare in the 1950s. Absent an influential tradition of left organizing in local communities seeking to connect neighborhood organizing with activism in the trade unions, the practices and strategies of emerging sixties radicals, like the Young Lords, increasingly fell in a vacuum. While the Young Lords launched an impressive course of grassroots campaigns in the late sixties, the larger radical movement to which they belonged failed to coalesce around a broad campaign calling for wealth redistribution, the mass creation of jobs, and an extensive housing construction initiative: the fundamental changes that would have been necessary to alter the structural problems of urban decline and economic inequality with which the movement was concerned. Moreover, the movement did not leverage the social power required to achieve these radical reforms.

The labor upsurge of the 1970s presented possibilities for a community and labor coalition that may have been capable of enacting significant socioeconomic and political changes. In fact, the Young Lords and many other groups began to organize in workplaces during this period, but their efforts were stymied by the inexperience of the New Left and the advent of recession, which undermined the mass character of the movement.

Political limitations of the period notwithstanding, the YLO represents the best of sixties radicalism. The group injected dynamism and excitement to the most pedestrian of local issues through their activism and were central to raising the political profile in New York of Puerto Ricans, the second largest racial minority group in the city. Organizing with the benefit of years of movement experience, the bold confrontational style of YLO campaigns was effective in achieving immediate local reforms. At their best, the Young Lords' community organizing campaigns attempted to extend the meaning of American democracy, especially as they put forth a new vision of society based on humane priorities.

Notes

1. For their comments on earlier drafts of this essay, the author would like to thank Manning Marable, Elizabeth Blackmar, Eric Foner, Jeanne Theoharis, Komozi Woodard, Gregory Baggett, Kouross Emaeli, Deborah Gershenowitz, Thea Hunter, Victor Maslov, and Susan Pensak.

2. For a discussion of the civil rights movement from its beginning in the postwar period, see Martha Biondi, "The Struggle for Black Equality in New York City, 1945–1955" (Ph.D. diss., Columbia University, 1997).

3. Phillip Foner, *The Black Panthers Speak* (New York: Lippincott, 1970), 2–4.

4. The RUM led workplace struggles among black automobile workers in Detroit. The HRUM had a strong community organizing orientation and was led by black and Puerto Rican hospital workers in New York. The Young Lords were Puerto Rican militants who first emerged in Chicago. The Brown Berets were Chicano cultural nationalists who attempted to work with gangs in California. I Wor Kuen was a Chinese militant group from New York's Chinatown that

worked closely with the New York branch of the Young Lords. The Young Patriots were white radicals from Appalachia who engaged in collaborative activist work with the Black Panthers and the Young Lords in Chicago.

5. Institute for Puerto Rican Policy (IPR), *Pablo "Yoruba" Guzmán on the Young Lords Legacy: A Personal Account,* Proceedings from the April 8, 1995 IPR Community Forum, ed. Joseph Luppens (1995), 11.

6. During most of the colonial period, Puerto Rico functioned primarily as a military outpost and had a diverse nonsegregated population consisting of a small number of slaves and Native Americans, a substantial number of freemen of color and poor white tenant farmers, and government officials. In Puerto Rico, rigid racial demarcations did not form part of the New World colony's social fabric in part because the slave plantation system was not a central feature of the island's economy. When a plantation economy did develop in the nineteenth century, severe labor shortages led to compulsory labor laws, which forced white land squatters to work alongside slaves and freemen of color in the fields. This development encouraged racial mixing and blurred racial differences as black slaves and white and colored laborers were compelled to intermingle with one another in the fields; an arrangement that eventually led each to find common cause with the other. See Sidney Mintz, *Caribbean Transformations* (New York: Columbia University Press, 1989), 82–94. For a discussion of racial ideology in the United States, see Barbara Jeanne Fields, "Ideology and Race in American History," in *Region, Race and Reconstruction: Essays in Honor of C. Vann Woodward,* J. Morgan Kousser and James M. McPherson, eds. (New York: Oxford University Press, 1982), 143–177, and Barbara Jeanne Fields, "Slavery, Race and Ideology in the USA," *New Left Review* 181 (1990), 95–118.

7. This does not imply, however, that racial identification does not impact the way Puerto Ricans perceive themselves. For a longer discussion, see Clara Rodriguez, *Puerto Ricans Born in the USA* (Boston: Unwin Hyman, 1989), 52–53.

8. In the aftermath of the Spanish-American War of 1898, the island of Puerto Rico became a colonial possession of the United States. Although Puerto Ricans were accorded U.S. citizen rights in 1917, the conditions placed by Congress on the island's political freedom compromised any suggestion of an equal and democratic relationship. Puerto Ricans living on the island were not allowed to vote in presidential elections, nor could they elect senators and representatives to Congress. This state of affairs engendered a radical tradition of nationalist movements on the island calling for national independence, which the Young Lords carried forward in their mainland struggles. The young radicals called for the self-determination of Puerto Ricans on the U.S. mainland and for Puerto Rico's independence, thus becoming the first Puerto Rican organization originating on the mainland to challenge the political status of the island nation.

9. Jack Bloom, *Class, Race, and the Civil Rights Movement: The Changing Political Economy of Southern Racism* (Bloomington: Indiana University Press, 1987): 173–179.

10. Our understanding of the movement is limited, specifically, by the periodization of the sixties in the historiography, the narrow geographic focus of the literature of the civil rights movement, and the popular conception of the civil rights movement as a purely African American phenomenon. Groups such as the Young Lords reached their zenith shortly after 1968. Since the dominant historical narrative of the sixties ends in 1968, the insurgent sentiment in poor urban communities, which found organizational expression thereafter, remains largely unexamined. Moreover, because the civil rights movement has been conceived as a uniquely Southern phenomenon, corresponding Northern movements have been broadly understood as eruptions of the discontented, with little holding them together in the way of consistent organizational forms and clear objectives. Additionally, the prominence of white students, urban rioters, and a narrowly conceived New Left as protagonists in accounts of the Northern movements has obscured the role played by the radical race-based formations of the period. While the civil rights movement is popularly imagined as a narrowly African American phenomenon, the example and success of African Americans inspired political movements among people of color. The emergence of movements led by Puerto Ricans and other historically oppressed racial groups suggests that as the possibilities for social change became increasingly evident with the legal and congressional watershed victories of African Americans, the movement became racially diverse. As the example of the Young Lords demonstrates, the Northern movements were multihued, mirroring the shifting demography of Northern cities.

11. This history of the Young Lords builds on the following pioneering works on the subject: Frank Browning, "From Rumble to Revolution: The Young Lords," in *The Puerto Rican Experience,* ed. Eugene Cordasco and Eugene Bucchioni (Totowa, N.J.: Littlefield, Adams, 1973), 231–245; Jennifer Lee, "The Young Lords, a New Generation of Puerto Ricans: An Oral History," *Culturefront* 3:3 (fall 1994): 64–70; Agustin Lao, "Resources of Hope: Imagining the Young Lords and the Politics of Memory," *Centro* 7:1 (1995): 34–49; Suzanne Oboler, "'Establishing an Identity' in the Sixties: the Mexican-American/Chicano and Puerto Rican Movements," in *Ethnic Labels, Latino Lives: Identity and the Politics of (Re)Presentation in the United States,* Susan Oboler, ed. (Minneapolis: University of Minnesota Press, 1995), Chapter 4; Carmen Teresa Whalen, "Bridging Homeland and Barrio Politics: The Young Lords in Philadelphia," in *The Puerto Rican Movement: Voices from the Diaspora,* Andres Torres and Jose E. Velazquez, eds. (Philadelphia: Temple University Press, 1998), Chapter 7. Retrospective accounts by former Young Lord activists have also contributed greatly to my work: Pablo Guzman, "Puerto Rican Barrio Politics in the United States," in *The Puerto Rican Struggle: Essays on Survival in the U.S.* Clara Rodriguez, Virginia Sanchez Korrol, and Jose Oscar Alers, eds. (Maplewood: Waterfront Press, 1984), 121–128; Pablo Guzmán, "Ain't No Party Like the One We Got: The Young Lords Party and Palante" in *Voices from the Underground: Insider Histories of the Vietnam Era,* vol. 1, Ken Wachsberger, ed. (Tempe: Mica Press, 1993), 293–304; and Pablo Guzmán, "La Vida Pura: A Lord of the Barrio,"

Village Voice, March 21, 1995, Iris Morales, "Palante, Siempre Palante! The Young Lords" in *The Puerto Rican Movement: Voices from the Diaspora,* Andres Torres and Jose E. Velazquez, eds. (Philadelphia: Temple University Press, 1998), Chapter 12.

12. For a full discussion, see William Julius Wilson, *The Declining Significance of Race and The Truly Disadvantaged* (Chicago: University of Chicago Press, 1990).

13. Although service industry jobs replaced blue-collar employment, the process of structural economic conversion failed to absorb large swaths of the urban population into the national economy. As early as the 1960s, the Department of Labor began to track the percentages of displaced workers using a new concept called "subemployment," a statistical index for tracking people who were either unemployed, underemployed, or permanently out of the labor force for lack of success in finding employment. United States Department of Labor, Bureau of Labor Statistics, "Labor Force Experience of the Puerto Rican Worker," *Middle Atlantic Region, Regional Reports,* 9 (June 1968): 21.

14. Seen in this light, Northern struggles transcend the restrictive framework of classification established by the civil rights historiography, which establishes black nationalism and integrationism as the two, often hermetically sealed, political currents in the movement. In dichotomizing the complex experiential process of a social movement, the framework fails to take into account the fluidity of social consciousness that characterized the period as well as the varied activities and unlikely alliances in which nationalist-identified groups (as politically diverse as they were) may have participated. Relatively absent from the dominant history of the civil rights movement is how and why, as the movement progressed, activists of different political persuasions in the nationalist/integrationist scale, such as Martin Luther King, Jr., of 1967 and the Black Panthers, began to connect the problem of racial oppression with class exploitation under capitalism.

15. This kind of structural unemployment among Puerto Ricans resulted from a myriad of factors including the higher participation of Puerto Rican males in declining blue-collar industries and occupations, lack of educational opportunities and retraining, racial discrimination, and the group's exclusion from the trade unions and government employment. Puerto Ricans encountered particular difficulty in the labor market because, as a considerably younger population, they lacked the experience and job market skills of their counterparts in the population at large. United States Department of Labor, Bureau of Labor Statistics, "Changing Patterns of Employment, Income, and Living Standards in New York City," *Middle Atlantic Region, Regional Reports,* 10 (June 1968).

16. Browning, "From Rumble to Revolution," 232.

17. "One Year of Struggle," *Palante* 2:8 (July 31, 1970), centerfold. Tamiment Library.

18. Michael Abramson, *Palante: The Young Lords Party* (New York: McGraw-Hill, 1971), 8. "The Young Lords Party: 1969–1975," *Caribe* 7:1 (1983): 10; David Perez and Arthur Tobier, *Long Road from Lares: An Oral History* (New York: Community Documentation Workshop at St. Mark's-Church-in-the-Bowery),

10; IPR, *Pablo "Yoruba" Guzmán on the Young Lords Legacy*, 11; Guzmán, "La Vida Pura: A Lord of the Barrio" 24; Alfredo Lopez, *The Puerto Rican Papers: Notes on the Re-Emergence of a Nation* (New York: Bobbs-Merrill, 1973), 324; Guzmán, "Ain't No Party Like the One We Got," 296.

19. Miguel Melendez was instrumental in establishing the group and persuading its members of the idea to build a radical organization dedicated specifically to the concerns of Puerto Ricans. Melendez's arguments proved influential for Pablo Guzmán and other Puerto Ricans and Latinos, many of whom were about to join the BPP just as the New York chapter of the YLO was born. IPRP, *Pablo "Yoruba" Guzmán on the Young Lords Legacy*, 11.

20. SEEK and the College Discovery program were instituted specifically in the City University of New York system and later extended to state universities to promote university enrollment of black and Latino students. See *Report to the Chancellor/City University of New York*, 1976; Lopez, *The Puerto Rican Papers*, 311.

21. Lopez, *The Puerto Rican Papers*, 320.

22. Radicalization was accelerated, in part, as large numbers of students witnessed the use of blanket repression by college administrations concerned with squelching protests and restoring normalcy on campuses. Disillusionment with their society spread as millions of students arrived at the conclusion that their universities were not removed from the realm of politics but rather collaborated in numerous ways with local police departments and FBI agents seeking to spy on radicals or aided the war effort by providing lists of matriculated students to the draft office.

23. Juan Gonzalez, Interview with the Oral History Program Archives at Columbia University, 1988, 45.

24. IPRP, *Pablo "Yoruba" Guzmán on the Young Lords Legacy*, 11.

25. "Interview With Cha Cha Jimenez, Chairman—Young Lords Organization," *Black Panther*, June 7, 1969, 17. The article is also referenced in Guzmán, "Ain't No Party Like the One We Got," 296; Abramson, *Palante*, 9; IPRP, *Pablo Yoruba Guzmán on the Young Lords Legacy*, 12. In the latter, Pablo Yoruba cites the *Guardian* as the newspaper that carried the interview with Cha Cha Jimenez.

26. It was not until 1972 that the New York organization, which by then had long severed ties with the Chicago YLO, would publish a comprehensive document outlining its politics and ideology. See the Young Lords Party, *The Ideology of the Young Lords Party*, Bronx, New York (1972) in Tamiment Library, Vertical Files.

27. On the reception of the Cuban Revolution within broad sections of the American Left in the 1950s and 1960s, see Van Gosse, *Where the Boys Are: Cuba, Cold War America, and the Making of a New Left* (New York: Verso, 1993).

28. Murray Schumach, "Seas of Garbage Engulf Islands on Broadway," *New York Times*, September 3, 1969, 1.

29. Abramson, *Palante*, 9; Guzmán, "Ain't No Party Like the One We Got," 298–299; "The Young Lords," *Caribe*, 11; Lee, "The Young Lords," 66; Jose Iglesias, "Right on with the Young Lords," *New York Times Magazine*, June 7, 1970, 32.

30. Perez and Tobier, *Long Road from Lares*, 11.

31. Miguel Padilla, "How N.Y. Young Lords Developed," *Militant*, January 30, 1970, 3.

32. The challenges the group confronted in this early struggle raised larger theoretical questions, which were rooted in the long-standing debate over the meaning and conception of socialism. That debate was first consciously articulated by American socialist Hal Draper in his pamphlet, *Two Souls of Socialism*. Draper traced the two major competing tendencies in the history of the socialist movement, which he defined as socialism "from below" and "from above." The former envisioned a system assembled and maintained through mass participation, while the latter depended on the self-sacrificing struggles and dedication of a politically edified minority. Hal Draper, *Two Souls of Socialism*, 1966, Pamphlet Collection, Tamiment Library.

33. For a discussion of the culture and structure of the Puerto Rican family, see Joseph Fizpatrick, *Puerto Ricans: The Meaning of Migration to the Mainland* (Englewood Cliffs, N.J.: Prentice-Hall, 1971), 77–100.

34. Abramson, *Palante*, 76; IPRP, *Pablo "Yoruba" Guzmán on the Young Lords Legacy*, 15; Guzmán, "La Vida Pura," 24.

35. Guzmán, "La Vida Pura," 24.

36. New York City Commission on Human Rights, *The Ethnic Survey: A Report on the Number of and Distribution of Negroes, Puerto Ricans, and Others Employed by the City of New York* (New York, 1964), tables 1.1–1.68; and [the New York City mayor's] Citywide Equal Employment Opportunity Committee, *Equal Employment in New York City Government, 1977–1988* (October 1988), 42, cited in Craig S. Wilder, *A Covenant with Color: Race and Social Power in Brooklyn* (New York: Columbia University Press, 2000), 226, 229.

37. Although the Young Lords were committed to militancy, they were not out to incite rioting. They were among a generation of radicals whose protest strategies embodied many of the same community organizing trends that swept through the decade. For activists such as the Young Lords, becoming revolutionaries in the course of the movements and confronted with the task of applying their newly acquired theoretical perspective to concrete circumstances, the fissure between theory and practice was partially bridged by adopting the radical models of action engendered by the period itself. In the North among Puerto Ricans, the YLO continued the tradition of full-time community organizing popularized by the SNCC's model of organizing against Jim Crow by mobilizing residents to assert their political rights in poor rural communities. As the radical wing of the sixties movements began to search for strategies of social struggle different from the increasingly contested nonviolent civil disobedience, SNCC's model was seen as the most effective avenue through which to achieve change. The young and inexperienced SNCC activists penetrating the deepest reaches of the South in their effort to register the black vote were exposed to the most desperate levels of poverty in the United States. This experience led many activists, who had previously held the country's political and economic structure in high esteem, to question the fundamental nature of the society in which they lived. Eventually, the effort to organize black Southerners at the community level grew into a desire to combat the most visible economic problems—poverty and unemployment, crumbling schools and hospitals—and the most flagrant

aspects of racial oppression, such as police brutality. SNCC also placed a strong emphasis on the mass participation of ordinary people in their fight against economic and racial oppression. From its inception, SNCC had represented the left wing of the civil rights movement. Because of the decimation of left organizations under McCarthy, SNCC, an organization with relatively little experience, was one of the few examples of an active, militant organization with a following. For a history of SNCC, see Clayborne Carson, *In Struggle: SNCC and the Black Awakening of the 1960s* (Cambridge: Harvard University Press, 1981). For critical overviews of SNCC's impact on the movement, see Manning Marable, *Race, Reform, and Rebellion: The Second Reconstruction in Black America, 1945–1990* (Jackson: University Press of Mississippi); Bloom, *Class, Race, and the Civil Rights Movement.*

38. Joseph P. Fried, "East Harlem Youths Explain Garbage-Dumping Demonstrations," *New York Times,* August 19, 1969, 86.

39. Carl Davidson, "Young Lords Organize New York," *Guardian* 22:3 (October 18, 1969): 6. For a reference to the series of demonstration held by the Young Lords Party, see also "Plastic Bags Given East Harlem in War on Garbage Pile Up," *New York Times,* September 13, 1969, 33.

40. Gladwin Hill, "Major U.S. Cities Face Emergency in Trash Disposal," *New York Times,* June 16, 1969, 1, 38.

41. For a discussion of the rise of American consumer culture, see Marty Jezer, *The Dark Age: Life in the U.S., 1945–1960* (Boston: South End Press, 1982).

42. Richard Reeves, "Lindsay: Learning About the Politics of Garbage," *New York Times,* August 24, 1969: Section IV, 4; Charles Morris, *The Cost of Good Intentions: New York City and the Liberal Experiment, 1960–1970* (New York: McGraw-Hill, 1980), 160–162.

43. For a history of New York's major municipal labor struggles in the 1960s, see Joshua Freeman, *Working-Class New York: Life and Labor Since WW II* (New York: New Press, 2000).

44. Morris, *The Cost of Good Intentions,* 104.

45. "The War on Rats," *New Yorker* (August 3, 1968): 23

46. The early civil rights movement in New York experimented with the issue of sanitation as a campaign; for example, the Brooklyn Congress of Racial Equality organized garbage-dumping campaigns at City Hall, and in 1968 the papers reported a garbage dumping demonstration at Lincoln Center.

47. "Residents in Flatlands Protest Spreading of Rats," *New York Times,* August 19, 1969, 86.

48. "Overtime Force to Clean Refuse," *New York Times,* September 6, 1969, 19; "1,509.9 Tons of Trash Taken in First of 4 Sunday Tests," *New York Times,* September 9, 1969, 93; "Mayor Enlarges Sanitation Drive," *New York Times,* September 14, 1969, 40; "City Concludes Experiment on Sunday Trash Pickup," *New York Times,* September 29, 1969, 44.

49. Davidson, "Young Lords Organize New York," 6; Abramson, *Palante,* 76–77.

50. For a study of childhood lead poisoning in the United States in the historical context of the politics of lead manufacturing and trade, see Siegfried Pueschel,

James Linakis, and Angela C. Anderson, *Lead Poisoning in Childhood* (Baltimore: P. Brooks, 1996).

51. Jack Newfield, "City Urged to Act in Lead Crisis," *Village Voice*, September 25, 1969, 24; see also Jack Newfield, "My Back Pages," *Village Voice*, October 9, 1969, 9, 24.

52. News Release, Department of Health of the City of New York, November 15, 1968, Vertical File: New York City, Poisoning, Lead (1960s and Earlier), Municipal Archive of the City of New York.

53. For other cases, see "Infant Dies After Eating Paint from Tenement Wall," *New York Times*, May 28, 1969, 18; "Brownsville Plagued by Paint Poisoning," *New York Times*, September 1, 1969, 1; Jack Newfield, "Lead Poisoning: Silent Epidemic in the Slums," *Village Voice*, September 18, 1969, 3, 39, 40.

54. Joseph Fried, "Paint-Poisoning Danger to Children Fought," *New York Times*, March 2, 1969: VI, 1, 8; "Lead Poisoning Is Affecting 112,000 Children Annually, Specialists Report," *New York Times*, March 26, 1969, 23; For more precise figures see Gary Eidsvold, Anthony Mustalish, and Lloyd F. Novick, "The New York City Department of Health: Lesson in Lead Poisoning Control Program," *American Journal of Public Health*, 64:10 (October 1974): 959. The last document was replicated as a pamphlet by the New York City Department of Health, Vertical File, New York City, Poisoning, Lead (1970s Folder), Municipal Archives of the City of New York.

55. Pueschel, *Lead Poisoning in Childhood*, 53.

56. The article also reported that African Americans and Puerto Ricans were paying the highest rent per square foot of all tenants living in the metropolitan area. "Can Anybody Run New York City?" *U.S. News and World Report*, 58:25 (June 21, 1965), 58.

57. Newfield, "City Urged to Act in Lead Crisis."

58. Jack Newfield, "Young Lords Do City's Work in the Barrio," *Village Voice*, December 4, 1969, 35.

59. Newfield, "Young Lords Do City's Work in the Barrio," 35.

60. Before the Young Lords Party launched its lead offensive, other groups attempted to bring attention to the issue in the city. In the late sixties, a series of local efforts were initiated by concerned activists, community groups, and politicians to pressure New York's government offices to implement preventive programs that had already been adopted in cities like Chicago and Baltimore. The Citizen's Committee to End Lead Poisoning, for example, was founded in August of 1968 to lobby local government to address the problem and educate communities most at risk. Fried, "Paint-Poisoning," 8; Jack Newfield, "Fighting an Epidemic of the Environment," *Village Voice*, December 18, 1969, 12.

61. Newfield, "Young Lords Do City's Work in the Barrio," 35.

62. Although the mainstream media had seldom reported on the problem, in September of 1969 a columnist for the *Village Voice*, Jack Newfield, became interested in the issue. A series of articles he wrote on the subject between September and December, in which he highlighted a series of plumbism

tragedies in the city and described the bureaucratic task involved in obtaining information on the subject from the Department of Health, helped set the stage for the Young Lords' actions in November and December. The crisis surrounding what many physicians increasingly referred to as a man-made epidemic had awakened even the medical profession to the idea of protest. A spring 1969 conference held at Rockefeller University brought physicians and scientists together to present social and medical solutions to the problem. Pessimistic about prospective government action, conference chair and Pulitzer Prize winner Dr. Rene Dubos stated, "The problem is so well defined, so neatly packaged with both the causes and cures known that if we don't eliminate this social crime, our society deserves all the disasters that have been forecast for it." Sandra Blakeslee, "Experts Recommend Measures to Cut Lead Poisoning in Young," *New York Times,* March 27, 1969, 25. Another meeting of approximately 75 doctors, nurses, and radical students was called by the Health-PAC (Policy Advisory Center) at Judson Church. At the long-time activist church near Washington Square Park, the radicalized health professionals discussed various action proposals including rent strikes and filling the hospitals with every child living in the slums between the ages of one and six, although no such actions were ever initiated following that meeting.

63. Newfield, "Young Lords Do City's Work in the Barrio," 35.
64. Eidsvold, Mustalish, and Novick, "Lesson in Lead Poisoning Control," 957.
65. Ibid., 97; Newfield, "Young Lords Do City's Work in the Barrio," 35.
66. Rafael Viera, radio interview, Pacifica Radio, California, 1970.
67. Guzmán, "Ain't No Party Like the One We Got," 301, 303.
68. Newfield, "Young Lords Do City's Work in the Barrio," 35.
69. Dr. Cornely made his comments after delivering a speech at the National Conference on Black Students in Medicine and the Sciences. See "City Held Callous on Lead Poisoning," *New York Times,* December 21, 1969, 40.
70. Henry Intilli, "False Hopes," *Village Voice,* December 11, 1969, 9.
71. Eidsvold, Mustalish, and Novick, "Lesson in Lead Poisoning Control," 957.
72. Jane S. Lin-Fu, *Childhood Lead Poisoning: A Pamphlet of the U.S. Department of Health, Education, and Welfare,* Health Services and Mental Health Administration, Maternal and Child Health Services (1970), 5. Vertical File, "New York City, Poisoning, Lead, 1970s," Municipal Archives of the City of New York. Repr. *Children,* 17:1 (January–February 1970): 2–9.
73. "Mayor John V. Lindsay to the City Council and the People of New York City," *New York City Mayor's Annual Report, 1969,* 6; see also Press Release, Office of Public Information—Office of the Administrator Gordon Chase, September 23, 1970:1, Vertical File, "New York City, Poisoning, Lead, 1970s." Municipal Archives of the City of New York.
74. Ibid.
75. Bayard Rustin, "From Protest to Politics: The Future of the Civil Rights Movement," *Commentary* 39:2 (February 1965): 26.

Chapter 11

It's Nation Time in NewArk: Amiri Baraka and the Black Power Experiment in Newark, New Jersey

Komozi Woodard

It is time for Beauty and Truth to rule the world again. It is time for the evolved beings to reorder this planet.

—*Amiri Baraka, "From: The Book of Life"*

In the political field, you have to know at each stage if you are doing the possible or not, and preparing the field for the possible for tomorrow or not. This is the problem.

—*Amilcar Cabral, Return to the Source*[1]

Pushing many of the feeble organizations aside, thousands of black youth stormed into militant Black Power organizations from coast to coast. Where there were only small Black Power organizations, they filled the ranks and made them bigger. Where there were no Black Power organizations in their locality, they established branches, and in that manner groups such as the Oakland Black Panther Party, the Los Angeles US Organization, and Amiri Baraka's Committee for a Unified NewArk (CFUN) became national phenomena in 1968.

Because the Black Power movement was experimental, the critical study of Black Power politics must begin with an inquiry into its most important experiments. This chapter is one effort toward that goal. The Black Power period in Newark lasted from 1966 to 1976, embracing both the 1967 Newark

Rebellion and the 1974 Puerto Rican Rebellion. Alongside the mounting political victories, those developments between 1967 and 1974 consolidated Baraka's standing as a pivotal leader, not only of the Newark black community but also of black America. His ascent to that rank was tied directly to the flowering of the Modern Black Convention Movement. Both locally in Newark and nationally in the U.S., the Modern Black Convention Movement was an essential component of the Black Power experiments, which included the cultural, political, and economic programs proposed and developed by the Black Arts movement, the Black Panther Party, the US Organization, the Republic of New Africa, the Revolutionary Action Movement, the Nation of Islam, the Organization of Afro-American Unity, the League of Revolutionary Black Workers, and Baraka's Congress of African People. Together, those cultural and political formations galvanized millions of black people in the broadest movement in African American history: High school and college youth organized black student unions, professors and educators created black studies programs, athletes mobilized protests against poverty and racism, workers fashioned militant unions, welfare mothers demanded power and dignity, soldiers refused army discipline, and during prison uprisings such as Attica, politically conscious inmates saluted Malcolm X and George Jackson. In other words, the Black Power movement was so thoroughgoing and the Black Cultural Revolution was so unprecedented that important historians such as Vincent Harding and Manning Marable have reached for such terms as *watershed* and *zenith* to calibrate its sustained impact during the Second Reconstruction in the United States.

So dramatic was Baraka's rise in the political arena that the *New York Times* could not fail to notice that at the March 1972 National Black Political Assembly in Gary, Indiana, "most convention officials acknowledged that ... the 38-year-old Newark native's influence predominated during the convention" and that "no one else had the organization or the strength that he had." In the same vein, Professor Vincent Harding noted Baraka's "tough-minded and powerful presence, based in a highly disciplined, Newark-based black nationalist organization, was the central force in the convention's leadership."[2] Actually, Baraka's core organization had chapters in 25 different cities from coast to coast, not to speak of the tens of thousands of dedicated activists in the allied groups such as the African Liberation Support Committee and the Black Women's United Front. Was all of that after the movement was officially pronounced dead by a number of experts?

In fact, the Black Arts movement, the ghetto uprisings, and an explosive African American sense of identity produced a new generation of Black Power organizations and leadership. The Black Power organizations were fashioned in the aftermath of the urban uprisings that supplied hundreds of new activists to populate the new organizations. The fusion between those leaders, organizations, and the intense consciousness of racial oppression became incredibly powerful in the context of the black urban uprisings of the 1960s. The hundreds of ghetto revolts of the 1960s marked a major turning point in the black revolt, highlighting the demand for African American self-determination. In neighborhoods people struggled for community control, in cities they fought for municipal power, and at the county, state, and congressional levels they sought proportional representation. During the first wave of unrest in the 1960s, 329 major rebellions unfolded in 257 different cities; after Dr. King's assassination on April 4, 1968, there were another 200 uprisings in 172 cities. In that context, waves of black youth demanding local autonomy were galvanized by the Black Power slogan, popularized by Stokely Carmichael and the Student Nonviolent Coordinating Committee (SNCC). "Black Power" was one of the most successful themes for political agitation in the twentieth century. Furthermore, Urban Sociology Professor Manuel Castells notes that Black Power "was not just a slogan. It was the practice of an excluded community that transformed the walls of its prison into the boundaries of its free city."[3] Then a third wave of youthful activists joined the black revolt following 500 racial confrontations in 1969.[4] Those hundreds of racial confrontations were the most violent expressions of ethnic conflicts that shaped black consciousness and spread the demand for African American self-determination. That is one brief general outline of the historical logic of that period.

The Newark Rebellion of July 1967 produced many Black Power organizations, including Baraka's United Brothers, the United Sisters, and CFUN, as well as the Black Women's United Front, and the Congress of African People. Those organizations incorporated the original Spirit House, a repertory group of actors and poets with perhaps two-dozen members. By 1972, the Newark Congress of African People had a cadre pf some 300 full-time members, with thousands of activist allies, filling the ranks of the CFUN Community Council, the African Liberation Support Committee, and the New Jersey delegation to the Gary convention in 1972.[5] A heavy torrent of activists was produced even after the 1969 racial confrontations gauged by the FBI. In cities like Newark as the African American community spread outward from the Central Ward ghetto, there were violent racial confrontations in the West Ward and North Ward schools that laid the basis for massive youth movements as well as wave after wave of recruits to the Newark branch of the Modern Black Convention Movement.

Before the Newark uprisings of July 1967, Amiri and Amina Baraka went to the Bay Area to help develop the first college-level Black Studies program in the United States. Militant student leaders such as Black Panther Jimmy Garrett called for that pioneering program at San Francisco State College. While in the Bay Area, the Barakas also helped develop the important Black Arts West at Eldridge Cleaver's Black House, alongside Ed Bullins, Marvin X, and Muminina Furaha. Once in California, Baraka was able to see the beginnings of both the Black Panther Party, led by Huey P. Newton and Bobby Seale, as well as the US Organization, led by Maulana Karenga. His contacts were made easier by his earlier associations with key people. Baraka met Bobby Seale much earlier during his book tour for *Blues People;* at that time, Seale was a stand-up comedian.[6] In early 1967, Baraka identified with the Black Panther Party because of the black nationalist influence of Malcolm X and the self-defense ethos of Robert F. Williams. Moreover, several of his close associates in the Harlem Black Arts movement had already become Black Panthers in New York City: Larry Neal, Ted Wilson, and Sam Anderson. When the police assaulted the Black Panthers, the Black Arts movement sponsored a series of plays and poetry readings to raise defense funds under the slogan: "Black Arts for Black Panthers." The other group that impressed Baraka was the US Organization. Its leader, Karenga had introduced himself to Baraka in Newark in 1966, during some meetings that led to the July 1967 Newark Black Power Conference. Both the Oakland Black Panther Party and the Los Angeles US Organization were successful at organizing ghetto youth into paramilitary groups that submitted to political leadership. Unfortunately, violence and gunplay overwhelmed the new Black Power groups that failed to discipline such youth groups. (Baraka's Harlem Black Arts Repertory Theater/School was one of the earliest victims; however, there were others.) Consequently, when Baraka returned from California to Newark in the spring of 1967, he was confident that he might model his movement along the lines of the Black Panthers and US. Ironically, over time, it would be Baraka and others who would forge more stable groups.

Background to the NewArk Rebellion

By the time Baraka returned to Newark in 1967 there was already a new militant mass Black Power movement stirring in that city around three issues: education, urban renewal, and police brutality. By 1967, African Americans and Puerto Ricans were the majority of the Newark population; however, their representation in the political leadership and educational establishment failed to keep pace. In fact, an Italian American political machine, headed by Mayor Hugh J. Addonizio had a stranglehold on political power, controlling not only Newark City Hall, but also dominating the Newark Housing Authority, the municipal courts, the police department, and the Board of Education. Looking at Italian American political power in the Northeast, in 1970, Chuck Stone wrote, "only Newark exemplifies total political control by [Italian Americans]."[7] To put things in perspective, Italian Americans had wrested political power from the Irish American political machine that had dominated in the 1950s. Thus, when Mayor Addonizio came to power in 1962, he mobilized against "Irish power." Significantly, Mayor Addonizio's major political ally against the old political machine was the African American community, particularly politicos like Central Ward Councilman Irvine Turner as well as Councilman Calvin West.

That white political machine held its power despite the unprecedented white flight from the city. The exodus of whites was judged as "cataclysmic." In 1940, there were some 384,000 whites in Newark, but in 1960, only 265,706. In the space of the seven years after 1960, the city lost another 70,000 white people. While whites were leaving Newark, African Americans were fleeing tyranny in the South for New Jersey's largest city. Blacks made up 17 percent of the city's population in 1950. About 130,000 migrated between 1950 and 1970. In 1960, blacks were 34.5 percent of Newark's population. By 1970, with 54.2 percent of the city's population, black Newark became the largest concentration of African Americans in New Jersey. In terms of cities with black majorities, Newark ranked among those with the highest percentages, beside Washington, D.C. and Gary, Indiana.[8]

The urban crisis was the principal economic, social, and political context for the ghetto revolts that fueled the Black Power organizations in the 1960s and 1970s. The burning issues of that urban crisis were housing, education, unemployment, and police brutality. Similar to the problems in Chicago and Detroit, Newark's housing crisis was heated by decades of segregated housing and brought to the boiling point by urban renewal policies aimed at the removal of the ghetto population.[9] In Newark, the issue that triggered public awareness was the proposed inner-city medical school campus slated to uproot a black community; this issue generated unprecedented interest and activity in black Newark. It became known as the "medical school crisis." The officials at City Hall and the Newark Housing Authority insisted that perhaps 20,000 black people vacate about 183 acres in the Central Ward to clear the way for construction of a campus for the proposed New Jersey College of Medicine and Dentistry.

The situation called for strong group leadership; however, there was a chronic leadership crisis in black Newark. With a few exceptions, for decades, the civil rights organizations made little headway in mobilizing the bulk of Newark's black community. Several studies found that most members of Newark's tiny black elite lived in the suburbs and took little interest in the tremendous problems of the inner city.[10] By 1966, a new grassroots leadership rooted in the community was developing in tandem with the rising neighborhood responses to the urban crisis. In contrast to the old leadership that resided in the suburbs, this new leadership located its headquarters and residence in the heart of the ghetto, particularly in the Central Ward. For instance, there was a militant Afro-American Association during this period. Moreover, SNCC set up headquarters on South Orange Avenue, adjacent to the medical school site, to organize for black liberation. A few blocks away, the Newark Community Union Project set up an alternative planning office to challenge the medical school land use plan. Several blocks away was Amiri Baraka's Spirit House, a cultural center at 33 Stirling Street. Two blocks from the Spirit House was the political headquarters of Baraka's CFUN at 502 High Street. And in close proximity, Baraka established the NJR-32 Project Area Committee office for alternative community planning to develop a neighborhood of garden apartments rather than high rise public housing projects. In the same vicinity, Amiri Baraka's comrade and wife, Amina Baraka, and her sisterhood established several African Free Schools, collective kitchens, and 24-hour nurseries. About two blocks from the African Free School on Clinton Avenue, the Black Youth Organization established the Chad School. Thus, between 1966 and 1970, numerous Black Power and Pan-African organizations and institutions emerged to provide leadership to a mobilized black community. When the new leadership called for mass presence at the public hearings for the medical school, hundreds of community people filled Newark City Hall to oppose the urban renewal plan. As the movement developed, so did the perception that the black community needed political power to defend its basic interests. Finally, the medical school crisis pulled together the many different classes that remained in the inner city and generated a militant sense of community identity in conflict with the forces behind the new medical school plans. For instance, there were small homeowners and tenants, industrial workers and welfare mothers, as well as small merchants and the unemployed.

Significantly, there were at least two activists from the Central Ward Democratic Party who identified with the community and consequently broke with the county and municipal political machine that would have destroyed much of their political base. The two leaders were Eulius "Honey" Ward and Russell Bingham. Ward had been a golden gloves boxing champion in the inner city. Bingham had been a veteran of the WWI. Both Ward and Bingham were seasoned veterans of the 1950s politics that led to the first black city council member in the city of Newark and per-haps in the state of New Jersey: Irvine Turner, a maverick newspaper reporter.[11] When Baraka's United Brothers and CFUN emerged, Honey Ward and Russell Bingham were among the first members.

The announcement that the secretary of the Newark Board of Education, Arnold Hess, would retire sparked a parallel struggle between Newark City Hall and the black community, bringing even more community forces into the political arena. While the black community proposed Wilbur Parker, a black certified public account, to replace Arnold Hess, Mayor Addonizio nominated James Callahan, a white high school graduate. The struggle over black representation on the Board of Education was just as heated as the medical school crisis. Although both the medical school crisis and the Board of Education controversy mobilized broad sectors of the black community, those two issues had dif-ferent class appeals. While the medical school crisis hit the grassroots where it lived, drawing many working people to black nationalism's strug-gle for control over urban space, the Board of Education issue was tailor-made to attract the African American middle class. Judiciously, Robert Allen noted, "This dispute over integrating the city's educational bureaucracy particularly incensed middle-class blacks, who viewed this bureaucracy as a potential vehicle for social mobility."[12] In theory, the seeds of one key element of black nationalism are in those failed attempts of the black middle class to integrate the official bureaucracy. That class was educated in the competitive ethic to covet such positions in the sys-tem. Once they had been told that they could not enter this world because they were not educated; so they continued their schooling. Now that they were educated, they had to face the ugly fact that exclusive white groups would use their political and bureaucratic power to monopolize those positions through racial discrimination. Thus, the "young, gifted, and Black" aspirants were discriminated against despite their educational credentials. This placed the black middle class and the civil rights move-ment in what sociologist Anthony D. Smith termed a classic "nationalist dilemma." Caught in this predicament, many in the black middle class contributed to the spread of black nationalism, particularly its political demands for proportional representation in the government. Professor Smith explains that in such situations people will opt for nationalism, particularly "where the alternatives of large-scale emigration or proletar-ian socialist revolution are ruled out, or hard to achieve."[13] Thus, the groundwork for a black nationalist movement, with mass appeals to a range of different social classes, had been laid before the July 1967 Newark uprising.

The NewArk Uprising, July 12, 1967: "It is Time for Beauty and Truth to Rule the World Again"

While the community struggles over the size and location of the medical school and over the quality of black representation on the Board of Education were heated, clearly the most explosive ingredient in the urban crisis in Newark was police brutality. The Newark Rebellion began on July 12, 1967. That was the night that fighting erupted in the Central Ward in the Fourth Police Precinct, after some people in the black community caught a glimpse of a badly beaten black cab driver, named John Smith, as the police dragged him into the police station. The Fourth Precinct station house, on the corner of 17th Avenue and Livingston Street, faced Hayed Homes, one of the largest public housing projects in the ghetto. Quickly, word of the arrest spread throughout black Newark, along with alarm over Smith's beating. A large and angry crowd gathered in front of the Fourth Precinct station house.

Standing only five-foot-seven, John Smith was not a particularly menacing figure, but the police beat him like a treacherous beast. After a police car stopped his taxi, supposedly for a minor traffic violation, the police officers told Smith's passenger: *"Get the hell out!"* Smith was placed under arrest, and as they drove him to the police station, one officer in the front seat turned around to face Smith:

> "He used his stick on me," Smith recalled, "The cop who was driving told the other one who was hitting me to stop.
> "No, no, *this baby is mine,*" the one who was using the stick said. When we got to the precinct I couldn't walk because he had also kicked me in the groin, and they started to drag me across the pavement. ...
> "You don't have to drag him like that," somebody called out. ...
> "Well, they carried me the rest of the way but once we got to the door they threw me in. There were at least six or eight policemen there who began hitting and kicking at me. They took me to a cell and beat on me some more until I thought it would never stop. They held my head over the toilet and one of them threw water on me [,] from the bowl [,] all over my head. Another hit me on the head with a gun butt and I was also hit with a blunt instrument in the side. Finally they just left me lying there."[14]

While Smith was being beaten, the black community was gathering outside, fearing that the worst had happened to Smith, and demanding to see him. Eventually, the mood of the crowd turned ugly. Before long, a hail of bricks, bottles, and Molotov cocktails hit the side of the police station.

After one officer was heard yelling, "How long are we going to wait?" 75 riot police, wearing helmets, stormed out of the station house, attacking the protest and clubbing anyone they could get their hands on. Robert Allen reported, "The cops beat everyone and anyone with black skin, including a black policeman in civilian clothes and several black newsmen. Cursing and mouthing racial slurs, the club-swinging cops indiscriminately smashed into the throng."[15]

The nonviolent phase of the struggle was over. After laying siege to the Fourth Police Precinct in the Central Ward, black people attacked a mile-long section of the Springfield Avenue shopping area and then headed downtown. The local newspaper reported that the weapons they used were bricks and pieces of concrete, which they threw at the police.[16]

The night after John Smith had been beaten like an animal, so was Amiri Baraka. Baraka's beating at the hands of the police during the Newark Rebellion took on a national significance, placing him on an important roster of political defendants that included Angela Davis, H. Rap Brown, and Huey P. Newton. According to biographer Theodore R. Hudson, "During the height of the confusion and violence, ... [Amiri Baraka], accountant Charles McCray, and actor Barry Wynn, riding in [Baraka's] Volkswagen bus, were stopped and arrested by police officers at South Seventh Street and South Orange Avenue" in the Central Ward. After they were savagely beaten, they were charged with unlawfully carrying firearms and resisting arrest. Baraka was scarred for life; a photo in *Jet* magazine, showing Baraka in police custody, pictured him handcuffed to a wheelchair, covered in his own blood.[17] He recalls, "I was left in the [hospital] hallway, handcuffed to a wheelchair, completely covered with the drying blood, my head on fire." That is the way his wife, Amina, saw him when she arrived. "The police attributed [Baraka's] wounds," writes Hudson, "to his having been hit on the head by a bottle thrown by some unknown person." Baraka, however, "accused the police of premeditated brutality," and as far as the guns were concerned, Baraka "claimed he did not know where they had come from but suspected that the police had 'planted' them."[18]

In his own autobiographical account, Baraka recalls:

> The blood felt hot in my face. I couldn't see, I could only feel the wet hot blood covering my entire head and face and hands and clothes. They were beating me to death. ... I was being murdered and I knew it. ... But then I could hear people shouting at them. Voices calling, "You bastards, stop it. Stop it. You're killing him." From the windows black people were shouting at the police. ... They started throwing things.[19]

Reporter Ron Porambo conducted his own investigation of the incident and turned up an eyewitness, a black police officer, who said he was:

> ... standing about thirty feet away when they snatched [Baraka] out of that little truck, knocked him to the ground and began to beat him so viciously that I don't know how that little man is still living today. I started to get over and butt in, but I just knew they were going to kill him from the way they were beating him and I figured they'd just kill me, too. *Man, I was crying.* That was all I could do without committing suicide.[20]

Feeling powerless and humiliated, the anonymous black officer who witnessed the police brutality never found his voice in the courtroom; he told Porambo that "he didn't testify at the trial because 'it would have been just another *nigger* telling lies on the whole Newark police force'"[21]

It was a desperate situation for both men and women. Amina Baraka explained that, fearing attack by the police during the insurrection, the women in the Spirit House boiled large pots of water and lye and waited for the assault at the top of the third floor stairwell. That is where she was positioned when her neighbors told her that she had better go to the hospital to see what the police had done to her husband. In a panic, she ran through the streets barefoot until she reached the hospital and screamed when she saw Amiri Baraka shackled to a wheelchair covered in blood. She protested that he was not receiving any medical attention. At City Hospital, the white doctor "peered at" Baraka and asked if he was "the poet." When Baraka affirmed that, the doctor said, "Well, you'll never write any more poetry!" Baraka recalls, "Then he gave me fifteen stitches on my forehead and another five in the hairline, with no anesthetic, like some primitive Gestapo butcher."[22]

While Baraka was imprisoned, he noted,

> the police and National Guard harassed my family, [Amina] and my baby son, Obalaji. One night they shot into the windows and [Amina] and the child had to get into a closet. Then the next night they broke into the theater and tossed things around and broke things up. They went down into the basement, where I had printing machines, and destroyed what they could, papers and materials. They went up the stairs, wandered around on the second floor, and started up to the third floor, where [Amina] and Obalaji lay crouched in the darkness. She was trying to keep the little baby quiet and he was quiet, remarkably for such a tiny baby. She had prepared some Afro-American napalm, lye and hot water, to throw on them if they came through the door, but fortunately they did not. Satisfied with the destruction they were able to commit, they left.[23]

At one point, Baraka did not think he would survive his imprisonment; there was word of a prison break, and during that time of desperation he penned these words about black self-determination to his wife, as well as to his son Obalaji and his daughters:

> Life Life LIFE is what we want. We want life more desperately than anyone. But where is it? There is no life without *honor!*
> We must choose the way we live. Under what laws and under what Gods! Our rule will be just ... because we *feel* (the need for) justice (dear wife you taught me) we understand the demand all Allah-God's creatures make for justice.
> It is time for Beauty and Truth to rule the world again. It is time for the evolved beings to reorder this planet.[24]

Not only did Amiri Baraka survive prison, but his movement also rose like a phoenix out of the ashes of the Newark Rebellion. His leadership and organization came to symbolize the politics born of the urban uprisings: "Black Power, the power to control our lives ourselves. All of our lives, Our laws. Our culture. Our children. Their lives. Our total consciousness, black oriented." Baraka made a plea for a different kind of black revolution, linking political power to the reordering of urban space: "We want power to control our lives, as separate from what [others] want to do with their lives. That simple."[25] Speaking of the new revolutionary black man, he wrote: "He will reorder the world, as he finds his own rightful place in it. The world will be reordered by the black man's finding such a place. Such a place is, itself, the reordering. Black Power. Power of the majority is what is meant. The actual majority in the world of colored people."[26] As Baraka spread his ideas of black self-determination and the redefinition of urban space, circles of black people gathered to defend him from the police and from the legal system.

On the heels of the Newark Rebellion of 1967, the first popular National Black Power Conference was held in New Jersey's largest city. The Newark meeting differed from the first Black Power Conference, held one year earlier in Washington, D.C., which was not a mass summit but a planning meeting convened by Harlem Congressional Representative Adam Clayton Powell, Jr. While Robert Allen's influential interpretation argues that the 1967 Black Power Conference compromised the radical thrust of the black revolt, the Newark conference that began on July 20 in the war-torn city helped advance a militant definition for the urban uprisings. In the shadow of the Newark and Detroit rebellions, the main theme of the summit was black self-determination and the debates centered on whether that would be achieved by reform or by revolution. Rather than split over the issue, the militant Maulana Karenga of the US Organization called for a united front, insisting, "We can all keep our individuality, our differences, and still move in the same direction."[27]

Originally the organizers expected some 400 delegates, but the attendance swelled to more than 1,000 during the four-day conference. The meeting highlighted a new generation of Black Power leaders. At the beginning of one session, Sam Anderson, a young Harlem poet and mathematician associated with the Black Arts movement and the New York Black Panther Party, mounted the stage and replaced the U.S. flag with a black nationalist flag. During that same session, the conference introduced the new chairman of SNCC, H. Rap Brown. Brown spoke about black liberation in a down-to-earth manner that everyone understood: "If this country doesn't come around, then black people are going to burn it down."[28]

At the same meeting, Amiri Baraka, still bandaged from the police beating, insisted that what had developed in Newark was "a rebellion of black people for self-determination," and then added, "The next time, don't break into liquor stores. Go where you can get something to protect yourself!"[29]

However, no one at that summit was fiercer than Karenga. According to one published account, looking over the audience during his speech, he tried to "Mau Mau" the throng. Karenga asked, "Any white people here who oppose our demands? Any Negroes who want to stand up for their white masters? *We're giving you a chance to die for your white master!*" The *Life* Magazine reporter noted, "no one stood up."[30]

Reporting for the *New York Times,* Earl Caldwell wrote: "As promised, the conference here brought together many of the diverse elements from Negro communities across the country. Nationalists, Muslims, and Mau Mau sat down with moderates and conservatives in workshops to help build black power programs for Negroes." Caldwell reported one moderate, who said, "some of these ideas sound radical, but when you study them they have a lot of validity" and that his understanding of what the black militants were saying was that "the system doesn't work for you so you must change the system." In essence, the Newark conference represented the spread of the legitimacy of the key themes of Black Power among African Americans: self-determination, self-respect, and self-defense. Few who attended the conference and were introduced to black radicalism were not transformed.

Perhaps the most radical sessions of the summit took place in the churches in the Central Ward, where the uprising had begun. One four-hour mass meeting was held at the Mount Zion Baptist Church at the end of the first day's downtown deliberations. At the rally, Floyd McKissick, the chairman of the National Congress of Racial Equality (CORE), urged a recall movement to rid Newark City Hall of Mayor Hugh J. Addonizio. The Newark commissioner of human rights, Alfred Black, set the tone for the rally, stating: "A black man today is either a radical or an Uncle Tom."

There were three resolutions passed at the rally: First, "to demand the release of persons still in jail after last week's rioting in Newark"; second, "to support the 'right of black people' to revolt when conditions made it necessary"; and third, "to ask the United Nations to investigate Newark under the authority of its charter on colonial territories."[31]

Rather than ending, mellowing, or "co-opting" the militant thrust of the Black Power experiment, the National Black Power Conference in 1967, coming on the heels of a wave of urban rebellions in Atlanta, Detroit, and Newark, marked the beginning of the Modern Black Convention Movement. The national call for Black Power and a black united front helped galvanize a new set of organizations in Newark, New Jersey, and beyond. While creating alternative schools and other institutions in the ghetto, those new organizations would mobilize community organizations to openly challenge the power structure in the political arena.

Out of a long tradition of fictive kinship groups of sisterhoods and brotherhoods, including the Moorish Science Temple Movement and the Nation of Islam, new groups took shape in the aftermath of the Newark uprising and the Black Power Conference.[32] Just as in earlier crises militant groups such as the Sons of Africa and the African Blood Brotherhood emerged, after the 1960s uprisings and the Black Power Conference the United Sisters and the Congress of African People (CAP) developed. These names suggest a long tradition in African American history as well as contemporary lines of international solidarity. In Newark, one early development was the growing circle of women gathered around Amina Baraka at the Spirit House to discuss black liberation and African culture as she took the lead in establishing the African Free School in 1967. Ultimately, that sisterhood developed into a full-time cadre in both CAP and the Black Women's United Front.

Throughout those developments, Amina Baraka forged a large circle of political activists as she nurtured a small circle of advisors at the helm in research, culture, administration, leadership, and strategic planning: Salimu Rogers, Jalia Woods, Staarabisha Barrett, and Jaribu Hill. The highest rank in the Women's Division was "muminina," in other words, a "true believer." Born in Newark, Muminina Salimu Rogers was the executive administrator of the central headquarters of CAP, the National Black Political Assembly, the Northeastern Regional Office of the African Liberation Support Committee, as well as the Black Women's United Front. Born in Montclair, Muminina Staarabisha Barrett was a college-educated member of the sisterhood. Staarabisha was part of the founding of the Black Women's United Front; she became one of the group's foremost national speakers. She became the leader of the Essex County Urban

League. Recruited from Kalamazoo College, Dayton, Ohio-native Muminina Jalia Woods was the principal of the African Free School and one of the founders of the Black Women's United Front and the Anti-Imperialist Cultural Union (AICU). At one point, Jalia Woods was a member of the Central Committee and the head of the Women's Commission for the Congress of African People. She was not only an expert in strategic planning, helping many Newark institutions survive the postindustrial economy, but also in 1972 she was elected a district leader on a rebel slate in the Essex County Democratic Party. Her hard-hitting campaign emphasized the crisis of garbage buildup and rat infestation in the ghetto. One of the most impressive leaders advising Amina Baraka in political matters was Cleveland, Ohio-born Muminina Jaribu Hill, the second most powerful officer in the Women's Division and a founder of the Black Women's United Front. Jaribu was a student activist at Central State in Ohio, and she ran for the U.S. Congress in the 1974 elections. After many successful elections, Jaribu led the community in the victory song, "Together We Will Win" (or, in Swahili, "Pamoja Tutashinda"), sung to the music of Nina Simone's "Four Women":

> We-ee are black
> Beautiful People
> To-ge-ther we will win
> Together we will win
> Together we will win

Similar to the United Sisters, the United Brothers idea emerged in late 1967. The United Brothers envisioned a black united front, an organization of organizers, and a political vanguard bold enough to lead the black community in a ruthless struggle for power. That development began when Harold Wilson, a childhood friend of Baraka, joined the poet at the Spirit House. Wilson was a small-scale community merchant, a retailer who at various times sold groceries, clothing, and furniture. Apparently, during the uprising the National Guard had riddled Harold Wilson's Springfield Avenue furniture store with bullets. With his extensive network of community contacts in Newark, Wilson began to mobilize resources and recruit men and women to form the core of a new political organization. Wilson would become the first elected spokesman for the group. According to oral tradition, John Bugg, a door-to-door salesman, was the first recruit, and it was he who thought of a name for the new organization—the United Brothers. Upon their initiations, John Bugg became Kaimu Safidi, and Harold Wilson, Sultani Mhisani. Thus, the

Newark Black Power movement continued a long African American tradition of building community and organization around a kinship motif. In that manner, they followed countless African blood brotherhoods and sisterhoods before them.

Probably in November 1967, Amiri Baraka, Harold Wilson, and John Bugg sent a letter to a list of black leaders in Newark, requesting their support in organizing a black convention:

> The United Brothers of Newark would like you to attend the initial meeting of interested citizens coming together to form a steering committee that would issue a call to Black Leaders for a citywide unity meeting.
>
> The meeting to form a steering committee will take place at Abyssinian Baptist Church—W. Kinney Street, 8:00 P.M. Friday, December 8, 1967. You are urged to attend. Don't let your people down!
>
> In Unity,
> THE UNITED BROTHERS.[33]

More than a dozen people attended the meeting. Eventually, the call drew Kenneth Gibson, Shirley Johnson, Earl Harris, Linda Wheeler, Harry Wheeler, Rosa Lee Gray, Junius Williams, Louise Layton, Donald Tucker, Golden E. Johnson, Theodore Pinckney, Jackie Bugg, Eugene Campbell, Carolyn Reed, George S. Reed, Jr., David Barrett, Eulius "Honey" Ward, and Russell Bingham. Many of those founders became the next generation of political leadership in the city, including mayors, city council members, and municipal judges, as well as the head of the antipoverty agency and the superintendent of the Newark Board of Education.

As the United Brothers built their ranks and committed themselves to Black Power politics, they pledged their families to a lifetime of struggle for black liberation. Thus, when a child was born into that organization, the sisterhood made a secret pledge during a ritual, some of it in Swahili. When Ndada Mali Dowdell was born, her mother, Muminina Asali Dowdell, and the sisterhood of activists, swore:

> On this day we commit our child Mali to the Black nation forever becoming. We promise to teach Mali her identity, support her in her purpose and provide her with the direction she needs to build a better place for Black people on this earth.
>
> Even as our forefathers believed that their children would be placed on a camel [which] would take them to Ahera (paradise) [,] So we commit our children by placing them on this camel [,] Symbolic of our organization which will build that paradise for Blacks on this earth where we can live in peace, walk in dignity and create in confidence.

And if we fail to keep this commitment may our children denounce us and may our names be forgotten. For Black people must survive in spite of all and anyone for as long as the sun shines and the water flows.

Recruitment and Self-Transformation in the Modern Black Convention Movement

Deep commitments, rituals, and radical visions alone were not enough to lead the black community in battle against its oppressors. The United Brothers and CFUN needed recruits to staff the Black Power organizations. The recruits to CFUN ranged in age from elders to adolescents. The oldest recruit was Russell Bingham, who was born in 1898 and fought in WWI. Bingham was a veteran not only of the war in Europe but also of the Harlem and Newark political machines. In Harlem he observed leader after leader, from Paul Robeson and Marcus Garvey to Adam Clayton Powell, Jr., and Malcolm X. Bingham became Baraka's most trusted long-term political mentor. Prior to the Black Power movement, Russell Bingham was a key political advisor to the veteran Newark Negro politico Irvine Turner. However, in 1966, when the medical school crisis stirred the black community, Russell Bingham began to feel torn between his allegiance to Turner, who backed City Hall, on the one hand and the grass-roots community opposition on the other hand. Consequently, when Bingham and Ward decamped, it caused a major breach in the Essex County Democratic Party, especially at the municipal level. His colleague, Honey Ward, was the chairman of the Central Ward Democratic Party. Thus, his departure weakened the central party machine for a time, and opened important possibilities for Baraka's black convention party. In other words, the early support from Honey Ward and Russell Bingham was one of the key factors in the phenomenal rise of the Modern Black Convention Movement. They had experience from the 1950s in working in independent black politics with the New Jersey Negro Labor Council and particularly with what was probably the first independent African American political convention that launched Irvine Turner's first official campaign as an anti-Joseph McCarthy and anti-HUAC (House Un-American Activities Committee) candidate.

After the Newark Rebellion, Russell Bingham attended the 1967 Newark Black Power Conference, where he met Maulana Karenga. Soon thereafter, Bingham became one of the founders of the United Brothers and CFUN, as well as the senior political advisor to Amiri Baraka. Upon joining Baraka's inner circle, Bingham was renamed Baba Mshauri (elder counselor, in Swahili). Explaining why he joined Baraka at the age of 69, Baba Mshauri said that he was struck by the "seriousness" of the organization that the poet was building and by the "sincerity" of the youth in the Black Power movement, particularly their dedication and selflessness. "That impressed me," he explained, "because as a rule, when you meet people, especially when [they are] becoming involved in politics, they have some ultimate goal that they want *for themselves.*"[34] Baraka recalls that Baba had "an undying love for his people."

As the Modern Black Convention Movement built momentum, it fashioned various means of recruitment, including its weekly Soul Sessions. The Soul Sessions were weekly meetings on Sunday evenings during which the United Brothers and CFUN congregated with their allies and celebrated at CFUN's headquarters at 502 High Street. The program alternated between music and speakers, featuring black nationalist lessons as well as cultural presentations. At times the Young Lions (Simba Wachunga) performed the South African boot dance or the Zulu dance; on other occasions, the women in the Malaika Singers moved the congregation with songs by their heroine, Miriam Makeba. Soul Sessions were also the place for the announcement of the naming of new recruits and the promotion of rising activists. CFUN had a ranking system that ranged from a new recruit, who was considered a kobe (turtle-a beginner),to mwanifunzi (student), and cheo (the first officer rank), up to such ranks as jelidi, sultani, kaimu, and the rare rank of imamu for men.[35] The women's ranks were simpler, ranging from ndada (sister) and malaika (good spirit) to muminina (true believer). At the end of the program, Amiri Baraka delivered a keynote speech or read poetry on special occasions. One member recalls that he was recruited immediately after one of those Sunday meetings: "I remember my first Soul Session. Matter of fact, I was real impressed. The first Soul Session, I joined *the organization.*"

> Baraka made a speech; I never will forget it. It was dealing with morality, like cleaning up your lifestyle—drinking and smoking and all this kind of stuff. *The new man,* an alternative *value system.* The speech was so strong and so convincing that I remember when I walked out from the Soul Session— because I was smoking cigarettes at that time—I remember that I got a block away from the place, I threw my cigarettes away. I never smoked a day since. *That was the impact it had on me.*[36]

In addition to Soul Sessions, Baraka spoke about Black Power in the schools. As the black community desegregated the schools in the West and North Wards of Newark surrounding the Central Ward, massive conflicts unfolded in the high schools. In the midst of those conflicts some students heard Baraka speak for the first time. That is where Larry Hamm encountered Baraka. Later to become the first student on the Newark Board of Education, Hamm knew little or nothing about black consciousness before he heard Amiri Baraka speak at Arts High School. There Hamm had learned from his white teachers to fear Baraka: "The white teachers really had bad opinions of him. The black teachers—I don't think they had an opinion at all! They rarely really expressed their opinions about anything, but the white people, you could hear them talking." Hamm recalled seeing Baraka in what was then rare African dress:

> I expected to see this, like, fire-breathing black *giant*, you know, this man who ... would literally make you tremble just to look at him. I tiptoed down there, and there was this little man down there, you know, he couldn't have been more than about five feet, six or seven. He was very thin...He had on these strange-looking clothes, and he was speaking at the podium, and he had these *two big dudes* on either side, you know. I guess they were watching the audience to make sure that none of us were going to do anything to hurt this man. And, ... he didn't look like he could harm anybody. But boy, when you heard him talk, you knew that this was a man to be reckoned with. ... That was my first [time] hearing, I guess, what you would call a race leader speak.[37]

Soon thereafter, Hamm organized a high school student movement, the NewArk Student Federation. The NewArk in this name, as well as in the Committee for Unified NewArk, came from Baraka's cultural redefinition, insisting that the "slave ship of Newark" would become a "New Ark" for the liberation of black people. The mass mobilization of the NewArk Student Federation reveals another dimension of what was meant by "nation building" as the Modern Black Convention Movement unfolded among youth: The students were ready for action. The federation used its extensive organization to launch many demonstrations at the Newark Board of Education by pulling thousands of black students out of high schools with militant chants. Hamm recalls:

> We would go over to Weequahic High School, and we would call out, literally call out, all the students from Weequahic High School, and they would come out because we had an organization. We had representatives of the New Ark Student Federation in every school in the city, and they would pre-arrange that all the students were going to walk out at 11 o'clock. And I would be up there at 11 o'clock and all the students would walk out. And we would march from Weequahic High School to South Side High School. The students of South Side saw these thousands of students from Weequahic coming, and they were at the windows, waving, you know, saying "*We are ready.*" And they

would come out and we would march those [thousands] over to Arts High and get those 500. And we would march over to Central [High School], and get a thousand more. The black students at East Side would march up from East Side to meet us at the Board of Education. *People would say that they could hear us coming before we got there—that's how many of us there were.*[38]

From the elderly Baba Mshauri to the youthful Larry Hamm, the Modern Black Convention Movement helped to transform members of the community as they struggled for self-emancipation. Some took on lifetime leadership responsibilities. For instance, Hamm is the leader of the People's Organization for Progress, a grassroots group that protested the New Jersey state trooper use of racial profiling.

Slowly, but surely, Baraka's movement developed a basic strategy. Identifying with the battles for self-determination in Africa, Asia, and Latin America, black nationalism proposed a strategy for black liberation involving struggles for regional autonomy in urban centers with large concentrations of African American population. It also insisted on alliances with other oppressed peoples, particularly Puerto Ricans and Mexican Americans. Tactically, the stratagem involved the fight for community control at the neighborhood level, self-government at the municipal level, and proportional representation at the county, state, and congressional levels. In the urban enclaves, black nationalist politics sought to accelerate the process of nationality formation, or what they called "nation building," through the rapid spread of independent black development. Because of the urban crisis, one driving force in that process was the collapse of basic government and commercial services in the "second ghetto." The cultural nationalist strategy of African American radicals was to develop parallel black institutions in the void left by the mainstream economy in providing basic services and offering black nationalism and cooperative economics as rational alternatives. Furthermore, in the international arena, Black Power politics supported national liberation for oppressed peoples and opposed colonialism and imperialism. As Baraka's CAP became a nongovernmental organization in the United Nations, it actively pursued those policies.

In line with that evolving strategy, Baraka's CAP fashioned a mutual defense pact with the Puerto Rican Young Lords Party in Newark against the persistent threat of white terror. The mutual defense pact between Newark CAP and the Newark Young Lords laid the foundation for a political alliance consolidated in the historic November 1969 Black and Puerto Rican Political Convention. After a protracted struggle for power, the Modern Black Convention Movement defeated the Addonizio political machine in June 1970. It had been a long and difficult dogfight. Although the black convention candidates received the majority of votes in the pre-dominately African American wards as early as the November 1968 elections, the white extremist candidates Anthony Imperiale and Anthony Giuliano outpolled them in the heavily Italian American wards.[39] However, in the May and June elections of 1970, with Puerto Rican allies and progressive white coalitions, Mayor Kenneth Gibson became the city's first African American mayor. Specifically, on June 16, 1970, Mayor Hugh J. Addonizio lost the election with 43,086 votes, and Kenneth Gibson won with 55,097. The voter turnout reached an unprecedented 73 percent of the electorate. Some 7,000 white voters felt uncomfortable with Addonizio on election day, casting their ballots for Gibson alongside some 48,000 African American and Puerto Rican voters. Thus, with the solid support of 19 out of every 20 black votes, Kenneth A. Gibson broke a key executive color bar in the power structure by becoming the first black mayor of a major eastern seaboard city.

Baraka's Modern Black Convention Movement used the municipal victory to set the stage for more mass mobilization around Black Power, Pan-Africanism, and anticolonialism in Africa. Instead of dismantling the political campaign apparatus, the convention movement employed similar techniques to mobilize black America for the first CAP on Labor Day weekend in 1970 in Atlanta, Georgia. Dozens of Black Power organizations from other cities had supported Baraka's leadership in the struggle for power in Newark. Those same groups joined in building CAP to replace the annual Black Power conferences. Rather than a paper structure passing annual resolutions, those activists wanted an ongoing political structure that could be a national voice for their black nationalism and an international voice for their Pan-Africanism.

With some 3,000 in attendance, CAP witnessed an unprecedented display of unity between civil rights organizations, elected officials, and Black Power groups. At the high point on the convention stage, civil rights leader Whitney Young and black nationalist leader Louis Farrakhan embraced each other before the assembly. In terms of civil rights leadership, the congress boasted not only the National Urban League's Whitney Young but also Reverend Jesse Jackson of People United for Self-Help and Ralph Abernathy of Southern Christian Leadership Conference. As far as black politicians and elected officials were concerned, the congress relished the attendance of John Cashin of the National Democratic Party of Alabama, Julian Bond of the Georgia legislature, Mayor Richard Hatcher of Gary, Indiana, and Mayor Kenneth Gibson of Newark, New Jersey. Finally, in the black nationalist camp, the congress celebrated the participation of the widow of Malcolm X, Betty Shabazz; the national representative of Elijah

Muhammad's Nation of Islam, Louis Farrakhan; the spokesman for Stokely Carmichael, Howard Fuller of the Malcolm X Liberation University; Imari Abubakari Obadele of the Republic of New Africa (an early champion of reparations), and Amiri Baraka of CFUN.

At least 200 local organizations from 40 cities were represented at the Atlanta congress. The new group targeted 30 urban areas with black concentrations of population, ranging from Newark (138,035) to Chicago (812,647) and New York City (1,087,931) in 1970. By 1974, CAP had local leadership and branches in at least 25 of those urban centers in California, Delaware, Washington, D.C., Illinois, Indiana, Indianapolis, Maryland, Massachusetts, Michigan, Missouri, New Jersey, New York, Ohio, Pennsylvania, and Texas.

By 1971, Newark CAP had established a block of community programs at radio station WNJR. *Black NewArk* was the name of CAP's local newspaper, as it was the name of its weekly radio program and its weekly television program on channel 47. CAP distributed 5,000 of its newspapers each month and reached thousands of people in the New York metropolitan area more regularly with its radio and television programs. Clearly, Newark CAP spread its ideas about an oppressed "Black Nation," African liberation, and Pan-Africanism, and the demands for Black Power, including self-determination, self-respect, and self-defense, quite extensively to the African American population centers in the New York metropolitan area. Beyond those population centers, CAP's national newspaper, *Unity & Struggle*, reached another 16,000 readers in dozens of cities.

The Black Power movement used that groundwork to sponsor African Liberation Day on May 19, 1972, establishing a bold new structure, the African Liberation Support Committee (ALSC). During that decisive period, tens of millions of Africans suffered under colonialism and apartheid. African Americans in the ALSC played an important role in supporting the independence and democratic struggles of the people of Angola, Mozambique, Guinea-Bissau, Namibia, Zimbabwe, and South Africa. That support work was part of a plan to isolate South African apartheid with its powerful military support for despotism and colonialism in Africa. Those victories required protracted struggles and sustained international support; and those successes illustrate what African American mass mobilization can do in international solidarity.

Conclusion

By now we can reassess the earlier historical judgments about Black Power and the politics of black nationalism. For one thing, it is easy to see that

Black Power proved itself effective in the mobilizing and political organizing that took place in the Northern ghettos—effective enough to overturn entrenched ethnic municipal political machines such as the one in Newark. The Modern Black Convention Movement was able to uncover and consolidate the issues around which African Americans could be organized and politicized. And, clearly, Black Power developed numerous alternative and parallel political structures: notably the Black and Puerto Rican Political Convention and the National Black Political Assembly. In addition to those structures, the grassroots movements developed their own structures and "levers of power for poor Blacks" in the youthful Black Youth Organization and the NewArk Student Federation and in the militant feminist Black Women's United Front. At the zenith of its development, the Modern Black Convention Movement attacked corporate capitalism and imperialism as the sources of the increasing gap between wealth and poverty. Moreover, Black Power called upon the support of moderate and progressive whites in political contests. In *Black Power: The Politics of Liberation in America,* Stokely Carmichael and Charles Hamilton were wrong in their prediction that coalitions with whites were out of the question. While Black Power called for white support of its objectives, it did not ask whites for their permission. In this sense, the politics of black nationalism was not essentially escapist, illogical, dysfunctional, or pessimistic. In other words, judged by its initial challenges, some of the Black Power experiments were substantial successes on the long road to black liberation.[40]

But Black Power did not supply the answers to a host of new issues and challenges that emerged in the tumult of the black revolt. In order to rise to those challenges, it is crucial to begin to sort out the strengths and the pitfalls of the Black Power movement. When the next rounds of battles in the ghetto mount, some of the lessons from the Black Power era may be invaluable. Because it was the source of unprecedented mobilizing power at the grassroots, it is important to resist the temptation of "throwing out the baby with the bath water."

As I have pointed out elsewhere, in terms of revolutionary mobilization, one of the worst mistakes made by some of the Black Power experiments was their attempt to demobilize black women, defining a "woman's role" in a limited fashion. Sexism proved a dangerous pitfall to black liberation. To the extent that women seized full political participation, the Black Power movement flourished. However, to the extent that some Black Power advocates stymied the dynamics of women's liberation, they damned the prospects for black liberation.

At another level, Robert Allen's influential judgment in *Black Awakening in Capitalist America,* that the 1967 Newark Black Power Conference marked the taming of the Black Power movement by corporate capitalism, is in serious error. As a militant mass movement spreads its hegemony, encountering reformism is not the same as succumbing to it. And neither is debating and winning over the reformists to more radical stands the same as corrupting the militants. Many people in the ghettos during the revolts were not staunch revolutionaries; but given the situation, they joined the uprising. The process unfolding all around them transformed even many that did not join the uprisings.[41]

In the remarkable epilogue to *Black Bolshevik,* Harry Haywood mistakenly follows Robert Allen's timetable in dating the demise of the radical thrust of the Black Power movement to the 1968 Black Power Conference in Philadelphia.[42] Anyone looking at the radical political thrust of the Philadelphia summit would see that the conferences were not only gaining large numbers of adherents, with some 4,000 people in attendance, but they were also advancing in radicalism with their strong condemnation of military conscription and the Vietnam War.[43]

However, the Black Power movement was never so weak or so gullible as to be compromised, as Allen argues, by the public relations department of Clairol![44] The serious work of assessing the black liberation movement requires a more professional political gauge than that one. Second, Clayborne Carson's proposition that the black revolt ended in 1968 with the assassination of Dr. King and with the urban uprisings is clearly wrong. After some very difficult moments, the black revolt ushered in a new generation of activists and organizations, as demonstrated in the Modern Black Convention Movement. Neither the black revolt nor its leadership was weak and one-dimensional. Quite the contrary: A review of the Black Power movement in Newark suggests that the movement and its various leaders were complex figures who rose to the enormous challenges of 1967, 1968, and beyond. To view the urban uprisings of the 1960s merely as destructive to the civil rights organizations does not capture the fullness of that historical moment for the African American freedom struggle. Black Power organizations arose from the ashes of the urban rebellions, from coast to coast. The Black Power movement was one of the largest mass initiatives in African American history; to trivialize its stature with a premature death notice is a serious intellectual mistake. In part because of those kinds of intellectual mistakes, the critical work of evaluating that great movement for black emancipation has only just begun.

Notes

1. Amiri Baraka, "From: The Book of Life," *Raise, Race, Rays, Raze: Essays Since 1965* (New York: Random House, 1971); Amilcar Cabral, *Return to the Source* (New York: Monthly Review Press/African Information Service, 1973).

2. Paul Delany, "Conciliator at Black Parley," *New York Times,* March 13, 1972, 30; Vincent Harding, *The Other American Revolution* (Los Angeles: Center for Afro-American Studies, UCLA, 1980), 215.

3. Manuel Castells, *The City and the Grassroots* (Berkeley: University of California Press, 1983), 54.

4. Joe R. Feagin and Harland Hahn, *Ghetto Revolts* (New York: Macmillan, 1973), 105–108.

5. The CFUN Community Council was a very large group of activists who worked to elect Kenneth Gibson as mayor in 1970. Numbering 1,000, their ranks included ministers, tenant organizers, welfare mothers, laborers, students, and activists.

6. Amiri Baraka, *The Autobiography of LeRoi Jones/Amiri Baraka* (New York: Freundlich, 1984), 191; LeRoi Jones, *Blues People* (New York: William Morrow, 1963).

7. Chuck Stone, *Black Political Power in America* (Indianapolis: Bobbs-Merrill, 1968), 125.

8. The best study of this background is in Robert Curvin, "The Persistent Minority: The Black Political Experience in Newark" (Ph.D. diss., Princeton University, 1975); reprinted (Ann Arbor, Michigan: University Microfilms International, 1975).

9. For Chicago, see Thomas Philpott, *The Slum and the Ghetto* (Belmont, Calif.: Wadsworth, 1991) and Arnold Hirsch, *Making the Second Ghetto* (Cambridge, England: Cambridge UP, 1983); for Detroit, see Thomas Sugrue, *The Origins of the Urban Crisis* (Princeton: Princeton UP, 1996).

10. Edward J. Wolak, "A Political Study of the Negro in Newark, New Jersey" (senior thesis, Princeton University, May 1948); Harold Kaplan, *Urban Renewal Politics: Slum Clearance in Newark* (New York: Columbia UP, 1963), 155–156.

11. Mindy Thompson, *The National Negro Labor Council: A History.* Occasional Paper No. 27 (New York: American Institute for Marxist Studies, 1978).

12. Robert Allen, *Black Awakening in Capitalist America* (New York: Anchor, 1970), 131.

13. A. D. Smith, " 'Ideas' and 'Structure' in the Formation of Independence Ideals," *Philosophy of the Social Sciences* 3 (1973): 19–39, citation 28.

14. Ron Porambo, *No Cause for Indictment* (New York: Holt, 1971), 101.

15. Allen, *Black Awakening in Capitalist America,* 132.

16. "New Violence in Newark: Stores Burned and Looted," *Star Ledger,* July 14, 1967, 1.

17. Komozi Woodard, *A Nation Within a Nation: Amiri Baraka (LeRoi Jones) & Black Power Politics* (Chapel Hill: University of North Carolina Press, 1999), 80.

18. Theodore R. Hudson, "The Trial of LeRoi Jones," in Kimberly Benston, *Imamu Amiri Baraka (LeRoi Jones): A Collection of Critical Essays* (Engelwood Cliffs, N.J.: Prentice-Hall, 1978), 49–50.
19. Baraka, *The Autobiography*, 262.
20. Porambo, *No Cause for Indictment*, 34–35.
21. Ibid., 35.
22. Baraka, *The Autobiography*, 265.
23. Ibid., 265.
24. Amiri Baraka, *Raise, Race, Rays, Raze* (New York: Random House, 1971), 52; Baraka, *The Autobiography*, 264.
25. Baraka, *Raise*, 41.
26. Ibid., 40.
27. Earl Caldwell, "Two Police Inspectors from Here Among the Newark Delegates," *New York Times*, July 22, 1967, 11.
28. *Life*, July 28, 1967, 26.
29. Ibid.
30. Ibid.
31. *New York Times*, July 22, 1967, 11.
32. See Herbert Gutman, *The Black Family in Slavery and Freedom* (New York: Vintage, 1976).
33. Amiri Baraka, "Creation of the New Ark," in *The Black Power Movement: Amiri Baraka from the Black Arts to Black Radicalism*, Komozi Woodard, ed. (Bethesda, Md.: University Publication Association, 2000). This is Baraka's unpublished but invaluable history of the Newark movement.
34. Woodard, *Black Power Movement.*
35. In Maulana Karenga's Kawaida rank system, the highest Imamu or "Spiritual Leader" was a Maulana. Unfortunately, detractors of Karenga translated this word as "god"; but any student of Islam knows that this is a high ranking scholar, as in Maulana Abul Kalam Azad (1888–1958), an Indian Muslim scholar (minister of education of the Republic of India at the time of his death), who developed some new principles for the interpretation of the Qur`an.
36. Saidi Nguvu interview in Woodard, *Black Power Movement.*
37. Lawrence Hamm interview, in Woodard, *Black Power Movement*
38. Ibid.
39. See Komozi Woodard, *A Nation Within A Nation*, chapter 3, for more details on the crucial 1968 election.
40. Stokely Carmichael and Charles Hamilton, *Black Power: The Politics of Liberation in America* (New York: Vintage, 1967).
41. Robert Allen, *Black Awakening.*
42. Harry Haywood, *Black Bolshevik* (Chicago: Liberator Press, 1978); see Woodard, *A Nation Within a Nation*, 107–108.
43. See Woodard, *A Nation Within a Nation*, Chapter 3.
44. Allen, *Black Awakening in Capitalist America*, 163–164.

Afterword

Robin D. G. Kelley

Shirley Clarke's remarkable independent film, *The Cool World,* shot in Harlem in 1963, opens with a black man standing on a stoop before a small crowd indicting America's "white devils" for centuries of slavery, Jim Crow, and racist violence. The listeners follow his every word, some nodding in confirmation, others fascinated but skeptical. As the camera pans we see a handful of people carrying signs as if they were preparing to launch a protest march, and one man holds up a newspaper with the bold headline "Exempt Negroes from Taxes." The speaker, probably a member of the Nation of Islam, really has one point to make: Our time has come and we are declaring war.

My students are always surprised by these opening scenes, especially when I tell them the film was shot the same year as the March on Washington. Those who claim to know American history cling to a narrative in which the civil rights movement begins below the Mason-Dixon line with the Montgomery Bus Boycott, followed by a decade of sit-ins, marches, prayer vigils, and voter registration drives. Not much happens in the North until the mid-1960s, when race riots erupt in Harlem, Watts, Chicago, and Washington D.C. and catch the attention of Dr. Martin Luther King, Jr. Urban poverty and Northern racism is added to the movement's agenda, but turning the other cheek doesn't work up north. A new urban militancy is embodied in figures such as Malcolm X and those who followed in the wake of his death, from the Black Panther Party to the Black Liberation Army. Meanwhile, the situation in the South begins to change as well. Young activists in the Student Nonviolent Coordinating Committee (SNCC) start to carry guns to protect themselves, and its black leaders, particularly Stokely Carmichael and Willie Ricks, begin to question the movement's integrationist agenda. During the summer of 1966, the slogan "Black Power" emerges full-blown among black SNCC and Congress of Racial Equality (CORE) militants. Tired and impatient with the slow pace of the civil rights establishment, a new attitude overtakes the movement: no more compromises, no more "deals" with white liberals, no more subordinating the struggle to the needs of the Democratic party. Out of bitter disappointment rises a new "Black Revolution."

The wonderful essays in *Freedom North* should put this neat, oversimplified narrative to rest once and for all. Each, in its own way, demonstrates that the civil rights movement was never merely regional; it was national *and* local. They show that movements in Northern and Western cities and towns were contemporaneous with events in the South and often struggled over the same issues—from school desegregation to police violence. But most importantly, *Freedom North* exposes the limitations of certain descriptive and analytical categories, notably "integration," "nationalism," "separatism," and even "civil rights" itself. When we look at Northern movements, we learn that the struggle for what was then called "Negro rights" incorporated a wide range of issues, from housing and job discrimination to reparations for slavery, from poor sanitation services for blacks to demands for better playgrounds, from battles over the treatment of black customers in retail stores to support for African independence movements. Sometimes the same folks who are picketing white-owned stores for refusing to hire the very black people who keep them in business are also supporting back-to-Africa movements or efforts to create an independent black nation in North America.

In other words, "civil rights" falls short of capturing the wide scope and vision of the post-WWII black freedom movement, not just in the North but throughout the country. *Freedom North* ought to make us rethink the *Southern* movement, for if we look beyond the usual suspects we will also discover that some activists below Mason-Dixon took up issues such as reparations, police brutality, African liberation, and the conditions of the poor and working class. Groups we associate with the "north," such as the Nation of Islam and the Black Panther Party, actually had a presence in Southern cities, including Birmingham, New Orleans, and Winston-Salem, North Carolina. And few Southern movement histories make mention of the fact that a radical nationalist group, the Revolutionary Action Movement, held its first Afro-American Student Conference on Black Nationalism at Fisk University in Nashville, in May of 1964.

Freedom North should be required reading, especially for those of us who are still committed to eradicating racism and inequality and believe that freedom is still worth fighting for. These essays compel us to challenge the North-South divide, look at the nation as a whole, and examine the relationship between the black freedom movement and the rest of the world. They demolish the myth that black people needed a "messiah" to lead them by introducing us to local leaders who rose from the grassroots but never found a place in the grand narrative. And, finally, they reveal a vision of emancipation so broad, so complex, and so fluid that it defies labels and categories. "Freedom" was a much bigger matter than integration; it was, and continues to be, a struggle for full citizenship *and* the right to determine our destiny, a struggle for power *and* the overthrow of the many oppressions we all experience, a struggle to remake the world *and* to ensure we never forget the past that made us. The *we*, I venture to say, might include all oppressed humanity—including white folks—for the black freedom movement at its best exposed the fragility of whiteness, shed light on how racism arrests the human potential, and sought to replace the values of individualism, accumulation, and competition with the values of community, cooperation, self-determination, love, and an unwavering commitment to social justice for all.

Index